FUTURE TEACHERS AND SOCIAL CHANGE IN BOLIVIA
Between decolonisation and demonstration

D1732164

Mieke T.A. Lopes Cardozo

Photo 1, front cover: students and trainers of urban teacher training institutes in a march through the streets of La Paz, 16 September 2008

This research project is part of the 'IS-Academie' programme on Education and International Development, jointly funded between the University of Amsterdam and the Dutch Ministry of Foreign Affairs.

Cover design: Maurits Lopes Cardozo & Rikjan Scholten
Illustrations: Mieke Lopes Cardozo

ISBN 978-90-5972-573-7

Uitgeverij Eburon
Postbus 2867
2601 CW Delft
Tel.: 015 – 213 14 84 / Fax: 015 – 214 68 88
info@eburon.nl / www.eburon.nl

I dedicate this book to my parents, for their love and support

CONTENTS

LIST OF BOXES, TABLES, FIGURES, MAPS AND PHOTOS

ABBREVIATIONS

ALBA	Bolivarian Alliance for the Peoples of Our America (*Alianza Bolivariana para los Pueblos de Nuestra América*)
ASEP	Bolivia's new Education law (2010) entitled *Avelino Siñani Elizardo Perez*
AECID	Spanish Development Cooperation Agency (*Agencia Española de Cooperación Internacional para el Desarollo*)
CDA	Critical Discourse Analysis, as developed by Fairclough
CEPAL	Economic Commision for Latin America and the Caribbean (*Comision Economica para America Latina y el Caribe*)
CEPOs	Indigenous Education Councils (*Consejos Educativos de los Pueblos Originarios*)
CPE/E	Cultural Political Economy (of Education) approach (Jessop/Robertson, see chapter 2)
COB	The *Central Obrero Boliviano*, or Bolivian Workers' Centre, the largest trade union (founded 1952).
CONMERB	*Confederación de los Maestros de Educación Rural de Bolivia* or Rural Teachers' National Confederation
CTEUB	*Confederación de Trabajadores de Educación Urbana de Bolivia* or Urban Teachers' Union
DANIDA	Danish International Development Agency
ECM	Extended Case Method
EDI	Education For All Development Index
EIB	Intercultural and Bilingual Education (*Educación Intercultural Bilingüe*)
EFA	Education For All, global movement initiated in 1990 in Jomtien, see http://www.unesco.org/new/en/education/themes/leading-the-international-agenda/education-for-all/
ESFMs	*Escuelas Superiores de Formación de Maestras y Maestros,* teacher education institutes or 'Normales'
ETARE	*Equipo Técnico de Apoyo a la Reforma Educativa* – technical support team for 1994 education reform
FEE	ALBA's Editorial Educative Council (*Fondo Editorial Educativo*), coordinated by Bolivia
GDP	Gross Domestic Product
GTZ	German organisation for development cooperation (*Deutsche Gesellschaft für Technische Zusammenarbeit*, since January 2011 integrated in GIZ: *Deutsche Gesellschaft für Internationale Zusammenarbeit*)
HDI	Human Development Index, developed by UNDP (see below)
HIPC	World Bank's Highly Indebted Countries initiative
IADB	Inter-American Development Bank
ILO	International Labour Organisation
IMF	International Monetary Fund
INS	*Institutos Normales Superiores* (now ESFMs)
JICA	Japanese International Cooperacion Agency (JICA)
MAS	Evo Morales' governing political party 'Movement Towards Socialism' (*Movimiento al Socialismo*)

MDGs	United Nation's Millenium Development Goals: http://www.un.org/millenniumgoals/
MERCOSUR	Southern Common Market, or *Mercado Comun del Sur*
MIP	Political party of Felipe Quispe, *Movimiento Indigenista Pachacuti*
MNR	The Nationalist Revolutionary Movement (*Movimiento Nacionalista Revolutionario*), founded in 1941.
MoE	Bolivian Ministry of Education
NEC	National Education Council, founded in 1992 by the MoE
NEP	New Economic Policy, neoliberal policy strategy in Bolivia since 1985
NGOs	Non Governmental Organisations
P	Research location 2: rural teacher education institute in **P**aracaya
PDI	Research and internship course for pre-service teacher students (*Practica Docente e Investigación*)
P-INSEIB	*Proyecto de Institutos Normales Superiores de Educación Intercultural Bilingüe*
PND	Bolivia's National Development Plan (*Plan Nacional de Desarollo*), 2006-2010
PROEIB-Andes	Program of Professional Development in EIB for the Andean Countries, UMSS, Cochabamba
PRSP	Poverty Reduction Strategy Paper, forms part of IMFs and WBs SAPs (see below)
SAPs	Structural Adjustment Programmes, neoliberal policies of large financial institutes (including the WB and IMF) implemented in low income countries.
SB	Research location 1: urban teacher education institute **S**imón **B**olívar
SENALEP	The 1982 introduced programme National Service for Literacy and Popular Education (*Servicio Nacional de Alfabetización y Educación Popular*)
SIDA	Swedish International Development Cooperation Agency
SIMECAL	System of Education Quality Measurement, 1996-2002
SJTE	Social Justice Teacher Education
SRA	Strategic Relational Appraoch (by Jessop, Hay and colleagues, see chapter 2).
TE	Teacher education
TCP	People's Trade Agreement (*Trato de Comercio de los Pueblos*) in the context of ALBA
TS/TT	Teacher student/Teacher trainer
UMSA/UMSS	Universidad Mayor de San Andres, La Paz/Universidad Mayor de San Simón, Cochabamba
UNDP	United Nations Development Programme
UNESCO	United Nations Educational, Scientific and Cultural Organisation
UNICEF	United Nations Children's Fund
UNNIOs	*Unidad Nacional de las Naciones Indigenas Originarias*
US	United States of America
WB	World Bank

WORDS OF THANKS

This thesis would not have been possible without the time, support and dedication of many people in Bolivia who were involved in this research project over the past four years. The numerous respondents, whose anonimity I will respect, my two local supervisors Anke van Dam and Maria Luisa Talavera and their families, my friends Ramiro, Andrea and little Emily, and many many others: *¡les agradesco mucho!* I have very much appreciated the guidance and support of my two academic supervisors. I want to express my sincere gratitude to Professor Michiel Baud. You have critically and encouragingly supported my academic development over the past four years and I will not forget how you have always reminded me of the importance of 'having Bolivia' central to my research and book. I am also particularly grateful to my 'daily' supervisor Mario Novelli. You inspire me with your genuine enthusiasm and dedication, intellectual support and confidence in my work, and I hope that we can continue to work together in the future. I also want to thank the professors in the external committee, Isa Baud, Xavier Bonal, Susan Robertson and Annelies Zoomers, for taking the time to read and comment on my work.

I have been privileged to experience first-hand how critical and passionate teachers can make a difference. I am grateful to Margriet Poppema, Graciela Paillet and Paloma Bourgonje for their encouragement and trust during my academic studies as lecturers and supervisors, and afterwards as caring colleagues and friends. My close colleagues also deserve a sincere *thank you*; Hulya, Toni, Joosje, Inti, Magali, Sanne, Edith, Iris, the other GID-colleagues, secretariat and co-teachers, thanks for your support and our chats, lunches and precious moments of silence and writing. I am grateful for my contact and discussions with students, who stimulate my thinking and writing on critical and reflexive teachers, but also inspire me to personally strive to become one. I am also thankful for the inspiration and learning experience I gained from working with several colleagues on co-authored pieces, including Mario Novelli, Inti Soeterik, Jesse Strauss and Ritesh Shah. I also want to thank the staff members and IS-Academie colleagues at DSO/OO at the Ministry of Foreign Affairs in The Hague, for your kind interest and support over the past few years. I thank Vicky Cardenas for her dedication and transcriptions in Bolivia, Joanne Lennon for her excellent editing and Julian Vargas Talavera for his translation of the summary in Spanish.

Finally, I want to say thanks to all of my dear friends – in the Netherlands and abroad – for your understanding and interest, for helping me to enjoy my life-besides-work, and for your patience, especially in the last year of this PhD-journey. I am also grateful for those who have taught me in my practices of reiki and yoga both in the Netherlands and Bolivia, which have helped me to develop and slow down at the same time. I am very grateful for the warmth and support of my family and everyone of my 'extended Scholten-family' on Rikjan's side. I especially thank my big brother André – for always being there, my even bigger brother Maurits – for your bright ideas and creativity, Anne – for your sincere support and Marlies – for your curious enthusiasm. I would not be who and where I am now without the love, confidence and support of my parents Eric and Nynke, to whom I dedicate this thesis. My warmest and dearest gratitude goes to Rikjan, my favorite partner in life and travels. *Dankjewel lief*, for your endless support, respect, humour and love.

PROLOGUE

Conducting 'fieldwork research' over different periods during the past four years in Bolivia as a young, Dutch female has been a daring, exiting, challenging and rewarding experience. When I first set foot on Bolivian soil in June 2002, the country made an everlasting impression with its extreme climates and landscapes, politics being played out in the streets, a chaotic infrastructure and high altitude together with an incredible variety of peoples and cultures. The daily battle against poverty and struggles for social justice were then, as they are now, highly visible in the streets of Bolivia's large cities and small villages. It was during this travel that I decided to focus my further studies on understanding these structures of inequality and people's struggles against it. Inspired by critical thinkers such as Freire and Sousa Santos, it is my conviction that education – and particularly educators – *can* pursue a 'practice of freedom', and make a difference towards more just societies. This thesis is dedicated to understanding the potentials, difficulties and limitations to Bolivian teachers being agents of change, with a particular focus on the role of teacher education institutes.

This thesis positions the case of Bolivia in a wider context of counter-hegemonic tendencies to processes of globalisation and neoliberalism, and focuses on the opportunities and challenges in working towards (or against) social change and justice within Bolivia's teacher education schools and its inhabitants: the teacher students and trainers. The research follows a multiscalar, interdisciplinary and historically informed approach (Dale, 2000; Dale, 2005) that aims to uncover Bolivia's 'politics of teacher education', by posing questions that reach beyond the education sector and the national state level. Since the inauguration of Bolivia's first elected indigenous president Evo Morales in 2006, the Bolivian government has proposed a new political ideology of '21st century socialism' which is aimed at radical transformations of Bolivia's politics, economy and society – so that all Bolivians can '*vivir bien*' (live well). Education is a crucial sector to bring about these transformations, and teachers are envisioned as strategic political 'actors of change' in Bolivia's new route to development.

Positioning this particular case study alongside other cases of social transformation (particularly in the Latin American context), the more general goal of this thesis is to understand the role of teacher education institutes and actors in underpinning, or opposing, emancipatory education and processes of societal transformation. By focusing on the new 'revolutionary' government of Evo Morales, the thesis intends to explore how, and to what extent, Bolivian pre-service teacher education institutes and actors develop strategies for, or against, the societal transformation that is envisaged by the new Bolivian Plurinational constitutional regime. Based on a four-year long empirical engagement with Bolivia's unique context, it tries to unravel the potentials, complexities, contradictions and pitfalls inherent in teachers' combined role as educators and potential socio-political agents for, or against, transformation.

Informed by insights from critical pedagogy, as well as Bolivia's new discursive engagement with education for transformation, the study departs from the assumption that social justice oriented teacher education, by stimulating reflexivity, critical thinking and socio-political engagement of future teachers, has the potential to contribute to the broader socio-political goals of respect for diversity and social justice. The research does not aim to 'measure' these contributions; instead it wishes to provide a better insight into the possibilities and challenges when forming future teachers as agents of (educational and societal) change. The knowledge and skills required from teachers in the Bolivian state's new vision of decolonising and inter-/intracultural education demand that Bolivian teachers become critical and reflexive public intellectuals – an expectation that is seemingly in contrast to the low status and acknowledgement Bolivian teachers are still faced with in their daily lives. In line with a global 'crisis in the teaching profession', the teaching profession in Bolivia has neither a social recognition nor a suited economic compensation. In addition, teachers have a lack of proper support in either their pre-service or in-service teacher education system.

This thesis seeks to understand these and other structural-institutional aspects of the governance of teacher education, as well as the agential features of Bolivia's teacher education system, in the context of a revolutionary transformation of Bolivian society. At the structural level, it explores the power relations and mechanisms in the teacher education institutions and beyond, so as to analyse the various obstacles to, and potentials for, transformation and innovation of these institutes that is envisaged by the current government. In addition, the study endeavours to appreciate the agential dimensions, including the motives, identities and strategies of Bolivia's future teachers and their trainers in coping with a highly tense and changing landscape. This book aspires to take the reader through a fascinating journey on the struggles of future teachers amidst revolutionary politics, demonstrations and decolonisation in Bolivia.

1

Introduction:
Bolivia, future teachers and social transformation

'Education as the practice of freedom – as opposed to education as the practice of domination – denies that man is abstract, isolated, independent, and unattached to the world' (Freire, 1970: 62)

1.1 Research relevance and rationale

The rise of Evo Morales: bringing change amidst continuity?

Dynamite is exploding on the corner of the Prado, the main street in the centre of La Paz in the Bolivian highlands. On a Friday afternoon, a large procession of urban schoolteachers is filling the streets with their presence and slogans. *'¡Contra la descentralización! ¡Contra la educación privada! ¡Contra la corrupción!'*[1] These teachers march the streets regularly on Friday afternoons in their fight against government reform initiatives. It is October 2007, and the first 'indigenous-led' government of Evo Morales is close to ending its second year of reign. Two years earlier, in December 2005, the election of president Evo Morales Ayma attracted the eyes of the world on Bolivia. The majority of Bolivia's population voted for the former coca-farmer, union activist and political leader of the 'Movement Towards Socialism' party (MAS). Not only was Morales elected as president, his MAS party also won a majority in Congress, enabling the formation of a new cabinet that supported him in his ambitious new political agenda for change (Postero, 2007: 2). Morales became famous, nationally and internationally, for different reasons. Besides being potrayed as the 'sweater-wearing president', the 'best friend' of both Castro (Cuba) and Chavez (Venezuela), and as a fierce opponent of America's anti-drugs war in international media, on a national scale Morales promised to put an end to the historical processes of exclusion and marginalisation of Bolivia's indigenous majority.

The government of Evo Morales is dedicated to change Bolivia amidst a context of deep and continuing processes of poverty, inequality and conflict. With a 'politics of change', the new government endeavours to radically restructure Bolivian economy, politics and society, with education as a major vehicle for this change. Through the 'decolonisation' of Bolivian politics, education and society, the government of Morales aims to overcome the ills of colonialism,

---

[1] 'Against decentralisation! Against private education! Against corruption!'.

1

racism and the structural stains of poverty and inequality caused by neoliberalism. Education is officially recognised as '*the highest function of the state*' (Proyecto de Ley, 2007), and it finds itself at the forefront of debates in the streets, media and parliament. The new education law that aims to decolonise the entire education system was finally approved in December 2010. During the public launch of this new law, '*that has been created by Bolivians, and not by the World Bank or the IMF*', Bolivia's president Evo Morales claimed that '*teachers are the soldiers of the liberation and decolonisation of Bolivia*' (Ministerio de Educación de Bolivia, 2010d). Being part of a larger Latin American '*region in revolt*' (Dangl 2007:7), change and transformation are on the tips of policy makers' tongues in contemporary Bolivia, not least when it concerns the role of educators for societal transformation. This relationship is clearly stated in an introduction to an early draft of the new law (Proyecto de Ley, 2006):

'*The processes of historical change taking place at present in benefit of the Bolivian people, propelled by the political will of the government and popular social movements, present a historic opportunity to deeply change education policy, making it the engine for sustainable development of the state and establishment of a new society based on solidarity, justice, harmony and complementarity of own cultural identities*' (translation by author).

Bolivia has always been a country of extremes and contrasts; it is '*demographically the most Indian country in the Americas*' (Zoomers, 2006: 1024) and, since its independence in 1825, the country has struggled to establish internal cohesion and a national identity in the face of substantial ethnic and geographic diversity (Kohl and Farthing, 2006: 40). Bolivia's unequal society is being described by some as '*a beggar on a throne of gold*' (Brienen, 2007: 27), contrasting the high levels of poverty with the rich resources hidden in the country's soil. The election and re-election of today's president Evo Morales, identified by many as an indigenous leader, is symbolic of the rise of indigenous social movements in the last few decades.[2] These emerged from a cry for change in Bolivia, as well as other countries in the region, including for instance Ecuador, Nicaragua, Uruguay, Brazil, Paraguay and Venezuela. Bolivia's political shift is thus part of a wider contemporary 'turn to the left' in Latin America (Lazar and McNeish, 2006: 157; Rodriguez-Garavito et al, 2008; Dangl 2010: 4). Inspired by both left wing and indigenous ideals, and in line with wider constitutional reforms throughout contemporary Latin America, a new Bolivian constitution was overwhelmingly approved in a referendum in January 2009. With this new constituion, the Morales government pushes for large scale land reforms, the nationalisation of natural resources and an alternative, endogenous development route based on environmental and social justice, which officially recognises Bolivia's 36 different cultures, each with their own language, together creating the Plurinational State of Bolivia. Map 1 illustrates Bolivia's nine departments, as well as its landlocked location in the heart of South America, in between its neighbouring countries Brazil, Paraguay, Argentina, Chile and Peru.

Eloquently put by Kohl and Bresnahan (2010: 5), the achievements of the Morales government are, so far, much like beauty in the eye of the beholder as Bolivia remains one of the poorest and most unequal countries of the Latin American continent. Huge inequalities, between rich and poor, between lowland and highland Bolivia, and between different ethnic-cultural groups, lead to social tensions and conflicts (Latinobarómetro, 2007; Lopes Cardozo, 2009).

---

[2] In August 2008 two thirds of the voters during a recall referendum decided to let the government continue, while Morales was re-elected for his second term of presidency in December 2009.

Although this moment is indeed a significant one in Bolivian history, in the eyes of Brienen it is also part of a longer historical process, as '*Morales follows in the footsteps of a long line of revolutionaries and reformers who have attempted to wholly restructure Bolivian society under some unifying banner*' (Brienen, 2007: 22). Brienen's observation echoes the discourse of Morales' inauguration speech, in which he purposefully declared how the '*democratic cultural revolution is part of the struggle of our ancestors; it is the continuity of the fight of Túpac Katari and Che Guevarra*' (Evo Morales in Postero, 2007: 17).

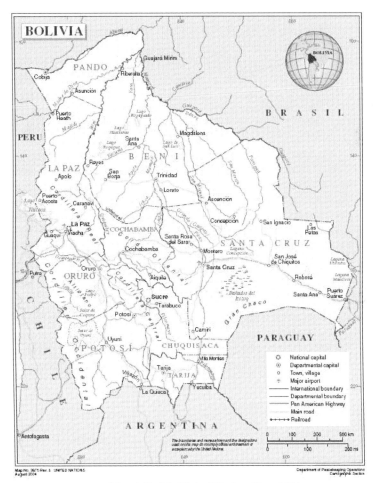

Map 1, Bolivia United Nations Map, 2004

Although democratically elected with a unique first-round majority vote, and a strong support base with social movements, Evo Morales' transformatory political line is not accepted uncontestedly by various groups in Bolivian society. With regard to the education sector, the tense political situation and the long process towards consensus on the new constitution results in a 'sense of waiting' for new policy directives to come, in a time when social tensions are rising. There is a strong divide between (richer) elites in the fertile lowlands who mostly disagree with the redistribution and nationalisation plans, and the pro-Morales supporters that predominantly inhabit the poorer and higher regions of the country. Not all groups in Bolivian society, and similarly not all teachers, approve of Morales' new project of decolonisation; some see it as a (new) imposition in to their lives, others as clashing with their interests or political views. Regardless of Bolivia's radical political sway, the Friday-afternoon demonstrating teachers of La Paz are determined to continue their struggle to stop the Morales government from radically transforming the education system – just as they have demonstrated against former government reform plans. In contrast, other groups of mostly rural and Morales-supporting teachers, and particularly their union-representatives, feel a sincere sense of ownership of the decolonisation project. It is important to reach an understanding of the role, potentials and difficulties of the envisaged transformation of Bolivia's teacher education sector, as a crucial vehicle for Morales' broader politics of change. In the context of this clear political will and transformatory discourse, how and why is it so difficult to accomplish revolutionary transformation of Bolivian society *and* its education system in practice?

Bolivia's unique response to development and social change

With its new political push for radical, structural, societal and educational transformation, Bolivia is marking an exceptional alternative route towards development that stands in stark contrast to mainstream (neoliberal inspired) global tendencies and generates an intriguing area for social science research. Morales, together with his colleagues Chavez in Venezuela and Correa in Ecuador, follow a model of '21st century socialism', as an alternative to market capitalism. 21st Century socialism provides an alternative development model, which does not fully reject capitalism (yet it does reject *foreign* imposed market policies), as it seeks to embed capitalism within a humanitarian project for social justice (Kennemore and Weeks, 2011).[3] In this line of thought, Bolivian vice President García Linera stated how '*we will never be like other places*'. He continued his speech, at the inauguration of the Constitutional Assembly in August 2006, with the following words: '*for 513 years we have tried a failed path. We have the right to try another way, to gain control*' (La Razon, 07-08-2006). Bolivia's National Development Plan (*Plan Nacional de Desarollo -* PND, 2006-2010) is consequently aimed at a '*sovereign, dignified, productive and democratic Bolivia where everyone can live well*'. Living well, or *vivir bien*, is an important concept also adopted in other leftist oriented Latin American countries, albeit in slighly different ways. In Venezuela, for example, '*buen vivir*' is aimed at 'supreme happiness' and forms an integral part of the 21st century socialism political project '*for national liberation, endogenous development, and for an alternative environmentally friendly and sustainable conception of society and development*' (see for instance Griffiths, forthcoming: 1). In Bolivia, 'to live well' is defined in the PND as '*access to and enjoyment of resources and material assets; affective, subjective and spiritual realisation; in harmony with nature and the wider community*' (Ministerio de Planificacion del Desarollo, 2006-2010). This '*alternative cosmovision*' presumes to: '*live in harmony with nature, to live a social life in solidarity, with a democratic and integral plurinational and diverse development, a multidimensional change departing from cultural diversity and with interculturality and diversity at the basis of the quality of life*' (National Development Plan in Yapu, 2009: 51-52).[4]

---

[3] The model of 21st century socialism emerged for the first time in the 1990s, as a response to the failures and damages caused by market-oriented policies throughout the Latin American region. It critiques the mistakes of both neoliberalism and twentieth century socialism (the latter one being dictatorial, and economic failure and no longer relevant) (Kennemore and Weeks, 2011).

[4] *Cosmovisión* translates as *Weltanschauung* or comprehensive world view.

Bolivia's engagement with these principles received international attention during the Climate Conference in Copenhagen in January 2010, when Morales defended the idea of respecting Mother Earth (or *La Pachamama*) and *'vivir bien'* – or to live well *enough*, and not to live well at the expense of other people and nature (see for instance Democracy Now, 2010).[5] In this sense, Bolivia's interpretation of 'social justice' – as a way to *vivir bien* (live well) – is a broad conceptualisation that includes environmental justice, social equality and respect for diversity, political/democratic representation for all and an equal economic system to the benefit of all Bolivians – and particularly not serving the economic interests of foreign actors. Or in the words of president Evo Morales on education's function to reach this situation of social justice or 'living well for all': *'patriotism should be encouraged in classrooms so that students [learn to] defend our national interests, and [to stay] far removed from demands which were to serve foreign interests. Education should foster solidarity, as it is more important to share than to compete'* (Ministerio de Educación de Bolivia, 2010d). With this statement, the government openly and strongly chooses to break from a Bolivian history of exclusionary and neoliberal inspired politics. The phenomenon of globalisation paints the broader picture in which societal and educational changes take place in Bolivia and elsewhere. Refraining from seeing globalisation as an *'unambiguous and non-negotiable structural constraint'* (Hay, 2002a: 164-166), this thesis positions the case of Bolivia in a wider context of counter-hegemonic tendencies to processes of globalisation. The research follows a multiscalar, interdisciplinary and historically informed approach that aims to reveal Bolivia's 'politics of teacher education' (Dale, 2000; Dale, 2005), by posing questions that do not solely examine Bolivian education but reach beyond the education sector and the national state level.

The role of education in Bolivia's social transformation

Teaching is a political act which can promote or hinder the realisation of a more just and humane society (Freire, 1970; Price, 2001). Social transformation in Bolivia is – at least discursively – high on the political agenda, as explained above. In Bolivia, education is perceived to play an important role in processes of change. In the same week that I witnessed the Friday afternoon teachers' demonstration, a Bolivian Ministry of Education (MoE) official explained to me during an interview how: *'society will not change if we do not change education, and education will not truly change when we do not change teacher education'*.[6] This comment provides a strong argument for the focus of this research: if we want to understand processes of social transformation in Bolivia, education provides an important entry point, and teacher education lies at the basis of any education system. In relation to processes of social transformation, education *can* provide a tool for emancipation, empowerment, tolerance, cohesion, strengthening of cultural identities and (indigenous) knowledge, integration into the national (and international) economy, reinforcement of national unity and a critical cultural, societal and political awareness. Education policies not only represent the state's vision on how its population can be best 'developed', it also defines what type of citizen is envisaged, or how Bolivia aims to deal with its diverse population and social inequalities. Practices in education institutes at different levels also provide valuable

---

[5] *La Pachamama* is widely recognised in Bolivia as a highly spiritualized and honored Mother Earth, which has a reciprocal relationship with humans. Kennemore and Weeksn (2011: 273) point out how recently the Bolivian government has a weakened reputation in the debates on climate change, as it continues to fund its own social policies through the extraction of natural resources.

[6] All quotes from respondents are interpreted and translated from Spanish to English by the author.

information on how these policies work in reality.[7] In order to understand the implications of education reforms, as part of wider state policies, we need to understand educators' roles and agency in developing strategies that either work to enhance or resist these processes.

Education policies in Bolivia historically have dealt with the issues of diversity and inequality in different ways, slowly shifting from a homogenising and modernising type of schooling to a more inclusionary system. Although the 1994 Educational Reforms for intercultural and bilingual education was seen as an innovative reform at the time, its design and implementation process was soon criticised by a range of Bolivia's education actors for a lack of genuine participation, and for being 'imposed' by foreign actors. As one of its first political acts, the Morales government immediately decided to replace the 1994 Reform and create a new Bolivian-owned and 'revolutionary' education law (which the thesis accordingly refers to as the ASEP law) to decolonise the education system, which carries the names of two historical indigenous educators: *Avelino Siñani* and *Elizardo Pérez*. On the one hand, Bolivia's new education reform, which forms a strategic part of Morales' government's 'politics of change', aligns with the global discourse of quality *Education For All*. It differs, however, in promoting a decolonised, inter- and intracultural, productive and communitarian education system, an approach that is unprecedented.[8] Building from debates in Latin America and beyond of education for liberation (including the well known work of Freire, 1970), Bolivia's new education law stipulates a '*liberatory pedagogy*', as it encourages personal development and a critical awareness of reality '*in order to change it*' (Article 3.14, ASEP law, 2010b).

Teacher education institutes are crucial spaces to bring about educational changes and should ideally work as a jump start for societal change, since this is where a new generation of future teachers are prepared. Several Bolivian based authors verify the importance and necessity to study, politically prioritise and radically transform (pre-service and in-service) teacher education (Speiser 2000; Talavera Simoni 2002; Nucinkis 2004; Albó 2005; Van Dam 2006). Generally, there is quite a negative image and low status of teacher education institutes in Latin America (Vaillant 2010). Concerns include a low quality of the training; low academic achievements of students that enrol in Normales; little '*actualizacion*' (in-service training); a disconnection between theorecical and practical training; a lack of sufficient infrastructure (buildings, libraries, computers); and a lack of cooperation and coordination of teacher training (at the national level) (see for instance Rama, 2004). Often teachers and their trainers are seen as part of the problem of this low quality education, rather than as part of the solution. Hence, many recent (neo-liberal) reforms demanded individual solutions by shortening the training and demanding more from teachers, instead of adequately addressing structural obstacles to educational qualities at the same time (Feldfeber, 2007; Tatto, 2007; Sleeter, 1996). Torres del Castillo argues for the need for a 'new model of teacher training' in the Latin American region. It is no longer possible to ask teachers to be well informed, creative, innovative, participatory, bilingual, interculturally sensitive, understanding, critical, and an agent for change, when their

---

[7] With most academic attention paid to the role of non-formal 'popular education' in Latin American processes of social change (Bartlett 2005), this thesis sets out to understand the potential for social change in the formal education field in Bolivia, in which the majority of students are enrolled.

[8] With 'communitarian education', I do not refer to a political philosophy of 'communitarianism', but rather to the Bolivian contemporary notion of 'community-based' education. I use the word 'communitarian' so as to stay close to the Bolivian discourse.

education in the teacher education institutes fails to adequately prepare them (Torres del Castillo, 2007: 10-12). However, it has to be noted that changing educational institutions, processes and actions is a difficult and slow process. Teachers, teacher trainers and training institutions – in Bolivia referred to as *Normales* – are not always welcome to radical changes. It takes a lot of time and investment, and lays a great burden on often already overburdened educators of all levels (Talavera Simoni, 2002: 305).

Bolivia substantiates its unique contemporary approach to the teacher education sector in a number of ways. Contrary to global mainstream teacher education reforms, in Bolivia the training of future teachers has been prioritised and extended (from three and a half to five years), instead of shortened, while teachers' salaries have increased significantly over the past few years.[9] In response to the fact that teachers – and particularly their training – have not been at the centre of the reforms taking place in Latin America (Speiser, 20009: 28), and based on the failure of the implementation of the Bolivian 1994 reform, the new ASEP law emphasises the need to start the reform at teacher training institute level – the Normales. In spite of this recent acknowledgement of the importance of teacher education in Bolivia, there is still a lack of academic, institutional, financial and statistical information in this area. In one of the few in-depth studies on teacher education in Bolivia, Lozada Pereira concludes that '*it is time for an investigation into the quality of teacher education not only by using standardised indicators, but also through an integral social science analysis of the complexities*' (2004: 161). This is exactly what this thesis aims to do. In addition to the need to explore the institutional mechanisms of teacher education, another pressing research area in the field of teacher education is to understand teachers' identities and motivations, particularly in diverse societies (Hamilton and Clandinin, 2011). In sum, the rationale of this thesis is to explain both these structural-institutional aspects of the governance of teacher education, as well as the agential features of Bolivia's teacher education system, in the context of the revolutionary transformation of Bolivian society that is currently taking place. The story of Ramiro in Box 1 effectively illustrates the relevance of this research motivation.

---

[9] Considering the very low level of teachers'salaries in Bolivia for a long time, the salaries still remain too low according to Bolivia's teacher unions (see also Talavera 2011). However, compared to other sectors, teachers' salaries are relatively high.

Box 1: Ramiro

The following story of Ramiro's life as an '*Aymara Bolivian, almost-teacher and taxi chauffeur*' as he refers to himself, perfectly illustrates the choices, strategies and tensions that Bolivia's future teachers face on a daily basis. Ramiro, 28, was born into a family with three brothers in the highland city of El Alto, the highly politicised support base of Evo Morales. His father was more dedicated to the bottle than to his young family and left when Ramiro was too young to remember him. His mother works in the food section of El Alto's gigantic market, where she sells various types of potatoes, quinoa and other goods. Every morning, Ramiro gets up at 5am to drive his mother to the local food distribution centre, where they load their daily merchandise in the back of the taxi. After Ramiro has dropped off his mother and her goods at the market, he usually manages to finish several taxi-rides before he drives down to the teacher training institute Simón Bolívar in the city of La Paz, where classes start at 7.30am.

Becoming a teacher was a logical, rational and vocational choice, Ramiro told. During a long interview at the kitchen table, he started to explain how '*my family wanted me to become something in life, and so I chose to become a teacher, because when you graduate you have a secure job and a secure salary, and I can support them*'. Moreover, he continued, '*I also wanted to become a teacher because I have good skills to teach, to laugh and communicate with young people. For two years, I worked on Isla del Sol [the Sun Island – in the Titicaca Lake] as an English and Aymara teacher, and there I became interested to enter the Normal*'. The final reason, he assured me, had grown during his training over the past years. '*In the Normal they teach you the theories, and it's very traditional. We just have to copy, and we get bored and tired. But this is not how we should teach our students later on. When I become a teacher, I want to give incentives to my students; I want them to enjoy school. I will talk about our Andean culture, we will play theatre in Aymara language, and I will let them make expositions of their own study projects*'. In addition to Ramiro's desire to improve the quality of education in his future classroom, he is also committed to the envisaged transformation of Bolivian society. '*I very much wish that my country Bolivia progresses. I voted for Evo, because he is an alternative for me. I keep having faith in my president, who is an indigenous, and he has suffered the same as we have. He comes from a very low class background, so he knows the suffering, and that is what he is fighting for. But, this change will need years; it is not an overnight change*'. However, together with many other (almost) teachers in Bolivia, Ramiro's political support to Evo and the MAS does not mean he agrees with all measures taken by the Ministry of Education, as is exemplified by the many demonstrations of both Ramiro's urban and rural colleagues. While Ramiro's older brother works as a full-time taxi driver, and his younger brother has recently joined the army, Ramiro is persistent about his future as a teacher.

It had, however, not been easy for Ramiro to get into the Normal. Like thousands of others, it took him three consecutive years before he finally passed the entrance exam and interview, and was lucky enough to be granted admission to the Normal Simón Bolívar, Bolivia's largest teacher training institute in the city of La Paz. When I first met Ramiro about four years ago, he was studying to become an English teacher, yet he suffered discrimination on the basis of his low language proficiency. This was partly due to the fact that he could not keep up with the level of English of other students, as he lacked the finances to pay for extra classes, which most other students did. He re-examined his destiny, and three years later he decided to switch his specialisation to become an Aymara teacher. '*Now, I am proud to become an Aymara teacher, because I identify with being indigenous, because I talk Aymara, because this is who I am*'. Ramiro's choice and feelings exemplify the current changes in Bolivian political discourse and education policy, in which indigenous cultures and languages are revalued. His story illustrates some of the various features around the future teachers' potential role, both as improvers of educational quality, as well as their latent political agency in processes of transformation in a highly inequal, diverse and conflictive Bolivian society.

1.2 Positioning this research within relevant debates in the literature

Teachers, like Ramiro, are either consciously or unknowingly strategic political actors, as they spend numerous hours with their students, and contribute to the way Bolivia's future generations will perceive their peers, neighbours, fellow citizens and foreign visitors. Also, becoming a teacher, and entering formal teacher education in one of the 'Normales', is perceived by many lower class and indigenous Bolivians as one of the few escape routes from poverty. This is clearly illustrated by groups of youngsters who see themselves as forced into going on hunger strike in protest at being refused entrance into a teacher training career. Bolivian teachers are often seen as important figures within communities (Canessa, 2004: 190) and as crucial actors in the implementation of nationwide education reforms (Van Dam, 2007: 5; Contreras and Talavera, 2003: 25). Hence, educators play a crucial role in constructing or deconstructing social imaginaries, such as the 'decolonised nation' the current Bolivian government envisages. In several places around the globe teachers have proven to be a potential *new intelligentsia* that can actively engage in transforming or reforming society, either in support of – or against – a hegemonic regime. From Sindhi nationalist teacher activists in Pakistan, to African-American civil-rights activist students in the United States, and Shining Paths' revolutionary basis at the University of Ayacucho in Peru; educators-with-a-mission can be found all over the world (Baud and Rutten, 2004: 213-214). In the words of Freire, the struggle to construct a more just society requires teachers who realise that their role is not a neutral one (Delany-Barmann, 2010: 193).

The knowledge(s) and skills required from teachers in the state's new vision of decolonising and inter-/intracultural education demand Bolivian teachers to become public intellectuals – an expectation that is seemingly in contrast to the low status and acknowledgement Bolivian teachers are still faced with in their daily lives. For a long time Bolivian teachers have been structurally undervalued, underpaid and underestimated with regard to their societal importance, and potential strategic importance in processes of development. Even though current policies have shifted their attention to the need to include (future) teachers in their strategies for social change, this discourse is not reflected in educational and societal reality in Bolivia, where teachers still struggle to cope with multiple jobs, conflicts-of-interest with parents and incertainty on what is expected from them with yet another reform. This situation has many resemblances to the situation in other parts of the world. Although teachers are commemorated annually on the 5th October on World Teachers' day[10], we still see a lack of recognition worldwide for the importance of the teaching profession. Many teachers – obviously in some cases more severe than in others – are given a low social and professional status, with low or even absent rewards and battle with a lack of quality training and support. Considering these global developments, we can speak of a *crisis in the teaching profession*, where a market model of education is pushing for an instrumentalist perspective on teachers as 'products', leading to stronger control mechanisms and a *new teacher accountability*, diminishing teacher morale (Vongalis-Macrow, 2007: 430-432).

---

[10] World teachers' day commemorates the UNESCO/ILO Recommendation Concerning the Status of Teachers of 1966.

A global crisis in the teaching profession

In line with a global tendency of a crisis within the teaching profession, the teaching profession in Bolivia neither has high social recognition nor adequate economic compensation (Lozada Pereira, 2004: 181). These factors are compounded by the presence of a problematic pre-service and in-service teacher education system. Due to processes of globalisation, since the 1990s a so-called 'global teacher reform agenda' is setting standards for a market oriented model of education in many places around the globe. Policies that 'deal with teachers' are borrowed and copied from one place to the other, sometimes without the necessary adaptations to another context (Apple, 2009: xi). Teachers are inserted into new systems of control, accreditation and certification, where incentives and rewards are linked to performance, all aimed to compete in a global market (Tatto, 2007: 8). Robertson (2011: 3-4) analyses how over the past decade, market-driven policy making by the World Bank and the International Finance Corporation has influenced teachers' work on a global scale, with evidence suggesting that these policies not only create '*a worse set of conditions for teachers in schools*', but that they are also '*likely to generate negative outcomes and diminished opportunities for learning*'. These organisations push for a market-oriented restructuring of education systems through mechanisms such as public-private-partnerships, often followed by reduced teachers' salaries (and training), which feeds into the World Bank's interest of a reduction of GDP (Gross Domestic Product) spend on teachers' wages and greater control over teachers' capability, by linking teacher performance to student outcomes (Roberston 2011: 4). Bolivia's recent policy shift endeavours to counter these global tendencies towards a commodification of the education profession.

When schools, within a neo-liberal human capital perspective, become mere factories with the aim to transmit certain skills (mathematics, reading and writing) in order to form productive citizens, teachers become 'interchangeable parts' in the production process, working with standardised formats (curricula, teaching to the test). Learning, then, becomes an instrumental means to an end (grades, certificates, job opportunities). Whereas most of these 'performance-based' and 'teacher-accountability' measures argue to pursue an improvement of the quality of education, we should question if limiting teachers' authority and autonomy to a one-size-fits-all market model will do this job. Following a market driven global education model, in many places teacher morale and quality is not enhanced but further unravelled by the shortening of teacher training courses or cutting teacher salaries – a situation that until recently was also reflected in Bolivia.

Bolivia's current ASEP law is an attempt to counter the global tendency of a standardised, market-oriented reform process, as its discourse proclaims to foster various forms of knowledges and a historical and contemporary socio-political awareness, through education a public education system. Yet, the data of this study reveals inadequate engagement of, and support for, teachers' meaningful participation in policy-making and implementation processes, limiting their spirit and possibilities to encourage critical and political(-ly aware) education. The thesis explores both the positions of resistance as well as support to the new decolonising reform process of the various actors involved in the (teacher) education arena, including teachers' unions and social movements. However, the potential impact of teachers' conscious or unintended strategies on processes of educational and social transformation is not to be overestimated either. It is important to bear in mind how on a global scale educators at all levels of the system – and not excluding those in Bolivia – suffer low status, low salaries and little to no support or training, even when they are supposed to be bringing about new education reforms or even societal transformation.

Teachers thus face a contradictory role, on the one hand being a 'professional' that is assigned with socialising future generations and expected to restrain from striking let alone collectively organising trade unions. On the other hand, as civil servant, teachers are faced with low wages and low status, forcing them to act collectively to defend their interests. Hence, teachers unions' work is very politicised, since they have to both defend their collective members interests, as well as some notion of 'public education' as an interest of the general public – which often clashes with state led (neoliberal) reforms (Novelli, 2009). Harvie's (2006) elaboration of teachers' struggle 'within, against and beyond capital' is useful here. Harvie explains how 'the classroom is a site of struggle' in which teachers produce new labour power for a capitalist mode of production in the school-as-factory (*within capital*), yet at the same time struggle against and even beyond capital, in collective (unionised) and individual ways. Harvie describes how in Africa '*students and teachers have engaged in countless struggles – student strikes, teacher strikes, exam boycotts, demonstrations, road blocks, occupations of schools and university buildings*' (2006: 22).

Likewise, such events of demonstrating teachers take place in Bolivia and other Latin American countries. In one of the few studies that critically analyses this topic, Kosar Altinyelken (2010) warns against simplifying teachers' resistance as something negative and argues how, in the case of Turkey, teachers' strategies to modify and resist the new curriculum is actually driven by a positive rationale. Instead of simply viewing teachers as conservative and problematic, she makes a case for perceiving teachers as inventive and knowledgeable decision-makers with well established beliefs, or 'good sense', about their roles and the needs of their students (Kosar Altinyelken, 2010: 196-198). She aligns with a growing body of literature that calls for a more nuanced view on the tensions between teachers' 'good sense', their 'principled resistance', their professional autonomy and growing organisational controls. Rather than putting aside teachers' resistance as a psychological deficit or basic reluctance, teachers' *can* also respond from their professional principles (Achinstein and Ogawa, 2006). In the case of Bolivia, as Talavera's (2011) work shows, teacher resistance from the urban union since the military dictatorships and the subsequent neoliberal period are not rooted in professional principles for improving educational quality anymore, but rather in improving working conditions and salary issues. In conclusion, we should avoid simplistic black-and-white accounts of teachers' resistance being either positive or emancipatory versus negative and un-principled.

Teaching for socio-educational change – a critical pedagogy of social justice

What, then, is the (potential) role of educators in Bolivia's national context where – at least rhetorically – the state supports a 'radical pedagogy'? Why do teachers still resist, even when policies seem to be more inclusive and just (at least in ideology)? Can we conclude that teachers are not necessarily a progressive force, but in some cases even more so a conservative one? The complexity of teachers' work is reflected in that it responds to both social and educational change. There is a present policy priority towards their educational role in the 'knowledge economy', downplaying teachers' social relevancy (Torres del Castillo, 2007). However, in the case of Turkey, Kosar Altinyelken shows how teachers' political affiliations, concerns for the

11

future of the regime, and more general criticism of the government, all influenced teachers' attitudes towards the new curriculum and their classroom practices (2010: 244). She suggests the need to study the political issues surrounding reform implementation, which is similarly important in contexts such as Bolivia. This research wants to stress the importance of both educational and societal roles of teachers, albeit very complex, especially in the unstable context of Bolivia. This idea is also brought forward by those authors in favour of (developing) social justice teacher education, which aims to combine both the 'professional' (knowledge and learning) tasks and the social justice tasks of teachers (Cochran-Smith et al, 2009). Grant (2009) reminds us of the story told by the American black social movement leader Baldwin in 1963 in New York, in front of an audience of around two hundred teachers. This speech became known as '*A Talk to the Teachers*' and it openly challenges teachers at a personal level to become '*workers for social justice*', by stating '*it is your responsibility to change society if you think of yourself as an educated person...*'. Baldwin was one of the founders of the idea that teachers *could* function as a critical mass in the struggle for social justice (Grant, 2009: 654-655).

In many places around the globe teachers are often attacked in the media, blamed and shamed as being the main cause of low quality education, instead of seeing teachers as part of a potential solution. In my view this is contra-productive in the endeavour for better quality and social justice oriented education. Teachers have an enormous, important and difficult task to fulfil, and they should be given the opportunity and incentive to develop themselves and to receive the status and compensation that they deserve (Lopes Cardozo, 2009). Both critical pedagogues Apple and Giroux thus warn for the devaluation and deskilling of the teaching profession, through increased productivity levels and control (Apple, 1982: 24; Giroux, 2003b: 47; Apple, 2009: ix-xii). According to Giroux, '*the deskilling that teachers experience across the world is further exacerbated by World Bank pedagogies that impose on countries forms of privatization and standardised curricula that undermine the potential for critical inquiry and engaged citizenship. Learning in this instance is depoliticized and often reduced to teaching to the test*' (2003b: 47-49).

Education for social change ideally contributes to both academic competencies and the democratisation of both institutions and relations within – and beyond – the walls of the school; students and teachers should not just study social injustices, but actively transform them (North, 2008). Educators, collectively organised amongst themselves, yet also together with other social activists, can employ a radical pedagogy of social justice as a constructive form of resistance, political intervention and to create opportunities for social transformation: '*learning is not about processing received knowledge but about actually transforming it as part of a more expansive struggle for individual rights and social justice*' (Giroux, 2003a: 11). Committed to the idea of social justice education, North writes about 'performative pedagogy', which challenges the distinction in learning practices between knowledge and action. In this view, education as a transformative tool is not about 'learning about', but 'learning from', or actively challenging deep internal beliefs and world views (North, 2006; North, 2006; North, 2008).

The insights from critical pedagogy literature are relevant when researching education and social transformation in the case of Bolivia, and have influenced the design and analysis of this study, as critical pedagogy sees education as an instrument to battle structural forms of marginalisation through the empowerment of agents of social change. During the past three decades, critical education theorists (to name a few: Apple, 1982; 2009; Banks, 2004; hooks, 1994;

Giroux, 2003b; Sleeter, 1996) have argued for a critical approach that can be loosely identified as 'critical pedagogy', although various other terms (radical pedagogy, democratic education) are also in use (Edwards Jr., 2010). Critical or radical pedagogy is an educational movement that has been largely inspired by Marxist theory, Gramsci's work on cultural hegemony and Freire's work on education for liberation. A critical pedagogy perspective is needed in order to tackle the fallacies of neoliberal inspired and market-driven education policies, and their exclusionary effects on marginalised groups. Giroux, for example, recalls how education is part of politics, power and authority, urging social scientists to analyse and explain how dominant discourses and social relations affect (non-)school going children and youth in societies characterised by deep structures of discrimination. What is particularly interesting of Giroux's work for this study, is his demand to '*make the pedagogical more political by identifying the link between learning and social transformation, provide the conditions for students to learn a range of critical capacities in order to expand the possibilities of human agency, and recover the role of the teacher as an oppositional intellectual*' (Giroux, 2003a: 7). This thesis builds from these theoretical insights, and places them in the contemporary context of Bolivian political tendencies against (globalised) neoliberalism and in favour of – at least ideologically – collective and individual rights and social justice.

The following quote from the Bolivian ASEP law (2007) shows the significance and relevance of the relation between education and social justice in the Bolivian context: '*Education is in and for life, with dignity and social justice assuming work like a vital necessity and an integrative and balancing relationship with the cosmos and nature, to live well (vivir bien).*' The new constitution further stipulates that teachers are expected to engage in community life by undertaking (action) research to '*solve productive and social problems*' in the community, to '*promote scientific, cultural and linguistic diversity*', and to '*participate side by side with the local population in all processes of social liberation, in order to create a society with more equity and social justice*' (Article 91 of the new constitution, 2008: 20). Recognising that social justice is a broad and multi-interpretable concept, this study explores the Bolivian interpretation of what a socially just education system – and society – looks like. The aforementioned Latin American coloniality debates are helpful theoretical tools to understand this Bolivian conceptualisation of social justice. Based on document analysis and interview data, for this study I identify the Bolivian conceptualisation of social justice in education as 'the process of transformation through decolonisation of the education system in order for all Bolivians to '*vivir bien*' (live well)'. As mentioned in the introduction of the book, *vivir bien* is a central concept in the National Development Plan, the constitution and the ASEP reform.

Similar to the link between justice and education in current Bolivian policies, at a global level over the past decade the term social justice is appearing more and more throughout the field of education – in literature and programme design of teacher education programmes, in educational conferences and in scholarly articles and books (North, 2006: 507). Social justice has become education's latest 'catchphrase' (North, 2008), not least in the field of teacher education (Zeichner, 2009). Zeichner, a key author in the subfield of 'Teacher Education for Social Justice', outlines the three main categories of theories about the concept of social justice: firstly, a liberal approach to social justice focused on the distribution of material goods and services, mainly based on the work of Rawls (North, 2006; Rawls in Zeichner, 2009: xvi; North, 2006: 511); secondly, recognition theories which emphasise the importance of social relations among individuals and groups within the institutions (based on the work of e.g. Young 1990, in

Zeichner, 2009: xvi); and finally, theories that combine both distributive and relational justice, such as Frasers' approach, which I find useful when analysing the present socio-political and educational development in Bolivia (further elaborated in the next chapter). In a case study on pre-service teacher training for elementary science teachers in New York, Moore's findings suggest that *'teacher education must play a more immediate, fundamental and emancipatory role in preparing pre-service teachers in developing science teachers identities and a stance toward social justice'* (Moore, 2008: 589). Moore, drawing from Lewis, Banks, Cochran-Smith and others, argues how in the pre-service preparation of teacher students, social justice involves exploring the social construction of unequal hierarchies, privileges and access to power, and consequently to deconstruct unjust and oppressive structures for marginalised groups of students (Moore, 2008: 591-592). Studying the case of Bolivia, then, becomes particularly relevant considering the present anti-neoliberal government and the new education reform, and the possible effects on a cultivation of social justice (teacher) education.

While positioning this research in the broader field of social theory, and particularly within international education debates, I find it useful to draw on the broader critique on educational research developed by Roger Dale (see also Novelli and Lopes Cardozo, 2008). According to Dale, most educational research falls under the notion of 'educational politics' – a somewhat narrower view on educational policies directed to improve the status quo. Rather than understanding education policies as 'applied education policy', this thesis endeavours to produce a 'political sociology of education' (Dale, 1994). It aims to follow the 'politics of education' approach – which sees education systems within a wider multilevel context, and poses questions that reach beyond the education sector and the national state level (Dale, 2000; Dale, 2005).

Drawing from this approach, some key arguments from the broader critique of mainstream educational research developed by Dale (2000; 2005) help to define four 'considerations' for carrying out research from a critical theory perspective. Firstly, research should avoid *disciplinary parochialism*, by conducting interdisciplinary research and combining insights from different sciences (e.g. for this thesis this includes literature from the fields of international development, international relations, educational sciences, critical pedagogy, conflict studies, etc).[11] Secondly, and in recognition of the globalised world we live in, a 'politics of education research approach' should focus beyond the state as a main actor, incorporating a multilevel perspective to avoid *methodological nationalism*. For instance, a narrow focus on the state as the main actor ignores other important players at the grassroots and international levels, above and below the state. Thirdly, research should overcome a persistent *ethnocentrism* within the literature as well as in development approaches, which continue to see the 'Western' state as a model, and the 'Western' way to development as the only one. In this study, I draw from the insights of Latin American coloniality debates (discussed in the following chapter), in acknowledging the existence and equal status of 'other knowledges'. Drawing from Sousa Santos' notion of the 'sociology of rebellion' and the need to 'start listening to the South', it can be argued how, in order to challenge the dominant role of western academia in producing 'valid' knowledge, we need to seek out alternative knowledges as a key task of strengthening critical

---

[11] Fairclough in his Critical Discourse Approach argues for 'transdisciplinary research', which entails a long term collaboration and dialogue between disciplines (Fairclough 2005: 923).

theory (Novelli, 2006). Moreover, in accepting that, research (design and results) will naturally be influenced by the geography, class, gender, and ethnicity of both researchers and research subjects, efforts should be made to value and support research undertaken by academics, grassroots movements, unions and so on from the Global South[12]. Particularly in educational research, alternative and indigenous non-Western schooling systems have been largely ignored since they were seen as 'falling outside of the parameters of "legitimate" study in the history of the philosophy of education' (Reagan, 2005: 6). Fourthly, we need to challenge a tendency to *a-historicism* in research.[13] This thesis aims to address these four considerations for carrying out social science research, by looking through a critical theoretical and political lense at radical processes of social transformation as exemplified in Bolivia's teacher education sector and beyond.

1.3 Research proposition and research questions

Even though this case study on the role of Bolivian teacher education and educators in processes of social change has a particular spacio-temporal specifity, it does carry a more general relevance as it aims to contribute to wider debates about the socio-political role of teacher education institutes, and its key education actors, in furthering or resisting processes of social change. Inspired by the thinking of Sousa Santos (interview by Dale and Robertson, 2004) on a contextualised and bottom-up ecology of knowledges, in contrast to a hegemonic monoculture of knowledges, this thesis endeavours to tell the story of Bolivian experiences of societal transformations through the lens of teacher education institutions and actors. Or in the words of Sousa Santos: *'we need alternative knowledges for alternative societies and sociabilities'* (interview by Dale and Robertson, 2004: 158). Bolivia's attempts to decolonise the education system therefore deserve closer attention from the global academic field.

With the aim to place this particular case study within its connections to other cases (particularly in the Latin American context), the more general goal of this thesis is to understand the role of teacher education institutes and actors in underpinning or opposing emancipatory education and processes of societal transformation. It takes the new 'revolutionary' government of Evo Morales as its case study. By doing so, the thesis intends to explore how and to what extent Bolivian pre-service teacher education institutes and actors – including teacher students and trainers – develop (un)intended strategies for or against the societal transformation that is envisaged by the new Bolivian Plurinational constitutional regime. Hence, the main research question of this thesis is:

---

[12] For this thesis, I refer to the Global South as a metaphor for a social, economic and geopolitical space where 'racialiced and subaltern peoples' are struggling to 'establish institutional structures that create a space for alternative theoretical projects that transgress europeanity' (Maldonade-Torres in North 2006: 529) and, regardless of geographical location, a site inhabited by those suffering from (and resisting to) global capitalism (Santos in Mathers and Novelli 2007: 234; Novelli 2006: 280).

[13] In practice, a critical and comparative historiography should be at the basis of any education system aiming to foster its positive face (Bush and Saltarelli 2000).

Main Research Question:

How do Bolivian pre-service teacher education institutes and actors develop strategies for or against the socio-educational transformation that is envisaged by the new Plurinational constitutional regime?

In order to answer this question, the book has been structured into five parts, and directed by the following guiding questions (Table 1):

	Guiding questions and book parts
Part I	*What are the main theoretical and methodological foundations of the research?*
Part II	*How can we understand the historical and present processes of continuity and change in Bolivia's socio-political, economic and educational context?*
Part III	*What are the main structural factors – historical and present governance mechanisms, main actors and power dynamics at different scales – that affect Bolivian teacher education?*
Part IV	*How can we understand the agential factors – teacher students' and teacher trainers' identities, motivations and perceived roles – in the context of an urban and a rural Normal?*
Part V	*What are (future) teachers (un)intentional 'strategies for/against change' and how do these relate to the strategically selective context?*

Table 1, guiding questions and book parts

1.4 Definitions of main concepts

A number of important concepts arise from these questions and deserve further attention. I provide a relevant definition for each concept in relation to the Bolivian context in Box 2. The following theoretical chapter further illustrates these main concepts and their relations in a conceptual scheme. At the start of Parts III, IV and V of the book, I provide an overview and discussion of the relevant debates in the literature that it is necessary to be familiar with in order to understand the data analysis in those book parts.

Box 2. The main concepts and operational definitions

Bolivian pre-service teacher education → the formal system of training for Bolivia's future teachers in preparation of their teaching career. The study focuses on one urban and one rural Bolivian teacher education institute (*Normal*), located respectively in La Paz and Paracaya (see Map locations in chapter 1). Teacher education has a duration of 3.5 years (recently changed to 5 years) and is defined as the responsibility of Bolivia's plurinational state (Asamblea Constituyente de Bolivia, 2008: article 96).

The new Plurinational constitutional regime → the democratically elected (December 2005) and re-elected (December 2009) government led by the first indigenous president Evo Morales, and a new Plurinational constitution as of February 2009, which proposes an Education Reform entitled *Avelino Siñani-Elizardo Pérez* (ASEP), which aims for decolonized, inter- and intra-cultural, communitarian and productive education and pursues social justice and a dignified way of living ('*vivir bien*').

Social Transformation → according to the new Bolivian constitution this forms part of the essential task of the state, as it should '*constitute a just and harmonious society, founded on decolonisation without discrimination or exploitation, with full social justice to consolidate plurinational identities*' (2008: article 9). In the Constitution, education is defined as '*liberating, revolutionary, critical and fostering solidarity*' (article 78), promoting '*gender equity, non-violence and human rights*' (article 79), and advancing the '*integral development of critical social consciousness in and for life, to live well*' ('*vivir bien*', article 80).

Social transformation and social justice are directly linked to the goals of higher education, which includes teacher education, as being: '*intracultural, intercultural and plurilingual, and has as its mission the integral training of highly qualified and professionally competent humans; to develop processes of scientific research to solve problems related to productivity and the social environment; promoting policies and social interaction to strengthen scientific, cultural and linguistic diversity; to participate with the community in all processes of social liberation to build a society with greater equity and social justice*' (2008: article 91).

Book part III: chapters 5 and 6
Structural factors → ***Teacher education institutes*** → historical and present governance mechanisms (with a focus on the past two decades), main actors and power dynamics at the different institutional, community, national, regional and global scales that enhance or resist transformation of Bolivian pre-service teacher education as envisaged in the ASEP reform.

Book part IV: chapters 7 and 8
Agential factors → ***Teacher students and trainers*** → includes the complex and hybrid identities of Bolivian future teachers and their trainers, the various perceptions of an ideal teacher by different actors, future teachers' motivations and perceived motivations (by other actors) and alleged roles of teachers in urban and rural contexts.

Book part V: chapters 9 and 10
Strategies for/against change → individual and collective (un)intentional strategies for, or against, change in relation to the strategically selective context – bringing together structural and agential factors.

1.5 Thesis layout

The book is divided into five parts, all related to one of the five guiding questions presented above. These sub questions have guided the design, data collection, analysis and writing, and are inspired by the 'three levels of education questions' proposed by Dale (2006: 190). The 'first level' of analysis focuses on the level of educational practice, and includes questions such as *who is taught, by whom, where and when, under what circumstances and with what results?* The 'second level' deals with education politics, and questions like *how, by whom and at what scale are these issues [the practice of teacher education] problematised, determined, coordinated, governed, administered and managed?* And finally, the more abstract 'third level' engages with 'the politics of education', and asks questions including *in whose interest are these practices and policies carried out; what is the scope of education and what are its relations to other sectors/scales?* The thesis does not aspire to cover all of these questions, but by engaging with various questions linked to all three levels, it does endeavour to open up *'extensions of the research imagination and of spaces of dialogue around other educations and education otherwise'* (Dale, 2006: 190).

In part I of the book, entitled 'THEORETICAL AND METHODOLOGICAL FOUNDATIONS', chapter 1 explores the ontological and epistemological foundations of the study, and aims to develop a meta-theoretical interdisciplinary framework to understand the role and impact of Bolivian teacher education institutional mechanisms and actors in relation to the government's transformatory discourse and policies of decolonisation. Drawing from Hay's (2002a), Jessop's (2005) and Dale's (2010) interpretations of critical realism, this study is further inspired by the Cultural Political Economy (of Education) (Jessop, 2004b; Robertson, forthcoming) and Dale's 'Politics of Education' approach (2000; 2005). The thesis departs from the idea that Bolivia's current political project of transformation not only covers economic redistribution, yet also includes cultural and political aspects of recognition and representation, and as such draws from feminist (Fraser 1995; 2005) and critical pedagogical theories (such as Apple, 1982 and Giroux, 2003). The chapter continues to explore neo-Gramscian insights on processes of state transformation, and the role of both organic intellectuals and education within them and links them to theoretical debates on 'education for emancipation and liberation' that have been applied to this study, including Latin American theoretical debates on coloniality and critical pedagogy literature on the role of education in social transformation. This leads me to discuss the main debates in current literature on Social Justice Teacher Education (SJTE), and I derive some key criteria that are relevant to the Bolivian context, including an action-research methododology that supports critical thinking and reflexivity of (future) teachers. The chapter then turns to discuss the Strategic Relation Approach as developed by Hay (2002a), Jessop (2005) and others as the main inspiration for the methodological approach of this study, and aims to apply this to the field of education by also drawing from the multiscalar 'politics of education approach' (Dale 2000; 2005) and critical pedagogy. The result of this is illustrated in a conceptual scheme. Finally, the chapter highlights the specific aspects of this thesis' research design, its methodological tools, units of analysis, research methods and ethics. More specific literature discussions are introduced at the start of Parts III, IV and V on respectively institutional change, teacher identities and motivations, and teacher agency.

The second part of the book includes chapters 3 and 4 on 'BOLIVIA, TEACHERS AND CHANGE: SOCIO-POLITICAL AND EDUCATIONAL CONTEXT', and directly applies the meta-theoretical insights discussed in Part I. Chapter 3 explores the diverse characteristics of Bolivian socio-political, geographical, ethnic and cultural historical and contemporary context. The chapter continues to define several dimensions of conflict in contemporary Bolivian society, which consequently impact – and are influenced by – the work of educators. Chapter 4 takes this discussion to the education arena, outlining the relevant historical developments in this field, with specific attention to the tensions over, and implementation challenges of, the intercultural and bilingual education reform of 1994. The chapter focuses on the specifics of the history of Bolivian teacher education from the early twentieth century up to the latest reform process in the 1990s. Part II thus provides the necessary historical and contemporary socio-political and educational background in order to further look into the issues of future teachers, their education and social transformation in Bolivia in the remaining chapters.

The third part of the book, 'STRUCTURAL FACTORS: INSTITUTIONAL GOVERNANCE', then engages with the current strategic selective context of the governance of teacher training institutes, its present mechanisms, actors and power-plays. Part III starts with an introduction on the main debates in the literature, which help to explain processes of institutional change and the main developments, strategies, opportunities and obstacles of teacher training governance. In doing so, it aims to react to the question of how and why teacher training is, or can be, changed according to the political ambitions of the new regime. Chapter 5 is dedicated to explain the current policy initiatives of the ASEP law for decolonising education, its implications for the teacher education sector, actors' various positions on and power struggles around the new policy and finally a set of challenges for future implementation of ASEP. Chapter 6 explores the politics of teacher education, portraying the governance in and around the Normales as a socio-political battlefield. The chapter first discusses the increasingly tense struggles for future teachers to get into these institutes. It continues to look at the way Bolivian actors perceive the various obstacles to institutional transformation, as well as potential opportunities for change, and several recent reform initiatives in the period between 2000 and 2010 are analysed. Consequently, the chapter zooms into the '*Practica Docente e Investigacion*' (PDI – teachers' practice and research) course and analyses the potentials and challenges of this course as a promising educational initiative for enhancing teachers' reflection, creative engagement and critical socio-political awareness geared towards social justice. The chapter ends by analysing if, and how far, the practices in Bolivia's Normales reflect the theoretical ideas of SJTE.

Addressing the institutional level is, however, only a part of this research approach, as the fourth part of the book 'AGENTIAL FACTORS: IDENTITIES AND MOTIVATIONS' aspires to understand and explain the agential factors underlying Bolivia's future teachers' agency for or against change. The brief literature discussion at the start of Part IV is needed in order to explain my findings on the motivations, identities and perceived roles of Bolivia's future generation of teachers, and the relation to the contemporary socio-political 'discursive context of change'. Chapters 7 and 8 aim to challenge the homogenising views that exist in the literature and society on Bolivia's teachers as poor and marginalised peasants and their efforts to become '*mestizos*', and reproduce homogenising educational tactics. Instead, in chapter 7 I demonstrate a more diverse picture of the internal identities of student teachers and their trainers, particularly highlighting a changing profile for Bolivia's future teacher force in terms of their increasing age and experience, as well as changing self identification processes. Chapter 8 continues to analyse the construction of Bolivian teachers' identities, by first outlining the various perceptions of future teachers' alleged roles in urban and rural environments. Secondly, the chapter analyses the various views on 'the ideal Bolivian teacher' and finally, it discusses teachers' actual motivations to enter the teaching profession. In doing so, it challenges the assumption that Bolivian teachers are only driven by economic reasons, and it argues for the need to acknowledge and act upon a latent vocation and socio-politically engagement of Bolivia's future teachers.

Finally, in the fifth part entitled 'AGENCY, CHANGE AND CONTINUITY', I bring together the insights on the structural and agential factors in a discussion of the potentials, difficulties and limits to Bolivia's future teachers' agency as agents of social change. In the introduction to this last part, I highlight the main issues from the debates on teachers as agents of change. In chapter 9, I take the discussion to the obstacles and niches for Bolivian teachers' individual and collective strategies for or against the governmental envisaged project of transformation. The chapter finalises by questioning whether in a structural and agential context of continuity and change, Bolivia's teachers could be perceived as 'soldiers of liberation' or rather as guards of continuation. As a way of conclusion, the final chapter 10 returns to respond to the main research proposition and question of *how Bolivian pre-service teacher education institutes and actors develop strategies for or against socio-educational transformation that is envisaged by the new Plurinational constitutional regime?* The chapter uses the outcomes of the data analysis of this research to reflect upon and respond to the theoretical approaches and insights presented in chapter 2, and the introductions to the Book Parts III, IV and V, in a modest attempt to contribute to further theoretical understandings of teachers' engagement in processes of educational and socio-political transformation.

PART I

THEORETICAL & METHODOLOGICAL FOUNDATIONS

2

Theoretical and methodological framework to understand social change, teacher education and teachers in Bolivia

'Hope provides the basis for dignifying our labour as intellectuals, offering up critical knowledge linked to democratic social change, and allowing both students and teachers to recognize ambivalence and uncertainty as a fundamental dimension of learning to engage in critique, dialogue, and an open ended struggle for justice'
(Giroux, 2003b: 49)

'You have to be committed to study, to become the light and hope that Bolivia needs for its development'
President Morales in an address to secondary school students in Santa Cruz
(Ministerio de Educación de Bolivia, 2011)

2.1 Introduction

'One state has died, and one state has been born. The colonial state is no longer, and the national state has arrived, bringing hope, for all the people of the world'. These are Evo Morales' dramatic words as he is inaugurated ritually as the first indigenous leader of Bolivia in the ancient site of Tiahuanacu in January 2006.[14] Hope is often mentioned in relation to processes of change, as the above quotes reveal. This hope-change nexus becomes particularly relevant in highly unequal societies, such as Bolivia, where historically marginalised groups with great anticipation struggle for a better future. This chapter discusses theoretical insights that help to understand the complexities and tensions between the discourses and reality of Bolivia's transformation processes, and the role of education and educators in working toward a better world.

Theory helps us to make sense of the (in)visible world around us. Theory is both time and space bound (Cox, 1996) and fluid rather than static, as it is constantly rethought and reshaped on the basis of fieldwork (Dale, 2010). 'Doing' social science research is, however, anything but a simple task. This is even more so the case for fieldwork research in Bolivia and its constantly changing society and politics. With this chapter I hope to make a modest contribution to creating a suitable theoretical frame for understanding contemporary transformation processes in Bolivian education and society. My approach to studying Bolivian teacher training in its changing socio-political context includes interpretations and variations of key aspects of critical

---

[14] See BBCs video reporting, 'Evo Morales sworn in as spiritual leader',
http://news.bbc.co.uk/2/hi/americas/8473899.stm (last accessed 01-04-2011).

ethnography such as reflexivity, (multiscalar) dialogue and solidarity – for this particular study interpreted as a longer term dialogue, engagement and dissemination strategy with various groups of respondents involved in the study. Research grounded in critical methodology is particularly suitable for understanding pre-service teacher identity, agency and the stance toward social justice because it seeks to document the process of empowerment of voice and human agency. This way, *'critical pedagogy constitutes an emancipatory and democratic function for school and research so that marginalized voices are heard'* (Moore, 2008: 590). Although the scope of this research is limited, in the sense that it cannot fully do justice by painting a generalisable picture of the whole Bolivian teacher education system, as it only includes two of the twenty-seven Normales in Bolivia, it does aspire to contribute to a better understanding of this under-researched field.

2.2 Meta-theoretical inspirations

With regard to ontological and epistemological perspectives, this study most closely adheres to the theoretical perspective of critical realism. More specifically, it draws from a particular version of critical realism, which has been at the basis of Bob Jessop's work on Cultural Political Economy (CPE). As Susan Robertson's book *A Class Act: Changing Teachers Work, Globalisation and the State* (2000) suggests, critical realism is a powerful methodology for studying the social world of teachers. Ontologically, critical realism affirms there is a reality that exists independently of our observation of it, since structures and processes can only partly be experienced at the empirical level (Fairclough, 2005: 922). It thus avoids a positivist assumption of empiricism (Hall, 2009), since multiple interpretations of this reality exist (Hay, 2002a: 122). According to a critical realist approach, theory is a tool that should be utilised to explore and explain the three domains of reality, being: 1) *the empirical* (visible experience of the real and actual); 2) *the actual* (visible and invisible events and processes); and 3) *the real* (or the invisible structures, causal mechanisms and powers) (Jessop, 2005: 41). Epistemologically, critical realism pleads for a critical constructivist approach, which starts from the appreciation that we cannot understand (political) behaviour and power relations without understanding the *ideas* actors hold about their environment. Thus, it recognises a complex and dialectical interaction between material and ideational factors (Hay, 2002a: 208). Furthermore, critical realism asserts that knowledge is produced through continuous confrontations between 'retroductive theoretical hypotheses' generated through processes of enquiry (Jessop, 2005: 43) by asking *'what needed to have happened for this to be the case'*? (Dale 2010).[15] This 'version' of critical realism aims to explain social phenomena and to make generalisable claims about them. Bearing in mind the intrinsic tension in case study research, between particularity and generalisability, the conclusions of this research, about social transformation and teacher education in Bolivia, should be located within a specific time and place, while at the same time, with great care, it outlines some generalisable insights in its conclusions.

Building on the critical realist recognition of the importance of both the discursive and the material, the Cultural Political Economy (CPE) approach developed by Jessop and colleagues at Lancaster University takes 'the cultural turn' in political and economic research seriously

---

[15] 'The social structures, institutions, mechanisms, rules, resources, etc. that human agents draw upon in order to initiate action, can in principle be *retroduced* and their operation uncovered and *explained*', Dale explained during a lecture at the University of Amsterdam in August 2010, '[From a critical realist perspective] evidential statements are the mediated results of investigation and so never directly reflect real or actual phenomena'. Statements derived from the lecture included in this thesis (Dale, 2010) were agreed upon by R. Dale in personal communication, May 2011.

(Jessop, 2004b: 160). Jessop's approach to CPE draws mainly from (critical) Marxist theoretical models, as it seeks to follow the cultural turn without disregarding '*the articulation of semiosis with the interconnected materialities of economics and politics within wider social formation*' (Jessop, 2004b:159). This perspective thus stresses the importance of including semiosis in political economic analysis, with semiosis being defined as 'the intersubjective production of meaning', including narrativity, rhetoric, hermeneutics, identity, reflexivity, historicity and discourse. Closely linked to Latin American coloniality debates (discussed below), CPE's epistemological stance emphasises the contextuality and historicity of knowledge claims (Jessop 2004b), whilst at the same time stressing the materiality of social relations, and the constraints agents face (Robertson, forthcoming).

A relevant interpretation of CPE for the field of education is provided by Susan Robertson, and carries the name 'cultural political economy of education' (CPE/E) (Robertson, forthcoming). The CPE/E, as well, takes the cultural turns seriously by also examining the role of semiosis. It sees education '*not as a pre-given container or universal and unchanging category of social relations and life-worlds, but as a complex terrain and outcome of discursive, material and institutionalised struggles over the role of education in the social contract*' (Robertson, forthcoming). From a critical pedagogical perspective, Robertson reminds us how education is '*a key site of cultural production and social reproduction*' (Ibid.). In summary, the CPE/E helps us to disentangle and disclose the complex (and contradictory) ways in which discourses/ideas/imaginaries (such as development, knowledge or decolonisation), actors/institutions (such as the nation state, international organisations, as well as sub-national educational institutions including the Normales) and material capabilities/power (resources, aid, information) are mobilised to strategically and selectively advance an imagined (decolonising Bolivian) economy and its material reproduction, within which education is now being re/constituted in particular ways.

Although this thesis has an empirical focus on the level of Bolivian teacher training institutions, it places these organisations in a broader local, national, regional and global context. The research aims to refrain from seeing globalisation and regionalisation as predominantly one-way processes of influence from the top (global and/or regional levels) down to the national and local levels. In order to avoid methodological nationalism, there is a need to explore the relationships between 'the different scales of governance' (Dale, 2005: 124), with governance being defined as '*the work of governing broken down into independent sets of activities*', not necessarily performed by the state (Dale, 2005: 129). Thus, instead of only applying a narrow analysis of Bolivian 'Education Politics', I aim to also engage with the 'Politics of Education' in Bolivia (Dale, 2005: 139-141). Dale's 'politics of education' approach seeks to understand and explain the 'social contract' for education: what does society give to education, and what is expected in return? Through what 'logic of intervention' does education work; *how* does it seek to deliver on its part of the social contract? Should it restore the status quo? And, should it modernise or control its population? (Dale, 2010; 2006). This thesis deals with the varying answers to these questions for Bolivian education over time, with the most current 'logic of intervention' being 'decolonisation through education'.

The thesis also embraces some of the ideas of Roger Dale's Globally Structured Educational Agenda, particularly his conceptualisation of 'Global', implying the '*social and economic forces operating supranationally and transnationally, rather than internationally, to elude, break down or override*' *national boundaries, while reconstructing the relations between nations'* (Dale, 2000: 428).[16] In order to understand Bolivia's new education reform for decolonising education, I both look at the 'Program' of the ASEP law (the content, the innovative policy itself), as well as the 'Program Ontology', or *how* this policy was designed and works (Dale, 2005; Pawson, 2002). In other words, it is not the ASEP policy itself that 'works', rather the actual implementation of the policy initiative depends on *'the nature of their subjects and the circumstances of the initiative'* and *'the resources they [the initiatives] offer to enable their subjects [teachers, curriculum developers, etc.] to make them work'* (Pawson, 2002: 342). This *process* of how various actors interpret the ASEP law is called the 'program mechanism'. Thus, it is this programme mechanism that triggers change, rather than the actual 'programme' (the ASEP law) itself. In summary, from a critical realist inpired politics of education approach, this thesis, in its design and analysis, engages with the various scales and actors of the Bolivian education field that are inherently involved in processes of societal change – either as drivers or resisting forces.

2.3 A social justice and (neo)Gramscian perspective on socio-political and educational change in Bolivia

Following from the rationale of this research presented in the first chapter, present day processes of social transformation in Bolivia are not just about an economic redistribution of wealth (and educational and work) opportunities among different classes, it is also very much about struggles for cultural recognition and political representation of large and varying groups that for so long have been excluded and discriminated against in Bolivian society. Struggles for social transformation in Bolivia are thus about a struggle for social justice, interpreted in this thesis by following the Bolivian understanding of the concept of *vivir bien* (to live well), which encompasses environmental and gender justice, a recognition of cultural and linguistic diversity, political/democratic representation for all Bolivians and the restructuring and redistribution of a fair and equal economic system that benefits the Bolivian nation.[17] I find Nancy Fraser's comprehensive understanding of social justice useful for interpreting and understanding the contemporary socio-political strategies in Bolivia. Fraser (1995: 82) defined two types of remedies to social injustices including: 'affirmative remedies' – correcting the outcomes without changing structural frameworks; and 'transformative remedies' – correcting outcomes by restructuring the underlying generative framework (Fraser, 1995: 86). Rather than an affirmative multicultural approach, or what Hale (2002) termed a form of 'neoliberal multiculturalism', Bolivia's current 'politics of change' with, at its core, the new 'revolutionary and decolonising' education law, are hence about a struggle for transformative social justice. Based on historical developments of gender (in)justice, Fraser (2005b) provides a three-dimensional normative framework of social justice, which includes the concepts of redistribution, recognition and representation (2005b: 300, 305).[18] As illustrated in Table 2 below, this social justice framework analytically distinguishes three

---

[16] Although Dale's Globally Structured Education Agenda approach is linked to the phenomena of capitalism as a common interest of transnational forces, I also find elements of his work useful for the analysis of ALBA's regionalism – a counter-hegemonic and anti-capitalist initiative – and particularly the dialectical interference of the Bolivian proposed education Reform and ALBA, as discussed in chapter 3.
[17] Though some might argue the concept of social justice is perhaps viewed as a 'Western' or 'neoliberal' in the Bolivian context, in my research I have not encountered such views.
[18] In her earlier work, Fraser (1995) made an analytical distinction between socioeconomic injustice (with redistribution as a solution) and cultural injustice (requiring culture-centred politics of recognition), while

interlinked dimensions: the socio-economic dimension (linked to *redistribution*); the cultural dimension (or *recognition*); and the political dimension (of *representation*), the latter one including three levels of misrepresentation.

Dimension	Socio-Economic	Cultural	Political
Remedy to injustices	Redistribution	Recognition	**Representation** 3 levels of misrepresentation: - Ordinary-political level - Boundary setting level of misframing - Meta-political level

Table 2, Fraser's three-dimensional conceptualisation of social justice (2005a,b; see also Muhr, 2008b: 58)

The third concept of representation is developed to open the framework of analysis to the multiscalar complexities of the political arena. Decisions taken at the state level, often impact the lives of people above and below the state (at local levels, but also in the wider region beyond the state). Similarly, international institutions and mechanisms may have an influence on processes of (in-)justice on national and local scales (Fraser 2005b: 304).[19] Fraser explicitly stresses the relevance of this three-dimensional approach to challenge maldistribution, misrecognition and misrepresentation for social movements, such as the indigenous movements who gained political strength since the 1990s in the Latin American context. Particularly in the *third meta-political level of misrepresentation*, large groups in society are excluded from participation in meta-discourses that affect them. Indigenous groups, environmentalists, development activists and international feminists have started to claim their rights to stand up against the non-territorial powers or structures (e.g. the international financial market, global governance on climate change, or exclusionary forms of schooling) that influence their lives. Similar to having a relevance to this study, Aikman applies Fraser's three-dimensional theory of justice to study indigenous education initiatives in the African continent (2011).

While social justice is nowadays a fashionable term in the education field, the meaning of social justice and its relation to education is far from settled (North, 2006) nor unproblematic.[20] In line with Fraser's arguments, more socially just education would need a combination of both redistributive and recognition approaches (North, 2008: 1187). Calls for redistribution in education often include equality of access to education, and an economic redistribution of material goods and social services to educational institutions. Education for recognition, then, seeks to respect and include all students while stimulating critical and meaningful dialogue. The

emphasising the two are intertwined (Fraser, 1995: 72-73). In her more recent work on feminism and gender justice, she goes a step further and presents the three-dimensional conceptualisation that is applied here.

[19] This dimension does not only deal with the first level *ordinary-political misrepresentations* (denying full participation as peers in social interactions), it also deals with a second level *boundary-setting mechanism of misframing* in the context of globalisation, criticizing the framework in which the national state is the sole political space that excludes marginalised groups from any influence. On a third level it states that many injustices in the world are not territorial in character, and that chances to live a good life are not fully dependent on internal (state) political constitutions, but also on, for instance, regional political agreements such as those constructed through ALBA (see chapter 3).

[20] There seems to be a separation in academic debates on how to approach a just society through education. On the one hand, there are the more conservative researches that argue for assimilation and maintaining educational philosophies that serve to continue the status quo (of a severely unbalanced power structures). On the other hand, critical theorists relate to the struggle for social justice in education with the specific goal of depicting and eradicating those power structures their opponents seek to hold on to (Boyles et al, 2009: 37).

liberal idea of individuals' entitlement to equal opportunities and rights will not do the job of creating a more just educational environment, let alone society. Equality in education does not necessarily lead to more justice, social cohesion or poverty alleviation, since the effectiveness and outcomes of education (policies) depend on the 'educability factors' (a set of material, social, cultural and emotional conditions) that facilitate *learning*, rather than *attending* schooling (Bonal, 2007).

From a social justice perspective, there is thus a need to look at both macro (institutional) and micro (interpersonal relations between staff, professors and students) levels of power, as well as the relations between those dimensions and power relations that extend beyond the school space (North, 2006: 523; North, 2008: 1190). Building from these insights, this study aims to gain insight into the complex power relations between the structures and the agents, the governance of teacher training institutes and their inhabitants, the macro and the micro levels, and beyond. By applying Fraser's approach I try to avoid methodological nationalism through the inclusion of the multilevel dimension of representation in the analysis (Fraser, 2005a). The effects of, and influences on, teacher education do not stop at the gates of the teacher education institution's premises. Rather, this study shows the interconnectedness and dialectics between what happens in Bolivia's Normales in relation to various political processes, discourses and strategies at the supranational, national and subnational scales.

Gramsci on hegemony and counter-hegemony

What theoretical inspiration, then, can help to further explain why radical processes of social transformation are a chaotic and troublesome undertaking, even when a newly democratically elected government drives these processes? Why are processes of social change aimed at social justice, in this case illustrated in the area of Bolivian teacher education, successful or unsuccessful? In order to understand Bolivia's present processes of social transformation, being part of a wider Latin American turn to the left (Rodriguez-Garavito et al, 2008), I draw from (neo-) Gramscian thinking on hegemony and counter-hegemony. Gramsci's work was originally written in the first part of the twentieth century and largely during his imprisonment under Italian fascist rule. Gramsci tried to explain how, in the case of Italy, taking state power was not enough to push for a nation-wide revolution, as the state was just one of the locations of power in Italian society. While traditional Marxist theories are criticised for being too economically focused in their analysis, Gramsci's work acknowledges the relevance of cultural hegemony, and the role of civil society and cultural institutions – including the education arena – in understanding balances of power and processes of societal change (Femia, 1975: 30; Bieler and Morton, 2004: 92; Bates, 1975: 353). Educators, in Gramscian thinking, are consequently seen as important transmitters in gaining political as well as cultural hegemony, or in other cases as working as an important counter-hegemonic force.

While recognising the obvious differences in time and geography between the case of early twentieth century Italy and the possibilities of socialism, and 21st century Bolivia under president Morales, Gramscian ideas are still useful when developing an understanding of contemporary changes and counter forces in the Bolivian society, through the lens of education. Various authors (for instance Morton, 1999: 5-6; Harris, 2007: 2) have suggested how Gramscian ideas on hegemony are particularly helpful in understanding the Latin American 'strategic sites of political struggle', where various forms of resistance to hegemonic structures (but not necessarily states) take place – for instance in the case of the Mexican Zapatista movement, as well as indigenous social movements in the Andes region.[21] Obviously, there is no single theory that perfectly explains the dynamics, complexities and (lack of) success of processes of social transformation around the world and to look for one assumes a reductionist approach to science (Harris, 2007: 23). There is, however, a need for understanding the 'democratic dialectic', which helps us grasp the dynamic interconnection between the state, civil society and the market in processes of social change, particularly in cases such as contemporary Bolivia and Venezuela (Harris, 2007). Exploring this relationship is also especially important for understanding the work of teachers (Robertson, 2000). The teacher training sector in Bolivia works and interrelates with all these terrains, and forms part of this democratic dialectic. In the words of Harris: *'If we hope to develop a relevant theory of social change, we need to study the important battles of today that have raised the banner of alternative globalisations. One such battle has been taking place in Bolivia'* (Harris, 2007: 11). I argue for the relevance of applying Gramscian thinking on hegemony and counter-hegemony to explain the complexities of the struggle for state power alongside cultural hegemony through the project of decolonisation of teacher education in Bolivia.

In the following chapter 3, I demonstrate how Gramsci's notion of an 'organic crisis' is apparent in contemporary Bolivia, where the majority of the population have given their vote to Evo Morales rather than the old ruling elite. Morales, however, might have taken state power, but has not yet succeeded in installing counter-hegemony in the cultural domain of civil society and education. Gramsci, in his Prison Notebooks, called this moment of an incomplete transition due to unprepared political forces an organic crisis, since *'the old is dying and the new cannot be born'* (Gramsci 1975, in Martin, 1997: 47). An organic crisis is manifested as a crisis of hegemony, in which the population cease to believe in the national leaders and traditional parties (Bates 1975).[22] Creating a counter-hegemonic culture, as is attempted by the current Bolivian government, is a long and conflictive process. Bolivia's current counter-hegemonic cultural-political project is uneven in its success and support amongst different socio-ethnic groups and geographical locations, as Morales' supporters are primarily (yet not exclusively) indigenous peoples inhabiting the Western and central highlands, as will be illustrated in chapter 3.

According to Gramsci, civil society – again including education institutes and educators – play a crucial role in a 'war of position', for which popular social forces need to build counter-hegemonic institutions that challenge capitalism and occupy autonomous social and political space. Besides this 'war of position', Gramsci developed the notion of a 'war of manoeuvre', defined as *'a frontal or insurrectional attack against the state or a period of intensive and active struggle, such as*

---

[21] Anderson (in Martin 1997, and in Kohl, 2006), one of the main critics of Gramsci's work, stated how Gramsci gave the notion of hegemony various and even contradictory meanings, and that we should rather perceive hegemony as a multiple concept that incorporates both civil society and state hegemonic strategies. This critique is addressed in Jessop's strategic-relational approach (SRA, see below) which employs a broad perception of 'the state' as a 'social relation' (Jessop, 2007: 1-9).

[22] There are various pitfalls of an organic crisis, according to Gramsci. The ruling class might for instance respond by blaming their own failure on the opposition – or in some cases on (ethnic) minorities – which can even go as far as an attempt to exterminate these forces (Bates 1975: 364). Inspired by Gramsci, Bates advocated the need for a strong moral rationale of revolutionary forces: *'the meek, the ignorant, the foolish, and the immoral, no matter how understandable their condition, will never be able to build a new order. Only those who are proud, strong, righteous, and who know how can organize a new society and create a new culture which, after all, proves its historical superiority only when it replaces the old'* (Bates 1975: 366).

strikes and mass protest (Harris, 2007: 3).[23] The title of this thesis, 'Between Decolonisation and Demonstration', already shows the relevance of Gramsci's notions of position and manoeuvre for teachers in Bolivia. Gramsci's three 'moments' of the 'relations of forces' in a society are helpful in analysing the troublesome and often long lasting processes of transformation (Crehan, 2002: 91-97; Gramsci, 1971: 175-185), and will be further elaborated in the discussion of Bolivia's social relations of production and Morales' complex and difficult alliances with social movements and the wider civil society in his project for decolonisation (Book part II, chapter 3 and 4). For the discussion here, I particularly draw from the Neo-Gramscian School of International Relations' theorist Robert Cox. He sees (Neo-)Gramscian thinking as a way to address the overemphasis on structures and consequently a neglect of agents and agency, of both traditional Marxist thinking as well as Wallerstein's World System Theory (Novelli, 2004: 26). Cox's critical theory broadens our understanding of 'hegemony', by categorising it within three spheres of activity: firstly the *social relations of production* as a starting point of analysis – including the (re)production of knowledge, morals, social relations and (educational) institutions; secondly various *forms of state* – consisting of historically constructed state-civil society relation; and thirdly, different (and alternative) forms of *world order* (Bieler and Morton, 2004). Similar to CPE discussed above, this perspective encompasses a totality of *material, discursive* and *institutional* forms of social relations that bring about social change. Thus, within the three spheres described above, the three reciprocal elements of 'ideas', 'material capabilities' and 'institutions' constitute a particular 'historical structure' or 'historical bloc' (Bieler and Morton, 2004), and will be demonstrated for the case of Bolivia in chapter 3.

Latin American theories on coloniality, knowledges and education for emancipation

The importance of the cultural and discursive domains of Bolivia's counter-hegemonic project is reflected in Latin American debates on coloniality. When writing about Bolivian politics of teacher education in the context of the new reform for decolonising education, one cannot avoid academic discussions related to coloniality theory. '*Decolonisation is at the centre of political debate in Bolivia and the wider Latin American region*', said Felix Patzi, a Bolivian sociologist and the first Minister of Education in Morales' government in 2006, when he opened a seminar on Decolonisation and Education in October 2008. Patzi was responsible for the very first drafts of the new ASEP law for decolonising education, which is clearly inspired by regional debates on coloniality. A growing number of academic debates on education in Latin America deal with issues such as coloniality, critical (border) thinking and 'other', 'alternative', or 'indigenous' knowledges (see e.g. Escobar 2007; Grosfoguel 2007a, 2007b; Mignolo 2000, 2007a, 2007b; Quijano 2005; Walsh 2007a, 2007b). These debates are connected to the global rise of social (including indigenous) movements, together with wider processes of economic and cultural globalisation that opened up alternative ways of looking at political, theoretical and epistemic approaches (Saavedra, 2007). Debates on the coloniality of societies and education systems aim to understand and at the same time deconstruct historical structures of injustices, and construct an equitable and socially, politically and economically just future. The interlinked idea of critical border thinking then suggests that an epistemic dialogue between Eurocentric and other approaches to thinking and knowledges is necessary in order to understand and deconstruct injustices (Weiler, 2003).

---

[23] It is important to mention Gramsci saw these notions of position and manoeuvre as dialectic and fluid, rather than static and unidirectional.

From this postcolonial perspective, modern educational systems are considered conservative, Eurocentric and exclusionary. The construction of knowledge, closely linked to educational processes, is central to the coloniality debate. The construction of knowledge relates to the 'politics of knowledge', or the control over and access to a diversity of knowledge cultures (Davies, 2006b: 1035). Walsh (2007) discusses the 'geopolitics of knowledge' in the context of Latin America and argues how, in this continent, the production of knowledge has been subject to colonial and imperial design for a long time. In Latin America, European thought is dominantly seen as scientific truth, while other epistemes, such as indigenous and Afro-descendent, have long been considered subaltern. Walsh (2007b) argues how social movements, and particularly indigenous movements, have worked on building a cosmology and epistemology based on their own knowledge, yet in dialogue with other knowledges (in plural).[24]

In relation to the acknowledgement of alternative 'knowledges' besides the dominant Eurocentric paradigm, as well as the idea of education for emancipation, I also draw from the critical theoretical perspective of Boaventura de Sousa Santos on 'oppositional postmodernism', which distinguishes two forms of knowledge: '*knowledge-as-regulation, whose point of ignorance is called chaos and whose point of knowledge is called order, and knowledge-as-emancipation, whose point of ignorance is called colonialism and whose point of knowledge is called solidarity, [with]colonialism being the conception of the other as object, hence not recognizing the other as subject*' (Sousa Santos, 1998: 128-129). While knowledge-as-regulation has been (and often still is) the dominant form, Sousa Santos' encourages to reinvent knowledge-as-emancipation and the need for 'alternative thinking of alternatives' (1998: 129). Embracing the reinvention of knowledge-as-emancipation as a paradigm of knowledge from a critical postmodernist theoretical point of view means shifting from 'monoculturalism toward multiculturalism', which requires a 'politics of translation' (Novelli, 2006: 280). This entails recognising 'the other' as a producer of knowledge, while bearing in mind a 'sociology of absences' – or an understanding of the hierarchy of the available hegemonic and sometimes silenced counter-hegemonic discourses; a move from decontextualised absolute knowledge to forms of contextualised knowledge; and to focus on the duality between conformist action and rebellious action – particularly attempting to reconstruct the idea and practice of *emancipatory social transformation* (Sousa Santos, 1998: 133).

2.4 A critical theoretical perspective on teaching – social justice, Gramsci and critical pedagogy

Part of the educational function and strategy of social transformation was Gramsci's idea that intellectuals – including educators – should instill a 'critical self-conciousness' in the masses of the population, to free them from the dominant hegemonic culture and to develop an alternative order (Bates, 1975: 360; Femia, 1975: 35).[25] Intellectuals, according to Grasmci, form a crucial group that can stimulate '*the passage from organic terrain of economic life to effective political organisation*' (Crehan, 2002: 95). Baud and Rutten (2004: 6) assert how since Gramsci, and even more so since

---

[24] Based on the thinking of Sousa Santos, Muhr and Verger (2006: 9) explain how alternative forms of knowledge from the Global South, or 'an epistemology of the South', are preconditions for alternative societies, since using various 'transformatory' forms of knowledge leads to a 'democratisation of knowledge'.

[25] Gramsci distinguished between 'traditional intellectuals' – officially independent, but in reality defending the interests of hegemonic groups, as opposed to 'organic intellectuals', possessing fundamental ties to, and defending the interests of, a particular class (particularly non-hegemonic, yet also hegemonic groups (Baud and Rutte 2004: 3).

the cultural turn in social movement studies, a broader conception of 'intellectuals' replaced the old dichotomy between the (educated) intellectuals and the masses. Education institutions, including schools, universities and teacher training colleges, can function as places of *creative ideological work and as places where activist intellectual networks may be formed*' (Baud and Rutten, 2004: 213). This thesis employs their comprehensive conceptualisation of 'popular intellectuals', being *persons who – educated or not – aim to understand society in order to change it, with the interest of popular classes in mind*' (Baud and Rutten, 2004: 2), and particularly their argument that individual agency is important in processes of social change, which applies to the analysis of Bolivia's future teachers as potential agents of change in chapter 9. Bolivia's attempt to decolonise the education system and teachers' presumed key role in this political project, could be perceived as such a strategy. However, this thesis also shows the limits to which teachers will be naturally engaged in these processes of transformation.

From a Gramscian perspective, education is part of the hegemonic functions of the state. This provides a theoretical justification for posing the research question whether, and how, educational institutions and actors – in this case in the area of teacher education – can be, and are, willing to actually change according to the ideologies of a new regime in Bolivia under Evo Morales. Following Gramsci, education institutes are sites of conflict and negotiation, in which both state and civil society actions come together and are mediated. Schools are, therefore, neither completely resistant nor fully cooperative to adopt policy reforms from the Bolivian state (Talavera Simoni, 2011: 19). Teachers, as popular intellectuals, tend to borrow from globalised ideologies and transform meaning to apply to their local contexts (Baud and Rutten, 2004: 208-209) and often adopt similar strategies of adaptation when it comes to implementing state reforms.

In addition to this state-to-school-level of reform adaptation Tabulawa (2003: 11-12), from a World System theoretical perspective, discusses the international level of transferring of certain education reform models. Teaching methods such as child-centred pedagogy and constructivism, according to Tabulawa, have been transferred from core to periphery states. As a result of these global processes of education policy transfers, the Bolivian 1994 Reform also strongly drew from the constructivist philosophy of knowledge production (Delany-Barmann, 2010: 183), and is consequently called a neoliberal and foreign-imposed reform by some. This critique fits Tabulawa's (2003: 12) criticism that the spread of the individualistic Western culture through constructivist based and child-centred pedagogical reforms are *deemed necessary for an individual to survive in a pluralistic, democratic capitalist society.*' Tabulawa claims this is part of a reproduction process of capitalism in peripheral states, and is indirectly adopted by international aid agencies that see education as an instrument for political democratisation (2003: 18). In response to these global tendencies, Bolivia's current educational reform undertaking is a search for an alternative way of pedagogy. This means an indigenous and context-specific pedagogy, which is inspired by a progressive tendency in Latin American pedagogical approaches – also known as popular education (or critical pedagogy in the US) – that particularly draw on Freire's Pedagogy for Liberation and broadly strives for progressive social changes and more egalitarian social relations. These approaches often entail problem-based learning and critical dialogue, the transformation of teacher-student relations and the incorporation of local or indigenous knowledges in teaching processes. Bearing in mind the premature phase of the decolonisation project for education in Bolivia, these alternative and indigenous pedagogies are a necessary field of research (Semali, 2001; Tabulawa, 2003).

Here, the work of critical pedagogues (see for instance Giroux's, 2003a/b; Sleeter, 1996; 2009; and Yogev and Michaeli, 2011) on transformative education and teachers as transformative or 'organic' intellectuals, provides useful ways to think about the complex roles of teachers in triggering or hindering processes of social transformation. The relevance of thinking about the transformative role of education and teachers is exemplified in, for instance, the recent special issue of *Development* on 'Education for Transformation' (Society for International Development, 2011), as well as the similarly entitled International conference of the Comparative and International Education Society in Montreal (May 2011). Robertson (2000:1) convincingly argues how transformation is what teachers are *engaged* in; change is the outcome of their labour. Building from a critical realist perspective, Robertson (2000: 11-13) helps us to understand the limits to teachers agency and strategies, in terms of the *'accumulated history'*, a historical path of events that shape and limit the changes possible in new institutional structures. Since the context of teachers struggles are time and location specific, a systematic analysis of the changing nature of teachers' work requires an exploration of the changing realtionship between the state, civil society and the market, and the way in which the state both mediates and is transformed through social and political changes. These relations between the state, the market and civil society are either fought out during periods of crisis and transition, or institutionalised through processes of compromises and consensus, into a 'social settlement' – which in turn is always vulnerable to resistance and thus impermanent.

Focusing in on the role of teacher education programmes, Yogev and Michaeli apply Gramsci's ideas on 'organic intellectuals' to a transformative teacher education model, that *'is intended to train teachers as "involved intellectuals" whose professional identity is based on strong intellectual self-image, awareness of social activism, and commitment to public activity'* (2011: 313). They argue how turbulent social and political contexts *'causes teacher training to apply conservative models that provide an illusion of security but obviate the possibility of developing dynamic, productive pedagogic thinking'* (2011: 315). Bolivia's rather conservative Normales (chapter 7), as well as a generally resistant attitude of a large group of teachers (chapter 5), show the relevancy of both Robertson's and Yogev and Michaeli's statements for this study. In order to bring about transformations in a problematic socio-political reality, Yogey and Michaeli suggest a teacher training model directed at nurturing teachers as *'active intellectuals'*, who are equipped with social and political awareness, by deepening future teachers' understanding of society, while at the same time having them engage in (accredited) *'experiential service learning'* (2011: 317-318). While building from Giroux's and others' 'American' critical pedagogy conceptualisation, Yogev and Michaeli also criticise its *'postmodern tendency to suspect each and every truth'*, thus moving away to construct a *'concrete system of values'*; something that is a necessary for student teachers in order to create a civic-social identity (2011: 316). In order to do so, teacher training institutes need to redefine their self-perception and responsibilities not only in the field of education, but also for the wider society. Hence, teacher education should challenge, rather than reproduce hegemonic conservative educational ideologies and practices (2011: 322).

A social justice pedagogy for teacher education

In the conclusion of her book, *Reforming Teaching Globally* (2007), Tatto draws attention to a main strategic dilemma for teacher education policy and practice; the question whether teachers should be seen, and thus trained, as professionals or as technocratic bureaucrats. This leads to the question whether teacher training is required to bring about critical reflection and extensive professional discretion/autonomy, or whether teaching is seen as more procedural, as a scripted activity that asks teachers to deliver the standards of a prescribed curriculum only. In a similar line of thought, Cochran-Smith (2004) explains how there are currently two fundamentally different debates about how to define the outcomes of teacher education. The first agenda is intended to reform teacher education through professionalisation, in order to guarantee fully-licensed and well-qualified teachers. This approach is based on the belief that public education is vital to a democratic society. Proponents of the professionalisation agenda refer to a *'professional teacher'* as a *'knowledgeable and reflective practitioner willing and able to engage in collaborative, contextually grounded learning activities'* (Yinger 1999 in Cochran-Smith, 2004: 206). The second agenda is based on a market approach to the problem of teacher shortages and through deregulation ensures that larger numbers of secondary school graduates (often with little or no teacher preparation) enter the teaching profession, resulting in an erosion of public confidence in education. In line with the increased popularity of including social justice in educational debates, Cochran-Smith, among others, promotes a third *'social justice approach'* to teacher education, that takes the professionalisation agenda a step further: *'it is important to ask, however, whether this emerging professional image also includes images of the teacher as activist, as agent for social change, or as ally in anti-racist initiatives [...] to adjust teaching practices according to the needs and interests of 'all children'* (2004: 207). Cochran-Smiths' triple division in approaches to teacher education seems legitimate considering the similar categorisation of Zeichner (2003), including *the professionalisation agenda, the deregulation agenda, and the social justice agenda.*

Social justice teacher education (SJTE), in the United States (US) context, originates from efforts for multicultural education since the 1980s. However, conceptually SJTE shifts the focus from cultural diversity issues to broader matters of social justice and social change, and teachers' individual and collective activities in struggles for that cause (McDonald and Zeichner, 2009: 596-599; Moore, 2008). The most extensive body of literature on interrelated themes of *'reflexive teacher education'*, *'teacher education for social justice'* and a *'social reconstructionist approach to teacher education'* comes from the United States (see for instance Greenman and Dieckmann, 2004; Liston and Zeichner, 1990; Lynn and Smith-Maddox, 2007; Price, 2001). In addition, we can also find relevant insights into critical forms of teacher education outside of the US and from contexts somewhat more similar to the Bolivian one. Especially the element of 'cooperation' – between teacher educators and students, between students and guiding teachers and among students and among teachers – is an issue mentioned often by other authors in relation to 'transformative' forms of teacher education (Talavera Simoni, 2002; Tatto, 1997; Pilar Unda, 2002). A review of this literature clearly shows the need for more research into the *what, how* and *why* of SJTE, and this thesis aims to build into these debates by portraying and analysing older and particularly the new developments of Bolivian teacher education.

Regardless of the popularity of the concept of social justice in education debates, there is, however, still conceptual obscurity on what SJTE exactly means (Cochran-Smith et al, 2009;

McDonald and Zeichner, 2009; Sleeter, 2009). The ambiguity in terms of the conceptualisation and practical implementation of SJTE allows a wide variety of programmes, with very different agendas, that claim to be part of this vision of preparing teachers (Cochran-Smith et al, 2009; McDonald and Zeichner, 2009). In an attempt to overcome the conceptual vagueness and plurality of interpretations of SJTE, Sleeter (2009) provides a useful analytical framework that includes three key strands of SJTE: 1) equitable access to high-quality, intellectually rich and culturally affirming teaching; 2) to prepare teachers to foster democratic engagement and dialogue; and 3) to prepare teachers as equity advocates for children and youth, challenging a dominant 'culture of power'. The author also outlines three 'key areas of action' of SJTE: recruitment; professional coursework; and guided fieldwork. These three strands and three areas of SJTE are further discussed and analysed for the case of Bolivia in chapter 7.

Key criteria for SJTE: developing teachers' agency through an action research methodology for critical thinking and reflexivity

Within the critical pedagogy debates, action research is recognised as an important tool in promoting reflective practice and educational change, as it aims to enhance teachers' agency – or space for manoeuvre in (passively or actively) adopting their strategies for or against transformation. Here, Vongalis-Macrow's tri-component model of teacher agency, which looks at teachers' obligations, authority and autonomy, is helpful. In the context of a global crisis in the teaching profession (chapter 1), in many countries teachers' obligations have been downplayed to a mere pedagogical role to 'deliver' well-performing students, leaving aside the societal roles of teachers. Often, policies add more regulatory tasks and tighter controls to teaching work, resulting in a '*commodification of teachers' agency*'. Likewise, teacher authority is being reterritorialised to the level of policy-makers. Teacher agency is 'reterritorialised', as teachers' authority is intentionally *within* the four walls of the classroom (Vongalis-Macrow, 2007: 431). In contrast to the '*commodification of teachers' agency*', the current government of Bolivia sees '*teachers as the soldiers of change*', and emphasises – at the discursive level – the importance of teachers' agency (obligations, authority and autonomy) in bringing about both pedagogical and socio-political roles of the ideal teacher (chapter 8).

A large number critical pedagogues concerned with social justice underline the importance of developing teachers' *critical thinking* and *reflexivity* (see for instance Avalos, 2002; Davies, 2005a; Davies, 2006a; Freire, 1970; Kane, 2002; McLaren, 1989; McLaren and Farahmandpur, 2005; Morrow, 1998; Robinson, 2005; Tatto, 1997; Tatto, 1999).[26] As explained by Greenman and Dieckmann (2004: 240), critical pedagogy serves to develop a critical lens and '*may be seen as pivotal for becoming a professional educator who is a reflective practitioner embodying a passion for equity and social justice*'. Reflection and critical thinking – both needed for *meaningful intercultural dialogue* – are also part of the decolonisation and critical border thinking ideas (Escobar, 2007; Sousa Santos in Dale and Robertson, 2004, among other authors) that are influential in current-day Bolivian discourse and politics. Relating to the discussion on Frasers' triple dimensions of social justice and the multiple tasks of education for social change, teacher education should provide future teachers with the opportunity to develop appropriate 'knowledge' (on subjects but

---

[26] According to Davies (2006b: 1035-36), reflexivity is the development of emotional intelligence that comes from dialogue and encounter, play (or protest as a game) and humour. Ideally this needs to be taken up in '*reflexive schools*' and '*reflexive teacher training colleges*'.

also on concepts such as social cohesion and social justice relevant to the local context), 'skills' (such as reflexivity, critical thinking and fostering intercultural dialogue), and 'values and attitudes' (such as respecting diversity, commitment to equality, a sense of identity) (Davies, 2006a).

The US debates often connect SJTE – and the key elements of critical thinking and reflexivity – to an action research approach (Liston and Zeichner, 1990; Price, 2001; Zeichner, 2009). Understanding the debates on the link between teacher education and an action research methodology is important, since action research is also applied in Bolivian Normales in the '*Practica Docente e Investigacion*' [teachers' practice and research] course (PDI, see also chapter 7). Action research – whereby research findings directly feed back into the environments from which they are produced – was developed as an answer to demands for more participatory and emancipatory research processes (Ritchie and Lewis, 2003: 10). According to Price (2001: 43) there is still a lack of investigation of what it would mean for pre-service teachers to engage in action research. Price argues that the goals of social justice and equity should be central to the action-research process, with the purpose of critically examining opportunities for the transformation of existing schooling practices. This critical view widens the goals of action research as a vehicle for educational change. The process of creating the conditions for change through action research should take place at three levels of the work of teachers: the personal; professional; and the political level (Noffke 1997 in Price, 2001). Action research has the potential to transcend the traditional schism between the theory and practice of teaching (Price, 2001: 48), an argument that similarly has been made in Bolivia as a rationale for the PDI course. The old 'exposition-assimilation-repetition' education paradigm was replaced by the 1994 Reform with an alternative education paradigm of 'experience-reflection-action' (Ipiña in Lozada Pereira, 2004: 71), employing action research as a teaching technique in the Normales, which is continued and further developed in the current ASEP law. Incorporating action research in teacher education is a way to build knowledge locally, and to make this knowledge more accessible to other educators (Noffke and Stevenson 1995 in Price, 2001), and this links to what is known in the current Bolivian education reform as productive education.

In short, action research can ideally function as and produce knowledge for change; it can enable future teachers to produce and control knowledge in order to enhance their agency, and act upon desired educational and societal changes in a critical and reflexive manner. However, it depends on the quality of the practical experience and the level of support teacher students receive during their 'guided enquiry' in school communities whether these actually help to build a social justice awareness and understanding, or if it will function as a reproduction of the status quo, merely reinforcing rather than challenging negative stereotypes (McDonald and Zeichner, 2009: 604; Sleeter, 2009: 619-620). The PDI course is thus an interesting entry point to gain insight into how and why in practice, the ideology of decolonised education actually works or fails to work, and is taken up in chapter 7.

Critiques to Social Justice Teacher Education
Zeichner wisely warns us to be cautious against uncritically accepting concepts such as social justice, reflection, action research and professional development in teacher education, without any closer examination of the purposes toward which they are directed in practice, and their actual consequences (Zeichner, 2009: xvi). The most commonly debated limitations and critiques

to social justice teacher education adhere to dominant conservative and neo-liberal thinking on education, often originating in the US but adopted at a global scale. These range from the *ambiguity critique* with social justice teacher education 'being anything and everything', and the *knowledge, ideology* and *free speech critiques,* criticising the content, purpose, gate-keeping issues and intellectual climate of teacher training programmes and institutes.

While acknowledging the powerfulness of these critiques in mainstream debates on teacher training, a number of authors in favour of social justice teacher education convincingly deconstruct these critiques, by arguing that there is no dichotomy between knowledge and social justice. Besides, the push for an apolitical teacher education system is invalid, on the one hand since these critiques are political in itself (coming from the neoliberal and conservative sides of the political arena) and on the other hand since any form of teacher education, including SJTE, is inherently embedded in and connected to (an understanding of) politics and society (Cochran-Smith et al, 2009). Relating back to Fraser's third dimension of social justice of representation, social justice teacher education is also concerned with the genuine levels of participation of teacher students and trainers in the design and implementation of teacher education policies, which in many cases is still very limited (McDonald and Zeichner, 2009: 605).

2.5 The Strategic Relational Approach (SRA) and a conceptual scheme

This section argues for the relevance and utility of the Strategic Relational Approach (SRA) as a heuristic tool. In this section, I position the SRA within relevant discussions of critical pedagogy, in order to be able to explain how both structural and agential factors affect teachers' (un)intended strategies in the classroom and wider society. The relevance of the Strategic Relational Approach (SRA) as a heuristic device lies in the fact that it supports the analysis of this study in its aim to reveal the open as well as the less overt structures, mechanisms and agency that support or resist the present changes in Bolivian (educational) politics. The SRA builds on both Bashkar's (and Archer's) critical realism and Giddens' structuration theory of the interconnectedness of structure and agency, and aims to go beyond a more 'dualist' perception of structure and agency (Jessop, 2005: 38, 40). The SRA pays tribute to Bourdieu's 'methodological relationalism'; an insistence on treating social phenomena in terms of social relations (Hay, 2002a: 89, 127). By re-formulating Giddens' theory of structuration, and the related concepts of *structure* and *agency*, the SRA tries to understand *the relationship* between structures (or contexts) and agency (or conduct), and sees this relationship as dialectical (Hay, 2002a: 89, 127).[27]

In the SRA, *structure* refers to context and to the fact that institutions, practices and routines appear to show some regularity or structure over time. *Actors* are conceptualised as 'concious, reflexive and strategic' within the SRA. *Agency* implies not only political action or conduct, but also a sense of free will, linked to concepts such as reflexivity, rationality and motivation. Jessop aims to bring agency in to structure – producing a 'structured context' – and to bring structure into agency – producing a 'contextualised actor' or 'situated agent' (Hay, 2002a:

---

[27] This dialectical relationship between structures, agents and their agency is also taken up in Robertsons' CPE/E approach, which is closely linked to the SRA, in that it aims to understand 'the structured and structuring role' of education in political economies, and how structure privileges some actors over others, while, at the same time, understanding how (individual and collective) educational actors might respond to this strategic selective context in their strategies (Robertson, forthcoming).

94-95, 128-129, 131). This 'structured context' is also explained as being a 'strategically selective environment', which favours certain strategies over others. *Strategy* is thus a central concept in the SRA, meaning *'intentional conduct oriented towards the environment [...] to realize certain outcomes and objectives which motivate action'* (Hay, 2002a: 129).

In the SRA approach, change is about the capacity of actors to shape their environment and about the ability of actors to make a difference. Both contextual and agential factors are central to explanations about social and political change, which is reflected in the design of this study.[28] Actors face an uneven distribution of opportunities and constraints in their contexts, thus different access to strategic resources (knowledge, capital) may be a significant determinant of the capacity of actors to realise opportunities. Agents acting in a routine manner are more likely to reproduce existing structures of social and political relations over time, while actors that resist norms and conventions will most probably transform existing institutions and practices (Hay, 2002: 166, 379-383, 390). Particularly during moments of socio-political change or crisis (like in Bolivia) 'new ideas' are important and interesting to analyse because of their potential political impact (Verger and Novelli, 2010).

In the SRA, ideas matter and so do practices. Actors must interpret and reflect on their context in order to act strategically, the context however determines strategic selectivity, and thus the discursive (ideas and discourses) is only relatively autonomous of the material (context, structures and mechanisms) (Verger and Novelli, 2010). Teachers' interpretations, or ideas, matter when we realise that most changes in policy are often preceded by changes in ideas (Hay, 2002a). This appears crucial when applied to Bolivia, particularly in the education field, where different political ideologies and the recent 'discursive turn' from *interculturalidad* to *inter-/intraculturalidad* and *descolonización* (Howard, 2009) play strong roles in the way people – including teachers – identify themselves and the world around them. Thus, in times of various competing and circulating discourses (Foucault in Luke, 1996), (future) teachers need to be able to reflect critically upon them in order to act strategically. However, while ideas matter, actors need a certain level of influence (power) and material resources in order to disseminate them and to formulate successful strategies (see below). In line with the thinking of Gramsci and Lukes, the SRA as developed by Hay argues how those that are able to shape *'cognitions, perceptions and preferences'* have a considerable influence over society (Hay, 2002a: 214). Thus the discursive and material are inherently and dialectically linked.

When we combine the SRA with perspectives from critical educationalists such as Apple and Giroux, we see that the dialectics between structure/agency and reproduction of knowledge and practices have also been discussed at length in the broader educational debates. In the early 1980s, Apple elaborated on structure-agency debates in relation to education. At the same time, he contributed to the ongoing debates around social, cultural, political and economic reproduction through education. Education was described *'as part of a larger economic and ideological configuration'*, in which *'reproduction and contestation go hand in hand'* (Apple, 1982: 6-8). Linked to the Gramscian perspective that education institutes are sites of conflict and negotiation, in which both state and civil society actions come together and are mediated (see chapter 3), Apple

---

[28] Part III focuses more on the 'structured context' of Bolivian teacher educational governance, Part IV on the 'contextualised agential factors', and Part V on the eventual strategies: (future) teachers' agency.

illuminates this relationship between the state, civil society and the education system, as being '*an arena of conflict over production of knowledge, ideology, and employment, a place where social movements try to meet their needs and business attempts to reproduce its hegemony*' (1982 in Scott, 2008: 65-66).

When applying the SRA to the study of (future) teachers, we should see *teachers as strategic political actors* that act according to their reflexivity, rationality and motivations, and are embedded in a *strategically selective context* that creates both opportunities and constraints to teachers' level of agency. Hay's notion of *strategically selective context* in educational terms can be understood in Apple's words: '*a space of schooling as a site of contestation, resistance and possibility*' (1980 in Giroux, 2003: 6); or as explained by Giroux (2003b: 48) we should: '*view schools as economic, cultural and social sites that are inextricably tied to issues of politics, power and control. [...] schools actually are contested spheres that embody and express struggle over what forms of authority, types of knowledge, forms of moral regulation and versions of the past and future should be legitimated and transmitted to students...*'. Although much of the critical pedagogy work is primarily engaged with the US context, these ideas nevertheless support my argument that the SRA is useful in viewing teachers, in the Bolivian context, as crucial *strategic political actors* in promoting or resisting progressive social changes.

From a critical realist perspective, and building from the SRA, we should see teacher training institutes as complex and emergent sites of struggle, contestation and mediation of power relations (Jessop, 2005: 28). From an SRA perspective, we can view teachers as active subjects who have a choice and can develop their own strategies. By applying the SRA an analytical distinction can be made between intuitive and explicitly strategic action. Both types of action are based upon teachers' perceptions of the strategic context, being, in this case, the Bolivian education system and within that the institutions of teacher training. '*Intuitive strategies and practices*' can often be described as routines, habits, rituals or other forms of un-reflexive action and contain a strategic component of 'practical consciousness' (adapted from Giddens, Hay, 2002a: 132). On the other hand, '*explicitly strategic actions*' rely upon the configuration of opportunities and constraints of the strategic selective context (chapters 6 and 7), and implies a conscious attempt to indentify and enact those options that will most likely bring about individual and collective intentions and objectives (Hay, 2002a: 132-133). In reality, most actions combine both intuitive and explicit strategic actions. Using SRA-terminology, teachers are knowledgeable and reflexive individuals who monitor the outcomes of their actions. These outcomes can be '*direct effects*' – producing a (minimal) and (un)foreseen transformation of the structured context – as well as '*strategic learning*' on the part of teachers – raising awareness of the opportunities and obstacles of structured context and informing possible future strategic actions. These relationships and effects are illustrated in the adapted version of Hay's conceptual scheme that is presented below.

Conceptual scheme

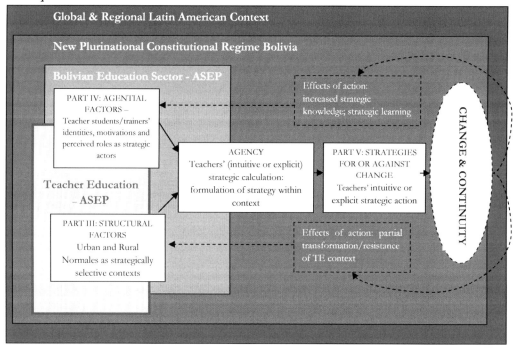

Figure 1, adapted from Hay 2002a: 131

The conceptual scheme (Figure 1) illustrates the main research concepts (see also definitions in chapter 1) and their relations, and is an adapted and extended version of the conceptual scheme of the SRA developed by Hay (2002a: 131). Teacher training institutes are, furthermore, located in the strategically selective context of local communities, the contemporary Bolivian education sector, Bolivian society and political economy, and the broader Latin American and global context. In an attempt to overcome 'methodological nationalism' (Dale 2000; 2005), the conceptual scheme presented below adds this multiscalar perspective to the figure; I have added various layers, including the global and regional context (outer layer), the national context of Bolivia's Plurinational Constitutional Regime, and the level of pre-service teacher education which is the focus area. As shown in the conceptual figure on the bottom left hand side, understanding and explaining *structural* factors – or the strategically selective context of the governance of Bolivian teacher education, is the core aim of chapters 5, 6 and 7 of the book (Part III). In addition, understanding the *agential* factors – or future teachers and their trainers as strategic actors – is taken up in chapters 8 and 9 (Part IV). Two arrows show the influence of both the structural and agential factors on teachers' agency. Chapter 9 (Part V) then combines all of these insights and looks into the (intuitive or explicit) *formulations of strategies* as well as the *strategic actions for or against change* that in turn will contribute (positively or negatively) to processes of societal transformation, as is shown on the right hand side of the figure. Considering the developing nature of the present day teacher training system in the context of a new education reform, it is perhaps too early to make clear statements about the *effects of these strategic actions* and that is why these boxes and arrows have dotted lines.

2.6 Critical theory in action

Having set out the meta-theoretical and methodological framework that informs this thesis, I now turn to the more specific aspects of this thesis' research design, its methodological tools, the units of analysis, research methods and ethics. With the aim to understand both the material and the semiotic, or the structural and agential interrelated factors, as set out by the SRA, the research design is influenced by insights of critical ethnography and critical discourse analysis. Particularly the insights and guiding principles of critical and engaged ethnography (Burawoy, 1998; Mathers and Novelli, 2007; Novelli, 2006) and Critical Discourse Analysis (Fairclough, 2005) have guided the design of the research approach. The following sections on research locations and units of analysis and (primarily qualitative) methods explain the choices of the research design. The chapter concludes by reflecting on the ethics and limitations to the research and the challenges I encountered doing fieldwork in Bolivia.

Critical ethnography

In critical ethnography, theory is not seen as static but it evolves through fieldwork.[29] To think of ethnography as 'the performance of critical theory' or 'critical theory in action' is an interesting and productive description (Madison, 2005: 13). Critical ethnography responds to the claims of Latin American coloniality theorists to give a voice to 'subaltern peoples'. Critical ethnographers *'will use the resources, skills, and privileges available to her to make accessible - to penetrate the borders and break through the confines in defense of – the voices and experiences of subjects whose stories are otherwise restrained and out of reach. This means the critical ethnographer contributes to emancipatory knowledge and discourses of social justice'* (Madison, 2005: 5). This relates to what Bolivian sociologist Saavedra mentioned in an interview in May 2010: *'The real validity of the information we collect during processes of investigation ultimately is determined by many factors, including personal ones; if there is no confidence, or even if there is no real solidarity, people will just give us the standard information, or they will tell us what they think we want to hear'* (114:19). This thesis was inspired and guided by the two main characteristics of critical ethnography: firstly *(self-) reflexivity* or *positionality* (or to acknowledge the power structures, privileges and biases of ourselves and our research subjects); and secondly, the notion of *dialogue* between the researcher and other participants in the study (Madison, 2005: 9).

From a loose genre of critical qualitative educational research, critical ethnography over the past decades became a more widely used term in other disciplines such as anthropolgy, sociology and cultural studies, yet there is no clear consensus on what it exactly entails (Carspecken, 2001). Therefore, this study draws from the insights of a specific version of a critical ethnographic approach, namely Burawoy's (2004; 1998) ethnographic approach called the Extended Case Method (ECM), and the interpretation of that in Mathers and Novelli's (2007) 'engaged ethnography' based on the work of Burawoy, Bourdieu and Sousa Santos. The benefit of ECM is to understand the micro-processes at the institutional level, while, at the same time, embedding these in a broader multiscalar environment in which macro processes (or 'macro resistance to neoliberalism') occur (Mathers and Novelli, 2007: 230). This leads to a methodological framework that aims to overcome the main criticisms of 'conventional

---

[29] Theorising – or the process of reconstruction – in critical ethnography involves moving from concrete to abstract (what is this a case of?), from simple to complex (how might this case be articulated with other cases?) and then to 'move back' in the reverse direction (retroduction): from the abstract back to the (newly theorised) concrete, from the complex to the (newly theorised) simple (Dale, 2010).

ethnography', being the value neutrality of research and the failure to capture power issues related to broader structures of inequality. Instead, ECM advocates a reflexive research technique with dialogue as a core principle, and intersubjectivity between participant and observer as its premise (Mathers and Novelli, 2007: 235; Burawoy, 1998: 14). The reflexive model of science embraces engagement rather than a positivist detachment to the world under study as the *'road to knowledge'*.[30] This way, it aims to extract *'the general from the unique, to move from the 'micro' to the 'macro', and to connect the present with the past in anticipation of the future, all by building on preexisting theory'* (Burawoy, 1998: 5).

In relation to Burawoy's notion of *intervention* or the extension from being an observer to becoming a participant, there are limitations to this study in the sense that as an outsider and visitor, I never was fully part of the teacher training system. In that sense, my 'engagement' had its limitations. However, because of returning to meet the same institutes and participants at various times over a period of four years, and by wide dissemination of the research results, I try to engage as a 'participant' in (opening) the debates on this topic in and beyond Bolivia, in academia, the policy and public domains.

Critical Discourse Analysis

In this thesis I draw from Fairclough's (2005) interpretation of CDA, in order to critically examine institutionalised beliefs, policies, practices as well as personal discourses, and to understand the 'how' of social justice in (teacher) education (North 2008). Discourse in this approach is interpreted as the analysis of 'texts' in a broad sense, including written texts, spoken interaction, multimedia texts as well as other forms of semiosis such as visual images (photos and murals) and body language (Fairclough, 2005: 924). Discourses are, for instance, essential to understand the 'politics of knowledge' – the knowledge-power relations that influence teacher education policies and practices; to reveal the different ideas on 'the ideal Bolivian teacher'; and to explore teachers' identities. Luke (1996:10), drawing from poststructuralist analyses of social history and contemporary culture by Foucault, mentions how teacher education has been re-examined as an arena where dominant socio-cultural discourses compete to construct and position teachers and students.[31] Fairclough acknowledges the causal powers of both structures and agency, and the potential of human agents (in this case teacher students and trainers) to transform or reproduce existing structures (of teacher education in Normales). I applied CDA to unravel the various perceptions of the influence of the new regime's ideological discourse and policy developments on teacher training. Although drawing from insights of CDA and partly employing its approach, it would, nevertheless, be unfair to claim a complete carrying out of CDA considering the lengthy and complex process of analysis this approach calls for (including interdiscursive and linguistic/semiotic analysis).

---

[30] It begins with dialogue between researcher and participants (often during interviews, and called *intervention*); it unpacks situational experiences and social interaction (the *process*, or situational comprehension of the discursive and non-discursive messages) and it embeds this within the external field of local processes and external forces (*structuration*), through a constant engagement with a dialogue with theory itself (*reconstruction*) (Burawoy, 1998: 5).
[31] 'Foucault described the constructing character of discourse, that is, how both in broader social formations ('epistemes') and in local sites and uses discourse actually defines, constructs, and positions human subjects. These knowledge-power relations are achieved, according to Foucault, by the construction of 'truths' about the social and natural world, truths that become the taken-for-granted definitions and categories by which governments rule and monitor their populations and by which members of communities define themselves and others' (in Lukes 1996: 10).

Due to its roots in critical realist ontology, and being closely related to Jessop's work on SRA in its dialectical understanding of discursive-material and agency-structure relations, I see Fairclough's version of CDA as a well-fitting tool for my analysis, particularly in relation to understanding institutional change (Fairclough 2005: 935). CDA is helpful to unravel the various constructions and perceptions of potentials and obstacles to institutional (or organisational) change in teacher education, as presented in primary and secondary documentation from the policy level, institutional level and non-academic Bolivian publications, as well as transcribed interviews concerning the governance issues of teacher education. CDA helps to understand and explain key questions relating to institutional change: '*when organisations change, what is it that changes? What makes organisations resilient in the face of change, resistant to change, or open to change? How are external pressures for organisational change internalised in organisations, how may members respond to them, and what outcomes are possible?*' (Fairclough, 2005: 935). He further argues how while change in discourse is often part of organisational change, this represents only a small part of the full and multifaceted picture in which social interaction and processes (including texts) are dialectically affecting and are affected by social structures. Basing himself on CPE, Fairclough developed a number of assumptions about institutional change, which basically see '*strategies*' as '*mediating the relationship between the change which is inherent in social interaction and texts, and change in organisational structures*' (Fairclough, 2005: 931). Or, in other words, strategies mediate between semiosis and materiality. Table 3 details out Fairclough's (2005: 931-932) assumptions for examining institutional changes.

Table 3 Institutional change: Fairclough's six assumptions (2005: 931-932)
1 **Organisational structures are hegemonic structures;** structures which are based in and reproduce particular power relations between groups of social agents, **which constitute 'fixes'** with enduring capacity to manage the contradictions of organisations in ways which allow them to get on with their main business more or less successfully.
2 **Organisational structures may come into crisis;** generally as a result of a combination of both external and internal changes and pressures, when the 'fix' is perceived as no longer viable.
3 **In situations of crisis,** groups of social agents develop their own particular (and opposing) strategies for achieving a new 'fix', and through a process of hegemonic struggle **a new hegemonic 'fix' may emerge.**
4 **Strategies have a partly discoursal character,** including particular discourses and narratives which represent in particular ways what has happened and is happening, and construct imaginaries for what could happen. Discourses and narratives may be 'recontextualised' from other organisations.
5 **Change in the social process, including change in texts, may have transformative effects on organisational structures** in so far as it becomes incorporated within successful strategies.
6 **The implementation of a successful strategy is a matter of the operationalisation of new representations and imaginaries** – or new discourses and narratives – in new ways of acting and being and new material arrangements.

These assumptions can be summarised in four analytical concepts related to institutional change, being <u>emergence</u>, <u>hegemony</u>, <u>recontextualisation</u> and <u>operationalisation</u> (Fairclough, 2005: 931-932). I use these four analytical concepts to explore the changing nature of the teacher education arena in Bolivia over the past two decades. In chapter 7, I take a closer look at how Fairclough's six assumptions, presented above in Table 3, help to understand institutional transformation in Bolivian Normales in the context of Morales' governments' politics of change.

Reflexivity and dialogue in this research

The insights and guiding principles from critical ethnography and CDA have guided the planning, intentions, practices and analysis during my fieldwork visits. The study employed a flexible research strategy (Ritchie and Lewis, 2003: 4) in the sense that the research design was constantly adapted throughout the process of fieldwork, reflection, analysis and writing. This thesis has a commitment to social and political change as the driving force when carrying out research. Consequently, it aims to engage with a 'critical public sociology' (Mathers and Novelli, 2007: 231-232), developing both theoretically grounded 'academic' outputs as well as publicly available research outcomes. The research thus endeavours to extend 'from monologue to dialogues' (Novelli, 2006), as it aims for a reflexive science approach and a commitment to processes of social emancipation, through dialogical engagement with various groups of Bolivian respondents, a (Spanish and English) academic audience and an extra-academic audience through involvement in policy and public debates. In line with the funding construction of the 'IS Academie', of which this PhD research is part, the overall research project aims to combine instrumental, critical and reflexive knowledge for a range of audiences in various contexts (Burawoy, 2004: 1608-1611).[32]

In the very first stages of the research, a primary one-and-a-half month visit to Bolivia helped me to explore a relevant and under-studied research area and to create the first networks and personal connections. Having developed a research proposal including the theoretical foundations, methodological approaches and first literature overviews of the societal and educational context of Bolivia, a second and more extensive visit followed in 2008. During those six months, the large bulk of data was gathered though various methods (see below) and staying for a longer period in Bolivia made me feel more connected and aware of the ever changing and fascinating Bolivian society, politics, culture and people. I received so much time, energy and valuable insights from Bolivian respondents and friends, and was therefore determined to stay connected and engaged with those involved in the research. In the following period back in Amsterdam, I combined analysing the data I had gathered with writing first drafts of the chapters and articles. I also started using the research as an input for lecturing and supervising students, which was helpful in structuring my research outcomes in an understandable way. At the end of the third year, I went back to Bolivia (one-and-a-half months) to present the preliminary outcomes of my analysis to various groups of respondents, both in the urban and rural institutes. I also went back to discuss my analysis and insights with policy-makers, academics and my local (academic and policy related) supervisors. I view this period as a valuable addition to the earlier 'data gathering visits' as it helped me to triangulate the findings and, more importantly, to share, discuss and further my ideas with the feedback of respondents. Although this thesis is clearly an expression and interpretation of my side of the argument, I wish to bring forward and represent

---

[32] Being committed to the idea that knowledge is a common good and its availability should not be limited to a privileged group of English speaking scholars, in addition to this English manuscript I also (intend to) produce research results in English, Spanish and Dutch, to disseminate through publishing in academic international interdisciplinary journals, to present and debate in academic and policy arena's (internationally and in Bolivia), to provide (online) publicly available free working papers and to insert research into teaching in university courses.

some of the ideas and voices of those that are not often heard in (international) debates on (teacher) education.

Data analysis

The data analysis of this research has been of a qualitative nature, consisting of coding and categorising main issues and themes out of the transcribed interviews, observations, field notes and documentation.[33] The data analysis software Atlas Ti was used for both data management and analysis. Whenever I quote from an interview or other transcribed document I refer to the (interview number: quote number) created in Atlas Ti. I have translated all English quotes from the Spanish transcriptions (carried out by a Bolivian research assistant). Where quotes from interviews are incorporated, they intend to illustrate broader held opinions, unless it is stated otherwise. To ensure anonymity, the numbers of the interviews in Atlas Ti, that I refer to in the text, do not correspond to the numbers in the list of interviews in Appendix 2. During the analyis and writing process, I used the output function of Atlas Ti, sometimes just for one code or sometimes combining codes, which provided the 'raw material' for analysis and input for the writing. Mind-map software was also helpful when structuring information and reflections both during the data gathering and in the analysis phase of the research.

2.7 Defining 'the case': research locations and focus of analysis

This research explores a small number of cases more in-depth, rather than looking for 'breadth'. I perceive Normales as crucial institutions in the process of knowledge production, of the production of 'knowledgeable individuals' and (future) teachers as 'strategic political actors' and the contestation and power struggles over what kind of knowledge should be (re-)produced. This study explores two cases (purposive sampling): the urban Normal 'Simón Bolívar' (La Paz) and the rural Normal 'M.A.Villarroel' in Paracaya, Cochabamba (see Appendix 7, Maps of Teacher Education Institutes in La Paz and Cochabamba). The aim of having two case studies is partly to be able to compare cetain aspects of urban and rural teacher training, but mostly to widen the source of information and to understand possible differences between the organisational contexts through qualitative methods (Ritchie and Lewis, 2003: 50). The urban Simón Bolívar forms the main case study and the rural institute Paracaya a secondary case (as illustrated in Map 2). The study is not comparative in the sense that it compares two similar types of cases, but rather the secondary case adds up to the information of the primary research location. Also, the cases were chosen because of their different ideological points of view and attitude regarding the new regime's education plans. During the first and last fieldwork periods I also visited four other teacher training institutes in different parts of the country, as demonstrated in Map 2. Information from interviews, photo registration and observations from these other Normales is also included in the analysis. I visited the two historically important institutes of Sucre (the first Normal created in 1909) and Warisata (where a basis was made for 'indigenous education' in the

---

[33] After reading through the transcriptions of fieldwork periods one and two, I made a list of codes I thought relevant for the analysis. I constantly kept in mind those 'search terms' (codes) that would later on help me to find relevant quotes for the writing process. I ended up with a long list of codes, because I decided to specify the codes according to theme as well as actors. This way, the same themes are listed several times: the codes 'Changes needed in Normal' and 'ideal teacher' – among many others – are included for teacher students (TS), teacher trainers (TT), other educators (E) and 'others', including policy makers and experts/academics), and so forth.

1930s). Furthermore, I gathered data in one day visits to the private Catholic Normal in Cochabamba and the Normal 'Enrique Finot' in the city of Santa Cruz.[34]

Map 2, Bolivia and research locations

The rationale behind choosing the urban institute 'Simón Bolívar' as the main case is based on a number of arguments. First of all, urbanisation flows led the majority of the population, including members of all different ethnic-cultural groups to live in the biggest cities – with the La Paz/El Alto region being one of the fastest growing and diverse urban areas. In this densely populated and diverse context it is especially interesting to see if, and how, the issues of respect for diversity and social justice are incorporated in teacher education. Secondly, basing the major part of the fieldwork time in La Paz made it possible to conduct interviews with policy makers, donors, unionists (with both the urban and rural unions' headquarters in La Paz), academics, university students, and educators at primary schools, but also to gather key documentation and join meetings, conferences, debates and book launches while I also worked

---

[34] From the 27 institutes that are operating today, I studied two Normales more in-depth, and another four institutes during shorter visits. Considering the diversity of the different geographical area's and Normales located within them, this thesis was too limited to provide an image of the entirety of 'the Bolivian teacher education system'. However, by avoiding a singular case study research approach I aspire to, at least to some extent, provide a somewhat more balanced view on the main issues for debate in the area of teacher formation in both rural and urban Bolivia.

46

with the students and trainers in the urban Normal. Besides, Simón Bolívar is seen in Bolivia as a powerful and leading institute in the field of teacher education.

After having decided to focus my study on Simón Bolívar, I felt the need to include another, preferably rural, institute to balance the outcomes of the study. Again, there were several reasons for choosing Paracaya as a secondary case. First of all, while in policy discourse there is no longer an official divide between urban and rural Normales, in reality their remains to exist stark contrasts between urban and rural teacher education institutes, and teachers continue to be confronted with contrasts between working in an urban or rural teaching and living context. This led me to include an institute that was rurally located and – according to its trainers – still focused on training future rural teachers. Secondly, I had already met the (then) general and academic directors of the institute during a meeting organised by the MoE in La Paz (discussing new policy directions for PDI, in October 2007). Both directors were interested in, and open to, participating in my research. Besides, they appeared to have a very engaged attitude toward the political developments around the ASEP law, which I had not witnessed in the other institutes in the same manner. Thus, including an institute that was already working on and with the new policy developments for decolonised education was an extra reason to choose Paracaya as my second location of study. Finally, the institute of Paracaya is located in a relatively populated rural area in the central valley of Bolivia and thus serves a relatively large population of teacher students.

Following a multiscalar approach to research, the thesis analyses these institutes as embedded in and dialectically related to their broader local, national, regional and global educational and socio-political and economic context. The data gathering process was not constrained within the gates of the Normales. The fieldwork research approach also included interviews, participation in meetings, observations and documentation of various actors outside the Normal, including policy makers (mainly national level and some local level), teacher union members (both urban and rural), primary school directors and teachers, (a limited number of) parents, indigenous CEPOs members, international bilateral donors and NGOs and academics. An overview of the (anonimised) interviews with these respondents is presented in Appendix 2.

Within the broader teacher training curriculum and programme, I decided to focus my data gathering around the 'PDI'-course (*Practica Docente e Investigación* – the internship and research course). The reason to centre on this PDI course, was because of the importance to bridge the theoretical contents to the educational practice through an action research model, and the potential stimulation of future teachers' reflection and critical thinking, particularly in relation to the direct school and its community – criteria that are linked to SJTE approaches discussed above (see for instance Liston and Zeichner, 1990; Price, 2001; Zeichner, 2009). Looking into the PDI course also permits an understanding of the (often complex and problematic) relationships between the teacher training institutes and the wider (school) community. Appadurai's (2006) idea of deparochialising 'the idea of research', and extending 'doing research' to a democratic potential belonging to the 'family of rights' (for all, and not just for higher educated academic researchers), also inspired my focus in the data collection phase on the PDI course: in my view, seeing (future) teachers as researchers and reflexive practitioners at the same time is a promising (policy) assumption, and deserves closer attention.

2.8 Methods

Following a reflexive science approach, both individual and group interviews and participant observation – or *'the study of others in their space and time'* (Burawoy, 2004: 25) – are included as key methods used in this study. In addition, focus group discussions and several types of workshops helped me to gather and *reflect on* the data. This research combines a 'panel study' (in which the same people are interviewed more than once) and a cross-sectional study (in which subsequent samples of new participants are interviewed) (Ritchie and Lewis, 2003: 55). For triangulation reasons, multiple methods were used, including: semi structured (individual and group) interviews; (participant) observations; focus group discussions; document analysis; a photo-workshop; participation in formal meetings and conferences; and informal accounts of teacher students' biographies. In addition, short surveys were carried out to gather data on teacher students' and teacher trainers' profile characteristics (chapter 7). The use and relevancy of these methods are now briefly explored.

Semi structured interviews

In total I carried out 119 semi-structured interviews; during the first fieldwork period I conducted 31 interviews, during the second fieldwork period 69 interviews and 17 during the last fieldwork period. An overview of all interviewees, their affiliation and their location is included in Appendix 2. The majority of these interviews were individual. However, 19 interviews were with more than one respondent (often in groups two or three). Most of these 'small group interviews' were with teacher students, as they sometimes showed up with friends/colleagues at the time of the appointment, or they asked others to join in when I asked them directly if they could sit down with me. At first I was unsure if the data from these small group interviews would be as valuable as individual interviews, but after a few of them I realised students actually opened up more in a small group, and even reflected on each others comments. This experience stimulated me to organise more group discussions with students (and trainers), particularly in the last visit (discussed below).

The semi-structured interviews of the first fieldwork period were open-ended, as my primary aim was to explore the main issues, problems and debates around teacher education. The (biggest number of) interviews I conducted during the second fieldwork visit were still semi-structured but, where possible and appropriate, I tried to cover the same themes in all interviews, in order to strengthen the analysis of various discourses and thematic issues later on. I also tried to create space in every interview to bring new issues to the table that I had not anticipated. The interviews during the last visit were still partially structured, in the sense that it was more of a discussion of the preliminary findings of my study and respondents reflecting and building on them. In some cases these interviews helped me to confirm (and triangulate) my results, but they also unveiled new insights and 'missing pieces'.

I used a flexible 'interview guide' for the semi-structured interviews during the second fieldwork visit, which specified the themes and questions I posed in interviews (see Appendix 4). The order in which these themes were discussed was always flexible and depending on the affiliation of the interviewee we spent more time on specific issues than others. This interview guide included the themes of: the new law; the main actors (including actors maps, as discussed below); teacher education's main goals; motivations to become a teacher; the characteristics of the ideal Bolivian teacher; institutional changes and challenges; societal change; critical thinking and social commitment of teachers; teachers as actors of change; perceptions of the PDI course; perceptions of social justice; and social justice in/through teacher education.

Most of the interviews were located in the working environments of the interviewees: in the Normal (usually in an empty classroom); in the *comedor* (cantine); or with trainers also in *la sala docente* (the teachers' room); in offices of MoE officials, unionists, bilateral donors, academics, NGO workers; at primary schools in director's offices; in the school yard or in (empty) classrooms. I also was invited to some of the homes of students and trainers, which was always a pleasurable experience. Somehow, these 'home interviews' always became very lengthy and not always as focused as in a working environment. Some respondents were also very generous in making the effort to meet me in a cafe or other public space, or in the house I was staying in, sometimes being very explicit about the benefits of being in a space without colleagues around, therefore making it easier to discuss more sensitive issues.

I generally did not encounter great difficulties in obtaining interviews at any level, although it took a few weeks before doors started to open up in the urban Normal. An exception to this was getting an interview appointment with the Minister of Education.[35] Before every interview, I would provide respondents with a leaflet describing my background information, contact details and intentions of the research (Appendix 3). This leaflet also stated that respondents' information would be treated confidentially, with anonymity and that they could withdraw from any specific topic, or the whole interview/discussion, at any given time. I also mentioned the fact that I would be returning to discuss and present the findings and that I would aim to publish the results in Spanish as well.[36] I always asked for consent to record the interview and in the great majority of interviews this was fine. The majority of the interviews (as well as some of the workshops and discussions) were transcribed by a Bolivian with Spanish as her mother tongue and a wide experience of transcribing (having worked as a secretary for the MoE before), and she signed a contract to treat all information with confidentiality.

Observations

Participant observations are a second important method of this research. Observations were conducted in the Normales, in schools, but also in political and social movement or union meetings. Usually, I would take pictures, sometimes videos and always make notes on what I saw and experienced. Firstly, inside the various Normales, I observed the institutional 'daily life'; the way trainers and students relate to each other; and the conversations and interactions in the *comedores* and communal places of students and teachers. I also conducted around 15 classroom observations (of approximately an hour), in various Normales and for different subject matters. Most class observations where carried out in Simón Bolívar, for the subjects of Social Sciences, English language, Literature and (the theoretical part of) PDI. During these observations, I did not use an observation checklist, instead I took notes on the following themes: teaching style

---

[35] I made the effort to call the secretary every day for about two weeks in a row, and eventually she called me one afternoon to say that the Minister was able to see me within the next half an hour. At that particular moment, I found myself in the middle of a teachers' march at the other end of the city centre of La Paz, but I managed to get to the Ministry in time. A few weeks later this Minister was replaced again for someone else.

[36] I often discussed with respondents the limitations of 'only' translating to Spanish, and not in any indigenous language. There is, unfortunately, no easy solution to this, as financial resources are limited and translation to one or two of the 27 official indigenous languages would also not solve the whole dilemma.

(traditional banking education, teacher or student centered teaching, innovative/participatory teaching methods); student-teacher relations; student-student relations; use of teaching materials (books, copied material, black/white board, other); and, when relevant, I also made notes on the content of the class, for instance during social sciences classes on relevant socio-political issues, and PDI classes that discussed the problems and successes of students' internships. Gaining access to the types of data used in this research – including observations of the daily routine and classes, joining meals, having informal conversations, organising conversation and discussion groups with students and trainers, and even taking over some English classes from absent teachers who asked me to do so – meant a considerable but worthy investment of my fieldwork time as it gave me a chance to look inside the institutional cultures of the Normales.

Also outside the Normales, the participant observation method was a useful tool. I joined various larger and smaller meetings/conferences/debates organised by either the MoE, by Unions, the CEPOs and/or by international donor agencies. Through my local supervisor Maria Luisa Talavera, who lectures at the Universidad Mayor de San Andres in La Paz, I joined a number of classes from university students working on anthropology in educational sciences. Here, I met students in the university courses whom I met again (and interviewed) inside the Normal since they were studying the two careers at the same time.

I drew together an important part of the data on PDI, and the link between teacher education and the actual 'educational reality' in schools, through visits to six primary schools during a period of one month. I particularly focused on one primary school located on the border between La Paz and El Alto called 'Colegio Italia'. I was introduced to the cooperative school director by a teacher trainer from the Normal who was assigned the task of following up on the internships of the teacher students. The director facilitated 'open access' to the classrooms where the interns were working (together with their guiding teachers), and the majority of 'guiding teachers' were open to interviews in their breaks or free time.

I joined in several teacher demonstrations and marches through the streets. These were quite intense and insightful experiences, as people were often very straightforward in their answers to my questions. Dynamite was exploding as we marched through the streets and the police were not hesitant in using tear gas or other means to control the crowd of protesting teachers. I actively interviewed people while walking down the streets and, during a march in October 2007, a befriended university student helped me to video-tape the whole demonstration while I continued to interview the demonstrators.

Focus group discussions, photo workshop and feedback workshops
Another method used for data collection and reflection was to organise thematic focus group discussions with teacher students. These discussions were often located in the classrooms of the Normal, in some cases after the official class hours, but sometimes also during class time if trainers explicitly asked me to do so (and some trainers used this as an excuse to disappear themselves). Between May and November 2008, I managed to have five of these group discussions with whole classrooms full of students (ranging from 20 to 40 students) or with a smaller group of around ten students on the theme of social justice. We discussed how students defined social justice, if they thought social justice was part of their training and the broader relationship between teaching and social justice.

In this same fieldwork period, I also organised a 'photo-workshop' with a smaller group of five final year students, all working on their final internship period and linked thesis/pedagogical project. We met four times over a period of one month, the first time simply to hand out the cameras and discuss the aim of the workshop. In line with the problem-based learning approach of the PDI programme, students were asked to explain in pictures what their main observed 'problem' was about and how they thought of a solution to this 'problem' in the school where they did their practice. The second meeting took place in the primary school where the students were doing their internship, to check whether students were encountering any difficulties or had questions. During the third meeting, students handed in the cameras so I could print the photos (for the students and for myself). The last meeting resulted in the actual 'workshop', in which the students organised their photos in categories and in this way they explained to both their peers and I how they experienced their final part of the PDI practice. The students were then able to use the pictures for their final thesis document and the cameras were left with their teachers for further use in the Normal.

During the final fieldwork period in April and May 2010 I organised another type of 'reflection and feedback' focus group, with both students (in total six discussions, with four in Simón Bolívar, one in Paracaya and one in Enrique Finot/Santa Cruz) and teacher trainers (one in Simón Bolívar and one in Paracaya). During these meetings, I usually started with presenting some of my preliminary findings. Participants then responded, posed questions and provided reflections. The atmosphere of these discussion meetings was often quite positive and informal. Following the advice of my local supervisor, I brought (coca) tea and cakes (as she was not entirely convinced people would show up or stay). The tea was nice but proved unnecessary, as people appeared genuinely interested to hear about the preliminary findings. At the same time, particularly in the rural institute, the group of trainers expressed that they had also expected this of me (since I had the funds to do so and because I had promised them to come back), and they took their time to critically question my methods, analysis and results. Although this was not the easiest experience I had, I am grateful for the serious engagement and critical attitude of these trainers, as they helped me to (already) defend my choices and research approach, as well as to think through the outcomes further.

Short surveys to help construct students' and trainers' profiles

With the purpose of creating a picture of the backgrounds and characteristics of teacher students' and trainers' profiles in my thesis, I designed a short and simple survey (see Appendix 5). In Simón Bolívar 164 first and third year students filled out the survey form and in Paracaya 158 first and third year students (with a balance between the number of first and third year students). These students were chosen arbitrarily by approaching their trainers at the beginning of their class and asking for 15 minutes of their time. The outcomes of these surveys were imputted into Excel and helped me to analyse and write about the student and trainer profiles presented in chapter 7.

Actor maps

During most of the interviews in the second fieldwork visit, I asked different respondents – including trainers, students, policy makers, unionists, donors and NGO-workers – to draw 'actor maps', portraying the main actors in the field of teacher education and their power relations. As soon as the discussion turned to the main actors in the field of teacher education, I asked respondents to take over my note book and pen, and instead of only speaking about their ideas I invited them to draw a scheme, a table or any sort of overview of the way they viewed the main actors. I always asked them to show what the most important actor, or actors, were in the field, and how they related to each other. Often, respondents would themselves draw and discuss those actors that are resisting or against the current policy plans. If they did not mention this themselves, I would ask them whether they thought there were also actors that were resisting current policies. With my notebook and pen in their hands, some seemed to take the role of a teacher, really trying to make me understand their points of view. Since the conversations were recorded as well, I could also use the transcribed recounts later on, together with the drawings. These institutional maps and the power relations they reveal are used in the analysis of chapter 5.

Teacher students' life stories

One of the most inspiring and satisfying experiences during my stays in Bolivia were the relationships and friendships I managed to build with some of the respondents and my local supervisors. Being able to be a small part of their lives during several periods helped me to understand better the personal side of becoming a teacher, or, for non-teacher students-friends, what it is like to live and work in Bolivia today. Stimulated by my local Bolivian supervisor, I started to write down reflections and accounts of the stories of the lives of my teacher student friends. In addition to these notes, I also kept a diary to write down fieldwork notes and other reflections on my stay in Bolivia and on the developments of the research. I also used Mind-map (MindManager) software to brainstorm and keep track of the different sources of data I collected, people I met and those that I still wanted to contact.

2.9 Limitations, ethics and challenges

Carrying out reflexive social science research is unavoidably 'trapped in networks of power'. There are various self-limitations of power effects that should be taken into account here, being *domination, silencing, objectification* and *normalisation* (Burawoy, 2004). Firstly, a social scientist that 'intervenes' by interviewing and observing cannot avoid *domination*, or being dominated because of the ever-present power relations. In my case, this was clear through, for instance, the bureaucracies of needing permission to do research and enter the Normales, which became easier with each time I returned. In the beginning mentioning some key names (of my local supervisor for instance) helped in gaining access, later on it was just a matter of passing by the right person in the MoE in order to get the correct letter and stamps. However, stamps do not guarantee *genuine* access. It took a couple of weeks to create an atmosphere of acceptance (first) and then trust (later on), particularly in the urban institute. The fact that my contacts spread according to a 'snowball effects' (of acquainted teachers and students), my study is 'dominated' by the (inter)views and observations of only a particular group of trainers. It was much easier to connect to trainers that showed an interest in my study and those were mostly the teachers of languages and literature, social sciences and pedagogy (which I, luckily, also see as the subjects most relevant to this study to observe).

A second limitation is what Burawoy calls *silencing*, and is related to those voices that are not represented and are absent from debates. Although this thesis aims to include the perceptions and voices of various actors, it is limited in terms of its scope (excluding for instance children taught by teacher interns and private schools), geographical coverage and, naturally, my choices in the way various voices are represented. Thirdly, Burawoy warns us that if we use *objectification*, or see social forces as natural and external instances, we should always be prepared for unforeseen and unexpected processes to erupt and break up the field of forces we identified. In my research, the constantly changing staff and Minister of the Bolivian MoE, as well as the staff of the Normales, shows how 'the policy level' cannot be assumed as a constant network of powers, as these changes in staff also bring about changes in power relations.

A fourth limitation brought forward by Burawoy is a process of *normalisation*, or 'double-fitting', in which complex situations are tailored to fit a theory and, in turn, theory is tailored to the particularities of the case under study, reducing the world into categories that can be investigated. Social scientists can challenge or mitigate normalisation by embedding the analysis in perspectives and categories that are designed from below, by those whose interests are supposed to be served by the study (Burawoy, 2004: 22-25). The ethnographic and multi-method approach – including observations, interviews, focus group discussions and various types of reflexive or feedback workshops with different groups of actors – was designed in order to address, to some extent, the limitations of silencing and normalisation. In addition, I constantly worked and reworked the theoretical frame that guided this study according to insights from the fieldwork. The scope and duration of this research did, however, not allow for a comprehensive inclusion of all of the actors in the (teacher) education sector – for instance with my decision that private education was not a key aspect of this thesis and only including a one-day visit to a private institute in the first fieldwork visit. Furthermore, the scope of this thesis was limited to only two main research locations, with some hints of practices in other Normales, yet far removed from a comprehensive study of the full arena of 'Bolivian teacher education'.

Another limitation of this thesis is its focus within the broad curriculum of teacher training on the PDI course. Instead of an in-depth analysis of the whole (old and new) teacher training curriculum documentation and implementation, I narrowed down to studying the 'practical and research part' of students education. I feel this choice was legitimate in the sense that PDI is a crosscutting course throughout the whole training of teacher students and part of every future teachers' training. Besides, it serves the purpose of creating an understanding of a Bolivian response to 'teacher education for social justice', as it directly engages with the wider community and applies a version of action research. The limitation of this choice, however, is clear in that I cannot make statements about the whole array of content and pedagogical approaches of 'Bolivian teacher training'.

As for the (security) situation Bolivia, I have not encountered serious difficulties during my stays in the country. However, the (sometimes country-wide) strikes, road blocks and (violent) uprisings have influenced the planning of my travels around Bolivia.[37] Last but not least, this research stops at a certain point in time, whereas the ever-changing developments in Bolivian society and education arena clearly continue. I therefore decided to 'stop' the data gathering process on the last day of my last fieldwork visit, 23rd May 2010. Of course, crucial and indispensable developments that took place after that period – such as the final version of the

---

[37] This was the main reason why only in the very last week of my last visit, I was finally able to visit a Normal in Santa Cruz.

ASEP law of December 2010 – are still taken up until the last writing and editing stages before publication. Some other limitations involve the challenges encountered during the research and my personal role in this research, as elaborated in Appendix 1.

As a final note for this chapter and relating back to the discussion on solidarity and engagement, whilst carrying out research in the diverse and partly 'indigenous context' of Bolivia, it is worth taking into account the arguments of Tuhiwai Smith (1999) about 'indigenous methodologies' and that *'research is not an innocent or distant academic exercise but an activity that has something at stake and that occurs in a set of political and social conditions'* (1999: 5). Bearing in mind that 'sharing knowledge' is a long-term commitment (Smith, 1999: 15-16), I intend to 'report back' and 'share knowledge' in different languages and for different audiences, extending the period of my PhD, including the publication of a Spanish and adapted version of this thesis for circulation in Bolivia.

PART II

BOLIVIA, TEACHERS & CHANGE:

SOCIO-POLITICAL AND EDUCATIONAL CONTEXT

3

Continuity & change in Bolivian society: a story of historical and present struggles

'Utopia is on the horizon. I go two steps, she moves two steps away. I walk ten steps and the horizon runs ten steps ahead. No matter how much I walk, I'll never reach her. What good is utopia? That's what: it's good for walking' (Eduardo Galeano 1993 in Las Palabras Andantes, in Dangl, 2010: 10-11).

3.1 Introduction

When I travel back from a day at the Normal Simón Bolívar, I find the streets of the centre of La Paz being taken over by a steadily moving mass of determined Bolivians. It is 20 October 2008, and thousands of government supporters endured days of walking without much food or rest as they marched into the capital to enforce the approval of a referendum on the new constitution. Many Bolivians working from the grassroots level know how to play politics with their feet: mass demonstrations have proven effective in changing the political direction of the country both before and during the current government. Large parts of the Bolivian indigenous population and social movements are walking towards their utopia, of a better, more just Bolivia. Moreover, *'utopias matter'*, because utopian discourse and actions can function as important instruments for social and political change (Postero, 2007: 12).

Bolivian teachers operate in a very complex and tense context, which historically has been characterised by continuous forms of conflict. Bolivia, situated right in the heart of South America, is a country of wide diversity, contrasts and struggles. Even though Bolivia experiences a period of economic growth in a global context of economic decline, it remains one of the most unequal and poor countries of the Latin American continent (World Bank, 2009). With a majority population that identifies as indigenous, and the rise of social movements over the past two decades, Bolivian society has entered a new stage in its history. This new phase is marked by the democratic election and re-elections of president Evo Morales since 2005. On the one hand, Morales' government radically wants to *change* Bolivia's socio-economic situation, through adopting a new political ideology and endogenous route to development. More than a mere political moment of transformation, the recent shifts in power have been connected to the Andean notion of *Pachakuti*, seen by many Bolivian as a traditional ritual and phase of change. This somewhat mythologised and stylised use of the Andean past, and reference to the imaginary of *Pachakuti*, is part of Morales' strategy (Postero, 2007: 3, 17).

On the other hand, Bolivia's society and education system are still confronted with *continuing* social tensions and deep structures of discimination and inequalities. The rise of Bolivia's social movements and their decisive roles in resource conflicts (e.g. over water and gas) are the results of a continuation of past clashes (Dangl 2007: 8). Under the new government of Morales, the education system is perceived as a crucial instrument to restructure and revolutionise Bolivia's society towards a decolonised ideal of *'equal opportunities for all Bolivian (male and female) to social justice in order to live well'* (Ministerio de Educacion de Bolivia, 2010b). These tensions, between *continuity* and *change* in Bolivian society, and the tensions or even gaps between a radical new *discourse* and social and educational *practices* are part of the main storylines of this thesis.

This chapter introduces and follows these story lines, as it provides an overview of the relevant aspects of the complex and conflictive strategic selective context of the past and present Bolivian society, in which (future) teachers – the main agents of this study – live and work. In the words of Gray Molina, *'the core of Bolivian democratic politics is about conflict and resolving conflict. Room for contestation is a driver for change'* (2009). The main objective of the chapter is to explore Bolivia's various conflict dimensions and to find out whether this room for contestation is indeed opening up new horizons amidst a context of continuing tensions and struggle. The chapter first outlines Bolivia's main socio-political historical developments, and paints the picture of continuous historical and contemporary political battle field for diverse state and non-state actors in a multiscalar setting that extend beyond the state level. I continue by outlining the characteristics of Bolivia's diverse demographical, geographical, economic and ethnic cultural context, leading to a situation of serious societal tensions. This leads us to the following section which stresses five processes of conflict defined for the purpose of this study, including: *poverty and inequality of opportunities; discrimination and exclusion; separatist discourses and identity politics; mistrust in the state and between societal groups;* and *popular protests and violent clashes between the state & social movements.* Finally, I begin to locate teachers – being the most important actors of this thesis – in this very diverse, unequal and slowly changing Bolivian context as an incitement for the next chapter, which deals with the education context specifically.

3.2 Bolivia's socio-political history of struggles for hegemony and counter-hegemony

Bolivian politics are a fascinating area of study, and this section provides a brief overview of the most important historical and recent political developments that are relevant in shaping the strategic context in which Bolivian (future) teachers live and work. Inspired by a relevant categorisation of Latin American politics of Rodriguez-Garavito et al (2008: 31-37), in this historical overview of socio-political struggles for (counter)hegemony I pay special attention to three important political players in Bolivia being: 1) political parties; 2) social movements – including unions, the (coca-)farmers and indigenous movements; and 3) the government..

Prior to the colonial period, the Andes region was inhabited by a series of civilisations; the Aymara civilisation took over from the Tihuanacu in the twelfth century and the Aymara were conquered by the huge Inca Empire. When the Spanish colonist arrived in 1532, in the region currently known as Peru and Bolivia, they used the fragility of the Inca Empire – disrupted by civil war – to take over control (Kohl and Farthing, 2006: 37; Morales, 2004: 245). The Spanish rulers found many ways to enrich themselves; through gold, silver, food stocks and coca leaves.[38] Bolivia was the first country to rebel against the Spanish oppressors, yet the last to achieve liberation. Eventually the struggle for freedom was won in 1824 guided by *criollos*, local elites with Spanish descent. The Venezuelan freedom fighter Simón Bolívar acknowledged this new state and it was named after him – the 'Bolivian Republic'. The colonial rule ended in 1825 when the Bolivian Republic was founded. However, the following period was everything but peaceful and stable. A small, white elite of military and large landowners, named *caudillos*, ruled the country. In this period large 'modernising' infrastructural projects were accomplished and most land was expropriated from indigenous communities (Malaver & Oostra, 2003: 13-16; Morales, 2004: 246). These developments – the appropriation of Bolivia's resources by the national and international elite, ongoing resistance by indigenous groups and tensions between the different regions of the country – form part of a shared process of colonisation and post-colonialism in many countries in the global South (Kohl, 2006: 34).

Photo 2. Fragment of a mural at El Prado in La Paz – artist Gonz Jove. On the left hand side the colonial repression is illustrated, from the centre to the right the struggle for independence

The year 1879 marks a sensitive period in Bolivian history; Bolivia lost its access to the sea to Chile. Bolivia still maintains it's naval forces (patrolling on Lake Titicaca) and politicians – including the current government – still try to gain popularity by 'dragging up' this subject. Bolivia's national self image was further hurt by loosing all of its wars with neighbouring countries from 1862 until 1935.[39] In the last two years of the nineteenth century the 'Liberal Revolution' laid the basis for a relatively stable political situation in Bolivia in the first decades of the twentieth century. However, the indigenous population remained marginalised and excluded

[38] The so-called *encomienda* system gave ownership of all land to Spanish aristocracy, while the Spanish colonizers maintained the so called *mita* system, used in the Inca period to ensure compulsory free labour by the lowest classes for the elite. The indigenous people had to work for their Spanish *encomenderos* in large agricultural estates (*haciendas*), in exchange for 'proper care'. However, the colonist made the indigenous population work all year long in harsh circumstances (Morales, 2004: 245).

[39] On 28 March 2011, the Bolivian newspaper *La Razón* reported how after failed negotiations with Chile Evo Morales plans to take this issue of access to the sea to the international court in The Hague. The BBC, on that same day, published a similar message, showing a picture of school children carrying boats with Bolivians flags, as they are taught 'they must reclaim the sea'.

(Morales, 2004: 247; Talavera Simoni, 2011: 32). The deterioration of the social and economic position of the indigenous populations led to further conflicts and violence, on both local and regional scales, in the beginning of the twentieth century (Baud, 2007a: 24).

In the 'Guerra del Chaco' (1932-1935) between Bolivia and Paraguay, different ethnic and geographic groups fought together on the Bolivian side, fuelling a new nationalist cry for change. This led farmers, miners, students and ex-combatants to join forces in a counter-hegemonic struggle against the oligarchy, as they formed the first revolutionary parties (among which the *Movimiento Nacionalista Revolutionario* – MNR). Bolivia's oldest political party MNR was founded in 1942 and since then developed from extreme left to extreme right. The Second World War deteriorated the situation in Bolivia, which was heavily dependent on tin export. In the years after the War, massive mobilisations and violent oppressions – under the command of Victor Paz Estenssoro – eventually led to the 1952 Revolution. A new alliance of armed farmers and workers, organised in unions and political parties, took over power from the military forces. The COB (*Central Obrero Boliviano*) became one of the strongest unions in Latin America and had a relatively strong political role at the time (Zavaleta 1998, in Talavera Simoni, 2011: 104). The highland region became the 'centre of the country', where modernisation and development processes were concentrated. The strong and powerful social movements of the miners were situated in the mountains and most of the governmental institutions were since then located in La Paz (Molina, 2008: 6; Talavera Simoni, 2011).

It took until 1952 to establish general voting rights and until 1956 before the first democratically elected government was in power.[40] Although the 1952 Revolution meant a first step towards full citizenship for indigenous groups in Bolivia, the dominant *criollos* of Spanish decent and the urban middle class *mestizos* created an exclusionary society with no space for indigenous participation in economic, political and social life. However, pressure from working class and indigenous groups ensured general voting rights, together with national education and healthcare systems (Kohl and Farthing, 2006: 35-36, 47). The revolution also changed the indigenous groups' 'title' (identity in my view is not the right term here), from the negatively associated *indio* to the term *campesino*, which refers to the rural background and lifestyle of many indigenous groups (Taylor, 2004: 9). In the decade of the 1960s, indigenous groups finally saw themselves represented through a formal political movement, when different groups of Aymara Indians – the Kataristas – organised themselves in a union that had its connections with the left-wing intellectuals in La Paz (Baud, 2007a: 32).

The wide differences of opinion among members of the revolutionary MNR eventually led to new oppressions and the involvement of armed parties. General Barrientos, chief of military forces, gained power in 1964. With United States support, the military stayed in power for the following 18 years (Morales, 2004: 248; Zavaleta 1998, in Talavera Simoni, 2011: 104). Resistance started to come from the 'revolutionary left'. Under the leadership of Ernesto Che Guevara a counter-hegemonic guerrilla battle was prepared in 1966-67, but this turned out to be

---

[40] According to the 1993 constitution, the president has the power to appoint ministers and prefects. He/she controls the military and state finances. The parliament consists of two chambers; a senate with 27 members, and a Chamber with 130 representatives. The parliament can authorise or hinder legislation processes. The national Ombudsman (*Defensoría del Pueblo*) investigates complaints of governmental actions since 1998 (Domingo, 2005: 1734; Morales, 2004: 241-242).

unsuccessful for the *guerrilleros*. The military were to keep their authority, and hegemony, until 1982. General Hugo Banzer ruled for most of this time. Bolivia was part of 'Operation Condor', a Latin American anti-communist pact between Argentina, Chile, Paraguay, Uruguay and Brazil. Many perpetrators of human rights violations from that time have never been condemned. A nation-wide hunger strike heralded the beginning of the end of military rule. A coalition of socialist, communist and revolutionary organisations called the *Unidad Democratica Popular* together with the Socialist Party and trade unions, pushed for a transition to democracy at the end of the 1970s. General Banzer was under so much popular pressure that he had to resign at the beginning of 1978. The transition back to democracy was rather troublesome, as many unsuccessful elections and very violent *coup d'états* followed each other. It took until 1982 to install a new democratic government, led by the leftist Siles Zuazo.

The 1980s are often called the 'lost decade' in Latin America, referring to a severe economic crisis in the region. Similar to wider developments in Latin America at the time, developments in Bolivia were characterised by: on the one hand neo-liberal Structural Adjustment Programmes or 'SAPs' (Kohl, 2006); and on the other hand the rise of indigenous social movements (Regalsky and Laurie, 2007: 242). During the first half of the 1980s, Bolivia's economy was in complete disarray and the newly elected president Siles Zuazo introduced an economic 'shock-treatment' (Brienen, 2007: 22, 30), in line with wider imposed and fairly brutal neoliberal programmes in Latin America (Klein, 2007). Advanced new elections gave the 1952 revolutionary leader Víctor Paz Estenssoro the opportunity to start a radical neoliberal experiment in 1985, named the New Economic Policy (NEP). Two influential international financial institutions – the World Bank (WB) and the International Monetary Fund (IMF) – in this decade used Bolivia as a 'social laboratory', as the SAPs were primarily designed by the economist Jeffry Sachs and Bolivia was even called a 'neoliberal success story' then. To minimise the negative social impacts of these neoliberal policies, social emergency funds were created. The Bolivian model was copied in many other countries in the global South (McNeish, 2006: 220, 224). However, there is consensus that this neoliberal programme in Bolivia (the NEP) has not reduced poverty and income inequalities, but instead had even deteriorated the social situation, despite the 'poverty alleviation programmes' and social emergency funds that accompanied it (Domingo, 2005: 1735; McNeish, 2006: 224-227). The NEP also undermined the power of the COB and other popular resistance groups (Morales, 2004: 249; Domingo, 2005:1735).

Throughout the twentieth century, labour unions formed the core of the opposition to the urban governing elites.[41] Historically, there has been a strong link between trade unions and political parties (Tapia, 2008: 215). The COB had an immense influence on politics in Bolivia from the 1952 Revolution until 1985, when the NEP was introduced. The class based labour movement formed a strong political opposition until the neoliberal policies negatively affected the unions' power. Due to its rigid male dominated and Marxist oriented structure, the COB was not able to succesfully navigate the SAPs.[42] In the decade of the 1980s it became clear that the link between the trade unions and political parties had its limits. Yet, at the same time

---

[41] In Bolivia's education sector, there are two influential teacher unions: a rural one and an urban one, which are discussed in more detail in chapter 5.

[42] According to Kohl and Farthing (2006: 153), the COB lacked flexibility to cope with a working force that turned more and more heterogeneous (including a large share of women). Together with the worldwide decline of communism, the decline of COB was irreversible.

decentralisation and political restructuring made space for indigenous and *cocalero* leaders to stand up. Bolivia's popular social movements emerged in response to forms of '*economic and military violence, leading neoliberalism to dig its own grave in Latin America*' (Dangl 2007: 8). Opposition movements since then often emphasised their identity and territorial demands. This illustrates the paradox of neoliberal policies; they both weaken and simultaneously stimulate active resistance (Kohl and Farthing, 2006: 75, 125, 153).

In line with the global post-Washington consensus model, the decade of the 1990s introduced a new era of socially oriented developments and reforms in Bolivia. The neo-liberal project was still going strong, from 1993 led by Gonzalo Sánchez de Lozada, or *Goni*, who was the original inventor of the neo-liberal experiment. He promoted sustainable development in a free market environment. Following international trends, human development (through education) and popular participation became key issues (Morales, 2004: 250-251). Goni also invented the *Plan de Todos*, or Plan for All, of which the 1994 education reform (see next chapter) was part of, together with privatisation, popular participation measures and the development of a new constitution in 1995 (Taylor, 2004: 21-25). These so called 'pro-poor' neoliberal reforms responded to the growing international and external pressures to tackle growing poverty levels. Subsequent to the World Bank's introduction of the Poverty Reduction Strategy Guidelines in 1999, Bolivia became the only country in South America to join the World Bank's Highly Indebted Countries (HIPC) initiative. This initiative included the formation of a more favourable debt repayment climate and capital investment, together with an involvement of the government in the creation of a Poverty Reduction Strategy Paper (PRSP) in 2003, as a response to the Millenium Development Goals (MDGs).[43] These neoliberal reforms recognised indigenous cultures and raised expectations of indigenous citizen participation. The reforms, however, rather channelled into a '*Western form of citizenship*' and did little to transform the status quo and structural forms of racism (Postero, 2007: 4-5). This led to growing dissatisfaction and unrest in Bolivian society as well as its political arena, in which old and new actors started to battle over a hegemonic neoliberal system and its failures.

Hence, the decade of the 1990s in most parts of Latin America was also characterised by the rise of indigenous movements. Indigenous movements had already come into being in the 1960s, but were only noticed internationally after 1992. That year, the 500 year 'discovery' of Latin America by Columbus was celebrated and indigenous groups in the whole continent took the opportunity to openly protest against continuing colonial relations. Internationally, indigenous rights and popular participation were given emphasis through the ILO 169 Convention, which was signed by Bolivia in its early stages. A strong '*collectively contrued social memory*' helped indigenous groups in the Andean region to develop an understanding of historical hegemonic systems of social and cultural domination, and to construct counter-hegemonic responses (Abercrombie in Postero, 2007: 13). While taking a critique on neo-liberalism and the nation state as the core of their protest agenda, these new social movements struggle for an alternative development model in different parts of Latin America. The highland and lowland indigenous movements differ from each other in terms of their organisational form, although

---

[43] Bolivia's local version of the global PRSP initiative was called the 'Bolivian Poverty Reduction Strategy' (McNeish, 2006: 223-224), which recently has been replaced under Morales' government by the National Development Plan (PND).

both are often organised following the labour union model. In the highlands, most organisations are based on family and community connections, the *ayllu's*.

The rise of social (and mostly indigenous) movements was encouraged by the installation of the 1994 *Ley de Participación Popular*, or popular participation law (Domingo, 2005: 1733).[44] Here we can see how through popular pressure methods – including massive roadblocks and protest manifestations (Harris, 2007) – the Popular Participation Law triggered space for contestation, as grassroots movements and unions could also make their demands heard through formal political channels (McNeish, 2006: 221). Although popular participation is highly valued in Bolivian discourses since the 1990s, and officialised through the Popular Participation law of 1994, large sectors of the population – and especially marginalised groups – have been excluded from real influence in (national level) politics and democratic participation, leading to social disintegration (Salman, 2006: 163; McNeish, 2006).

Thus, in the context of the failed neoliberal SAPs, a decline of trade unions and a rise of indigenous movements in the 1980s, during the 1990s a range of new players entered the political arena. This plurality of political actors is one of the main characteristics of 'the New Left' in Latin America, not excluding Bolivia, where different types of (mostly rural) social movements became to form a strong coalition on the left (Rodriguez-Garavito et al, 2008: 8-17). In Bolivia, Evo Morales has played a key role in the rise of the New Left. Based on his union-based political career (Sivak, 2008), he became one of the two protagonists of the Bolivian protest movement who converted their mobilisations into a political party; respectively the governing party *Movimiento al Socialismo* (MAS) of Evo Morales and the *Movimiento Indigenista Pachacuti* (MIP) of Felipe Quispe. Morales and Quispe, although not described to be best friends, gained electoral successes with their parties despite being portrayed as extremist, subversive, un-democratic and irrational (Assies and Salman, 2003: 150-155; Domingo, 2005: 1737-1738).[45] Morales spent quite some time abroad, where anti-globalisation movements and other indigenous movements (including the Zapatistas) inspired him to use his '*indigeneity*' strategically. As a consequence, he has been criticised for adopting a '*strategic essentialism*', because he '*romanticizes indigenous culture for political ends*' (Canessa 2006: 252-255). Interestingly, the process of transformation of the party system is being commenced from the rural areas into the cities (Tapia, 2008: 219-221) and the MAS came to power in a context of '*ruralisation of Bolivian politics*' (Zuazo, 2008).[46] Using the coca leaf as 'their symbol of struggle and Andean traditions', the coca-growers, or *cocaleros*, gained ground in electoral politics with the MAS (Dangl 2007: 49). The MAS is often brought forward as an example of the merge of indigenous social movements and (coca)farmer trade unions into a political party (Gray Molina, 2009).

---

[44] Through municipal decentralisation, this government sought to strengthen national legitimacy, to fight corruption, and to empower historically marginalised rural indigenous groups by giving them a voice. Through a system of redistricting, 311 new municipalities were created. They all had a rural majority, even though the rural population only counts for 42 per cent of the population (Taylor, 2004: 17-22).

[45] According to Canessa (2006: 241, 250), the political rhetoric of Quispe is mostly radical, exclusionary and particularistic; Morales' rhetoric, instead, is inclusive and broad as he lets *mestizos* into his party, and he is connected to both Aymara and Quechua cultures. In Bolivia, the term *Mestizo* refers to those from a mix of both Spanish and Indigenous descent.

[46] Zuazo (2008: 17) analyses how the MAS emerged out of four historical factors: 1) a strong urban-rural rupture; 2) the crisis of the neoliberal economic model; 3) a crisis in representativeness of traditional political parties; and 4) the decentralisation process towards 'municipalisation' from 1994 onwards.

Economic crises within Bolivia and in neighbouring Argentina at the turn of the century laid a basis for growing frustrations among the population. Kohl and Farthing (2006: 149, 175) explain how the neoliberal hegemony in Bolivia started to unravel in the period between 1999 and 2003, when the country staggered from one crisis to another. In this changing social and institutional context social movements emerged to (re)gain access to political processes (to the state) and to secure local autonomy issues (Yashar, 1998: 34). Three large social movements were the main players at that time. The (urban) teacher's union, by then the backbone of the COB, showed its strength and wide support through various protests. Secondly, new urban movements arose, especially in El Alto, the mostly indigenous city situated right above La Paz. Finally some ad hoc committees came into being in order to defend the rights of Bolivians to water (in 2000 in Cochabamba, see for instance Assies and Salman, 2003: 146-148), a fair tax system and natural gas in 2003. Recent history tells us how neoliberal governments have not survived the pressure of Bolivia's social movements, how the state was unable to *sell the idea of the common sense of neoliberalism to the mass of the Bolivians* (Kohl, 2006: 321) and how neoliberal hegemony started to unravel.

Following a 'politics of protest'[47] or 'direct democracy', the popular masses, movements and unions became a strong force within Bolivian politics at the start of the 21st century (see for instance Brienen, 2007; Domingo, 2005; Gamboa Rocabado, 2009). Since the so-called Water War in 2000 in the city of Cochabamba, counter-hegemonic popular struggles in Bolivia more and more began to focus against neoliberalism (Domingo, 2005: 1736; Harris, 2007: 12) and foreign domination, with Evo Morales as one of the fore runners of these struggles. The Water War in Cochabamba in 2000, through their successful mass mobilisation and victory of social movements, created counter-consciousness to neoliberal hegemony, giving rise to further battles over the recovery of gas resources and the extension of democracy. This illustrates a crucial aspect of Gramsci's 'war of position', since a new level of confidence and self-awareness stimulated people to organise and become agents of change (Harris, 2007: 11). Besides this 'war of position', Gramsci spoke of a 'war of manoeuvre', defined as *a frontal or insurrectional attack against the state or a period of intensive and active struggle, such as strikes and mass protest* (Harris, 2007: 3). Before taking democratic power, the political party MAS of Evo Morales were both employing a war of manoeuvre – with its massive demonstrations – and a war of position – becoming a leading social movement that eventually won the elections. One of the most famous events was the 'Red October' (because of the bloodsheds) mass demonstrations and blockades by popular movements, which eventually led to the resignation of the president Sanchez de Lozada in October 2003. When Lozada fled to Miami, he left vice president Carlos Mesa to take on a year-long interim presidency in a context of continuous battles and protest, until new elections were held in 2005 (Kohl and Farthing, 2006: 12; Postero, 2007: 5). In the words of Canessa: *The events of 2003 mark a profound change in the nature of indigenous protest, mobilisation, and identity in Bolivia* (2006: 243). Or, as El Alto based sociologist Pablo Mamani said about the overthrow of the neoliberal government in October 2003, *the state died, here in El Alto* (in Dangl 2007, 151), radically changing the legitimacy of governments in Bolivia.

---

[47] Or 'Protest politics' as referred to by Domingo (2005). Alternatively, the term 'politics of protest' has been used by David Meyer in his book on social movements in the US (in Krinsky 2007).

In Gramscian language, the Water (and later on also the Gas) Wars were a war of manoeuvre with the various represented sectors creating a new historic bloc of actors (Harris, 2007: 13). These events in Bolivia at the beginning of the 21st century can be seen as part of a '*new historic moment with resonance beyond its borders*' in which opportunities have opened for marginalised and especially indigenous groups to take a vital role in the formation of the agenda, which is both concerned with a politics of recognition and a politics of redistribution (McNeish, 2007: 889). Gramsci wrote about three different 'moments of relations of forces', which help to understand historical and contemporary formations of 'historical blocs', being particular forms of state, with specific attention to the role of social forces (through social relations) and civil society in these processes (Harris, 2007: 4). The first 'moment' refers to the level of structure, or the material forces of production, which forms the basis for the emergence of various social classes such as the rise of new political players since the 1990s in Bolivia. The second 'moment' is the relation of political forces, which reveals the homogeneity, self-awareness and organisation of various social classes (Crehan, 2002: 92).[48] The increasing political conciousness of Bolivia's indigenous and *cocalero* movements described in this chapter illustrate this stage. The third 'moment' marks the stage of effective political organisation. In Bolivia this can be illustrated by the example of Evo Morales' party MAS, as this third moment comes about when a class, or coalitions of classes, have organised themselves in a political party that incorporates the interests of the various social classes. The following political statement of Evo Morales in an interview – in ideological terms – could be seen as part of what Gramsci terms the 'third moment' of relations of forces: '*the new constitution is not created to retaliate to anyone, or to create a new elite. We don't have the ambitions to subordinate anyone, or to take revenge. We simply want everyone to enjoy the same rights*' (Journeyman Pictures, 12 May 2008). Effectively creating a new 'historical bloc' is, however, anything but a 'simple' undertaking. Part III elaborates on the specific power plays between the government and non-governmental actors (educational institutions, indigenous movements, unions etc) in the field of teacher education that both reinforce and undermine this development of a new historic bloc.

Viewed from a neo-Gramscain perspective, the Bolivian state can be perceived as a site of contestation and a 'strategic terrain' upon which both left and right political actors and wider civil society strive for their causes (Rodriguez-Garavito et al, 2008: 21, 34). The relationship between the state and social movements can be understood as a dialectical one (Rodriguez-Garavito et al, 2008: 35). Bolivia has a 'jammed' political culture, where individual leadership, mostly by men, and corruption still form important elements of the functioning of the system (Salman, 2006: 228; Dangl 2010: 26). This mistrust in the state is deeply rooted in historical struggles between governments and popular movements (Brienen, 2007; Salman, 2006; Domingo, 2005; Dangl 2007; 2010), and remains an important dimension of social and political tensions. Considering the majority votes Morales continues to receive, the change in government since 2006 appears to have contributed favorably to the legitimacy of the Bolivian political system (Seligson et al, 2006: 28; Tapia, 2008: 224). Morales' political and now governing party MAS has remained close ties with its social movement base, creating rather blurred boundaries between the party and social movements as they '*at times work for, with and against each other*' (Dangl, 2010: 16, 19). The

---

[48] This second political moment covers three faces of political consiousness: from solidarity within the corporate level; to solidarity among all members of a social class; and finally when corporate and class interests are transcended to a solidarity that encompasses the interests of all subordinate groups (Crehan 2002: 92).

relationship between the social movements and the current government is '*a two-way street*', since social movement's goals are largely supported and taken up by this government, while the MAS receives support for passing legislation and policies through (sometimes even MAS-funded) mass demonstrations (Dangl, 2010: 22). Yet, in spite of Morales' background as a social movement leader of the coca growers union before becoming president, he cannot count on an absolute support from all social movements. Several trade unions, neighbourhood movements (especially in El Alto) and landless movements have protested from the beginning against certain appointments within the Morales cabinet.[49] Zibechi warns for the '*dangers of seduction by the state*', as he emphasises how the new Bolivian government can be '*the bearer and voice of change*', yet it should not disempower social movements in their key roles (2010: 7).

Gray Molina, who was involved in Bolivia's UNDP Human Development Report 2007 '*El Estado del Estado*', claims that the '*lack of institutionality*' is actually a strength of Bolivian democracy. It creates a hybrid kind of democracy, according to Gray Molina, and makes accommodation and contestation possible. The next crucial steps for this accommodated hybrid democracy would be to integrate the former elites into the 'new society' under Morales and to recognise an emerging middle class with a mixed indigenous identity (Gray Molina, 2009). Or in Gramscian terms, the new government seeks to create hegemony, a consensus on their new route to a decolonised state transformation. Instead of the historical unifying policies of *mestizaje* – the creation of a unified *mestizo* nation (Canessa, 2006: 255; Zoomers, 2006: 1023-1024) – the Bolivian government now strives to create a decolonised and pluriethnic state, with equal rights and opportunities for its diverse people. The present government is facing the difficult task of creating consensus and a new 'social settlement' (Robertson, 2000). The new political discourse is clearly radical in nature, but critics point out the limitations of Morales' revolutionary politics of change. Regalsky (in Kohl and Bresnahan, 2010: 8-10), for instance, argues how Evo Morales' current political agenda does not coincide so much with indigenous demands for (certain forms of) autonomy. He argues that Morales' goal is to build a centralised nation state, by balancing indigenous demands with those of former elites, instead of radically transforming the state apparatus. While recognising the validity of this statement, alternatively it can also be argued how Morales sees himself forced into, and strategically uses this balancing of indigenous and former elite demands, in order to reach his goal of a radically restructured Bolivian society, for instance through a newly written constitution and education reform.

Bolivia's current political situation, in which the Morales government is struggling to install a counter-hegemonic project after a long history of elite domination, falls under Gramsci's notion of an 'organic crisis of the state'.[50] From a neo-Gramscian perspective on social transformation, the Bolivian state is certainly in a moment of transition, at the same time as the new 'revolutionary' government struggles to convince various groups in society of the validity of their new ideology. In Bolivia, an organic crisis of the state can be interpreted, in my view, in two ways. The neoliberal governments that ruled the country until Morales experienced an organic

---

[49] The (urban) teachers union for instance rejected the appointment of Felix Patzi Paco as the first Minister of Education under Morales, because he would lack a background in teaching (Petras 2006).

[50] Although critics wonder about its current applicability (Martin, 1997), as Gramsci's ideas on the 'organic crisis of the state' were based on his reflections on the weakness of the Italian bourgeoisie in the first part of the twentieth century, it is still useful to analyse the case of Bolivia, notwithstanding this is a very different geographical and temporal context.

crisis of their hegemonic regime, when social movements through mass demonstrations enforced an ending of their reign in the first few years of the 21st century. Secondly, the new, and not yet fully prepared, government since its installation in the beginning of 2006 up to the time of writing faces another version of an organic crisis, as it struggles to move a yet 'incomplete transition' further on. Based on empirical findings on the Bolivian education sector, the boundaries between 'political society' and 'civil society' are rather fluid, and the government is also internally struggling to create a cohesive strategy, since social movements leaders have now become officials within governmental institutions and work alongside an older generation of policy makers. Furthermore, the government is confronted with serious popular resistance to the new 'politics of change' and a decolonising education reform (see chapter 5). Due to this long-term transition phase at present in Bolivia (Harris, 2007: 13-14), or what I refer to in this thesis an impasse in the education sector, we cannot (yet?) speak of a new installed hegemony.

3.3 Bolivia in the world and in the region

With the aim to provide a multiscalar analysis of Bolivia's context, I now briefly turn to explain how these political developments are reflected in Bolivia's external relations. Although Bolivia's societal conflict has deep historical roots, it is the effects of wider processes of globalisation in the last few decades that have further intensified poverty and inequality in the country. In trying to overcome such negative outcomes of certain exclusionary globalisation processes (see for instance Duffield, 2001; Castles, 2001) and in response to the failure of certain 'pro-poor-policies' accompanying neoliberal structural adjustments, many Latin American countries have chosen to follow their 'own' regional and nationalist development strategies. It can thus be argued that the case of Bolivia is illustrative of a wider process of transformation in the Latin American region. The National Development Plan (2006-2010) summarises Bolivia's new external relation strategy: *'the state becomes a sovereign and self-determined actor, with an own identity, as it formulates its foreign political doctrine for diplomacic actions, providing an international framework of solidarity and complementarity, acknowledging a presence of indigenous peoples and in defense of sustainable use of natural resources and biodiversity'* (authors' translation). Especially in Bolivia, the sense of the need to protect 'the national' against 'the international' has recently become strong. Since Morales came into office in 2006, this tendency led – at least for the education sector – to the exclusion of the World Bank and the International Monetary Fund in decision-making and financing mechanisms. There also seems to be a break in the traditional 'back yard' relationship between the United States (US) and the Latin American continent. As explained by the Bolivian ambassador in the Netherlands, American domination in national politics is no longer tolerated in Bolivia (Calzadilla Sarmiento, 2009, translation by author).

Besides the 'global' influences on Bolivia, perhaps even more important nowadays are Bolivia's regional ties. Various Latin American leaders cooperate in South-South regional and global blocks (for instance Chavez from Venezuela, Lula from Brazil, Kirchner from Argentina, Correa from Ecuador, Ortega from Nicaragua and Morales from Bolivia), 'in order to alter the international economic rules of the game' (Rodriguez-Garavito et al, 2008: 27). We can distinguish between 'open regionalisms' with a more neoliberal character and new forms of regionalisms through 'counter-projects' (Muhr, 2008b). An example of the first form of open regionalisms is the Free Trade Agreement that was signed between Bolivia and MERCOSUR in

1996. On the other hand, and exemplary of the second form of counter-hegemonic regionalism, Bolivia also forms part of the 'Bolivarian Alliance for the Peoples of Our America' (ALBA), together with Cuba, Nicaragua and Venezuela.[51] Bolivia became an official member of ALBA in 2006, the same year Morales started to govern. Critics have called Bolivia's foreign policy schizophrenic, because it is driven on one hand by an ideological block (being ALBA), and on the other hand by pragmatic choices (linked to MERCOSUR) (Gray Molina, 2009).

Fairclough (2005: 931-932) speaks about *recontextualisation* as the dissemination of emergent hegemonic discourses across structural boundaries (e.g. between organisations) and scalar boundaries (e.g. from local to national or international scale, or vice versa). With regard to crossing scalar boundaries, Bolivia's decolonising education discourse is propagated at the regional level through Bolivia's coordinating role in ALBA's Editorial Educative Council (*Fondo Editorial Educativo* – FEE). Bolivia's relationship with ALBA has been reciprocal; while regional solidarity through the TCP (*Trato de Comercio de los Pueblos* or People's Trade Agreement) has offered Bolivia models for political, social and cultural engagement, the country has done the same for other ALBA member states (Lopes Cardozo and Strauss, forthcoming). In the 'Cochambamba declaration' of April 2008, the 'Margarita Declaration' of March 2009 and the 'Managua Declaration' of June 2009, several ministries of education of ALBA-members – Bolivia, Venezuela, Cuba, Nicaragua, Dominica and Honduras – declared the importance of fighting inequalities and social injustices through education throughout the ALBA region and to find alternatives to the commodification of education driven by 'the North' (ALBA, 2008; ALBA, 2009). So far, ALBA's actual education activities have been a focus on higher education, with around 6000 Bolivian students participating in exchange study programmes in Cuba and Venezuela (Muhr, 2009).[52] Bolivia has also engaged ALBA in its educational advancement through the *Yo Si Puedo* literacy programme, which brought Cuban teachers to areas with low literacy rates. Due both to that programme and Bolivia's own initiatives, the country was declared free of illiteracy on December 20 2008 (ALBA, 2009b: 5). Although the ASEP law was not directly related to the ALBA agenda in interviews, we can still see some convergences (see Lopes Cardozo and Strauss, forthcoming). For instance in relation to teacher education, the ALBA-Education plan presents aligning teacher training as one of the main goals (ALBA, 2009b) and Bolivia has recently changed the system from three and a half to five years, leading to a university level '*licenciatura*' (Bachelors degree), as is the case in various other Latin American countries.

3.4 Characteristics of Bolivia's diverse and tense context

This section shows an overview of the different dimensions of Bolivian diversity and inequality that have contributed to the countries past and present conflictive situation.

Geographical and demographical diversity
Bolivia's diversity is determined by its geographical variety and its multiethnic population; by its many different languages and cultures; and by its biodiversity and rich resources. The country is thinly populated with 9.7 million inhabitants (2008 estimates by UNESCO)[53], on a surface 26

---

[51] For more information see also http://www.alba-tcp.org/.
[52] Courses that are developed include Community Medicine, Education Sciences, Comparative Education and Oil Geopolitics (all at post-graduate level) and a PhD in Education (ALBA 2009a).
[53] http://stats.uis.unesco.org, last viewed 24-03-2011.

times the size of the Netherlands. While just about 95% of the population is officially counted as belonging to the Roman Catholic Church[54] and the remaining 5% to Protestantism, many Bolivians consider themselves to practice a contextualised interpretation of Christianity, where Christian traditions are mixed with various indigenous inspired traditions and the worshipping of Morther Earth. There is a heterogeneous church presence in Bolivia, including Jesuits, Silesians, Fransiscans, Protestants and the Summer Institute for Linguistics, among others. Often these religious institutes work in the areas of education, media or cooperation with indigenous movements and NGOs (Malaver and Oostra, 2003: 37; Yashar, 1998: 37-38).

Bolivia has nine departments (with a representing prefect) and these departments are divided into provinces. Since the 1995 decentralisation, the municipalities – more than 300 in total – form important administrative institutions. The country can be divided into three main geographical areas (see Maps 1 and 2): the Andes Highlands (*Altiplano*) in the West (20 per cent of the total surface); the valleys in the central part (15 per cent); and the lowlands of the tropical Amazon and Chaco in the North, East and South (60 per cent) (Malaver and Oostra, 2003: 60; Morales, 2004: 243). Bolivia remains the least integrated country in Latin America; huge geographical differences and an ongoing power struggle between the urban 'centre' and 'the regions', and between the '*media luna*' and the highland regions, prevent integration processes and interregional communication. As argued below, one of the dimensions of Bolivia's present conflict is the divide between the economically dynamic lowland movements (primarily in Santa Cruz, Tarija, Beni, Pando and Chuiquisaca) and social movements from the highlands and the valleys (McNeish, 2006: 234; Seligson et al, 2006: 35; Molina, 2008: 5). There is substantial migration within Bolivia, and many other Bolivians leave the country to work in Chile, Argentina, Spain or the United States. Within the country, people migrate to the bigger cities of La Paz, El Alto, Cochabamba and Santa Cruz. Especially young rural youth leave their homes to find job opportunities in the cities or in the lowland coca farming. International migrants, either seasonal or longer term, send back remittances to support their families back home (CEPAL, 2005: 55; Morales, 2004: 243). Due to this historical and present internal migration flow, no demographically 'uncontaminated' areas exist in Bolivia (Salman, 2008: 98).

Economic Development in Bolivia

The Human Development Report 2006 shows that 63.7 per cent of the Bolivian population lives in urban areas, with an estimate for 2015 of 68.8 per cent. The country ranks 95 (out of 169 countries) on the UNDP Human Development Index 2010 (HDI) and is placed in the 'medium human development' segment.[55] While poverty levels have decreased over the past few years, just a few years ago Bolivia was still in position 117 of the HDI 2008.[56] Data presented by Latinobarómetro (2007: 110) showed an increasing trust in (parts of) the economy since Morales came to power. Indeed, even in a global context of economic crisis, Bolivia's economy has grown: according to the World Bank (2009) the gross domestic product increased from 9.3 US$ in 2005 to 17.3 US$ in 2009.

Nevertheless, Bolivia remains one of the poorest and most unequal countries of the Latin American continent. Regardless of an increased popularity of the government after the

---

[54] See http://www.minbuza.nl/nl/Reizen_en_Landen/Landenoverzicht/B/Bolivia.
[55] See http://hdr.undp.org/en/statistics/.
[56] See http://hdr.undp.org/en/reports/global/hdr2007-8/ (out of 177 countries).

installation of Morales in 2006 (Kennemore and Weeks, 2011), Bolivia's democratic system continues with a broken legitimacy due to a failure to successfully integrate socio-economic developments (Zuazo, 2008: 13), slow economic development and the fact that a majority of the Bolivian workforce are employed in the informal sector. Without going into detail, there are a number of obstacles for Bolivian economic development including: low national savings and investments; national budgetary deficits, a negative trade balance and deteriorating terms of trade; export of resources with low added value; growing foreign debts and a crack-down on coca production (during the Banzer government 1997-2002); scarce employment opportunities; growing income inequalities; increased regional inequalities; and continuing social exclusion and inequalities (see for instance Domingo, 2005: 1735). While foreign or elitist exploitation of the countries' natural resources are usually seen as a main obstacle to poverty alleviation, Brienen argues that there is a danger in this singular focus and the overestimation of the productivity of Bolivian subsoil, since these expectations (when foreign dominance disappears, poverty will diminish) are too high (Brienen, 2007: 28-29).

Although political rhetoric might mislead us to think otherwise, Bolivia's interpretation of 21st century socialism in practice has not signified dramatic shifts towards a pure socialist model. According to Kennemore and Weeks, Morales follows a model of *'Andean capitalism'*, a pragmatic strategy of a centre-left government that aims to *'capture the capitalist surplus necessary for state spending'*, mostly from the country's natural resources (2011: 271). The nationalisation scheme of the MAS has made it possible for the government to fund various social policies, including the *'Bono Juancito Pinto'*, a cash transfer programme for school going primary education students of around twenty Euros a year. Both from an ideological 21st century socialism point of view, as well as a means to deal with a global volatile economy, Bolivia participates in various regional trade relations, such as the Back of the South and ALBA (discussed above). Venezuela, for instance, has provided financial support to Bolivian municipalities. The country also negotiates (for instance of gas deals) with various partners outside of Latin America, including Russia and Iran (Kennemore and Weeks, 2011: 271-272).

Within the National Development Plan (PND), education is considered a crucial instrument to strengthen development. In the PND, the current government also emphasises the need to live in harmony with the natural environment, with respect for Mother Nature and avoiding environmental degradation (Calzadilla Sarmiento, 2009). Drawing from Ramirez' world (education) cultures theory and Wallerstein's world-systems theory, Griffiths (forthcoming) analyses how, in the case of Venezuela, the relation between educational planning to benefit national development planning may be seen as an example of Venezuela both drawing on world-system level cultural scripts about education, as well as part of the governments attempts to achieve higher levels of endogenous economic development. A similar analysis applies to Bolivia, where we find a comparable reasoning that sees education as a core vehicle for national development.[57]

---

[57] A similar argument is presented in the Latin American regional overview of UNESCOs Global Monitoring Report 2011, which describes the link between mortality rates of under-5 year olds, which are three times as high for those children having mothers with no education. 'More educated women have better access to reproductive health information and are more likely to have fewer children and to provide better nutrition to their children, all of which reduce the risk of child mortality'. See http://unesdoc.unesco.org/images/0019/001914/191433e.pdf.

Cultural and ethnic diversity: developing indigenous identities

The country has struggled since independence in 1825 to create internal cohesion and a national identity in the face of significant ethnic and cultural-linguistic diversity. Depending on the source, Bolivia has between 34 and 36 official languages (Morales, 2004: 244; Taylor, 2004: 25; Delany-Barmann, 2010: 181). However, not all these languages enjoy the same amount of power, as often only four languages are referred to: Spanish; Quechua; Aymara; and Guaraní.[58] There are also different figures on the numbers of indigenous groups; Albó (2005) for instance mentions 34 groups, while other studies describe 37 indigenous groups in Bolivia (CEPAL, 2005: 9; Nucinkis, 2004: 4). A CEPAL survey of 2001 shows that 65.8% of the population who older than 15 years of age auto-identifies as indigenous, with the highest concentration in the urban areas of La Paz and Cochabamba because of urbanisation flows (2005: 32, 44, 45). A study named 'Democracy audit' in 2006 showed that 71% of the population identified themselves as belonging to indigenous groups (Seligson et al, 2006). In the 1992 census, few Bolivians identified themselves as indigenous, showing a change in self-conception over the last decade (Drange, 2007), a process that continues to date among future teachers as will be illustrated in chapter 7. This links to a change in identity formation from becoming white – or *blanqueamiento* – to becoming indigenous again – or *reindigenización* – as it is called by Chaves and Zambrano (2006).

The largest indigenous groups are the Quechua and the Aymara, respectively 49% and 41% of the indigenous population. The linguistic Map 3 below shows how Aymaras and Quechuas generally live in the Andean region, with the Aymaras on the higher plateau and the majority of Quechua people in the valleys (see also Speiser, 2000: 225). Yet, although Bolivia is often referred to as being an 'Andean region', a great part of Bolivia's territory and ethnic groups are Amazonian (D'Emilio, 1996: 13). In this lower part of Bolivia, many different smaller (a few hundred people) and larger (a couple of thousand people) groups have their own languages and (cultural) identities, and since the 1990s the Bolivian Amazon region has been an active site of indigenous organisation (Yashar, 1998: 25).

Despite the fact that the poor are primarily indigenous, they are everything but a homogenous group. What they have in common is '*a shared history of exclusion and a common frustration with the promises and the failures of neoliberal globalization*' (Kohl and Farthing, 2006: 4). Although at first sight it might seem clear which groups in Latin America can be identified as being indigenous, this is far from an easy task in reality. Identifying one self as being indigenous is highly subjective and at the same time it is contextually defined (Canessa, 2006: 243-244). Besides ethno-cultural classifications, in Bolivia a variety of other aspects are also adopted to define someone's identity, including language, geographical references, clothing and social class (Delany-Barmann, 2010: 182). Canessa points to the paradox that even though a majority of the Bolivian population identifies with being indigenous, the majority of Bolivians have Spanish as their mother tongue (Canessa, 2006: 256).

---

58 For instance on the webpage of the Dutch Ministry of Foreign Affairs,
 http://www.minbuza.nl/nl/reizenlanden/landen,landenoverzichten/westelijk_halfrond/bolivia.html, last viewed 17-07-2007.

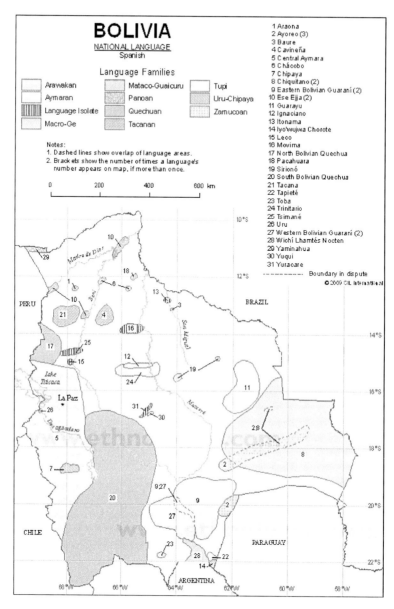

Map 3 Linguistic map of Bolivia (Lewis 2009, www.ethnologue.com, © SIL International)

Thus, language is a poor indicator of indigenous identity. Still, it is a factor for discrimination, as *'linguistic competence, or the 'correct' manner of speaking Spanish, seems to be an important mechanism of social discrimination that goes beyond ethnic and socio-economic differences in Bolivia'* (Seligson et al, 2006: 32). Fieldwork experience also revealed the difficulty and sensitivity of the identity discussion. The following quote, from a graffiti-painting from 'Mujeres Creando'[59], illustrates how discussion

---

[59] Mujeres Creando (Women Creating) is a feminist activist organisation working from La Paz. More information can be found on http://www.mujerescreando.org/. See also Dangl 2007, chapter eight.

continues on the claim that the majority of the Bolivian population is really indigenous, since it is unclear who identifies with being indigenous and why.

'Pachamama, tu y yo sabemos que la única originaria es la papa'
'Mother Earth, you and I both know the only native is the potato'

There are various ways of reflecting on 'indigenous-ness'. Van Dam and Salman's work (2003) helps us to understand different 'moments' of reflection, in which they first saw indigenous-ness as something of the past which could be overcome through modernisation. The second way of reflection departs from a multicultural and human rights perspective, widely adopted in mainstream international development debates, that sees difference as both valuable and necessary to overcome racism. The category 'indigenous' can also be viewed as a context specific social construct, often closely linked to political interests (see also Howard, 2009), especially in urban areas. This connects to what van Dam and Salman call the 'third moment' of reflection on indigenous identity. Postero (2007: 9) argues this 'third moment' is particularly relevant when reflecting on Bolivia's current politics of 'strategic essentialism', in which indigenous and Andean cultural aspects are appropriated to strengthen political power. As a result of major socio-economic inequalities, rougly since the 1990s, there has been an 'indigenous awakening' in Bolivia, but also in Ecuador, Guatemala, Mexico and to a lesser extend in Peru (Canessa, 2006: 242; Zoomers, 2006: 1043; Baud, 2007a). The issue of identity and ethnicity has only since the 1990s been recognised as having an impact on Latin American politics and conflicts, in contrast to earlier acknowledgement of it in other parts of the world (Yashar, 1998: 23).

Ethnic, political, social and educational discrimination and exclusion of indigenous population groups – that constitute the majority of the Bolivian population – are deeply rooted in Bolivia's society and politics, which in other cases are often linked to 'minority problems'. Zoomers (2006: 1025) argues that while indigenous groups are now actively involved in mainstream politics, the majority of these groups are still the poorest of the poor. Yet, while indigenous identity has long been 'equated with backwardness', nowadays a somewhat more flexible and dynamic perception has replaced this (see also Yashar, 1998: 23). A new middle class is emerging, of formerly lower class citizens who claim to be (at least partly) from indigenous descent (Gray Molina, 2009). Evo Morales is the most prominent example of this new middle class, as a former rural coca-grower who has, through union leadership and politics, worked his way up to becoming president.

3.5 Five processes of conflict

This context of huge diversities and large inequalities, between rich and poor, between lowland and highland Bolivia, and between different ethnic-cultural groups, lead to social tensions and conflicts in the country: as in indication about 80% of the population expresses that there is a conflict between rich and poor people in the country (Latinobarómetro, 2007: 67). For the purpose of this study, Bolivian conflict is defined as a combination of the following five processes: 1) high levels of *poverty and inequality* of opportunities; 2) *discrimination and exclusion*; 3) a regional struggle linked to the use of *separatist discourses* and *identity politics*; 4) a severe *mistrust* in the functioning of state (institutions) and between groups in society; and 5) reoccuring *clashes between the state and social movements*, that sometimes turn *popular pressure methods into violent encounters*. These processes are all historically rooted, as has been highlighted in the first part of this chapter, yet they also carry on under the current government of Morales.

First of all, high levels of poverty continue to exist, as was highlighted above. In the words of the Bolivian scholar José Luís Saavedra: *'poverty is a form of violence'*. Although poverty is not a direct cause of conflict, it can be seen as a trigger mechanism for frustrations with, and mistrust in, the state (Salman, 2006: 164, 171). Moreover, because of the wide gap between rich and poor people, ensuing severe inequalities lead to tensions amongst different population groups. Because of a lack of jobs, there are limited career opportunities for unemployed youth, which can lead to a process in which youngster's exploitation is reproduced, for instance for young, poor, female – and often indigenous – house servants (Kohl and Farthing, 2006: 190-191).

Secondly, discrimination and exclusion continue to leave deep marks on society and cannot be changed over night. Estimates illustrate that 71% of Bolivians label the tensions between the different ethnic and cultural groups as 'strong' or 'very strong' (Latinobarómetro, 2007: 70). Discrimination is not only directed towards a heterogenous group of indigenous peoples, but extends to gender issues, class issues and regional prejudices – with Andean inhabitants negatively called *'collas'* and inhabitants from the plains called *'cambas'* (D'Emilio, 1996: 22). Discrimination is apparent in political struggles and in clashes between societal groups, and it appears that concealed forms of violence over the past decades have become more 'open' and direct. Recently, on the 12 September 2008 for example, violent clashes between supporters and opponents of the 'indigenous president' at a demonstration in the Pando region regretfully resulted in deaths and wounded. Not only political preferences, but also 'racial' issues are said to have triggered the violence between civilians. One of Bolivia's ex-presidents described in the Spanish newspaper *El País* how regional, racial and cultural differences in Bolivia are at a critical stage. He argued how Morales has pushed his pro-indigenous constitution through, thus creating more tensions among the non-indigenous population and the risk of more violent confrontations (Mesa, 2008). Within the education sector, discrimination and exclusion of certain groups of (indigenous) students has been called 'indirect' or 'symbolic' forms of violence (Bourdieu in Regalsky and Laurie, 2007: 241). Although at the policy levels attention is being paid to solve these problems, in reality discrimination and social exclusion in educational institutions continue to exist. According to Gamboa Rocabado in UNESCO's report on Bolivian education, the function of present day education should be to *'identify a sentiment of reconciliation to overcome the inter-ethnic conflicts that have affected Bolivia'* (2009: 70).

A third aspect of present day conflict in Bolivia is the use of *separatist discourses* and *identity politics* that are linked to vast regional differences leading to tensions, the demand for autonomy in parts of the country by both the political (fomer elite) opposition and indigenous groups and the use of an exclusionary discourse by political leaders on both sides. Some sectors were, for instance, in favour of the new constitution and nationalisation of the gas reserves, whilst other sectors (those mobilised by the entrepreneurial elites of the department where the gas reserves can be found) claim regional autonomy and against nationalisation (Salman, 2006: 163). Zuazo (2008: 19, 24) discusses the urban-rural rupture in this context of regional and political tensions, originating from a colonial 'installation' of a lack of trust between (rural) indigenous people and the (urban) central state. She argues how decentralisation to the municipal levels from 1994 onwards resulted in a 'ruralisation' of Bolivian politics, aggravating the urban-rural divide and differences. There is also a partition between the economically dynamic lowland movements in the western *media luna* (half moon) – controlled by a powerful elite – and the indigenous and working-class based movements from the highlands and valleys (McNeish, 2006: 234; Seligson et al, 2006: 35; Molina, 2008: 5). According to Molina (2008: 10), the '*Cruceña*'[60] call for autonomy is a necessary step to liberate this relatively wealthy region from the political domination, the ideology and the poverty of the *altiplano* (highlands). However, we should avoid a simplistic vision on 'for or against autonomy', since different indigenous groups also strive for different forms of autonomy.[61] As president Morales explained in an interview with Al Jazeera: '*it is not a matter of east versus west, but of opposing groups in society*' (Al Jazeera, 2008).

Political leaders have started to use separatist discourses to mobilise their support against 'the other part' of the country. Although president Morales at the discursive level claims to work for a unified Bolivia, the opposition and other critics argue that his pro-poor and pro-indigenous strategy is a new form of exclusionary politics, fostering polarisation by excluding the non-indigenous and mostly urban inhabitants of the country (Molina, 2008: 8; Gamboa Rocabado, 2009: 23, 69). Besides, the present government announced to the press how the *prefectos* (provincial state representatives) of Santa Cruz are working towards a *coup d'etat* (La Razón, 2008). During another speech in March 2009, Morales addressed a crowd of supporters and urged all union leaders to '*define themselves*': '*If they aren't with the government, they are with the opposition. If they are with the opposition, then they are on the right, they are racist fascists, they are neoliberals*' (as quoted by Molina, 2009 in Kennemore and Weeks, 2011: 273). Such discourses can obviously lead to growing mistrust among the population against 'the other', claiming power on the bases of a particular identity. Within Conflict Studies, Kaldor (1999) uses the term 'identity politics' to explain such processes.[62]

Fourthly, there is a severe 'culture of mistrust' in society. Not only does part of the population lack confidence in the government to govern well, mistrust can also be signalled between groups in society, in the messages of the media and, importantly for this research, also in the education institutes. The fast majority of Bolivian daily press and television channels are controlled by private enterprises that have little trust in Evo Morales and the MAS (Howard, 2010: 186). The severe lack of trust in poorer peoples' opinions according to McNeish indicates an '*often hidden, but nonetheless potent structural violence of class, racial and gender prejudice that many Bolivian social scientists highlight*' (McNeish, 2006: 228). Regardless of his electoral success, over the past few years a lack of trust in the Morales government has also gained ground, even under Morales'

---

[60] From Santa Cruz

[61] Autonomy struggles are also fought out in the education sector, were alternative education policy initiatives – the so-called '*estatutos autonomicos departamentales*'– were created in the lower regions of Bolivia. These documents are highly debated in terms of their legitimacy, congruence with the national Constitution and influence on education. It could be stated that they '*ignore the common, emphasize their own truth as the only truth, and impede an open dialogue between different groups and cultures in society*' (Van Dam & Salman 2009).

[62] In some cases, it might be argued that certain forms of identity politics could be legitimate for a period of time, for instance when linked to the improvement of the lives and power positions of marginalized and discriminated groups. Although the concept of identity politics is a useful one, we should be careful not to treat it in a simplistic and solely negative sense. Hale (1997) elaborates on how the 'politics of identity' evolved in Latin America, and links it for instance to the rise of indigenous politics as opposed to unified national-popular projects.

supporters.[63] In contrast to the sense of hope when Morales came to power in 2006, it was estimated that only 29% of the population believes that the state is actually able to solve current problems (Latinobarómetro, 2007: 29). Relating back to Bolivia's turbulent politics described above, the country's 'political conflict' (McNeish, 2006: 225, 237), or 'crisis of belief in democracy' (Salman, 2006: 163), has led to a continuing unstable political environment and a lack of a 'culture of trust' in democratic institutions (Domingo, 2005: 1740; Zuazo, 2008: 14). Historically deeply rooted forms of corruption seem to persevere at different levels (national and local/institutional), only creating a deeper mistrust in state actions and official institutions (for a discussion on the lack of trust in teacher education institutes see chapter 7).

The fifth and final dimension encompasses the unceasing tensions between the state and social movements, sometimes leading to violent encounters. These events are usually portrayed in the national and international media by showing the clashes between police/military forces and social movements using popular pressure mechanisms such as demonstrations, roadblocks, hunger strikes and crucifixions. These popular pressure methods are particularly adopted by Bolivia's teachers' unions, as is explained below. Similar to other Andean countries, these instruments are primarily used to enforce popular power as opposed to state power. As Sousa Santos argues, in the case of these forms of direct popular action, we can distinguish between violent and non-violent and between human and non-human objectives (Sousa Santos, 2008: 269). Though popular uprisings have shown to be effective, even in overthrowing the government in 2003, they nevertheless also had – and have – their downsides. Particularly the poor can be viewed as both protagonists and victims of the effects of the numerous roadblocks and violent confrontations with the police and military. Furthermore, the economy suffers from the withdrawal of foreign investors who lose trust in the Bolivian situation.

Recent research has shown how education can both contribute to processes of conflict, as well as work against them (for an overview see Novelli, 2008: 478-481). A conflictive society and education are dialectically related to each other, since education is usually reflecting, influenced by and affecting society. The work of Bolivian teachers is embedded within and responds to this conflictive multilevel (global, national and local) context, and is the topic of the following section.

3.6 Teachers' life and work in relation to the five processes of conflict

Similar to many other education systems worldwide, Bolivian educators face the challenge to better understand the relationship between education and the tensions within society; to analyse the roots of inequalities, discrimination, mistrust, exclusion and the use of violence. Of course, it cannot be argued that education is the only cause of Bolivia's troubles, nor can it be seen as the sole medicine. Yet, we do need to take into account that the historically embedded inequalities within the education system will not change from one day to the next, that these structures do form a basis for tensions and frustrations in society and that there is a potential space for educators to work *against* these processes, as is taken up in chapter 9.

---

[63] For example, indigenous protesters who first thought the new constitution would be a ticket to inclusion in Bolivia's future, later on stated that Morales and 'his' constitutional assembly have not dealt with issues of greater autonomy and representation (Almudevar, 2007, BBC 06-08-07).

Both rural and urban teachers are faced with the first process of conflict – poverty and inequality – in both their private and working life. Teachers and students alike live with daily realities of poverty in their homes and in their classrooms. Teachers in both urban and rural contexts complained of poor teaching materials and a deprived infrastructure, such as insufficient or badly maintained school buildings and long and difficult journeys to get to school for both students and teachers. Some statistics show how inequalities still persist in the Bolivian education system, particularly in the more remote areas such as the Amazon region. Although only 8% of all primary schools are private (Contreras and Talavera, 2003: 9; UNESCO, 2011: 318), it has been argued by several education actors that there are significant inequalities between the quality of education in private and public schools. It was, for instance, mentioned by the former Minister of Education how *'most ministers of education – and Bolivia knows many of them – all came from private schools. Thus, the political decisions are in the hands of those who enjoyed a private education. Public schooling should open up these opportunities for others. Around 90% of society, including the social movements, demands changes for better quality in public education.'*[64]

Based on UNESCO's Global Monitoring Report statistics (2011) learning achievements in Bolivia differed between indigenous and non-indigenous students, and inequalities remain to exist over the past decade based on students' ethnicity, gender, regional and urban/rural location, and their level of wealth. The average years of schooling are calculated based on factors including wealth, location and gender, with an average of 11.5 years of schooling for a richer, male and urban student on one end of the continuum, and an average of 5.5 years of schooling for a poorer girl living in a rural area in Bolivia. Educational inequalities are further influenced by factors such as ethnicity and regional location within Bolivia, as becomes clear in UNESCO's most recent available statistics: particularly those groups with a Quechua ethnic background and those living in Cochabamba, Potosí or Chuquisaca face the highest levels of educational marginalisation in Bolivia.[65]

The work of Bolivian teachers is also strongly linked to the second dimension of conflict, as one of the principle problems that educators are faced with in Bolivia nowadays is not just *'the presence of multiple identities and languages but rather the existence of mechanisms of discrimination and exclusion'* (D'Emilio, 1996: 12).[66] Discrimination, the so-called 'diseducational function' of the school, thus presents an alarming feature in a country such as Bolivia with an indigenous majority (D'Emilio, 1996: 18). Until fairly recently, popular or indigenous knowledge was not seen as equally valuable compared to western-based knowledge (Gandin and Apple, 2002: 259). Some Bolivian teachers tend to disqualify indigenous knowledge as backward, since it is not based on modern science and technology (Regalsky and Laurie, 2007: 240). D'Emilio (1996: 17) observed how teachers would for instance ask their students *'if you want to be an Indian or if you want to be intelligent'*. Drange likewise signalled how a large part of Bolivian teachers assert that *'children from the city are more intelligent than children from the countryside'* and that *'intelligence depends on the race you*

---

64 Interview with the former Minister of Education, Lic. M.M. Cajías de la Vega on 16th September 2008.
65 For more detailed information and visual illustrations see UNESCO's GMR website, http://public.tableausoftware.com/views/PageFourNew/Pg4Dash?:embed=y&:toolbar=no&:tabs=no
66 However, it has to be noted that the complexity of interculturality also forms a huge challenge for teachers and policy makers (see for instance Albó 2003, the three dimensions of intercultural education).

belong to' (2007: 3).[67] A feminist and indigenist activist explained in an interview how teachers are protagonists in reproducing discrimination, forming one of the major obstacles to a genuine intercultural, bilingual and just education system in Bolivia: *'there exists a blindness in the political ideological vision of teachers: while most of them have black faces, in their minds they see themselves as even whiter than the whitest citizens of this country'* (70:5).

Both government offices and schools are identified by Bolivians as important scenes of discrimination (Seligson et al, 2006: 33). Bolivian schools, similar to Bolivian society, are characterised by a wide diversity. The integration of children with different backgrounds in the same school can – under certain circumstances – have positive effects on learning how to live together, as the case of Sri Lanka shows (Lopes Cardozo, 2008). However, when not negotiated well by teachers, these differences can trigger discrimination, stigmatisation and exclusion against those who learn more slowly, or those who do not understand the language of instruction (D'Emilio, 1996: 15). Discrimination and exclusion of certain groups of (indigenous) students has been called 'indirect' or 'symbolic' forms of violence (Bourdieu in Regalsky and Laurie, 2007: 241). Violence unfortunately does not only take place outside of schools. Often, schools themselves form places where direct and indirect violence is committed. A study by Regalsky and Laurie (2007) showed how local community members developed strategies to neutralise the unwanted effects (including racism and violence) of their local school. Furthermore, violence in the form of physical punishment, or even sexual abbuse has been – and in some cases still is – used in schools to punish low-performing or disobedient students. These punishments were 'tolerated' by the state until the 1994 reforms, in line with the goal to increase the number of girls in school. Since the creation of parent committees there is a larger control on what happens inside the school area. Teachers have been reported to be expelled by the parents associations because of – true or false – accusations of maltreatment of students. Finally, Seitz (2004: 51), drawing on the work of Salmi, uses the relevant concept of 'alienating violence', referring to culturally biased curricula, and suppression of linguistic and cultural diversity.

The third process of conflict (identity politics/polarising discourses) has a more direct influence on teachers' life and work. On the one hand, teachers' own identities (chapter 7) and being part of a certain community influences the way they perceive the situation in the country: a Bolivian Aymara highland teacher is more like to be in favour of the current Morales government discourses than an only-Spanish speaking teacher living in the city of Santa Cruz. The way teachers themselves experience the societal tensions and their own political views often influence the way they (do not) deal with these issues in school. Chapter 9 discusses teachers' potential agency to counter stereotyping and polarising discourses, by enhancing levels of trust and promoting open and critical dialogue.

The issue of mistrust can be illustrated by looking at the difficult process of the implementation of the 1994 Educational Reform (discussed in the next chapter), and the foreseen difficulties of the implementation of the new ASEP law (see chapter 5). According to the teachers' unions (and especially the urban one) the 1994 reform process lacked participation of teachers and was imposed by neo-liberal actors. Similarly, teachers currently complain again

---

[67] The issue of race in the Bolivian context is usually discussed in terms of ethnicity and/or indigenous background, culture and languages.

about a lack of genuine participation, ownership and a lack of information about the new ASEP law, which rather decreases than improves teachers' trust in government policies. In addition, mistrust in the quality and effectiveness of teacher training institutes can be signalled since the general view is that teachers are not being prepared well enough for their job. Several teacher trainers, as well as student teachers, explained how corruption and 'political favours' (in different forms and at different levels) and the malfunctioning of state institutions also increased a sense of mistrust (chapter 7).[68]

Bolivia's teachers unions are notoriously known for their use of popular pressure methods to push for their demands (see also chapters 5 and 11). I witnessed several marches, usually on Friday afternoons, organised by the urban teacher union in La Paz. This section of the teachers' union is known for the somewhat radical nature of their demonstrations.[69] On one occasion (September 2008), although there were no signs of this demonstration turning violent, police forces vigilantly controlled strategic locations in the city centre (including the MoE) because, as one police officer explained, these demonstrations by teachers 'might escalate'. Chapter 9 elaborates on teachers' possibilities and challenges of their collective agency related to this fifth process of conflict. In addition, in their desperate attempts to become a teacher – as a main way out of poverty – hunger strikes were organised by students who tried to push the MoE to let them enter the already full Normales.

As a final note on these five dimensions of the Bolivian conflict and its relation to the education sector, it is worth mentioning how the new ASEP reform aims to directly or indirectly tackle at least the first two processes through and in education, as a decolonised education system strives to create equal opportunities for all to live well, without discrimination (Ministerio de Educacion de Bolivia, 2010b). The final three processes are, however, not so much taken into account in the current education reform plans, while changing identities, misrust, corruption and strong feelings of resistance among educators are described in this thesis as pressing issues in the (teacher) education sector that deserve political attention.

3.7 Bolivian society in summary: continuing tensions, new horizons

A new political and ideological wind seems to be blowing through Bolivian territory, creating new spaces for contestation of historical structures of inequality and injustice. Change is the buzz-word in Bolivian media, politics and even in the streets and markets. Also, we can observe real changes taking place since president Morales' installation in 2006, such as a new constitution as of February 2009. A very important change in relation to this study is an emerging new profile of an indigenous middle class, with Evo Morales being the most prominent example (Gray Molina, 2009). Building on the work of Sahlins, Postero (2007: 12-13) rightly notes how there is continuity in all processes of social change, while in cases such as Bolivia, indigenous peoples are

---

68 Mistrust at the personal level was also visible in some of the schools I became acquainted with. Schools are often used in two or three 'turns' a day. In many cases, there are different management teams in the morning, afternoon and evening turns. Teachers and students reported a lack of communication between these managers, and the (mis)use or destruction of educational material in the classrooms by 'the other' users. Consequently, children who sit in classroom 1B in the morning, get to perceive their fellow students using the same room in the afternoon as unmannered and rude children, because their teacher is afraid to leave anything behind.
69 Data exists that show how between 1996 and 1997, in 17 encounters with the police, more than 170 people were detained, 2 people died and 62 were wounded (Contreras and Talavera 2004).

active agents in these processes of counter-hegemonic change. In addition to the need to build an alternative economic vision and activity, as Harris (2007: 19, 22) suggests, I argue it is similarly important to follow Bolivia's attempts to build a new education system that supports this alternative vision and a 'counter-hegemonic' culture. Struggles in Bolivia revolve around economic, environmental, social and democratic justice, and Morales' 'politics of change' envisions bringing these struggles for justice forward, with education being one of its core instruments for transformation. However, this is far from a smooth process, as various processes of conflict discussed in this chapter continue to dialectically affect the education sector and various social groups, including teachers, disagree with Morales' new project. These processes of conflict are also creating certain room for contestation, opening up a horizon of potential progressive changes in a context where change is – slowly – beginning to take place.

This context makes the focus of this study on the link between these envisioned processes of social justice and the role of teacher education and future teachers very relevant. Especially now the education system has a crucial function in preventing and coping with the effects of these conflictual processes. Drawing from debates in the field of 'Conflict and Education', it is relevant to refer to Pigozzi (1999) here, who emphasises that situations of crisis, emergencies and post-conflict reconstruction should be viewed as opportunities for positive transformation of education systems. In situations of societal transition, education systems – which might have contributed to the root causes of conflict – should not just be rebuilt, but be transformed (Bush & Salterelli, 2000: 24; Seitz, 2004: 56), as is anticipated in Bolivia's new ASEP education reform. The next chapter therefore turns to discuss how processes of *continuity and change* in the education sector eventually led to the recent developments of the new ASEP reform under the Evo Morales government, which will be the core focus in the chapters of Part III, IV and V.

4

Continuity & change in twentieth century Bolivian (teacher) education: from indigenous denial to Education For All

'I think a country does not become rich because they have mines full of gold. It is preferable to say that countries make progress when education is given priority'
(Member of the national rural teachers union CONMERB, 83:14)

4.1 Introduction

On a cold and rainy afternoon in La Paz, I meet with a senior teacher trainer in the canteen of the urban Normal. While warming our hands on a cup of coca tea, he started to talk: *'I was born in the highlands in an indigenous family. We spoke Quechua at home, and my parents worked as farmers and servants of a richer and land owning, Spanish speaking family. I am the oldest son, so I was sent to the village school'.* He stopped for a sip of tea, before continuing to tell about his memories of early days in school: *'For a long time, I did not understand what the teacher was saying, as she only spoke Spanish. The first few weeks were exiting, but then I started to get bored. I was sitting next to the son of the upper class family who my parents worked for. So what I did, was just copying the stripes and circles he was drawing in his notebook. I did not really get the point of it. Only when I started to become friends with the neighbouring Spanish speaking boy, slowly I started to learn to understand Spanish. This is when I came to understand that those stripes and circles is what people also call 'letters'. Later on, I started to learn how to write myself'* (108). Regardless of this unfair start to his education career, he is now a very passionate and engaged trainer at one of the biggest teacher training institutes in the country.

Education in Bolivia has historically developed from a unifying and discriminatory system to a slowly changing, more open, intercultural and multilingual type of schooling that, in line with a wider global push for Education For All since 1990, aims to provide relevant education to all its citizens. The story above of the older trainer exemplifies the importance of relevance of education for all students. While education has the potential to contribute to processes of societal transformation, educations impending role in society is not unproblematic either, since *'millions and millions of children in Bolivia, and in the whole world, are concentrated every day in classrooms. Nowhere is it so easy to reach massive amounts of people as in schools. But you know, every day they listen to nonsense, so it is a waste of time'* (Cuban researcher based in La Paz, 65:6)[70]. Although Bolivian reality in schools is more nuanced, the point made is valid in the sense that education's potential is clear, but it has not always been a political priority.

---

[70] The numbers indicated between brackets refer to the codified and anonimised transcriptions of interviews in the data analysis programme Atlas Ti.

As a basis for the analysis of the contemporary education situation and new decolonising education reform in chapter 5, this chapter explores the most important developments in Bolivia's educational history until 2006, or *before Morales*, and pays specific attention to the teacher education sector. After a condensed examination of Bolivia's education context until the 1990s, the chapter continues to discuss the rationale, mechanisms and implementation challenges of the Intercultural and Bilingual education law of 1994, a reform that internationally was given close attention due to its innovative nature at the time. The chapter paints the picture of a changing education context in the twentieth century that started off from a strong indigenous denial in its initial approach, while developing slowly into a more inclusive education system towards the beginning of the 21st century.

4.2 'Modernising' education in Bolivia (1900-1952)

Historically, Bolivian education has been aimed at linguistic and cultural assimilation – or *castellanización*[71] – and the incorporation in modernity of indigenous groups (Drange, 2007). A first official attempt to ensure free and mandatory (primary) education through the constitution was made in 1880. Throughout the last part of the nineteenth and the first part of the twentieth century, teacher training institutes, often referred to as Normales, were created in various countries in the Latin American continent. Most institutes were free of charge, public, under the control of a MoE and did not provide university degrees. The creation of these institutes was closely related to the construction of national identities and a unified nation state, and with this ideal in mind teachers were trained accordingly. In Bolivia, the first initiatives toward the education of teachers took place in the middle of the nineteenth century. There are recounts of teacher education initiatives in 1835, which is remarkable considering that *'on this side of the world the first Normales were established in 1839 in the United States and in 1842 in Chile the first Latin American Normal was created'* (Talavera Simoni, 2011: 16). However, due to a lack of finances and experts in this field, nothing concrete was established (interview (anonymous) historian UMSA, 25:4).

Elite resistance and political instability obstructed any systemised education for indigenous population groups (Taylor, 2004: 7)[72]. By the end of the nineteenth century, the first (rural) indigenous educational initiatives – *'escuelas clandestinas'* – arose, without any governmental support (UNNIOs, 2004: 11-12). The clandestine use of bilingual education, using the indigenous mother tongue to learn the Spanish language, was a pragmatic and insubordinate measure in the context of an exclusionary education system (Taylor, 2004: 7). In 1905 an endeavour was made to establish a nation wide and centralised education system; the 1905 law promoted teacher training, a primary and secondary curriculum, commercial and technical education and education availabilities for girls and indigenous people. Perspectives on the rise of indigenous education in the first half of the twentieth century vary. One the one hand, most authors refer to education in that period as a state controlled attempt to 'civilise' indigenous communities, and destroy indigenous identities and traditions. The state ensured its own interests – a unified and modernised Bolivia – through education (Taylor, 2004: 8), and made *'productive peasants out of the*

---

71 Translated literally this would mean something like 'enspanishment' of the population, aimed at imposing the Spanish language and culture.
72 Since the land and mine owning elite classes depended on the cheap labour of the indigenous population, they feared the 'liberating effects' of literacy (Soria 1992 in Taylor 2004: 7).

indigenous peoples'. Schooling was organised in a dual system, where 'urban education' was separated from 'rural education' (Drange, 2007).

The 1908 'General Education Plan' of Sanchez Bustamante initiated a new phase of the liberal education project (Talavera, 2009: 62). The 1908 Plan was different from the 1905 one in that it sought to create two different types of Normales: urban and rural ones. At the time of the creation of Bolivia's first Normal in Sucre in 1909, Franz Tamayo's ideas and the new the liberal Plan of 1908 gained ground and instead of a unified education system, a differentiated system of both teacher training and other levels of schooling was constructed. As an illustration of a contradictory and complex liberal paradigm, a MoE official in a Parliamentary speech recalled the danger of putting a book or a rifle in the hands of the indigenous, because with any one of these weapons the *indio* could leave aside its natural occupation as a farmer and that way disturb the political system' (Talavera, 2009: 64-65).

In June 1909, the first Bolivian teacher training institute *'Escuela Normal de Profesores y Preceptores de la Republica'* (now called *'Universidad Pedagogica'*) was created in Sucre, by a foreign Belgian educator named Rouma. This 'mission Rouma' has been critisised – particularly by the European educated *indigena* Franz Tamayo – for being too European centred and for disqualifying the capabilties of indigenous people (Del Granado Cosio, 2006; Lozada Pereira, 2004; Talavera, 2009: 64-65). The institute started with 28 students, first only men and in the second year a 'co-education system' was created for female teacher students. Also in other Latin American countries foreigners were involved in the creation of teacher training institutes: Argentina in Venezuela; and Spain in Mexico (Rama, 2004). In the period of 1915-1917 several other Normales were created in the surroundings of La Paz and Cochabamba. In 1917 the same Belgian man Rouma was also involved in the founding of the Normal Simón Bolíviar in La Paz, the main case study of this thesis.[73] The Belgian mission expanded with other missionaries who operated under the control of Rouma between 1910 and 1948. *'With Rouma, Bolivian schooling for a long time has been one of the most advanced of the continent'*, however reinforcing the divided urban-rural system by creating different and less successful Normales in rural areas (Talavera, 2009: 67).

Alongside these developments, several indigenous education initiatives developed in the beginning of the twentieth century, mostly in rural communities. The indigenous population viewed literacy teaching as an important step towards their liberation and they also wanted to reproduce the traditional *ayllu* system, which was based on collective agriculture and kinship relations. On the other hand, Brienen argues that we cannot view the development of indigenous education as a simple *'indigenous attempt to ward of the state's modernisation or as a state attempt to destroy indigenous culture'*.[74] He shows how the school actually functioned as a bridge between the state and the indigenous communities, with *'school teachers becoming representatives of the state in the communities, and representatives of the communities in the state'* (Brienen, 2002: 645-646). On the 2nd of Augst 1931 –

---

[73] The Simón Bolívar institute served under the authority of the 'Ministry of Public Instruction' (Del Granado Cosio, 2006), and it was created then to train secondary school teachers (Talavera, 2009: 67). The Normal Simón Bolívar was closed down for a period of 12 years from 1932 to 1946 because of the socio-economic effects of the Chaco War with Paraguay. Interestingly, it already had ties with the University Mayor de San Andres (UMSA) in this first period (25:4), which would (unsuccesfully) be repeated between 2000-2005 (see chapter 6).

[74] In his later work (2011: 320), Brienen claims that – rather than being victims of state led modernisation attempts – the indigenous communities were actually active agents in bringing 'modern' schooling into their communties, with the clear rationale of wanting to participate in 'modern society'.

which would later become the National Day of the Indian – the most famous and influential rural Normal in Warisata was established.[75] This teacher training institute was created in collaboration with the surrounding communities, and its students mostly came from this area. As a response to Tamayo's earlier critiques on the Belgian founded Normales, the Warisata institute did not merely copy a European model, but instead it created its own model focused on 'productive education', or education for work, now forming one of the pillars of the new ASEP law. The founder Elizardo Perez, a student who graduated under Rouma in Sucre, wrote down the historical development of the creation, functioning and the final destruction of the institute in 1940 (Talavera, 2009: 74-75). When the state realised that the development of local authority over schooling was inconsistent with their policies of (cultural) assimilation, the *escuelas-ayllu* and the *Normal de Warista* were forcibly closed down (Regalsky and Laurie, 2007: 235; Taylor, 2004: 8; UNNIOs, 2004: 12). The closure of Warisata was not only caused by elite fears of the *indigenal* education, as in this same period the first disputes between groups of teachers arose (Talavera, 2009: 75). The still ongoing cleavage between the mostly urban 'normalistas' (teachers trained in Normales) who strive for a unified system and the predominantly rural normalistas that struggle for indigenous forms of education is thus not only a recent struggle, but originates in the 1930s and 1940s of the last century.

4.3 National revolution, the *Código* and the *Escalafón* (1964-1960)

According to Paz Estenssoro, the 1952 revolutionary leader, a new kind of education was needed. The 1955 education reform – pushed through by the MNR (Regalsky and Laurie, 2007: 235) – envisioned diversity in terms of class, rather than ethnicity, culture or language. Baud explains that this is a form of irony, since *'these Bolivian reforms, revolutionary as they were, tended to address the rural population as peasants, not as Indians. After 1952, Indians were accepted in the nation as exploited masses, not as a culturally different population'* (Baud, 2007a: 29). Where the 1905 education reform sought to 'civilise' the indigenous part of the population, the 1955 '*Código*' reform aimed to assimilate indigenous people – by then named *campesinos* – into the dominant culture.[76] Regalsky and Laurie (2007: 242) argue that education since the 1955 reform only intensified ethnic boundaries between different groups in Bolivian society. Moreover, the teaching at that time was teacher-centred, based on memorisation techniques and especially relevant to an urban context (Drange, 2007).

In this period, the so-called *Código* was developed by an educational reform commission, including the MoE, the Ministry of Rural Affairs (for indigenous education), researchers from the university, and the urban teachers union[77]. One of the main goals mentioned in the *Código* was to create a single national identity. In contrast, the reform reinforced the two parallel education systems reflecting an urban/rural divide; the MoE was responsible for the (better equipped) urban system and the 'Ministry of *Campesino* Affairs' for the rural *Educación Fundamental Campesina* system. Interestingly, the two systems strived for different goals, and reflected a rather racist dualist system. Urban primary education promoted individual development, independent

---

[75] The Warisata experience was influential in the creation of (among other institutes) the second case study of this thesis, the Normal in Paracaya *'Ismael Montes Ascencio Villarroel'* in 1948 (Lozada Pereira, 2004).
[76] Similarly, the educational reforms of 1969 and 1973 promoted one national language (Spanish) and culture.
[77] According to Talavera 2011: 181 the urban unionists were the main authors of this document, resulting in a document that mostly reflected the urban educational context and not so much the rural one.

learning, as well as personal and social responsibilities. The rural version aimed for personal hygiene, literacy, vocational goals, more efficient agricultural practices, civic consciousness and national folklore (Taylor, 2004: 9-11).

With regard to teacher education, the *Código* established that the Normales were the only institutions in the country that could train teachers and provide them with a diploma (Del Granado Cosio, 2006: 12-13). A new wave of the creation of Normales took place after the Revolution into the beginning of the 1960s, both in urban and rural area's '*in order to guarantee the formation of principal subjects [the new teachers] that would valorise and reproduce the revolutionary reality*' (Lozada Pereira, 2004: 41). As a breeding ground for contemporary ideas about the ideal teacher in Bolivian Normales (see chapter 8), the *Codigo* stated how teachers needed to have a strong *compromiso social*, a social commitment. Article 95 for instance mentioned how: '*Normales are oriented to train a type of professional teacher with a broad cultural awareness, scientific preparation, a technical-pedagogical capacity and a social susceptibility with regard to collective problems and elevated moral conditions*' (quoted in Lozada Pereira, 2004: 43). The 1955 *Codigo* also established that the state, for her part, had to guarantee employment once a teacher had obtained the national teachers title. Therefore, teachers need to subscribe to the *escalafon*, which is a 'vertical' seniority or grade scale that ever since has been one of the main objects of defence of union struggles.[78] New teachers can registrar after they have completed their obligatory first two (in the case of urban students) or four (for rural students) years of working 'in province'.[79] After obtaining the official title, teachers receive payments and welfare arrangements from the state. In order to ascent in category (nowadays running from five to zero, followed by the last category '*al merito*'), teachers' need to complete an exam for the first three categories and are automatically promoted to the last categories.

Because of large teacher shortages at that time, article 234 of the *Codigo* authorised that all *Bachilleres* could teach at primary level and all University graduates at secondary level. They only had to pass a 'capacity exam'. After five years of working experience, these teachers could registrar as well to the *escalafon* as '*maestros interinos*' – a special scale for untrained teachers that comes before the first scale of the graduates (category 5) (CTEUB, 1957-2007; Del Granado Cosio, 2006; Lozada Pereira, 2004). In 1962, estimates of the total number of teachers vary between 12,762 (according to government at that time) to 9,551 (according to UNESCO), with respectively 45.4% and 47.9% of them being *interinos*. From this period on, (future) teachers organised at a collective level to struggle for a lower approbation grade for the entrance exam. The current demonstrations and hunger strikes of applicants, who try to push the MoE to let them enter the already full Normales because they have gained this minimum grade, thus have strong historical roots.

4.4 Education under military rule and transition back to democracy (1964-1990)

The military governments integrated the two parallel education systems back into one system for formal education, with a national curriculum (Taylor, 2004: 11-12), but in reality the two subsystems remained separate. During the 1970s a conductivist pedagogical reform gradually

---

[78] I use the term 'vertical' scale here, to contrast it with the 'horizontal' system of salary promotion that is for instance used in Mexico, which rewards teachers for extra training and professional development rather than only the years of experience (Tatto et al 2007: 156-157).
[79] Nowadays, *all* graduated teacher students have to work for two years in a remote area in order to enter the *escalafon*.

transformed practices of teachers, with a focus on memorisation and copying of contents, this way deprofessionalising teachers' roles. Teachers criticised the military rulers alienating and 'antinational' education policies and pressed for a more inclusive system at the second National Pedagogical Congress in 1979 (Talavera Simoni, 2011: 10, 147). Interestingly, in the broader Latin America region education systems were on the rise (late 1970s and 1980s). Illiteracy rates went down, enrolment rates went up and the number of female students rose relatively strong. Paradoxically, in this same period there were remarkable reductions in government spending on education. Governmental budgets for education dropped and many teachers lost their jobs. The 1980s saw concurrent social unrest and economic instability, which led to a crisis of the (rural) education system. Both unions and peasant social movements pressed the state to reform the education situation (Regalsky and Laurie, 2007: 242).

During military rule from 1964 onwards, government policies for teacher training aimed at a unified (integrating urban and rural teacher education), hierarchical and 'depoliticised' teacher education system. The number of humanities subjects was brought down, and pedagogical classes were added. The Higher Institute of Pedagogy was created to compile statistics relating to the teachers force (Contreras and Talavera, 2003: 21). This reform was called the 'contra-reform' by teachers, since in their eyes it counteracted their union movements and it thwarted all revolutionary ideals of the former reform. These hierarchical structures become clear when looking at the different titles used: at primary level teachers were called '*maestros*'; at secondary level '*profesores*'; and at higher education levels '*catedraticos*' (or '*cate*'), or '*licenciados*' (or '*lice*'). During my stays, I realised how much this hierarchical structure is still in use. Teacher students consequently addressed their trainers with '*cate*' or '*lice*' and when they found out I was also teaching at my University in the Netherlands some even used these terms when they turned to me. In 1967 teacher students started a '*Revolución Normalista*', which was '*a pedagogical movement that sought to change both the contents and the organisation of teacher education, in which students would have a bigger say in the determination of the politics of teacher education*' (interview 86:1 with a senior teacher trainer, currently employed at the MoE). In 1970, a massive and first time National Pedagogical Congress was organised, with participation of teachers (Talavera, personal communication May 2011).

The agreements never made it to an implementation phase, because of the *coup d'etat* and the beginning of a seven year dictatorship of Banzer in 1971. In 1975 the educational 'Banzer law' together with the 'law for Normales of 1975' were launched. Both university autonomy and teacher union activities were abolished. Teacher training was aimed at national security and the creation of '*a nationalist state, order, work, peace and justice*' (Lozada Pereira, 2004: 49). Self-development of teachers, a 'research spirit' and permanent evaluation and control were seen as important elements. According to a MoE official in 1995, since this period of dictatorship '*teachers are no longer great teachers, they have turned into mere unionists*' (Chavez 2007 in Talavera, 2009: 76). The law separated normal school administrative functions from technical schools. Party members and union leaders saw openings to enter management positions in this new structure (Contreras and Talavera, 2003: 21). Drawing from the data of this study, we can see how Banzer's law laid many of the foundations for the structure of teacher education as organised under the 1994 reform; the training is six semesters long, organised in both urban and rural Normales, with a concentration of decision-making power at the MoE.[80]

Until 1982, children were punished at school for speaking their own languages rather than Spanish (Albó and Anaya, 2003: 36). As a result, indigenous groups have lost many of their cultural and linguistic traditions (Albó, 2005). After the return of democarcy, the first elected government (Siles Zuazo 1982-1985) initiated the 1982 National Education Plan, including the first large scale literacy program SENALEP. Leaving behind linguistic homogenisation in educational planning, indigenous languages were taken into account as being both beneficial mother tongues in educational settings and contributions to national culture (Taylor, 2004: 14). In the first years of the 1980s, a National Plan of Action for Education was designed, that was part of the regional UNESCO Principal Education Plan for Latin America and the Carribean. These plans aimed for a minimum of eight to ten years of education, an elimination of illiteracy and improving the quality of education through reforms (Contreras and Talavera, 2003: 22-23).

The following elections in 1985 gave way to the neoliberal government of Victor Paz Entenssoro, and a severe economic crisis meant an increase in foreign influence and increased levels of foreign aid in the education sector. A situation of severe economic crisis, massive debts and hyperinflation was to be 'cured' by Jeffrey Sachs' shock treatment of the economy, with devastating social effects, particularly for the already marginalised (Klein, 2007: 178-179), severely affecting the social sectors, including education. Due to rising poverty levels, many children were taken out of the classrooms because they had to help their parents raising the family income (Talavera Simoni, 2011: 154). Teachers' salaries were decreased severely, a situation that lasted from 1983 to 2003, which has pushed the teachers' unions into a defensive and 'salarial' attitude (Talavera Simoni, 2011: 12-13). Teacher training institutes still mushroomed, especially in the rural areas. During the 1980s, the teacher training system was further separated, distinguishing between rural and urban teachers. Moreover, the problem regarding *interinos*, or untrained teachers, remained to exist and became a more pressing issue (Contreras and Talavera, 2003: 22-23). The MoE published the white (1987), pink (1988) and blue booklets (1988), respectively describing the pre-project of the upcoming education reform (of 1994), the various meetings and documents around this pre-project. Finally, the blue booklet discussed a diagnotic of the teacher education situation in the Normales. It pointed out how the administrative structures established through the 1975 Normales Law had several shortcomings: a vertical and badly communicated top down decision-making process; a disturbed implementation process as well as a lack of coordination of the urban and rural sub-systems (the 'blue booklet' (1988) in Del Granado Cosio, 2006: 22-23). From the 1980s on, small scale initiatives (some by the state, yet mostly by NGOs that aimed to fill the gaps left by the government) paved the way for the 1994 Reform (Van Dam and Salman, 2003: 23). The international interference in the (teacher) education sector was extended into the decade of the 1990s, with the preparations and creation of the 1994 reform.

---

[80] This situation still resembed the organisational structure of Normales until the first implementation of the new ASEP Reform's structure of five years of study in Februari 2010.

4.5 The 1994 Education Reform – Intercultural & Bilingual Education for All (1990-2005)

At the beginning of the 1990s, and being part of a wider global movement to reach Education For All, Bolivia was the first country in Latin America to make intercultural education an official state policy 'not only for indians', but for all children, according to the Bolivian researcher Albó (in Drange, 2007: 1). The rationale behind *Educación Intercultural y Bilingüe* (EIB, Intercultural and Bilingual Education) was to provide indigenous children with the self-esteem, security and creativity to achieve better results, while maintaining their communities' cultural values and practices (Albó, 2005). In this way, new generations could strengthen their cultural identity, of cultures that were about to perish and establish a better foundation for entering into intercultural encounters (Albó 2004:42 in Drange, 2007).

There seem to be different opinions on when, how and by whom the first proposals towards EIB were initiated. Different actors claim different starting points. The most often mentioned version starts in 1988. In this year a pilot project for EIB was started by the MoE and UNICEF (PEIB 1988-1995), with the support of the Swedish development cooperation (D'Emilio, 1996: 26). The Project-EIB (PEIB) showed a shift from monocultural and multicultural educational ideologies to a pluricultural ideology, at least for the role of language in education (Taylor, 2004: 14-15). This programme was partly inspired upon an earlier EIB project in Peru, supported by the German development coopration agency GTZ (called PEEB-P, 1979-1990).[81] Another source mentions that in 1989 the urban teachers' union CSUTCB presented the document *'Towards an intercultural and bilingual education'*, which was influential in further developments of the PEIB (UNNIOs, 2004: 13-14).

After several failed attempts to initiate the reform process under the MoE, a task force (ETARE – *Equipo Técnico de Apoyo a la Reforma Educativa* – technical support team for the education reform) was created in 1991, which fell under the Ministry of Planning and Coordination. ETARE was comprised predominantly of highly qualified Bolivian experts, assisted by external consultants, and received World Bank financial support and technical assistance. However, there were several disagreements between ETARE and the World Bank – who demanded an emphasis on curricular and pedagogical changes rather that administrative and institutional ones – but these were resolved in mid-1993; how remains unclear (Contreras and Talavera, 2003: 9-13, 15). Taylor argues that this reform differed from other Latin American education reforms because it specifically called for transforming two dimensions of the education system concurrently; not only the curricular-pedagogical approach but also the institutional-administrative dimension (Taylor, 2004: 17). This might be explained by a focus of ETARE on the former and a WB focus on the latter dimension.

Time apparently was running short. The EIB reform was officialised in 1992 (*Decreto Supremo* 23036) in a rush, without a validated EIB curriculum and without genuine grassroots participation. According to Taylor, the government felt pressure to officialise EIB coming from increased mobilisation of indigenous movements and because of the (early) signatory of the ILO

---

81 Bolivian linguists and anthropologists were trained in Peru and an agreement with the Peruvian government in 1990 gave access to textbooks and methodological guides. In Bolivia, around 114 rural schools were reached through the training of supervisors, directors and teachers at the national, regional and local levels. Different opinions seem to disagree on the number of schools reached in this pilot project (for instance 114 schools according to Albó & Anaya 2003: 43; D'Emilio 1996: 24; and Nucinkis 2004: 2; and 140 schools mentioned by Taylor 2004: 14,15).

169 Convention concerning the rights of indigenous and tribal populations (Taylor, 2004: 16-17; D'Emilio, 1996: 25). Following the 1992 Pedagogical Congress, the MoE created a National Education Council (NEC) with participation from teachers, parents, the Catholic Church and universities (Contreras and Talavera, 2003: 17). Though the NEC played an important role in the developments of the new Education Law, a teacher and curriculum developer claimed how all NEC results were '*thrown in the dustbin*' by the MoE, which in his view made this a fake process of teacher participation that was '*undemocratic*' (8:35). Although there were some structural differences between the ETARE and NEC, in July 1994 the education reform became law (*Ley* 1565).

Textbox 3. Education Reform 1994

- Main goals were to improve:
  - quality and efficiency
  - relevancy
  - coverage and equal access
  - permanence of educators in system
  - equal gender rights
  - individual and collective identity development
- Main 'tools' to reach these goals:
  - Intercultural and Bilingual Education (EIB)
  - Student-centred teaching and learning methods ('constructivist' approach to education; teacher is facilitator of learning process)
  - restructuring of education, teacher training and administrative systems
  - prioritising primary education
  - popular participation mechanisms (*Juntas Escolares*)
- Two main 'pillars': interculturality and popular participation
- Five crosscutting themes: democracy, gender, environment, health and sexuality.
- Curriculum divided in two parts:
  - *Tronco común* = common core; EIB national curriculum.
  - *Ramas complementarias diversificadas* = complementary diversified branches; determined by local educational authorities.

Sources: (Speiser 2000; Contreras and Talavera 2003; Taylor 2004; Van Dam and Poppema 2005, Van Dam 2006)

Textbox 3 shows a clear alignment between the 1994 Reform and tendencies in global education reforms (see for instance Altinyelken, 2010). The Reform focused on primary level education, a combined approach for quality and access for *all* children, it encouraged gender equality and introduced student centred/constructivist teaching and learning methods. In line with these international discourses[82] largely focusing on 'inclusive education', the Bolivian education reform sought ways to include all children – including children from different cultural groups, and especially girls and disabled children – in the education system (Canessa, 2006: 189-190; Contreras 1999 in Taylor, 2004: 28). The 1994 law was followed by a set of regulations on popular participation in education in 1995. Special 'boards of education' (*Juntas Escolares*) were organised by officially recognised local community based organisations (*Organizaciones Territoriales de Base*). Again in line with global developments, emphasis was given to monitoring the quality of education: in a period of eight years the SIMECAL (System of Quality Measurement, 1996-2002) was created and ended again, mostly due to political reasons – since there was little progress in

---

82 The 1990 Jomtien International Education Conference and the ILO 169 Convention on popular participation inspired this new discourse (Regalsky & Laurie 2007: 242; Speiser 2000: 226).

the implementation of the Reform – and 'institutional malfunctioning' (Gamboa Rocabado, 2009: 40-41). Still today, teachers are well aware of the influence of international reform 'conditions' on the 'neo-liberal' and 'imposed' 1994 Reform. For example, a (urban female) teacher trainer argued, and her agument was confirmed in other interviews, that '*Law 1565 stipulated the state only to take care of primary level education, which was a recommendation from the World Bank, from outside. In the new law they will take this out, and focus on secondary and university education as well*' (13:102).

Reforming Teacher Education 1990-2000: slow implementation and challenges

In the first period from 1994-1997, some initial attempts were undertaken to change the institutional structures of the Normales. Teacher education institutes in rural and urban areas were 'unified' in terms of their administration and status (Del Granado Cosio, 2006), aiming to put an end to the 'balkanisation' of the education system in Bolivia.[83] Out of the 25 institutes in existence then, 23 created an Academic Institutional Project document, which were revised by the MoE. Only eight institutes were selected to enter the process from *Escuelas Normales* into *Institutos Normales Superiores* (INS), with decentralised administration at the level of the *prefecturas*.[84] The juridical instrument that accompanied the Reform initiatives for the Normales '*Estatuto Nacional de Formación Docente*' was approved in 1997, and pressed for a '*democratic, participatory and socially committed*' teacher training that would: '*strengthen the valorisation of the teaching profession as a dignified and crucial profession for Bolivian society*'; '*strive to be a vanguard in educational innovations*'; and offer '*permanent opportunities for (peer) evaluation and in-service training*' (*Estatuto Nacional de Formacion Docente*, quoted in Del Granado Cosio, 2006: 38-39). Besides, a plan for an 'institutionalisation process' was created (and since 2006/2007 taken up again, which is discussed below). Nonetheless, these intentions were not concretised (Del Granado Cosio, 2006). The transformation process was slow and difficult, particularly because the Normales had '*established practices far removed from the teaching and learning processes*' (Contreras and Talavera, 2003: 22-23). Moreover, an evaluation done by the MoE showed how in Simón Bolívar the curriculum and intercultural education were interpreted in various ways, there was a lack of cooperation between teacher trainers and trainers received a lack of guiding materials to implement the 'abstract and theoretical' ideas of the reform (Ministerio de Educacion de Bolivia, 1999: 25, 28).

At the end of the 1990s, the MoE together with the CEPOS, GTZ and international consultants started the project P-INSEIB (*Proyecto de Institutos Normales Superiores de Educación Intercultural Bilingüe*), in which eight Normales were targeted to become INS-EIB (Von Gleich, 2008: 95-97; Delany-Barmann, 2010: 187). From these eight Intercultural and Bilingual Normales, four specialised in the Quechua laguage, two in Aymara, one in both Quechua and Aymara and one in Guaraní. Teachers were trained here to teach in indigenous languages and to teach Spanish as a second language (Van Dam, 2007: 10). The projects were supported by GTZ and later also by UNICEF and DANIDA (Denmark). The objective of PINS-EIB was to '*implement a sub-system of Intercultural and Bilingual teacher education to improve primary education in the fields of Quechua and*

---

[83] This term 'balkanisation' was introduced by Mario Yapu in his *En tiempos de Reforma Educativa* report, quoted in Lozada Pereira 2004: 76.

[84] The institute in Paracaya (this study's second case study) was not selected for this first process, Simón Bolívar in La Paz (case study one) was, although it did not hand in an Academic Institutional Project document (Del Granado 2006). The Ministry decided to include this institute in the transformation process due to various reasons, according to Lozada Pereira (2004: 107), being its location in La Paz; the large numbers of both students and trainers; and the protagonist role of the Simon Bolívar as a site of contestation/ gremial resistance.

Aymara' (Albó and Anaya, 2003: 201-202). Evaluations on the progress of the P-INSEIB project have been relatively positive, with regard to the internal capacitating of the trainers and the development of more relevant curricula (Von Gleich, 2008: 101). However, after conversations with some parties involved in the training of teacher trainers, such as the Spanish development cooperation AECID, some critical concerns were revealed as well (the programme is further discussed in chapter 5). A staff member for instance explained how the majority of the teacher trainers that received training to update their knowledge and pedagogical skills had already left the Normales due to massive reorganisations (81).

The first large scale evaluation in 1998, concluded that none of the institutes understood or implemented the 1994 curriculum and the management was brought back to the central level of the MoE. Studies also showed several Normales operated inefficiently with few students and often irrelevant curricula. The MoE started a new reform phase. It converted the oldest training institute in Sucre into a pedagogical university and selected sixteen training institutes to become part of the National System of Teacher Training as an INS. They worked towards reforming their curriculum, administration and exam system (Contreras and Talavera, 2003: 23). It took until 1999 before some actual changes were taking place at the level of the Normales. Although changes proceeded slowly, some positive developments were noticed in several INS, and specifically in INS-EIB, since the 1994 reforms (Van Dam, 2007; Concha 2002 in Contreras and Talavera, 2003: 24). The EIB-institutes started to use the new curriculum, which was created in 1999. The administration and enrolment system were 'modernised' (Albó and Anaya, 2003: 201) and the number of new applicants rose. By 2002, the PINS-EIB graduated over 4,000 teachers who were able to teach the intercultural curriculum bilingually (Contreras and Talavera, 2003: 24).

From 2000 onwards, the government started to launch several reform programmes for the teacher education sector. One of them was the *bachillerato pedagógico* (pedagogical baccalaureate); a teacher training programme in the last two years of secondary education. This project was the result of an earlier successful project for indigenous women in Mizque, Cochabamba. It was designed in the rural Amazon and Andes regions, to find an alternative to the large number of untrained *iterinos*. Also, it was designed to give young rural youth an opportunity to receive their training closer to home. Graduates must work for two years in a rural area and may continue their training at an INS afterwards. The teachers unions were not in favour of the creation of these institutions (Albó and Anaya, 2003: 205). Regardless of these efforts, Nucinkis (2004: 12) states that 23% of the teachers at bilingual schools are still untrained *iterinos*.[85] Moreover, even during interviews with MoE officials in 2007 and 2008 it was expressed that *iterinos* still form a pressing issue.

In that same period, from 2000 onwards, the government initiated a programme through which the administration of part of the Normales was taken up by both public and private Universities. An additional attempt to structurally change the (teacher) education sector was to expand access to the teaching positions from solely those who held a teacher training school degree, to all professionals with four-year university degrees. All prospective teachers would have to pass a competency test. These reform initiatives aimed to eliminate the historic monopoly that Normal school graduates held within the teaching community, but these were met with fierce

---

85 For further critical remarks see Nucinkis 2004: 30-31.

resistance at the institutional level of the Normales, as is elaborated in chapter 6. These issues were highly debated and the continuation of the 'monopoly' of *normalistas* (graduates from the Normales) in the teaching profession is up to today a point of discussion, resistance and demonstrations. This is an illustration of how struggles about continuity and change are also played out in the education sector (see chapter 6).

Critiques on the 1994 law

Many of the critiques on the 1994 reform emphasise the contrast between policy and implementation, and consequently reflect how the political attempts for transformation were met with resistance and continuity of practices in educational reality (UNNIOs, 2004: 15; Van Dam, 2006). This section discusses the main critiques from the literature combined with interview data, which will help to frame and understand current challenges with regard to prospective implementation of the ASEP law. [86]

With regards to bilingual teaching, the reform resulted in *'the right to bilingual education for all whose mother tongue is other than Spanish'* (Speiser, 2000: 227). Protests of *Mestizo*-parents against bilingual education of their Spanish-speaking children influenced this one-way implementation. These parents feared that their indigenous-speaking children would not learn the Spanish language when they would be taught in their mother tongue in the early years of schooling (Contreras 1999 in Taylor, 2004: 20; Van Dam, 2007: 24; Van Dam and Salman, 2003). Similarly, indigenous parents were afraid that education in local languages would only serve to keep their children backwards. This resistance appears quite logical when bearing in mind the three most mentioned arguments of rural parents as to why their children *should* go to school: to learn how to read and write – so as not to be betrayed by urban traders; to learn other skills and assets than solely agricultural ones; and (especially stressed by community leaders) the need to acquire 'the power (and language) of the other' (Regalsky and Laurie, 2007: 236-237). Although participation in rhetoric was very important, in practice there was minimal involvement of teachers, parents and civil society groups (unions) in the Reform process (Contreras and Talavera, 2003: 1).

Similar to the outcomes of this study for the present ASEP law, D'Emilio noted a wide variety of teachers reactions to the 1994 reforms; *'from passive compliance to militant defence of EIB, and even from tacit [resistance] to active boycotting'* (D'Emilio, 1996: 56). The majority of teachers went through an initial stage of scepticism; some experienced the advantage of better communication with students through bilingual education, while other mono-lingual teachers feared their positions (D'Emilio, 1996: 57). So-called 'pedagogical assistants' – teachers with an extra training and higher salary than school directors – were sent into schools by the MoE to help implement the reform. These pedagogical assistants were trained to introduce the content of the reforms into schools and train teachers on site. This resulted in numerous conflicts and thus the work of these 'assistants' was abolished. Teacher unions' resistance has been based on ideological ideas (of working against the reforms because they are part of a neoliberal package deal) and because their social rights got under discussion (Speiser, 2000: 237; Contreras and Talavera, 2004b). A possible fear for change and the 'unknown' new teaching styles might have triggered resistance as well (Talavera Simoni, 2011). A teacher trainer and member of the La Paz teachers' federation

---

86 Lozada Pereira warns that we need to take into account how many of the evaluations and critiques developed then and later on were neither neutral nor objective, because of personal involvement and/or political and ideological perspectives (Lozada Pereira 2004).

explained two main reasons for the union to resist the 1994 law, being firstly a lack of participation of '*the most crucial actor in educational change, the teacher*' and secondly, because '*the Law 1565 responded to the neoliberals, to the IMF, the World Bank*' and was thus seen as an 'imposed' law (48:18). Talavera explains how Bolivian teachers are caught in between two fires; having to navigate between pressure from resisting unions and actual changes in their teaching practice (1999: xxxii).

The epistemological ideas behind the reform are based on constructivist theory, which – among other ideas – emphasises the need to build knowledge based on the existent context and knowledge of the student (Lozada Pereira, 2004: 130). Some authors stress the usefulness and appropriateness of (radical and social) constructivist epistemologies to understand knowledge construction and processes of learning as both '*socially mitigated but personally constructed*' (Reagan, 2005: 8-10). Others, however, criticise the constructivist philosophy of knowledge to have been hijacked by international powerful actors and aid agencies whose (indirect) aim is to disseminate child-centred pedagogies. These child-centred pedagogies, which were also part of the 1994 Bolivian Reform, according to Tabulawa are part of a global spread of 'capitalist democracy'. With their 'technical rationality' and false 'value-neutrality', these student or child-centred pedagogies have been promoted in various contexts as a one-size-fits-all solution to making education 'more democratic', and students better suitable for an individualised market-led society and economy. These measures are often justified in terms of educational and cognitive terms, such as the improvement of learning outcomes and efficiency, yet there is no evidence of this (Tabulawa, 2003: 9-10).

Regardless of this (international) push for constructivist, child-centrered and participatory learning processes, and the intended tranformation into an intercultural and bilingual education, the practice in Bolivian schools continued to be teacher-centred, using memorisation techniques, a traditional banking approach and leaving problem-solving competencies underdeveloped (Speiser, 2000: 236; Regalsky and Laurie, 2007: 236). This situation was illustrated by a former teacher and school evaluator, now working at one of the CEPOs. '*Since the [1994] Education Reform, I visited schools in my function as a technical supervisor for the Reform, and it is a shame…to be honest we do not teach the children to think, we teach anything but how to think for themselves. For example, a teacher explaining about the digestive system of the body, he would for instance draw on a piece of paper, paste it to the Blackboard and say: students, this is the digestive system, and he would stop there. He immediately looses all the interest from the students, they will not even look at the drawing. You see, this is what is lacking, teaching to think, to think reflexively, critically*' (24). Even up to today in some areas this low quality education situation continues to exist, as a Bolivian researcher explained: '*One month and a half ago I visited many schools in the Northern Highland region, and it was really depressing to see the outdated teaching practices in classrooms, with zero biligualism. There is nothing of that now. They have returned to teacher centred teaching, so we have a very serious recession*' (61:15).

While the newly promoted intercultural teaching about local indigenous culture was less associated with an old fashioned banking approach, and allowed more room for the creativity of teachers (De Koning, 2005: 53), the concept of interculturality has not been sufficiently operationalised and has remained '*a slogan with little concrete meaning, a general discourse that is highly political but at the same time conceptually poor*' (Speiser, 2000: 227).[87] A first step towards interculturality in Bolivian education, according to Speiser, is '*to clarify one's own [cultural] position and to question the values attributed to different possible positions*' (2000: 231), a position that is currently reflected in the 'intra-cultural' dimension of the new education reform (see chapter 5). However, a narrow focus on the 'own identity' mirrors a lack of a critical approach to education, in which students learn how to *reflect* on their own (and other) cultures, norms, values and power relations (Van Dam, 2006: 7). Van Dam and Salman (2003: 24) added to the debate that within teaching materials, cultures were only portrayed in relation to traditions and rites rather than daily activities. In addition, the *ramas difersificadas*, which should contain the context specific part of the curriculum, were not fully developed everywhere (Nucinkis, 2004: 47; Van Dam, 2006). The incorporation of the new educational initiatives in textbooks has been a long and difficult process, thus leaving many teachers without these new materials (Albó, 2005: 15; Nucinkis, 2004). These new materials did not always reach the teachers and, even when new textbooks were provided to them, there was a lack of teacher manuals and further guidance (Van Dam, 2006). While in the initial process of textbook development representatives of different indigenous groups were participating (Nucinkis 2004), the textbooks were still developed through a centralised top-down approach, with only limited participation from teachers in the validation process of the textbooks, when they had already been written (Van Dam 2006).

The elaboration of a new teacher education curriculum for primary teachers similarly was a long and complex process that lasted for almost a decade (1989-1999). Most of the work was done in 1996, but it took until 1999 before it was made official. The '*Diseño Curricular Base*', or principal curriculum design, was only designed for the training of primary level teacher students (Lozada Pereira, 2004:77, 129). In the years that followed, a team of national and international experts and educators, led by Nicole Nucinkis, worked on a revised text for the basic curriculum for primary level teacher education. The document was finished in 2004, but according to Nucinkis it has never been used in practice (personal communication, November 2008).

Regardless of the reform initiatives in the Normales (mostly after 1999) teacher education predominantly continued to function according to former traditions and laws (Drange, 2007). In 2000, the German organisation for development cooperation GTZ signalled that gender inequalities, in relation to interculturality, were not addressed in teacher education practice at the same level as they were expressed in the materials. Moreover, PROEIB researchers showed the persistence of old-fashioned 'vertical' teaching methods, and the tensions and restrictions for genuine participation of guaraní organisations in Normal Superior schools in the Orient and Chaco regions (Alcon 2001 and Arispe 2003 in Albó and Anaya, 2003: 203). Albó and Anaya also stated that the majority of the teachers who graduated from an INS-EIB do not teach afterwards in bilingual schools for different reasons. Often, they end up working in an urban setting, where living and working conditions are better than in rural areas (Albó and Anaya, 2003: 203-204). Also, the hiring of new teachers, done by *Directores Distritales*, is said to be based on political and personal preferences rather than educational skills. The new teachers who do end up teaching in remote areas, often lack classroom experience and an understanding of the local context and language (see also Tatto, 1999: 18).

---

[87] Interculturality is conceptualised in the 1994 reform as a 'relationship of respect and appreciation for different Bolivian cultures that transcends regional and national borders' (Anaya 2002 in Taylor, 2004: 18).

Photo 3. Two girls in grade 3   *Photo 4: A fifth grade urban classroom*

4.6 In conclusion: towards the creation of an endogenous Bolivian education reform

Historically, education in Bolivia has been tightly linked to the reproduction of class differences as well as open and hidden forms of discrimination and exclusion, particularly of indigenous groups. The start of Bolivian teacher education was foreign driven, with the first Normal created in Sucre in 1909 by a Belgian missionary. During the 1930s, alternative forms of indigenous education and teacher training were developed, particularly in the highland village of Warisata, but soon these were closed down. During military rule, the urban-rural divided system was further reinforced and the institutional basic structure of today's Normales was created. The 1994 Reform for Intercultural and Bilingual education was an attempt to overcome exclusionary and homogenising forms of schooling. The reform process was complicated, lengthy and only to a limited extent successful. Teacher education was left behind during the initial implementation phase; to fill these gaps, some (short term) international initiatives took place to improve teacher education quality. The 1994 Reform did open up space for other discourses and various forms of resistance to these plans arose. Many teachers resisted the envisioned pedagogical and managerial changes in their daily practices and they did not receive proper support. Parents often perceived (and often still see) education as *the* way out of poverty and therefore preferred their children to learn Spanish, the 'Modern' language of business. Moreover, social movements, including teachers' unions, felt left out of the creation of a largely 'imposed and neo-liberal' reform. In conclusion, the actual implementation of the 1994 Reform was a thinly disguised assimilationist approach to culture, offering relational skills to indigenous peoples but allowing *Mestizos* and the indigenous populations to communicate only through *Mestizo* cultural norms and language (Spanish). EIB's ideology cannot fully develop if only rooted in educational policy (and not in daily life, such as media, street signs etc), especially when limited to elementary education (Albó 2002 in Taylor, 2004: 29; Van Dam and Salman, 2003: 25).

When Morales became president at the end of 2005, one of his first decisions was to do away with this 'foreign' education law, to create a new Bolivian-owned reform for decolonising education. The *emergence* of new 'indigenous' discourses (Fairclough, 2005: 931-932) that aimed at a revaluation of indigenous cultures, languages and rights had already started in the 1990s and was taken to the political arena by emerging political movements, including the MAS of Evo Morales. After a democratic victory, intellectuals in the new government under Morales developed a new political direction inspired by Latin American coloniality discourses for the entire education sector, including teacher education, slowly working towards a new hegemonic policy discourse (Fairclough, 2005: 931-932). The historical education context described in this chapter has thus led to the current political perception that '*a revolution in education*' is needed, as the new ASEP law proclaims.

PART III

STRUCTURAL FACTORS: INSTITUTIONAL GOVERNANCE

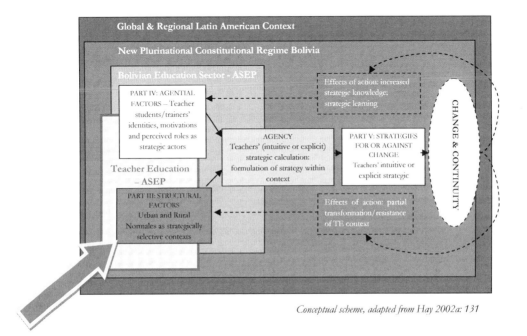

Conceptual scheme, adapted from Hay 2002a: 131

In the third part of the book, I aim to respond to questions related to the historical and present-day governing and inter-institutional relations of *Normales*: their institutional governance (Jessop, 2005: 35) and the structural institutional obstacles and opportunities for change (as illustrated in the conceptual scheme above). Over the past two decades there has been an increased recognition (within and beyond the social sciences) that 'institutions matter' in theoretical, empirical or practical contexts (Cummings, 1999; Jessop, 2004a). Before this 'institutional turn' their existence or relevance has been largely ignored and denied. Methodologically, this means the discovery that the institutional aspects of social life provide a rich entry point for exploring and explaining the social world, without excluding other themes or explanatory factors in research. Ontologically, institutions constitute the essential foundations of social existence in this approach. Without doing justice to the full elaboration of the debates on institutionalism, this research draws from some of these insights, in particular Fairclough's (2005) theoretical considerations on institutional change through the lens of Critical Discourse Analysis.

Furthermore, I draw from Jansen's (2001, 2005) 'politics of policy' and his ideas on political symbolism and non-reform in educational practice. In response to *'the under-exploration of a potentially powerful theoretical construct in third world sites'*, Jansen developed a 'politics of policy' theory to explain the (non)transformation from educational policy into practice in contexts of *'third world transitions'*, where *'politicians do not always invent policy in order to change practice'* (Jansen 2001b: 210, 212). His insights on non-reform and continuing policy-pratice gaps in low income contexts help us to understand Bolivia's earlier and current reform implementation challenges and 'non-reform' at the institutional level, and continuing policy-pratice and discourse-practice gaps in Bolivian education. In this thesis, I both draw from and criticise this interesting account. Drawing from a set of case studies on the transition to post-Apartheid in South Africa, according to Jansen, education policy making demonstrates a *'preoccupation with settling policy struggles in the political domain rather than in the realm of practice'* (2001b: 200).[88] In addition, the 'symbolic value' of education policy *'is revealed by the way that politicians and the public lend credence and support to the production of policy itself, rather than its implementation'* (2001b: 201). A relevant part of Jansen's analysis of political symbolism is the use of 'participation' as a process of legitimisation of policies, rightly emphasising the impact of unequal power and expertise of the 'participants' (2001b: 207).[89] Another relevant aspect for the case of Bolivia is Jansen's recognition that while financial constraints are pertinent to explaining educational non-reform, researchers need to look for other and different explanations for reform failure as well, including local and global constraints (2001b: 212). While Jansen's insight on the idea of political symbolism in many of its features is relevant to the Bolivian case, there are, nevertheless, also some divergenes with Jansen's analysis, perhaps not surprisingly considering the differences between South African and Bolivian histories and societies. Drawing from the outcomes of this study, in the final concluding chapter (11) I will suggest some ways to nuance or elaborate the idea of political symbolism.

I also find Cummings' (1999) theory on the InstitutionS of education useful in informing my analysis of Bolivian teacher education.[90] Cummings' framework of the 'InstitutionS of Education' (1999) perceives educational institutions as comprised of *'complex norms and procedures'* oriented toward realising a specific ideal. The capital S in InstitutionS emphasises the recognition that there is not one single institution of education, but that education systems are constituted out of several institutions. The specifics of these various institutions, including teacher training institutes, vary greatly. They have different incentive structures, with *'some that are favourable and some antithetical to development'* (Cummings, 1999: 422). According to Cummings, education varies across regions depending on a number of factors such as their historical underpinnings, the 'representative schools' (embodying new ideals), the definition of the ideal person, learning theories, school and classroom technologies (including curriculum), the system's administration and style, its sources of finance, and its systems of accountability. In Cummings' framework, the

---

[88] Jansen argues the first four years of the new political configuration in South Africa (1994-1999) can be typified as a period of 'political symbolism', geared primarily to an ideological-discursive shift, which *'is disconnected from immediate concerns about educational practice'* in South Africa's classrooms (2001b: 200-201).

[89] Similar to the situation of 'non-reform' in Bolivia after the 1994 Reform (discussed in chapter 4), in South Africa a clear implementation plan was not immediately there, and studies showed how revised syllabi often never made it to the schools, or went without accompanying training and support (2001b:203).

[90] As argued by both Cummings and more recently by Clandinin et al (2009: 151), there is a need for a shift in studies on and approaches to teacher education, moving away from questioning the what and how of teacher education, by moving to understanding the why of teacher education. This study aims to combine these suggestions, by examining the when, what, why, who, how of teacher education policies and practices in the Bolivian context.

concept of the ideal person is the core of the education system and educational reform emerges as a result of rapid ideological, political and economic change and is often aimed at the creation of a new concept of the ideal person. Notions of '*who should be taught, what they should be taught, how people learn, and how education should be organised follow from a society's conception(s) of the ideal person*' (Cummings, 1999: 426). This study shows how in the light of Bolivia's changing socio-cultural and political context, the discourses on the ideal Bolivian citizen and teacher are shifting and informing the development of a new decolonising education reform. Even though Cummings' theorisation of the InstitutionS of education is relevant input for my analysis, his framework for comparison between states has, however, some limitations for its application to this study, as I will demonstrate in chapter 6.

More recently, Tatto in her edited volume 'Reforming Teaching Globally' (2007) underlines the relevance of Cummings theoretical frame specifically for research on teacher education, since the education of teachers mostly occurs within institutions. Tatto adds to Cummings' theory by arguing for the need to understand both new conceptualisations of the ideal person, as well as conceptualisations of *the ideal teacher for the ideal person* as envisaged by teacher training institutions (Tatto, 2007: 15, 269). She (2007: 12) stresses how the effects of any reform for teacher education institutions are highly variable. Basing herself on Cummings theory, change in these institutions is '*conditioned by strongly ingrained institutional patterns*' and educational models that evolve around the culturally defined notion of the ideal person in a particular society. In line with Cummings, Tatto brings forward how teacher training institutes are by no means homogeneous, nor should they be seen as passive entities. Teacher educators use their agency to actively or passively resist reform initiatives in their institutions. A variety of rationales behind teachers' resistance, ranging from '*good sense*', '*social justice struggles*' to '*defending working conditions*' are reflected in Tatto's work on resistance in teacher education institutions: '*this resistance to change can be seen as a legitimate attempt at cultural preservation and to maintain control in defining national identities, indigenous knowledge and pedagogy, and 'locally grown' accountability mechanisms. [...] In other contexts resistance can be seen as a way to maintain power over teachers' lives, such as the teacher union in Mexico*' (Tatto et al, 2007b: 12-13). Tatto also discussed the different power relations that play out in the field of teacher education. Education systems are shaped by well-distinguished institutional patterns that in turn provoke 'counter-patterns' (Tatto, 2007: 16). The impact of these counter patterns, that often fill the gaps left by the dominant or traditional system, depends on the openness of the political system and the strength of the opposition parties.

5

An education system in turbulent times –
clashing views on decolonising Bolivian (teacher) education

'We radically need to change these modern types of traditional, disciplined and therefore violent forms of banking education, and start to pay attention to the mind and the body, not to obediently sitting still in classrooms, but to movement and play, to [cultural] expression, rituals and emotional intelligence. Education is not just about pure rationality, but about emotions, feelings and thus... our totality as human beings'
(Bolivian sociologist Saavedra, interview in May 2010)

5.1 Introduction

On Friday morning, 24 October 2008, a cold and empty lecture room in the *Monobloque* building of the Universidad Mayor de San Andres in the centre of La Paz slowly starts to fill. A rather mixed crowd, consisting of primarily Bolivian scholars, policy-makers, social movement leaders and students, as well as academic colleagues from Brazil, gather for a chat or finds their seat. Being one of the organisers of the seminar on *'Decolonisation and Education: reflections from Bolivia and Brazil'*, I get a bit nervous about the absence of our two main speakers of this morning: the former Minister of Education Felix Patzi and his Vice-Minister at the time, José Luis Saavedra. The seminar is supposed to begin in about five minutes and I soothe myself by remembering that punctuality is a flexible concept in Bolivia. To our relief, we see Patzi coming out of the elevator wearing sun glasses and a black *sombrero*, and carrying his notes for the speech he is about to give. Without Saavedra being present, nor responding to our phone calls, we decide to start the meeting. *'Since 2006, and initiated from within the Ministry of Education, Bolivia has put a stamp called 'decolonisation' on its politics'*, Patzi addresses his audience, *'Decolonising the education in Bolivia means reflecting on both the organisation of education as its contents. A fundamental problem in Bolivian education is the enormous inequalities, since people's educational opportunities are determined by their race, ethnicity, culture and language, resulting in a separate urban and rural system. Content-wise, decolonisation means we need to change our curricula in order to change our mental constructions that are based on a Eurocentric vision and to revalue the knowledges and conceptualisations of the indigenous populations'*. Precisely as Patzi rounds off his speech and apologises for his early departure due to other obligations, Saavedra enters the room. Presumably, the broken relationship between these two academics, after their short period as MoE colleagues, has resulted in this unwritten agreement to avoid each others' company.

In Saavedra's talk, the limits to the decolonisation approach are added to the debate, since *'decoloniality in itself does not provide a proposal. An authentic decolonising proposal can only emerge from those that were actually colonised, the indigenous populations.'* While not in full agreement to all elements of Patzi's position, Saavedra presents a corresponding vision of what decolonising Bolivian education would mean in practice. *'On the institutional level, decolonising education means opening up traditional educational environments, so that the whole community around the school becomes a pedagogical space for learning. At the curricular level, decolonisation means deconstructing the modern and colonial segmentation of educational disciplines, and departing from a holistic comprehension of reality, an epistemology of complexity, which is how indigenous populations see reality.* Saavedra concluded by stating how *'most importantly, we need to realise that at the level of human attitudes affection and values are crucial, as the main teaching technique should be through dialogue'.* Both Patzi's and Saavedra's views are embedded in the broader coloniality debates discussed in chapter 3, and both speeches show the diversity in interpretations of what decolonisation of education actually means.[91] As this chapter will show, this conceptual vagueness forms a pressing issue for the successful implementation of the new ASEP law for decolonising education.

The ASEP reform is part of Morales' politics of change and education is seen as the core vehicle for a thorough social, political and economic restructuring of Bolivian society. The Bolivian government has tried to construct a progressive reform in terms of its ideological underpinnings and a sector wide restructuring of the education system in cooperation with a range of civil society groups. The ASEP reform's close engagement with the idea of decolonisation has its roots in the ideas of coloniality theory. ASEP re-imagines education for, among other concepts, critical analysis and *'vivir bien'* – to live well enough – which can be connected to the debates on critical pedagogy of a social justice oriented education (see chapter 2). Many Bolivians see ASEP as an articulation of the Plurinational Constitution's and National Development Plan's more general goals (see for instance a reflection on the National Development Plan in Yapu, 2009: 51-52). Together these initiatives offer a new definition of citizenship, as education is an important factor in forming students' relationships with the world around them. ASEP can be considered a powerful part of the state's 'agenda for change', taking up articles 77-107 which constitute a considerable part of the constitution (which consists of a total of 411 articles).[92]

This chapter deals with three processes of (envisaged) transformation in the current Bolivian (teacher) education system and the various and clashing views on this project: firstly, the new education law entails a radical, ideological and epistemological reorientation of Bolivian education (and society) under the header of 'decolonisation'; secondly, these initiatives take place in a shifting context of continuous struggles between the government and civil society actors – with important roles for the MoE (Ministry of Education), the Normales, the teachers (urban) union and the indigenous education councils; and finally, while the new reform builds on earlier attempts to improve educational quality and relevancy there are serious foreseen challenges for the implementation process. I first outline the main characteristics of the new ASEP Law and

---

[91] These quotes are based on fieldwork notes and the 'Memorandum of the International Seminar', that can be retrieved from http://educationanddevelopment.files.wordpress.com/2009/02/memorandum-del-encuentro-internacional-sobre-descolonizacion-y-educacion.pdf.
[92] In this sense, the new Plurinational Constitution forms the legal basis for the re-founding and transformation of the Bolivian nation.

secondly the specific developments (so far) in the field of teacher education. This is followed by an introduction of the main actors that are relevant for this thesis and their respective views and power struggles in relation to the creation and implementation of this new law in the field of (teacher) education. Finally, I elaborate on the anticipated obstacles for the execution of the ASEP law and its new education pedagogy and curriculum.

5.2 The road to decolonising the Bolivian education system

The most recent available statistics show both a promising and alarming situation for the future of Bolivian education. In 2008, Bolivia's public expenditure on education accounted for 5.8% of its Gross National Product, which is just above the average public spending of 5% in the wider Latin American region (UNESCO, 2011: 349). On the global Education For All Development Index (EDI) Bolivia ranks 78 (out of 127 countries) and is considered a medium EDI country (UNESCO, 2011: 278). Bolivia is estimated to reach the Universal Primary Education goal by 2015 and is also likely to achieve the EFA literacy goal in 2015, according to UNESCO's Global Monitoring Report (2011: 80). Over the past decade (1999-2008) there has, however, been little change in the enrolment, survival, drop-out and repetition rates in primary education, as around 94% of Bolivia's children are enrolled in schools and approximately 80% of them continue to complete their primary education (UNESCO, 2011: 60).[93] Thus, there are still Bolivian children that miss out on education, or fail to complete their educational career once in school. These educational inequalities in Bolivia can be attributed to factors including ethnicity, gender, urban/rural descent, geographical location and wealth.[94] This challenging context forms the background to which the new ASEP law has to be implemented.

Between March and early June 2006 a first proposal for a new education law '*Avelino Sinani y Elizardo Perez*' (ASEP) was shared and discussed with 332 local civil society institutions. Consequently, it was officially started up during the National Educational Congress in July 2006, in which 26 organisations participated (Drange, 2007: 4). The first proposals for a renewed education sector were born in the educational commission of the constitutional Assembly from mid 2006 onwards (Gamboa Rocabado, 2009: 67-69). This resulted in a long process of consultation and approval that continued throughout the period of this research, until the ASEP law was finally approved in congress on 20 December 2010. This section aims to provide a broader understanding of Bolivia's new education reform 'Program' (the content and the innovative policy) by also looking at the 'Program Ontology', or *how* this policy was designed and works (Dale, 2005; Pawson, 2002). The *process* of how subjects interpret, negotiate and familiarise or reject the ASEP law is called the 'program mechanism' and is discussed in the sections on the new Law and power plays below, as it is rather this programme mechanism that triggers change, than the actual 'programme' (the ASEP law) itself (Pawson, 2002: 342). This section first introduces the most important developments for the entire education sector, while the next section elaborates specifically on the consequences of the ASEP reform for teacher education.

---

[93] Net Enrolment Ratio in primary education is the number of children of official primary school age who are enrolled in schools as a percentage of the total children of the official school age population. UNESCOs statistics show a slightly decreased NER from 95 in 1999 to 94 in 2008.
[94] See UNESCO's GMR website,
http://public.tableausoftware.com/views/PageFourNew/Pg4Dash?:embed=y&:toolbar=no&:tabs=no.

Morales' first Minister of Education, Felix Patzi, was one of the creators of the first versions of what now constitutes the ASEP law for decolonising education. In his controversial efforts to create a decolonising education system, Patzi pushed for diminishing the role of the Catholic church in education, or for an end to a 'Catholic Doctrine' in Bolivian education, which resulted in fierce protests from Catholics and evangelicals alike (Postero, 2007). The approved version of the ASEP law still refers to a *secular, pluralistic and spiritual* education model, as it *promotes mutual respect and coexistence between peoples with different religious backgrounds* (Article 3.6, ASEP law, 2010b). While some see a danger of worsening tensions between different ethnic and religious groups (see below), Article 3.12 stresses the need to *promote peaceful coexistence and the eradication of all forms of violence in education, for the development of a society based on a culture of peace, with respect for individual and collective rights for all*. The division between rural and urban Normales, according to Patzi, *reflects the differentiation between Indians and whites*. Therefore, he asserts, *decolonisation, as we defined it at the Ministry of Education, in practice means unifying educational institutions into one system, to put an end to ethnically defined separations.* [95] The law makes reference to broader debates in Latin America and beyond of education for liberation (see chapter 3), as Article 3.14 states Bolivian education aims to follow a *liberating pedagogy* as it encourages personal development and a critical awareness of reality *in order to change it*.

These new policy lines for a decolonised education system are embedded in the ancient indigenous, and primarily Andean spiritual values, or *cosmovisión*. This concept of *cosmovisión* for instance came up during an interview with an indigenous social movement leader: *'The law Avelino Siñani is telling us that the indigenous wisdom, their cosmovisión, is the strength of Bolivia. It is the essential basis of Bolivia, and the discourse of President Evo says the moral base of Bolivia is with the indigenous peoples'* (14). Indeed, the ASEP law refers to an education that *'develops knowledges and expertise from the worldview [cosmovisión] of indigenous peoples, peasants and afro-Bolivians, in complementarity to universal knowledges, to contribute to the integral development of society'* (Article 3.10, ASEP law, 2010b). More specifically on this *cosmovisión*, Article 3.13 specifies that education should build from and promote the ethical and moral values of the plural society, including for instance *'ama qhilla, ama llulla, ama suwa'* – do not be lazy, do not lie or steal, and *'suma qamaña'* or the earlier mentioned notion of *'vivir bien'* (to live well). Bolivian education, then, is based on *'the values of unity, equality, inclusion, dignity, freedom, solidarity, reciprocity, respect, complementarity, harmony, openness, balance, equal opportunities, social and gender equity in participation, welfare, responsibility, social justice, distribution and redistribution of social goods and products to live well'* (Article 13.3, ASEP law, 2010b). At a discursive level, the law thus covers all three dimensions of Frasers' conceptualisation of social justice, including distribution (the economic dimension of justice), recognition (the cultural dimension of justice) and representation (the political dimension of justice) (Fraser, 2005a; Fraser, 2005b). With regard to 'gender justice', similar to the gender-equity emphasis in the former 1994 Reform (chapter 2), the current government gives considerable (discursive) weight to issues of gender.[96]

---

[95] Source: 'Memorandum of the International Seminar', that can be retrieved from http://educationanddevelopment.files.wordpress.com/2009/02/memorandum-del-encuentro-internacional-sobre-descolonizacion-y-educacion.pdf.

[96] A number of constitutional articles for instance refer to gender equity, including 8, 11, 14, 15, 26, 48, 58, 78 and 79 (relating directly to education), 104, 147, 172.22 (gender equity in parliament), 210, 270, 278 and 402. Similarly, the ASEP education reform includes Articles 3.13, 4.2, 4.6. 5.7 and 10.5, which all directly refer to the importance of gender equity.

More specifically, the reform is built around the following four pillars, as identified by the Bolivian MoE: 1) decolonisation; 2) intra- and inter-culturalism along with plurilingualism; 3) productivity; and 4) communitarian education. While the government uses these four categories, the data of this study shows there are various interpretations of each pillar, lowering the prospects for creating a strong new curriculum, at least for the moment. In the interest of gaining an understanding of Bolivia's current educational and political processes, explorations of these concepts follow.

'Decolonisation' can be seen as an umbrella-pillar. The official explanation of decolonising education is *'putting an end to ethnic borders that influence opportunities in the area of education, work, politics and economic security, where no one is privileged on the basis of race, ethnicity and or language. It also signifies to avoid favouring conceptualisations of the Western world as if they are universal, yet valuing the knowledges, skills and technologies of the indigenous civilisations, both of the Amazonian and Andean regions'* (Congreso Nacional de Educación, 2006). Another official definition of decolonisation as used in the area of public policy is in line with the discourse of the ASEP law: *'Public policies need to be created based on values, principles, knowledges and practices of the Bolivian people; the actions of civil servants need to be oriented at preserving, developing and protecting cultural diversity through a intracultural, intercultural and plurilingual dialogue'* (Estado Plurinacional de Bolivia, 2009). Specifically, ASEP rejects parts of the 'colonial' education reform of 1994, which was developed in Bolivia with cooperation from international consultants (see chapter 4). However, supporters of the law see ASEP as a continuation of an emancipatory educational process, that already started with the intercultural and bilingual reform of 1994 (96: 25), and others – such as La Paz's teacher union – perceive it as a mere copy of the 1994 reform with some 'indigenous additions' (49:17). However diverse the interpretations and reactions to this reform, it is clearly a response to the need for a Bolivian-owned reform, as the former section showed how different groups of actors believe the 1994 reform was created – or 'imposed' – without enough genuine participation of civil society and teachers.

ASEP's second pillar builds on the 1994 reform's use of the concepts of inter-culturalism and bilingualism. The new form of inter-culturalism is linked to the notion of intra-culturalism. Rather than a narrowly-defined (American and European) notion of multiculturalism (Delany-Barmann, 2010: 186), or what Hale (2002) called neoliberal multiculturalism, the ASEP reform builds on Latin American social science and educational literature on the concept of 'interculturalism' and has developed the interrelated concepts of inter- and intracultural education. While inter-culturalism offers students skills in relating to other cultures, intra-culturalism engages reflection and growth of one's own identity. Various MoE officials and Bolivian academics have assured that the two aspects being part of a single pillar is very intentional, as neither can be successful in defining a plurinational citizenship without the other. Intraculturality is defined in Article 6.1 as *'promoting the restoration, empowerment, development of and cohesion between the cultures of the nation and indigenous peasant, intercultural and Afro-Bolivian populations for the consolidation of the Plurinational state, based on equity, solidarity, complementarity, reciprocity and justice.'* The law continues to state how the national curriculum incorporates the various knowledges of the different worldviews' (*cosmovisiones*) of these nations and communities. Secondly, interculturality is defined as *'the development of interrelationships and interaction regarding the knowledges, skills, science and technology belonging to each culture, which strengthens their own identity but also an equal interaction between all cultures in Bolivia and with the rest of the world'* (Article 6.2, ASEP law, 2010b).

As the most practical part of ASEP, plurilingualism exemplifies the inter- and intra-cultural process: students will learn the native language local to their area, Spanish and a foreign language (most often this will be English). Even though the (approved) law still talks about a plurilingual (teacher) education system, it is no longer trilingual. Depending on the context of the school, the first language of instruction will either be Spanish or an indigenous language (in cases where more languages spoken by different students, a communitarian committee will decide upon the language(s) of instruction). In addition, all students have the right to learn a foreign language and all teachers will be taught sign language (article 7, ASEP law, Ministerio de Educacion de Bolivia, 2010b).

Productive education, the third pillar, offers Bolivians a new type of engagement with the local and national economy. As the previous education reform geared students toward either technical or humanistic education, ASEP bridges the two. Under the new reform, students will finish secondary school with a technical-humanistic degree, allowing them to utilise either practical knowledge which can apply to the workforce, or to produce intellectually through attending university. While this is the practical application, productivity will also theoretically enable any secondary school graduate to produce new knowledge in whatever area they go into, through processes of critical analysis and reflection. Ideally, this critique will allow students to bring innovative change to the country, to be engaged in every sector, including economic growth. Another way productive education is explained, for instance by an indigenous movement leader, is by emphasising the function of education to create workers that have the skills and motivation to use *'the countries enormous potentials in the agricultural production or the production of hand-crafted goods'* (96:23). Nevertheless, vagueness still exists as in how to intepret this third conceptual pillar. An urban local governmental officer (and ex-teacher and teacher trainer) explains: *'in the rural areas people often confuse the idea of productive education with learning how to grow potatoes. They do not captivate the real essence of what it means; it also implies an intellectual production for people, to construct their own knowledge. This has to be worked out very well in the new curriculum design.'* He continues by saying how *'it is the same with adding intra- to interculturalism. For the community, it will just remain interculturality as long as it is not clear how this should work in the reality of the classroom.'*(72:19)

Communitarian education is perhaps ASEP's least defined and fourth pillar. While it relates to the larger, non-school community, it is not entirely clear to everyone how it does so. The three general interpretations are that either: the community actually plays a recognised role outside of the school day, which is especially important as Bolivia's schools operate on half-day schedules; schools engage indigenous community values and invite 'guests' from the community into the classroom; or some combination of the two. This has implications for the role of the teacher as well, particularly in rural communities, since *'the teacher is not only there for the student, but also for the family. This is the new teachers' profile, the practice of education is not only between the four walls of the classroom, but in the community, in the neighbourhood'* (14:16, quote from an indigenous movement leader, presently an official in the MoE). This centrally puts even more pressure on the quality of teacher training in order to prepare teachers for such an encompassing future role. Crucial in relation to communitarian education is the engagement of *'an equilibrium between the human being and nature in the individual and collective, to live well in the community'* (author's emphasis, Proyecto de Ley,

2007). The environment, or Mother Earth, is central in ASEP's vision of an integral education (see also Introduction).

Perhaps equally as important as the pillars and the law itself is that it applies to every formal education setting, from private, public and *de convenio*[97] schools, as well as from kindergarten through all post-secondary schooling. Special attention is being paid to those who had been falling out of the system previously, and thus educational institutions offering different levels should be created in remote areas, as well as for disabled students everywhere. There are three different 'forms' of education: regular education (from early childhood to secondary levels of schooling); special education (for people with special needs) and alternative education (for those who cannot participate in the regular system); and finally higher and professional education (Article 8, ASEP law, 2010). The different levels of the administrative structure of the education system include the: Ministry of Education and Culture; General Directions for Pluricultural Education; Departmental Directions for Education; Zone Directions; Nuclear Directions (cluster of schools); and Educational Unit Directions (*Consejos Educativos Comunitarios*). The ASEP reform organises the regular education system in three main educational levels:

1) **Early childhood development** in the form of '*Educación inicial en familia comunitaria*': 0-5 years; physical, affective, artistic, symbolic, spacio-temporal development.
2) **Primary education** – '*Educación primaria comunitaria vocacional*': 6-11 years; including maths, languages and communication, natural sciences and social sciences.[98]
3) **Secondary education** – '*Educación secundaria comunitaria productiva*': 12-17 years; focused on integrating theory and practice ('*educación integral*') of science, humanism, technology, ethics, spirituality, arts, physics and sports, as well as 'vocational and productive training' in the areas of productive technological sciences, human sciences, medical sciences and artistic sciences, physics and sports. In order to narrow the gap between rural and urban education, boarding schools and '*tele-centros*' in rural areas and marginalised urban areas will be constructed (Congreso Nacional de Educación, 2006; ASEP law articles 12-15).

The 'sub-system' of higher or tertiary education – '*Educación superior de formación professional*' – includes all (public and private) higher education institutions – including military, police and teacher education colleges. For all institutes, including the Normales, Technical Colleges, Art Colleges and Universities, it is obligatory to incorporate indigenous knowledges and technologies into 'modern knowledge'. Public universities are obliged to decentralise their faculties to rural and remote areas in response to the needs of each region (Congreso Nacional de Educación, 2006; ASEP law articles 28-30). The specifics of the new ASEP law for the '*formación de maestras y maestros*' (teacher education) are now explored.

---

[97] *De convenio* schools are cofounded by the state and private institutions which are often religious. Because of this funding scheme, these schools offer free attendance.

[98] The natural sciences should be directed at demythologising 'Darwinist racism', dismissing social inequalities constructed by society. Social sciences contents should relate to indigenous civilisations, their sufferings due to the process of the 'conquista' (colonial rule) and new tendencies with respect to sociocultural diversity (Congreso Nacional de Educación, 2006).

5.3 Cleaning up the snakes breeding place: decolonising teacher education[99]

In contrast to, and as a result of, the lessons of the implementation process of the 1994 reform (chapter 4), the Normales are the first institutes to be transformed according to the new policy guidelines. The Normales are perceived to play a crucial role in the foreseen transformation processes. The new system is defined as *'unified, public, free of charge and diversified. [It is] unified with regard to the professional hierarchy, pedagogical and scientific quality without the division between an urban and rural system, [and] diversified in the sense that it responds to the productive economic, socio-cultural and linguistic characteristics of indigenous populations of each region on Bolivian territory'* (Congreso Nacional de Educación, 2006). In anticipation of the approval of the new law six months later, in June 2009 a special decree (*Decreto 156*) was established to already begin the transformation of the Plurinational system of teacher education (106:1). The teacher training institutes are still called Normales in daily speech, however the institutes changed names recently and are now officially called *'Escuelas Superiores de Formación de Maestros y Maestras'*.[100] These higher institutes of teacher education will provide students with a *licenciatura* degree, equal to the university *licenciatura* degree, as becomes clear from this section from the National Congress of Education in 2006: *'The 'Institutos Normales Superiores' will be transformed into 'Escuelas Superiores de Formación de Maestros' and post-graduate Pedagogical University that all dependent on the Ministry of Education. The higher teacher education institutes grant a 'licenciatura' degree after 5 years of study. The New Law respects and guarantees the 'escalafón' as a major conquest of Bolivian teachers'* (Congreso Nacional de Educación, 2006).

Thus, contrary to global tendencies to shorten teacher training, Bolivia's new law installs a longer teacher education trajectory of five years in total, equal to other university level *licenciatura* degrees. Most teacher students seem to be happy with receiving a higher degree, but many of them are not content with the longer period of study. Teacher trainers need to have a *licenciatura* degree and management staff are obliged to have at least a Masters degree (Article 35, ASEP law, 2010b). There are some concerns about the fact that Normales can provide a university-like degree of *licenciatura*. One trainer and management staff member of the (private) Catholic Normal explained that *'those who can give licenciatura degrees should be the universities, not the Normales. But here we can see the power of the unions, they do not want all Normales to become Pedagogical Universities, because they say then the profession will be open to anyone with a licenciatura. So they want Normales to provide licenciatura degrees that are comparable to the university licenciaturas'* (90:17). This quote reflects wider concerns over which institutes should be allowed to give out university degrees, which is closely linked to the discussion on the 'opening up' of the teaching profession to all university graduates. The unions continue to struggle for an exlusive right of Normal-graduates (*normalistas*) to teaching jobs, which is further elaborated in chapter 6.

The discourse on decolonisation, intra-, intercultural and plurilingual education, communitarian and productive education are reflected in chapter III of the ASEP law that deals with higher and professional education, including teacher education (Articles 31-40, ASEP Law, 2010b). Textbox 4 provides an overview of the core principles and objectives of the ASEP reform for the field of teacher education.

---

[99] This title is inspired on an idea from a Bolivian researcher, who stated that if colonisation is a snake, the *Normales* would be its hotbed (114:11).
[100] Throughout the thesis I use the term Normales to refer to the teacher training institutes, like is common in Bolivian daily speech and debates.

As set up in the 1994 Reform programme, the initial training starts with an 'introductory' semester, called *nivellación*, aiming to get all students to the same level. Students who started before February 2010 followed a programme of six semesters after *nivellación*, with all semesters running for approximately half a year. Since early 2009, new batches of students have started in the new ASEP system of five years. These five years include 5,000 study hours (1,000 hours per year), equalling 300 credits (or 60 credits annually). The first two years are dedicated to a general training. During the second year, 360 hours are dedicated to an elected specialisation. The last three years are fully focused on the specialisation of the student teacher (102:2). In contrast to earlier documents of the ASEP law, in its final version the law no longer expects *all* teachers to be trained in a tri-lingual system. However, all teachers will be trained in sign language.

The image (6) illustrates the core principles, relevant concept and focus areas of the new curriculum for primary level teacher students. The five boxes include the subjects of each of the five years of training. A full elaboration of these subjects/disciplines is still being developed (at the time of writing – January 2011). The new curriculum includes subject matters such as traditional medicine, and 'food and nutritional security', in line with this extended role for teachers in communities. The new curriculum also has a clear political agenda, as it expects future teachers to 'decolonise politically', as they are trained in their first and second year in subject matters including '*cosmovisión*', 'political ideology', 'decolonisation' and 'communitarian mathematics' (La Prensa, 22-12-2010).

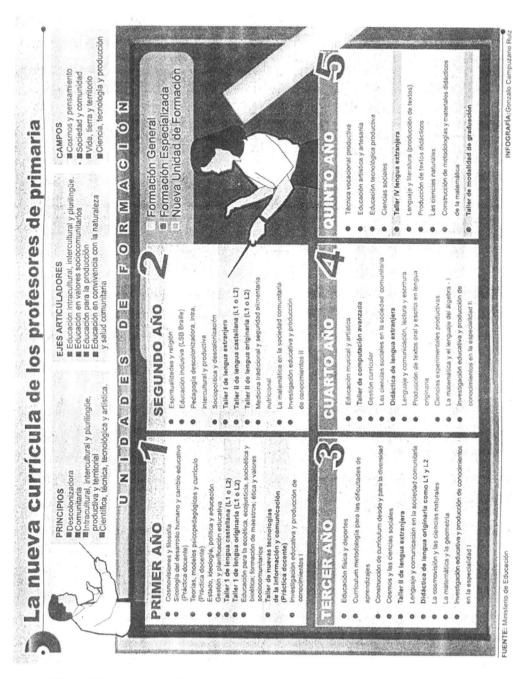

Photo 5, The new curriculum for primary teachers, source: <u>http://www.laprensa.com.bo/noticias/22-12-2010/noticias/22-12-2010_1220.php.</u>

5.4 Teachers' and trainers' in-service training

According to the new policies of the MoE: '*teacher education is a gradual and continuous process of personal and professional development*' (Medinaceli, 2007). In response to the need for better trained and 'updated' teachers and teacher trainers alike, in Bolivia the importance of in-service training was already established in 1997. Under the current government, teacher education is organised in three phases: the initial (pre-service) phase; the permanent (in-service) phase of conceptual and practical training; and the third phase of continuous training, provided at various academic institutes. According to a Ministry official who is responsible for the permanent and in-service training programmes, '*the projection of training the in-service teachers is backed up constitutionally with article 96.2 of the Plurinational constitution, which states teachers are obliged to take part in continuous actualisation programmes*' (106: 2). Articles 39 and 40 of the ASEP law also include the right and duty of teachers to take part in in-service training programmes (Ministerio de Educacion de Bolivia, 2010). He continues by sketching the scale of the foreseen activities: '*There are about 120,000 teachers in service now, including 17,000 untrained teachers ['interinos']. [...] The Ministry will centrally organise the offer of thematic courses for which teachers can subscribe voluntarily. [...] In contrast to the sporadic courses now offered by the Ministry and NGOs, the new courses will be in line with the new law's central policy lines, for example about how to implement decolonisation in the classroom. [...] We will generate a corresponding regulation, for instance for UNESCO who have a proposal for in-service training now. We are also still working on the role of the Pedagogical University [in Sucre], and the role of possible other existing or new universities, even foreign univeristies. [...] We will also control more closely the work of NGOs, because there were some instances of falsified papers and degrees. [...] But we will not homogenise and centralise all training possibilities, bearing in mind the diversity of this country*' (106: 3 - 106:6).

From this quote, it seems the MoE is aiming to develop new in-service training opportunities and to coordinate those initiatives that have existed so far. A young teacher in an interview told me that this coordination was absolutely needed, since she was spending – and in her eyes partly wasting – her money on different, but not officially recognised, training programmes and workshops by NGOs, because of a lack of a coordinated and officially certified system (128). Plan International, CEBIAE[101] and Save the Children, among others, were mentioned by a MoE official as NGOs working in the area of in-service training for teachers and trainers (106:8). Simultaneously, both the MoE as well as the urban Normal were in contact with the regional organisation Convenio Andres Bello for their training programmes for teacher training staff.[102] Some of these programmes had already started for the trainers of Simón Bolívar in 2008, and it was not yet clear as to what scale the Convenio Andres Bello would take up similar programmes for teacher trainers in other Normales. Despite these initiatives, many teachers complain of a lack of opportunities for in-service training, particularly outside of the urban areas.

During a presentation of a MoE official at an international seminar in October 2007 in La Paz, a strategy to implement these long-term training plans (in the period 2008-2011) was presented. The strategy included the creation of 'permanent training centres' as well as

---

[101] Centro Boliviano de Investigación y Acción Educativas, see http://www.cebiae.org/.
[102] Convenio Andres Bello is an international and intergovernmental organisation that works in a number of Latin American countries, including Bolivia, to 'strengthen and develop educational, scientific, technological and cultural integration'. See http://www.convenioandresbello.org/.

Pedagogical Universities in various regions, that would enable teachers to continue their professional development through the accomplishment of various university degrees (ideally the *licenciatura* is followed by a masters, PhD and Post-Doc title) (Medinaceli, 2007).[103] However, a MoE official mentioned in May 2010: '*we are in a transformation phase, we still have to define and create regulations on permanent and continuous training. There are various things missing, but we are proceeding*' (106:11). Various interviews and observations confirmed that to date, little has been done to implement the in-service teaching programmes on a nation wide scale.

5.5 Using Cummings InstitutionS framework for contrasting 1994 and ASEP reforms

Cummings theorisation of the InstitutionS of education (see introduction to Part IV) is relevant for providing an overview of the differences and continuities between the 1994 Reform (discussed in chapter 4) and the current ASEP reform, and their respective policies for the teacher education arena. Cummings framework has, however, some limitations for its application to this study. Cummings developed a framework in which he compared the various historical education models of different hegemonic states. He also develops a set of core principles that aim to help understand and compare different models of the InstitutionS of education, including: the period of genesis; the pedagogical ideal; the representative school; the scope; its dominant learning theory; the school and classroom technologies; the institute's administration and administrative style; the unit costs and source of finance (Cummings, 1999: 423-424). I draw from and adapt part of Cummings' comparative principles, in order to compare the impact of the two most recent Bolivian reforms on teacher education institutions (see Table 4). Different from Cummings principles, I included 'Scope' into 'Ideals' to avoid an overlap I see in his analysis. Also, I changed 'Administrative styles' into 'System of accountability' and I left 'Unit costs' out because of a lack of clear data that could make any valuable statements on that issue for this case. Moreover, drawing from Tatto's work, I added 'resistance and counter-patterns' into the table, as these tendencies are crucial in understanding the current field of Bolivian teacher education (TE).

Over the past few years the (envisaged) role of the Bolivian government has changed considerably from the way it was described by Regalsky and Laurie (2007: 239-240), as '*a foreign power that has spoken a foreign language and has given urban answers to rural problems with schools functioning to legitimate the state criollo hispanicizing hegemony through its hidden and explicit curricula*'. With ASEP, the MoE has designed a counter-hegemonic project for decolonisation, which aims for social justice – or to *live well* – for all Bolivians, and recognition and inclusion rather than an expulsion of indigenous values, knowledges and languages. In that sense, it can be considered a 'revolutionary reform', which seeks not only to produce genuine improvements in people's lives, but also to build popular political capacity (Rodriguez-Garavito et al, 2008: 24). While Bolivia's new constitution and the ASEP reform work toward addressing historical social injustices, especially concerning the marginalisation of indigenous populations with regard to economic distribution, political representation and socio-cultural recognition processes, the decolonial ideas are certainly not uncontested, as will be now elaborated.

---

[103] And those teacher trainers that I spoke to whom were indeed working toward a Masters or PhD, were often not comfortable enough to share this with their colleagues, and most of them asked me to keep this information secret, or as '*a surprise*', as one trainer assured. This might have to do with the fact that it is not an easy nor a fast process to obtain a Doctors title in the Bolivian social sciences context, as one respondent explained.

Models of Teacher Education	1994 Education Reform 1565	1994 policies on TE	2006-2010 Reform ASEP	2006-2010 policies on TE
Period	1992 – 2010	Mostly after 1999	Developed since 2006, approved December 2010	Institutionalisation process since 2007; new 5-year TE programme since 2010
Ideal	Intercultural and Bilingual Education	PINS & PINS-EIB (chapter 4)	Decolonised, Inter-/intracultural/pluri-lingual, productive and communitarian education	Integral system for all *Institutos Superiores de Formacion Docente* (chapter 5)
Representative school	–		Warisata	Warisata
Learning theory	Constructivism, Vigotsky	Constructivism Vigotsky	Freire, Action research, coloniality theories of knowledge	Freire, Action research, coloniality theories of knowledge
School and classroom technologies	Child-centered, participatory, core & additional curriculum	Child-centered, participatory, core & additional curriculum	Community involvement, productive education, core & additional curriculum, problem-based learning	Community involvement, productive education, problem-based learning, action research methodology
Administration	Quasi-decentralised	Administration by MoE or University	Quasi-decentralised	MoE still central role in policy making, planning. Normales (again) have relative autonomy.
Source of finance	MoE, foreign funding (including WB, IMF, UNICEF, GTZ, AECID, NL)	MoE, foreign funding (including GTZ, AECID, UNICEF), institutional income	MoE, foreign funding (Basket*)	MoE, institutional income, small part of Basket
System of accountability	Parental Councils	Student Federations	School, community, municipal and departmental committees	Student Federations, community involvement (chapter 5)
Resistance or counter-patterns	Unions, parents, SIMECAL Quality evaluation	Problematic transformation of Normales 1994-2005	Urban teachers union, groups of parents, anti-Morales politicians, church etc.	Powerplays in the TE field (chapter 6)

Table 4, Models of Teacher Education, adapted from Cummings (1999: 42)
* The Basket Fund is a largely unconditional fund (12 million US $ per 4 years) from the Netherlands, Denmark, Sweden and Spain for the Bolivian Ministry of Education.

5.6 Main actors and their views on education reform

Having set out the main characteristics of the new ASEP law in the (teacher) education field, I now introduce the main actors involved in the Bolivian governance mechanisms of the area of teacher education, and I analyse the tensions and power struggles between those actors and their positions with regard to the ASEP reform project for decolonising education. As set out in the theoretical chapter 2, I draw from Dale's understanding of the pluriscalar nature of educational governance (2005), by taking the national level policy making of the ASEP law as a starting point, while simultaneously engaging with the importance of processes and actors above and below the state level. Since actors are involved at various levels and with varying resources, changes cannot be attributed to any single actor or scale. So, with the above information about the various actors in mind, this section discusses the – sometimes conflicting – points of views and struggles over the new ASEP law.

Normales

Presently, pre-service teacher education in Bolivia is provided in 27 Normales, or as they are now labelled ESFMs (*Escuelas Superiores de Formación de Maestras y Maestros*), as well as in 20 smaller scale Academic Units (UAs), which are dependent on a larger ESFM institute and that are created to serve those living in more remote areas. The two private and religious Normales will be closed down, and new ones have been opened. An indicative overview of the current institutes is provided in Table 5.[104] The table shows both Normales (ESFMs) and UA's. Where foundation years are missing, in most cases this means that these institutes were (re)created recently, without any specific data available. The last column indicated the urban and rural *location*, and not so much its focus area, as currently all Normales are supposed to be unified under one system. While there is no official division between urban and rural Normales in policy narratives anymore, in reality these differences are still influential and relevant for the purpose of this research.

In general, there is little contact and exchange between these institutes, except for contacts between the management staff during official meetings organised by the MoE (36:2, 62:20, 122:12). According to the regulations for Normales of 1997, the organisational structure of every institute consists of three levels: a consultative; an executive; and an operational level. At the first level, each institute has a consultative board. Yet, they are not only given different names, they also function differently in the various institutes. Reports from the period before 2006 showed for example the hierarchical/vertical advisory boards in the institutes that were administered by universities (and that were financially dependent of these universities) in the period 2000-2005. In Warisata, this was one of the main reasons why the contract for external administration of the University San Francisco Asis was not prolonged in 2003 (Yapu in Lozada Pereira, 2004: 125-126). At the second level of executive power the General Director carries responsibility with regard to the training and professional development of the teacher trainers' staff, and internal evaluation mechanisms. Thirdly, at the operational level there is an Academic Director – whom is responsible for curriculum development – and an Administrative and Financial Director (36:2, 67:18). Earlier research criticised the organisational management

---

[104] This overview is more indicative rather than precise data, since it was difficult to acquire data on the presently existing, closed down or to be closed down Normales.

structures in general to be bureaucratic and centralised (Lozada Pereira, 2004), which was confirmed by respondents of this study, as is discussed in chapter 7.

In an evaluation report from the MoE (1999), the urban institute Simón Bolívar was described as the leader in processes of resistance and the 'permanent conflict' between the government and Normales in the period between 1997-1999. The evaluation took place during a turmoil period in which the MoE had just announced the Simón Bolívar would be administered by the public University (UMSA – see chapter 6). Yet a small number of teacher trainers did not resist or refuse to accept all governmental policies, as they also saw the benefits of the involvement of the University. A number of teacher trainers in recent interviews similarly spoke out against their unions' attitude of resistance to the new Reform plans, arguing that not all of their colleagues supported this position of refusal of the La Paz union (7:2). Thus in line with Tatto's claim mentioned in the introduction of the chapter, we cannot judge either of the Normales included in this study as homogenous, particularly not in terms of their political stance and attitudes.

Table 5, Teacher training institutes: ESFMs and UAs	Department	Foundation	Urban-rural location
1	ESFM Riberalta	Beni	1965	Rural
2	ESFM Clara Parada (Santísima Trinidad)	Beni	1976	Urban
	UA: San Ignacio de Moxos	Beni	—	
3	ESFM Marsical Sucre/Universidad Pedagogica	Chuquisaca	1909	Urban
4	ESFM Franz Tamayo (Villa Serrano)	Chuquisaca	1961	Rural
5	ESFM Simón Bolívar de Cororo	Chuquisaca	1966	Rural
6	ESFM Ismael Montes (Vacas)	Cochabamba	1946	Rural
7	ESFM Manuel Ascencio Villarroel (Paracaya)	Cochabamba	1948	Rural
8	ESFM Simon Rodriguez Carreño	Cochabamba	—	Rural
	UA: Cercado, Villa Tunari, Tarata, Sacaba	Cochabamba	—	
9	ESFM Simón Bolívar	La Paz	1917	Urban
10	ESFM Warisata	La Paz	1938	Rural
11	ESFM Bautista Saavedra (Santiago de Huata)	La Paz	1938	Rural
12	ESFM Mariscal Andrés de Santa Cruz de Calahumana	La Paz	1958	Rural
13	ESFM Antonio Jose de Sucre	La Paz	—	Urban
14	ESFM Vila Aroma	La Paz	—	Rural

15	ESFM Tecnologico Humanistico El Alto	La Paz	–	Urban
	UA: Caranavi (Simón Bolívar), Ancocagua, Corpa (Mariscal Andres)	*La Paz*	*–*	
16	ESFM René Barrientos Ortuño (Caracollo)	Oruro	1965	Rural
17	ESFM Ángel Mendoza Justiniano	Oruro	1970	Urban
	UA: Corque (Angel Mendoza), Machacamarca, Pampa Aullagas (Rene Barrientos)	*Oruro*	*–*	
18	ESFM Puerto Rico	Pando	–	Rural
	UA: Cobija, Filadelfia	*Pando*	*–*	
19	ESFM Franz Tamayo (Llica)	Potosí	1961	Rural
20	ESFM Andrés de Santa Cruz	Potosí	1971	Rural
21	ESFM José David Berrios	Potosí	1938	Urban
22	ESFM Eduardo Avaroa	Potosí	1985	Urban
	UA: Atocha (Eduardo Avaroa), San Luis de Sacaca (Andrés de Santa Cruz)	*Potosí*	*–*	
23	ESFM Enrique Finot	Santa Cruz	1959	Urban
24	ESFM Multietnica intercultural Concepción	Santa Cruz	–	Rural
25	ESFM Plurietnico del Oriente y Chaco	Santa Cruz	–	Rural
26	ESFM Rafael Chavez Ortiz	Santa Cruz	–	Rural
	UA: Vallegrande (Enrique Finot), San Julian (Rafeal Chavez Ortiz), Charagua (Plurietnico)	*Santa Cruz*	*–*	
27	Juan Misael Caracho (Canasmoro)	Tarija	1938	Rural
	UA: Tarija, Gran Chaco	*Tarija*	*–*	
	PRIVATE INSTITUTES: CLOSING DOWN			
	Normal Catolica Sedes Sapientiae	Cochabamba	1956	Urban
	Normal Adventista	Cochabamba	1971	Urban

Sources: Del Granado anexo 1ª, Lozadae Pereira 2004 anexo 1, website of the viceministry of higher education[105]

---

[105] Websites: http://ves.minedu.gob.bo/ves/index.php?ID=dgmaestros and http://www.dgfm-bo.com/pages/escuelas/beni.ph, last visited 20-04-2011. From the above mentioned institutes in the table, I have visited five in total: the Simon Bolívar in La Paz, the (private) Normal Catolica in Cochabamba, Manuel Ascencio Villarroel in Paracaya, the Universidad Pedagogica (which is 'treated' as a Normal and not a university, but with extra training possibilities) and the Normal of Warisata. Simón Bolívar is the main case study, and Paracaya is a secondary and additive case, as was discussed in chapter 4. See also Appendix 7 for two maps on these institutes' locations in the departments of La Paz and Cochabamba.

The Normales are usually large institutions with more than a thousand students. Both rural and urban institutions tend to have very little equipment, poor libraries and, at least in rural areas, boarding school systems that allow students from remote areas to take part, as is elaborated below. Besides the management and administrative staff, there are two other important groups of actors in the institutes: the teacher trainers and the teacher students (see part IV).

Funding mechanisms of Bolivia's Normales

Teacher education in Bolivia is public and funded from the National Treasury. It is, however, not easy to acquire (reliable) data on finances.[106] This was confirmed in the MoE evaluation report of 1999 for the case of Simón Bolívar, where data on the annual spending and budget were not retrieved (1999: 22-23), and the external evaluation of Concha et al (2002: 22) claiming how *'there is confusion about the financing of infrastructure and equipment of the Normales'*. In recent interviews with MoE officials of the financial department of the MoE, it became clear that salaries of teaching, management and administrative staff are still paid through the MoE, from the funds of the National Treasury. The infrastructure and water, gas and electricity bills of the institutes are financed through the municipal levels (112:1, 113:1), or through the external resources of the Basket fund.

Normales also generate sources of income themselves. The 2004 UNESCO report findings still reflect the situation today, where these resources range from (international) donations to – particularly in rural Normales – income through renting out (class)rooms, the selling of agricultural products (produced on the premises of the institute) or payments from students and staff to cover electricity and other bills (Lozada Pereira, 2004: 156-157). Besides these forms of income, the data of this study discloses how a considerable part of the institutes' budget is raised through the payments for certificates and other formal paperwork. In two rural institutes (boarding schools) students affirmed that they also had to pay for their daily costs, but that services were insufficient; there were complaints of a lack of functioning and clean sanitation facilities, very small rooms and a low quality of nutrition. Currently, the MoE evaluates the spending of the Normales, through annual 'POA's' (*Annual Operation Plan*) that examine the income (from the Treasury as well as own resources) and expenditure of each institute (112:1). However, the budget reporting of Normales has been criticised for being rather 'rough estimates' including 'unregistered spending', rather than *'reflecting the real financial situation of the institutes'* (Concha et al, 2002: 47). In 2004, Lozada Pereira's report revealed how political pressure, teachers' unions' leading roles and consequent conflicts determined the way finances were distributed among the various institutes. The increase of the budget of Simón Bolívar in La Paz was, for instance, higher than rural and Amazonian institutes (Lozada Pereira, 2004: 102-103).

Overall, there is little foreign investment in the teacher education system, except for smaller investments in some Normales (such as laboratories and libraries) paid from the budget that the MoE receives from the 'Basket Fund' of the Netherlands, Denmark, Spain and Sweden

---

[106] Lozada Pereira (2004) provides some data of the period right after the 1994 reform: the amount of money spent on teacher education increased from 4.511.282 US$ in 1994 to 6.880.810 US$ in 1999, while interestingly changes in teacher education only started to take place after this period, which leads us to assume that investments have increased since.

(101:6). A MoE official from the financial department mentioned that between 2007 and 2010, the MoE received about 10 million US dollars through this Basket Fund, and a small part (which he could not trace down) of that was invested in improving the facilities of some Normales (113:1).

When having a closer look at how foreign organisations provided funding and support in Bolivia's teacher education system, we can observe how already in 1972 and the following year, UNESCO and UNICEF organised two seminars for the improvement of the quality of in-service teachers (Lozada Pereira, 2004: 47). After UNICEFs role in the reform process of the 1990s, they now run a project for pre-service, in-service and long distance training on EIB in the Amazon region. In this region, there is still a lack of trained teachers, particularly for the secondary level of education (interview with a former MoE official now working at UNICEF (3:1)). The Spanish international development cooperation agency (AECID) cooperated with the MoE in a quality improvement programme for teacher trainers at the Normales from 1999 onwards, in 21 Normales and with 1,011 teacher trainers (81). The involvement of AECID in this initiative ended at the end of 2007, as the MoE was supposed to take over the responsibilities of this programme (AECID, 2007). I did meet some teacher trainers and management staff members that were enrolled in the AECID programme, but many of the participants had left the Normales. A Normal Director told me they had to leave because these participants were not *normalistas* but 'University-teachers' that participated in this programme during the University administration in some Normales. When Normales became autonomous again, many of these trained participants accordingly had to leave the teacher education sector (64:4). Two AECID staff members (89) and a MoE official verified this statement (Del Granado Cosio, 2007). While Lozada Pereira's report states it was not the (relatively small) increase in budget of the rural Normales that made changes from 1999 onwards, but rather the programmes and interventions of foreign actors (Lozada Pereira, 2004: 161-162), the report also mentions how (international and national) consultancy reports on the 1994 reform critique these forms of foreign funding in Normales to have been badly distributed nor widely used (Lozada Pereira, 2004: 119). In line with this last observation of Lozada Pereira, I encountered only a few, small scale, examples of cooperation with or donations from foreign donors in the Normales I visited.

Student teacher federations

In Normales, student teachers are (supposed to be) represented through representative bodies called student federations. On its website, the MoE for instance proclaimed how in the beginning of 2010 several of the student federations were involved in negotiations with the MoE on issues such as transparency and anti-corruption in the Normales, the delivery of equipment (computers, sports facilities), and incentives for further studies, among other things (Ministerio de Educacion de Bolivia, 2010a, 8 February). However, in both the urban and rural institute, students complained of a lack of accountability, contribution fees that 'disappeared' and a general feeling of malfunctioning of these federations. During the fieldwork period 2010, elections for a new federation were planned for in the urban institute, '*after three years without a functioning representative body*' (student teacher 103:8). In these elections, different student parties present themselves, like the one in Photo 6, in the Normal Enrique Finot in Santa Cruz. It was reported in both institutes that once these 'student fronts' are elected, they often do not (or, cannot) live up to the promises of their electoral programme. One student explained that this was due to the power relations between the federation and the management. A radically different point of view came from a Ministry official in an interview in 2007, who talked about a 'dictatorship of the students', commenting how – when indeed functioning – student federations had significant power both in relation to staff and other students. '*I am sure they [student union leaders] use this power more for their own interests, which is neither beneficial for the majority of students nor the quality of teacher education*' (76:17).

Photo 6. Representatives of a student party present themselves at the Normal Enrique Finot in Santa Cruz

Below, I briefly introduce the nature of Bolivia's national teaching force, which also resembles the main characteristics of the teacher trainers and teacher students at the Normales.

In-service Teachers

According to the statistics of the Bolivian MoE (2009) Bolivia has 137,817 teachers, with 60% women and 40% men. There are 122,294 primary and secondary level teachers or school directors, and 11,321 have administrative or official functions. In total, 4,202 teachers work in Normales, including trainers and administrative personnel. Between 2005 and 2009, the national teachers' population increased by 10.5%, from 125,820 teachers in 2005 to 139,134 teachers in 2009. Of all teachers, 59% work in urban areas and 41% in rural areas. According to the MoE, 16% of Bolivia's teachers are said to be 'young' (below 30 years), 31.32% between 30 and 40 years old; 26.03% are between 40 and 50 years old; and 26.84% are aged above 50.

Due to a lack of good retirement arrangements, a fairly large group of relatively 'older' teachers see themselves as forced into continuing their work. According to the teacher unions, teachers (and teacher trainers in Normales alike) see themselves forced into continuing to work at a relatively old age, because there are no good arrangements in place for when they stop. Various respondents connected this lack of retirement arrangements to a deteriorating educational quality and outdated teaching styles. In addition, they linked it to the fact that there is a surplus of trained primary level teachers now; because on the one hand, the older generation continuing working, and on the other hand, the training system does not seem to respond to the needs of the education system by training too many primary level teachers, while failing to deliver enough secondary school teachers (13:113).

Contreras and Talavera (2004a: 64) provide an overview of the composition of the Bolivian teacher force having the following characteristics: there is a growing 'feminisation' of the teacher profession; a strong indigenous presence; continuing deterioration of their socio-economic status; continuing poverty among teachers; it is often a second career choice; many teachers have extra jobs, inside or outside of public and private schools; and often Bolivian teachers come from a marginalised background. My fieldwork research confirmed this situation in which a majority of Bolivian teachers have other jobs (such as taxi drivers, waiters, guards, child care workers), or they run second turns (often in private schools) in the afternoons and evenings. Being forced into extra jobs leaves them little or no time to prepare their classes, or for *actualización* (updating professional knowledge). Due to changed entrance regulations and a pessimistic economic situation, many teacher students are not young secondary school leavers anymore, but people with former studies and professions that seek a secure job opportunity (see chapter 7). The growing group of older students often have family responsibilities, leading to child care problems, especially when both partners are studying and working.

School, community, municipal and departmental committees

Being an important part of the new law, and part of the decentralised system, community participation is organised through '*Concejos Educativos Comunitarios*', including parents, teachers and community organisations. They change their formation every one or two years. These school councils are responsible for (local) educational management and the delivery of quality education for all (Congreso Nacional de Educación, 2006). Already since the 1994 Reform, parents gained relative power in the context of primary and secondary schools committees. They help, among other things, with organisational aspects of school feeding programmes, cleaning school premises and organising festivities, but they also keep an eye on the work of teachers. According to Van Dam (2007: 6), in some cases, tensions arose between these school councils and the teaching staff, because the councils accused teachers of bad performance or issues such as sexual intimidation. Although the school councils were also meant to have educational roles, so far, this is often limited to the cleaning of classrooms or preparation of school meals. At the municipal level, the so-called *Núcleos* (schools clusters) can develop joint projects for the improvement of educational quality, which are then funded partly by the MoE and partly by the municipality. Within the cluster, there is usually one 'head school' which provides a group of other smaller schools with facilities such as a library, media centre and a full eight year primary education programme (Van Dam, 2007: 7, 10). While teachers' salaries are arranged at the central administrative level, the nine departmental education sections (*Servicios Departamentales de Educación – SEDUCA's*) are in charge of managing the local assignments of teachers' positions. In general, there is little connection between the schools, SEDUCA's and the Normales, as discussed in chapter 7.

Ministry of Education of Bolivia

The MoE is a powerful actor in a centrally organised education system. It is the main driver behind the new Education Reform. The mission statement of the MoE in the new Plurinational state is to '*design, implement and execute politics of inclusive, equitable, inter-intracultural, plurilingual, scientific, technological and quality education strategies, with social participation on the basis of a territorial, communitarian-productive and decolonizing Plurinational education system.*' This is followed by their vision statement, which states '*the Ministry of Education ensures a productive, communitarian and quality education for everyone with socio-cultural relevance, contributing to building a just society, and a balanced and harmonious relationship with nature that supports the development of the plurinational state, to live well (vivir bien), through strengthening educational management*' (Ministerio de Educación de Bolivia, 2010c). The teacher training department (*Dirección General de la Formación de los Maestros*) is part of the vice-ministry of higher education and professional training.[107] The MoE carries the main responsibility for the teacher education system (Lozada Pereira, 2004: 181; Ministerio de Educación de Bolivia, 2010b).

There exist internal differences in the MoE on interpretations of the rationale and ways to implement the new ASEP Reform for decolonising education. The ex-minister, who was still in her position when interviewed, acknowledged that resistance was not only coming from teachers and their unions, but also from people within the MoE itself (46:2). According to some authors, the MoE remains an island with a lack of touch with reality (Van Dam, 2006); and an institution with a lack of coordination and clear strategy (Nucinkis, 2004: 51). This position was confirmed by an ex-teacher trainer, who explained how the MoE itself is still a very conservative institution, at least in regard to some officials who have stayed on since the change of government (8:43). In interviews in 2007 and 2008, several MoE officials expressed their concern and sometimes disapproval, for instance of the 'indigenous and rural' focus of the reform project, or the fact that Normales would be allowed to hand out university-level degrees (76:7). One MoE officer for instance shared that: '*the problem with this new law is that is only takes the indigenist point of view as a reference, and it bases everything on the experiences in Warisata in the 1930s. It is too much focused on changing educational management to become more communitarian, and its lacks a proper pedagogical paradigm*' (76:9). Because we had interviews in 2007, 2008 and 2010, the openly negative attitude of this person eventually changed over time into a milder, and even a mildly supportive, stance to the ASEP law. Perhaps a growing cluster of pro-ASEP staff members, and thus some institutional pressure, had to do with this change. These interpretations stand in stark contrast to another group of officials in the MoE, by now perhaps the majority, who strongly support the new ASEP reform. For example, a former social movement leader, now working in the MoE, is a strong ASEP ally. He affirmed the MoE had a strong political role in the development and promotion of the new decolonising policy lines.

Combined with interview data, the analysis of actor maps provides some interesting insights into the position of the MoE and the existing power plays in the field of Bolivian teacher education (for illustrations see Appendix 6).[108] Around half of the drawing respondents focused on the key role of – and power plays between – both the MoE and the teachers' unions (see for example Actor maps 2 and 3, Appendix 6). These maps were typically drawn by academics and policy makers, but also some of the trainers. In most of these latter maps, the MoE takes a central position, while teachers unions were placed in a similar position and size, while respondents would illustrate the tensions and power struggles between the two. Interestingly, the

---

[107] Other vice-ministries include: Vice-ministry of Primary and Secondary Regular Education; the Vice-Ministry for Alternative and Special Education (including adult education, specialised education for diabled students and (post)alfabetisation programmes (Ministerio de Educacion de Bolivia 2010c). The Teacher Education department recently created its own website (http://www.dgfm-bo.com/pages/normas/pag_01.php), with a potentially interesting (but not yet fully operating) digital space for sharing information.

[108] I invited 34 of the respondents to schematically draw out an overview of the way they viewed the main actors, their relative power and their relationships in the specific field of teacher education. In the interviews, when entering the discussion on the main actors in the field of teacher education, I asked respondents to take over my note book and pen instead of only speaking about their ideas. Usually, this was a point in the interview where people opened up more. With my notebook and pen in their hands, people tended to take up their teacher-role, really trying to make me understand their points of view. Since the conversations were recorded as well, I could also use the transcribed recounts later on as a further explication of the drawings. Of the 34 respondents who drew an actor map, 14 were teacher trainers, 8 student teachers, 4 policy-makers, 5 academics and 3 social movement members.

other half of the respondents, being mostly teacher students and teacher trainers, position themselves centrally as core actors in the field (see for instance Actor map 1, Appendix 6).

As illustrated in Actor map 4 (Appendix 6), one of the MoE officials responsible for teacher education explained how the MoE has actually lost a lot of its decision-making power. She pictured the MoE of Education and its Teacher Education Department ('*DCFD*') almost falling off the page of the note book, perhaps accidentally reflecting how the MoE now finds itself in a position '*with its back to the wall*' because of the pressure from the unions, and to a lesser extent from parents and other civil society groups – positioned in between the MoE and the unions. She reflected, '*we are on the sideline with all these social movements, we have to find consent for all decisions but in many cases we do not even create a consensus, we are just forced to take a decision*' (6:26). Actor map 4 shows the central position of the union (*confederación*), whom on the one hand '*do not present proposals for improvement of the quality of education*' (on the left side), while on the other hand they want to '*take back their decision-making power*' in the Normales. Particularly with respect to struggles around the number of students that should be allowed to enter the Normales she felt the MoE is losing its strength (6:27). Clearly frustrated, she continued to talk about the difficult position the MoE finds itself in, especially with regards to the conflict with (the urban) teachers' union: '*the quality of teacher education is low, and why? Because there is no time to work on proposals, all the time we have to resolve conflicts*' (6:27).

Hence, the MoE not only struggles internally, but even more so externally with various actors who resist the new education reform. Based on analysis of interview data and the Actor maps, various groups of educational stakeholders are resisting the ASEP reform, including: the urban teachers union; parts of the teacher corps that are not well informed and do not feel ownership of the new plans; some groups of parents; the political opposition and 'old' elite/oligarchs in the lowland regions; the Catholic Church; conservative forces within universities; and private education institutes.[109] However different the positions of these actors might be, they share a fear that the current government plans will clash with their own interests and power positions. In an interview, an ex-Minister of Education explained how creating a coherent new policy based on consensus was one thing, but the most pressing and difficult challenge was to overcome the disintegration at the national level, and the resistance to the (then proposed) new law (46:6).

Teachers' unions

In terms of the representation of in-service teachers, Bolivia has two main teachers' unions: The *Confederación de los Maestros de Educación Rural de Bolivia* or Rural Teachers' National Confederation (CONMERB); and the *Confederación de Trabajadores de Educación Urbana de Bolivia* or Urban Teachers' Union (CTEUB).[110] Only CONMERB is a member of Education International.[111] All teachers are obliged to join the teachers' union (urban or rural, depending on their location) and (automatically) donate 0.5% of their salary to the unions (Contreras and Talavera, 2004b; Regalsky and Laurie, 2007). Education International in their online barometer show the following facts on trade union rights (in general) in Bolivia: '*Government workers can form trade unions. Some*

---

[109] These results came out of the drawings I asked various respondents to draw in response to questions concerning the most important actors and their position towards the new ASEP law.
[110] See CTEUB's website http://www.cteub.com/, CONMERB has no website.
[111] http://www.ei-ie.org.

25% of workers in the formal economy are union members. Mediation is required before a strike or lockout begins. Strikes in public services are banned but do occur, most commonly strikes by teachers, health care and transportation workers' (EI, 2007). Bolivia's teachers' unions have proven to be powerful players in the field of (teacher) education. Similarly, in Mexico, the power of the teacher union lies in the fact that teachers work under very poor conditions and have a low (societal) status (Tatto et al, 2007b: 145).

For a long time the relationship between Bolivia's teachers' unions and the government has been, and to a large extent still is, mildly speaking, uneasy. This was, however, not always the case. From their creation around 1909 (Anaya, 2009: 14), roughly until 1960, the teachers' unions and government '*interacted on an equal basis and brought about pedagogical initiatives and proposals*'. The military dictatorships, the financial crisis of the late 1970s and the neoliberal political direction (including Structural Adjustment Programmes) afterwards provoked a defensive attitude of the teacher unions, fighting rather for their salaries than for educational quality issues (Talavera Simoni, 2011: 11-13). The unions have played strong roles in reform processes in the last two decades, while the focus on workers' rights and salaries has remained. The resistance from the side of the urban union largely continues to date, but the rural confederation supports the new ASEP reform, as will be shown below. In addition, we have to recognise that while all teachers are automatically subscribed to one of the unions, the union's demands and strategies are not necessarily supported by all teachers at their 'base' (Anaya, 2009: 43). Even though the central level representatives of the national rural teachers union (CONMERB) strongly feel that the new law was created in close cooperation with them, the experience of talking to various (rural and urban) teachers shows how even living up to Fraser's 'ordinary first level of representation' is in reality a huge challenge (Fraser, 2005a; 2005b). Participation of teachers in the creation of the law in effect means the participation of higher level representatives of the unions, and as a result many teachers do not feel engaged. The findings show that even when a participatory discourse is implemented, by including representatives of societal groups, this still does not necessarily mean all members of these groups have a sense of ownership over the process.

For this study, I have particularly engaged with respondents from the urban federation of the teachers union in La Paz, because of their relationship with the Normal Simón Bolívar. According to one of the union leaders in an interview in October 2007, '*this is the most important federation of the whole country, both because of its high number of affiliates, between 4,000 and 5,000, and because of its organisation and combative attitude. This union works from a Trotskyite perspective, and all leaders are part of the Revolutionary Workers Party*' (79). In another interview the unionist continued to explain how for this La Paz federation, it is currently a tough battle to maintain their independent union position (of resistance to current government plans), since the national CTEUB is closely aligned to the Communist Party, which co-governs with the MAS. '*We feel like a lonely drop in the ocean*', the unionist explained, since the COB and the mining unions, and even the national teachers unions, have become '*officialistas*'. According to the La Paz unionists, the large 'officialista' unions are controlled by, and work in conjunction with, the governing party MAS (49).

The feelings of ownership of the rural union's active members stand in stark contrast to the resistance that is felt by the national urban teachers union; and even stronger in the Trotskyist inspired La Paz section of this union. The urban union was also invited to all national level reform meetings, but they have left the conference table many times. The urban unionists do not support the plans for further decentralisation that are proposed in the Law, as this would place too much power in the hands of parents and local organisations, threatening both teachers' autonomy and a unified education system. Also, they fear that a pluricultural, communitarian and productive education will exclude those living in urban areas and even lead to new forms of exclusion. Besides, an urban union leader was very critical of the design process of the new teacher education curriculum, as those that were invited by the MoE were paid 10,000 Bolivianos (around €1,000), *'while as a senior teacher I only get 1,500 Bolivianos per month. We are thus very sarcastic when the government states the curriculum was created on the basis of indigenous knowledges. These indigenous 'connaisseurs' were paid 10,000 Bolivianos, that is a shame! In a national congress we decided that from the union we would put sanctions on those that participated in this process with the government'* (49). An ex-teacher trainer who participated as a curriculum designer confirmed that he faced great difficulties when trying to gain access to a new position as a trainer in a Normal again, as he was often 'vetoed' out of application procedures (8).

The La Paz unionists specifically oppose the plans for decentralisation of the education system, already started in the 1990s and continued to some extent in the ASEP law. Decentralisation, the union leader explained, on the one hand gives too much power to parental commissions to decide on teachers' positions, while on the other hand, it *'will lead to a very unequal division into tiny pieces of the pie, called education'*. It is feared that with departmental and local forms of autonomy, *'everyone will organise their own type of education'*, leading to a splintered national education system, in which *'poorer regions will consequently have lower quality education'*. Moreover, *'the right wing old elite, and via them the transnational corporations will take over control of Bolivian education. Like everywhere in the world, they want education systems to decentralise and privatise, but we need a centralised system'* (49). From a more distant point of view, it is interesting to conclude that this last argument is actually very close to the current governments' aims through ASEP, and it seems the same argument is used for different sides of the debate.

However, in contrast to a general negative and conservative image of the urban union, after conversations with their national level head quarters in La Paz, I think a more nuanced view is appropriate. For example, financally supported by Education International, the national urban union has constructed its own reform proposal in order to generate further discussions on the design of ASEP. This response, titled *'Schooling to liberate the country'*, was published along with an analysis of the differences and commonalities between the governments' views and the urban unions' views on ASEP (CTEUB, 2006; CTEUB, 2007).[112]

There are, thus, close ties between the unions and the Normales. There is a particularly (in)tense relationship between the countries largest Normal Simón Bolívar and the radical teacher's federation of La Paz. Studies on the situation of Normales before 2006 repeatedly state how political conflicts and the powerful position of unions hindered the realisation of a number of governmental plans (see for instance Del Granado Cosio, 2006; Lozada Pereira, 2004). One union leader of the federation in La Paz explained this relationship: *'We see the Normal primarily as part of the federation, and when its suits them, they follow all our instructions. But when it does not suit them well,*

---

[112] This analysis called *'Debate sobre la educación Boliviana'* presented a long list (102 pages) discussing all articles of the 1994 reform. These initiatives were financially supported by Education International, the global teachers unions federation: http://www.ei-ie.org/.

they distance themselves from the federation and take their own stance'. The unionist continued to explain how this resulted in a conflict over participating in the design of the new ASEP teacher education curriculum, which they do not support.

One unionist explained the conflict between the La Paz federation and the urban Normal over participating in the design of the new ASEP teacher education curriculum: *'We as the urban union, we rejected this new law. So when the Ministry saw we would not collaborate in their curriculum design, they started to personally invite some individuals at Simón Bolívar. The Normal should have obeyed the resolution of our union, but instead they have sent delegates and so the Ministry could say Simón Bolívar participated'* (49). The union leader was clearly unhappy with these independent developments of the Normal they had supported in their struggles against University administration just a few years ago. Viewed from the perspective of a trainer and delegate of the Normal, the situation is even more complex because of internal struggles within the institute. The trainer explains why, according to her opinion, participation in these meetings is still important: *'I was sent to represent this Normal in a congress on the new law and its curriuclum, and the directorate of this institute rejects the proposal. I think this is dangerous because once we do not accept it, it will just be imposed on us, and imposition is not good at all. This will not help us to change. Contrarily, when we stay involved along the way we can influence, and come to a consensus'* (urban teacher trainer 13:4).

The unions, and particularly the attitude of this La Paz federation, received critique from the various academics I interviewed. For instance, a University lecturer in political sciences and former director of the Simón Bolívar under its University administration between 2000 and 2005, shared his critique, that is rooted in *'an educational and political frustration, because we have not been able to put an intercultural education renovation in practice. We did not know how to seduce the unions, although I get more and more convinced that our unions are not seducible, there is no way we can have an affective relationship with them, as they only work from a logic of struggle, and not from a logic of dialogue'.* Clearly frustrated, he continued to state *'the union is like a dinosaur. It does not belong to this world anymore, it should be in a museum, but instead, they continue to live among us'.* He further critiques the COB and the teacher unions to carry on with a national ideology of unification and homogenisation originated in the 1952 revolution, while *'this has been substituted with a diverse and intercultural state model. The union thus loses its position, as they continue to believe in a homogenous education and society'* (23).

Since many teachers do not have enough access to information about the policy developments, they follow their union leaders in their opposition to the law. An urban union leader for instance told me that they organise weekly Wednesday-evening sessions in their union recidence called *'casa social de los maestros',* these meeting are for their members to discuss current issues in the education sector, including the new law, as: *'they need to have a good knowledge basis to be able to debate this law. Sometimes, teachers just follow their union leaders who represent them at the national level. But this is not how it should be, in order to fight, our bases need to be convinced of something, and its our duty to educate them in this direction'* (49). An Ex-Minister of Education explained the polarisation of the urban and rural unions through their respective visible actions: *'It's very difficult. For instance, now we have demonstrations. On the one hand there are road blocks from the side of the rural teachers who ask for approval of the law, and on the other hand we see the urban teachers marching the streets to hinder approval of the law'* (12:17).

In summary, the unions have a relative, powerful role in negotiating, changing or resisting government policies, as well as their influence in the placement of staff at Normales. The unions are, nevertheless, far from two homogeneous organisations for urban and rural teachers, and internal differences have led to various strategies of departmental and local confederations (46:5). An indigenous MoE staff member in an interview in May 2010 brought forward how power relations are slowly shifting: *'it is no longer only the Ministry and the unions who decide on the [teacher] education sector, now there are also other actors [like the CEPOs] involved. The power the unions once had in deciding which students, trainers and directors were placed in Normales is now broken with the institutionalisation processes'* (115:6). At this point in the interview we heard a loud blast outside the building. The urban teachers' union was protesting outside the MoE and teachers used dynamite to enforce their demands. Loud exclamations were repeated over and over again: *'we are against decentralisation! We demand higher salaries!'* In an attempt to maintain the validity of statement he just made, my interlocutor replied *'but its only a few, most of them are at work'*.

Indigenous Education Councils – CEPOS

Civil society organisations – and particularly indigenous movements – play an important role in the Bolivian education sector, particularly since the 1990s. The *Consejos Educativos de los Pueblos Originarios* (CEPOs – Indigenous Councils for Education) were established in 1994. The CEPOs represent Bolivia's numerous cultural and linguistic communities and their current organisation is based on long historical roots. The movement has been financially supported by the Netherlands and Denmark.[113] Already during the former 1994 Reform process, but similarly right now, the CEPOs have a genuine influence on policy plans, representing the indigenous populations' educational needs. The CEPOs support the new Reform in its focus on revaluing the various indigenous cultures and languages in education. According to the CEPOs, they too have been main protagonists in the creation of the new law, including the key pillars of communitarian, productive and pluricultural education.[114] A CEPOs representative expressed their engagement with the design of ASEP law as follows: *'This reform is the first real experience with how society really participates in the formulation of educational politics. Various societal groups were involved, such as teachers, professionals, parents, the catholic church and even the military'* (96:19). The CEPOs are also currently engaged with the design of the curriculum for teacher training institutes. According to a member of the CEPO in Sucre (CENAQ), there are seven different CEPOs from different regions working on their curriculum proposals, and these are then merged together with input from the MoE. It is interesting to note that both the leaders of CONMERB and the CEPOs emphasise their foundational roles in the creation of this law. Although the CEPOS seem to have gained important influence on educational policies these days, it remains an issue for further research to analyse what space is available for, and negotiated by, this and other civil society organisations in order to create change and improvement, towards more equitable educational and societal opportunities, respect and tolerance and in general a higher level of social justice in society.

---

[113] This was the case until the time of writing, when Denmark continued their funding while the Dutch future funding is insecure considering the political decision of the Dutch Ministry of Foreign Affairs to phase out the donor relationship with Bolivia.

[114] For more information see www.cepos.bo.

International and religious organisations

Chapter 4 already described a variety of international and, importantly, regional actors involved in Bolivian education. Bolivia has long been a so-called 'donor darling'. Numerous international NGOs (non-governmental organisations) and international donors have been, and to some extent still are, involved in Bolivian development processes. NGOs – often funded by the Catholic Church – became active in Bolivia in the 1970s. Similar to other Latin American and Southern countries, the government of Bolivia for example accepted the educational projects in remote areas of the Summer Institute of Linguistics.[115] Major non-governmental players in the education field (especially with regards to the 1994 reforms) were UNICEF, UNESCO, GTZ (Germany), SIDA (Sweden), DANIDA (Denmark), Finland, World Bank (WB), International Monetary Fund (IMF), Inter-American Development Bank, JICA (Japan) and the Netherlands.[116] For example, UNICEF supported the development of teaching materials (Laurie et al, 2003: 480), GTZ and AECID (Spain) supported intercultural and bilingual teacher education, and DANIDA offered their support particularly in the Amazonian region.

Many of the NGOs who started to work in Bolivia in the 1970s were funded by the Catholic Church. Historically, the church has played a role in providing primary, secondary and higher education, including teacher education in two private Normales. However, at the time of writing, the final document of the ASEP law enforces the closure of the two religiously oriented (and the only two private) Normales, since all teachers should be trained in a neutral and non-religious way (Ministerio de Educacion de Bolivia, 2010). This is supported by some teacher trainers (8;13) who see the current private education system, of around 10% of the schools, as very unequal and unwanted. However, other teacher trainers are themselves closely involved in religious education institutes, such as *Fe y Alergía*. They explained how most of the religious schools were already part of the public system, while they adopted a parallel curriculum that was closely linked to the 1994 reform. In the current context, the church has a fairly big role in the education sector in Bolivia, although their role in the education sector is becoming more limited with the ASEP law that aims for non-religious and public education, triggering protest from the side of the religious organisations.

---

[115] This protestant US based missionary organisation sought to evangelise more effectively through the instruction in and development of indigenous languages. Additionally, USAID's PER-1 (1975-1980) and the World Bank's PEIA (1978-1980) also conducted bilingual education programmes. The first programme to genuinely develop indigenous language skills through education was carried out by the Catholic Comisión Episcopal de Educación (CEE) in 1981 (Taylor 2004).

[116] Considering that this research is part of the Dutch funded IS-Academie programme (University of Amsterdam and Dutch Ministry of Foreign Affairs), I briefly outline the role of the Dutch in Bolivia here. Bolivia has had relations with the Dutch government since 1941, when the Dutch representative was positioned in Buenos Aires. Yet, it took until the return of democracy in 1982 before diplomatic relations became a bit warmer. In the second half of the 1980s a Dutch development office opened in La Paz, which became an embassy in 1993, with an independent ambassador since 1997. The Dutch government is at the time of writing still one of the major international donors in Bolivias education sector, yet considering the changing policy directions of the new Ducth government the continuation in a similar form is very questionable. With the aim to enhance sustainable development, and in order to improve overall economic growth and the lives of the poor, Dutch aid so far has focused on several sectors including education, water management, environment, agrarian productivity, good governance and support for the constitutional assembly.
http://www.minbuza.nl/nl/Reizen_en_Landen/Landenoverzicht/B/Bolivia/Betrekkingen_met_Nederland, last accessed on 25-01-2010. Currently, Bolivia is being phased out as it is not longer one of the partner countries of the Dutch government.

According to the (WB funded) study of Contreras and Talavera, in the 1990s the role of multilateral banks and donors was important, yet there was also Bolivian leadership and the degree of local ownership was *'sufficient to do away with any former perceptions that multilateral banks and donors imposed the reform'* (Contreras and Talavera, 2003: 2). Nonetheless, with the present government perceptions of a 'foreign imposition' of the 1994 Reform seeming to have gained ground, the WB and IMF do not play a significant financial role anymore in the education sector. The World Bank's last big project on 'Education Quality and Equity Strengthening' closed in 2006.[117] Although various MoE officials and non-governmental actors spoke of 'no cooperation at all' with the Bank any more, the World Bank 2009 Report on the Status of Projects in Execution reports a (small scale) project to support access and quality of secondary education at the Municipal level of La Paz (World Bank, 2009). New forms of cooperation between the World Bank and MoE were established during 2010, *'but only on the initiative of the Ministry'*, a MoE official explained, *'and not with the idea of them [the World Bank] telling us what to do'* (115:9). The World Bank is currently, in some cases, accepted as a 'strategic ally' if they agree to finance the Ministries' initiatives. As an illustration of this, the World Bank provided finances for an international seminar on decentralisation in the education sector in May 2010 (115:9). The Interamerican Development Bank (IADB) continues to play a role in the external funding of Bolivian education proposals. It supported a range of Reform programmes of the 1994 Reform and continued to finance a programme for Child Friendly Schools in 2007, a Microenterprise and training programme for women in 2008, and a US$200,000 funding for institutional support to the MoE in 2010.[118] The MoE currently works on a proposal for financial support from the IADB on Productive Communitarian Secondary Education, which includes support for institutional reform, teacher training, diffusion of the new Reform's advantages in communities and evaluation.[119]

Thus, although Bolivia aims for a genuine Bolivian education reform now, it does not mean foreign assistance is thrown out of the window fully. According to UNESCO (2011), in 2007-2008 Bolivia was still one of the largest recipients of aid to education in the region with US$72 million, together with Brazil (US$85 million) and Nicaragua (US$71 million).[120] Both the 2004-2008 Multiannual Operative Programme (POMA) and the 2010-1014 Strategic Institutional Plan of the MoE, that is aimed at increasing the quality of education, uses the (unconditional) 'basket funding' of US$92 million donated by the Netherlands, Denmark, Sweden and Spain for a period of four years (106:8)[121]. Besides, several small scale international initiatives still continue. For example, in March 2010 a team of Belgian, German and Austrian experts came to La Paz to train teacher trainers for a couple of days on special needs education (La Prensa, 18-03-2010b).

---

[117] http://web.worldbank.org/external/projects/main?Projectid=P006204&theSitePK=40941&piPK=73230&pageP K=64283627&menuPK=228424 last visited 26-03-10.
[118] For more (financial and project) details, see IABD's website on former and current funding in Bolivia for the education sector: http://www.iadb.org.
[119] See IADB's website, http://www.iadb.org/en/projects/project,1303.html?id=BO-L1071. The Ministry of Health and Social Development prepares a funding proposal for Early Child Hood development: http://www.iadb.org/en/projects/project,1303.html?id=BO-L1064.
[120] See also the regional overview of the Report for Latin America, http://unesdoc.unesco.org/images/0019/001914/191433e.pdf.
[121] The current Basket funding runs from 2010-2014.

Since 1996 the research institute PROEIB-Andes, located at the premises of the Universidad Mayor de San Simon (UMSS) in Cochabamba, was created with funds from Germany (GTZ). The fact that these university studies in EIB have been created shows an interest in this theme from Bolivian-based academia as well (Nucinkis, 2004: 21). In 1998 a master course in EIB was started, in cooperation with the UMSS, and this still runs to date. Between 1998 and 2008, 132 students subscribed to the programme and 110 completed their degree. Of these students, 98% identifies as indigenous. The majority of the graduates continued working in universities or Normales, while others reported to be working in government positions, NGOs or as consultants (Limachi, 2008). Besides, the institute cooperates in various research projects with countries in the region, such as Peru, Colombia, Ecuador, Chile and Argentina. In 2007, the leading role of GTZ stopped, yet the institute continues to exist. Their main aim is to *'strengthen intercultural and bilingual education from the perspective of, with and for the indigenous populations, in order to respond to the necessities and demands for more and better education in a context of more and more indigenous political participation.'*[122] However, a MoE official in May 2010 claimed that *'PROEIB ANDES is not a priority for us anymore. We stopped the cooperation in 2006. In our view, they do not exist anymore'* (106:13). At first I was surprised by this lack of connection because of the apparently logically shared goal of intercultural and bilingual education. However, interviews revealed that the political rationale that PROEIB-ANDES was a product of the former 'imposed' reform and was therefore not suited to the new reform plans (89; 106). Considering the need for more conceptual clarity on the new concepts used in ASEP, more (academic) and Bolivian-based research on the various power plays and implementation challenges of ASEP, as well as a need for highly qualified EIB teacher trainers, this is a missed opportunity.

In sum, the role of foreign actors in the field of education in Bolivia has changed and diminished over the past few years. I think the following quote from a Bolivian academic explains this new situation and role for international donors: *'if international development cooperations want to provide a helping hand [in terms of finances], they are very welcome, but their logic has to change, it has to be in line with our new logic of education'* (61:34). A former social movement leader now working in the MoE adds to this how current policies are *'all initiatives of the Ministry itself'*. He continued with, *'if there is [external] financial support, we are the ones who decide. We are looking for strategic allies, not for those that do not support or undermine our national political strategy'* (115:9).

The picture I have provided so far of the power struggles in a polarised and heterogeneous field, leads me to discuss the actual and foreseen implementation challenges of the ASEP Reform.

5.7 Challenges to implement the ASEP reform in practice

This section discusses a range of envisaged challenges for the implementation of the ASEP law. First of all, Bolivia's MoE maintains the position that ASEP has been created by educational actors themselves. Moreover, it has used this position to differentiate ASEP's creation process from the 1994 law, which was mostly built by high-up government officials and foreign consultants, with some consultation from civil society groups. Embracing the decolonial opposite, then, would mean an intense amount of participation by the people at the 'bottom' of

---

[122] Information from interviews and from http://www.proeibandes.org/.

the educational power structure, being teachers, their unions, parents, administrative staff of educational institutions and social movements.

Fraser's three-dimensional theory of social justice (Fraser, 2005a; Fraser, 2005b) is helpful here to analyse in how far social justice is indeed part of both the policy programme (the actual law) as well as the programme ontology (Pawson, 2002: 341-342) of ASEP, or the process of the creation of the law together with its prospect for implementation. Fraser's theory of social justice (see also chapter 2) starts from the principle of 'participatory parity', which is appropriate for my analysis of the difficulties of genuine participation and ownership of ASEP at different levels. Representation, the political dimension of social justice, does not only deal with the first level ordinary-political misrepresentations (denying full participation as peers in social interactions). It also deals with a second level boundary-setting mechanism of misframing in the context of globalisation, criticising the framework in which the national state is the sole political space that excludes marginalised groups from any influence. According to Fraser, there is a third meta-political level of misrepresentation, where the majority of people are excluded from participation in meta-discourses that affect them. Because the Bolivian *government* is representing all Bolivians in the meta-political level of ALBAs Declaration meetings (see chapter 3), within these ALBA processes there is a lack of a genuine participation and ownership of educational actors at the local level. ALBA is a supranational development, which has little to no connection to the lives and work of the Bolivian educators I spoke to. My fieldwork outcomes coincide with this analysis, revealing discontent in regard to low levels of participation in the design of ASEP.

While the government maintains that the ASEP reform was not exclusively designed by experts and officials, numerous teachers described the opposite. For example, during the 2006 National Education Congress – with 26 organisations and 628 delegates – the urban teachers union, among others, left the meeting. Many of the delegates felt the *'government was forcing their proposal and ideology on the Congress 'in communist style' without giving possibility for debate'* (Drange, 2007: 4). This illustrates the gap between the government's participatory discourse and educators' own experiences. Respondents confirmed that rather than honest teacher ownership and reform design through participation, they felt that the ASEP law has again been imposed from above. While the government defines participation as central to the process of decolonisation, its own analysis of decolonisation, to some extent, calls into question its own actions. This relates to what Jansen describes as an aspect of 'political symbolism', using 'participation' as a process of legitimisation of policies, rather than an instrument aimed at successful implementation (2001b: 207). While emphasised at the discursive level of the ASEP law, Fraser's third political dimensions of social justice (representation) in practice does not work very smoothly yet. In this sense, the process of national level frame-setting has been only partly successful, as only the representatives of the rural union and the CEPOS feel genuine engagement with the new law, while many of the (mostly urban) teachers experienced a lack of involvement in decision-making processes (Fraser 2005a). In this sense, we can see a difference between a participation-oriented Programme of the ASEP law and a Programme ontology that does not fully carry out the principle of parity of participation as described by Fraser (2005a).

There were also signs of a more quiet form of teacher opposition to the reform, dictated by an unbroken political support to the indigenous president Morales and an unwillingness to openly critique his 'politics of change'. As a result, some of the MAS supporters might have refrained from speaking up against the education reform or the surrounding discourses, even if they had disagreements with it. This is not an uncommon thing among MAS supporters, claims sociologist Mamani, as in some circles it is considered a 'moral sin' to speak against Evo Morales, '*as people's support is not critical, its just idolatry*' (in Dangl 2010: 33). This seriously questions whether teachers will do their part for the implementation of ASEP, if they continue to feel a lack of ownership of the law that the government describes.

The education law also aims to strengthen 'recognition', or Frasers' cultural dimension of social justice, as it aims to include historically marginalised and indigenous people by supporting their cultural logics. However, some of these people are much more interested in engaging with the cultural logic that they have learned to engage with for centuries, often referred to as 'modern' or 'Western' culture, or what Sleeter terms the hegemonic 'culture of power' (2009). An ex-minister of education and academic in La Paz explained that through Bolivia's process of colonisation, a cultural, political and economic hierarchy came into being, which has been a strong force in society ever since. The current state of consciousness of Bolivia's indigenous population imagines their future as part of the modernising approach to development rather than the coloniality approach. Many Bolivian teachers and academics explained that students and their parents are interested less in the decolonisation project and rather in the project identified as 'colonial' by the Morales administration, which offers personal economic success through engaging in 'colonial' hierarchies, such as (Spanish) language, geography/migration and 'modern' cultural norms. The decolonial project is unwanted by some, as it is seen as an imposition into their lives, and since impositions could be considered colonial tactics, the design process and prospects for implementation of the reform, or the ASEP reform ontology, could be considered the same way.

This is a position which should be respected, as Bolivia is one of the poorest countries in the Latin American region and many indigenous peoples, and those in rural areas, are the poorest of the poor. These marginalised groups simply want to make sure that their children grow up to have a better life than they have had. Similar to parents' opinion in the 1990s, this often means focusing on Spanish in school rather than their indigenous language, as well as supporting migration to the cities and effectively contributing to indigenous assimilation into *Mestizo* culture. Exploring these parental positions on 'modernity' and perceptions of 'development' through education, as well as the (lack of) governmental engagement, needs further study. True dignity, which has been a central part of the indigenous demands in Bolivia, must be tied to significant improvement at the material level. Postero (2007: 22), based on the work of Fraser, convincingly argues how Morales' followers thus not only want their president to enact a politics of recognition, but also a politics of redistribution.

Another major challenge is the need to create a universally accepted curriculum as part of the ASEP reform. Even if the curriculum is adapted to be locally relevant, according to a MoE official, there is a lack of capacity among indigenous groups to systematise their cultural heritage (1:10). In addition, many are concerned with the lack of knowledge of indigenous languages of teachers, in regards to full implementation of the plurilingual character of education. There are not enough teachers able to teach (in) native languages (see chapter 7). Another complicating factor is that some of the indigenous languages only have an oral tradition, which supposes a problematic relationship between the use of Spanish and those languages in the classroom.

An additional issue of concern is the general sense of uncertainty and an impasse in the education sector. Ever since the previous education reform of 1994 was repealed by the Morales government soon after it took power, teachers faced great insecurity regarding what guidelines to follow and how long they would have to wait for new ones to be introduced. When discussing these reflections with an educational scholar, he both confirmed and expressed his frustration: '*In this context of change that we are living in, it is inexplicable that after more than four years of a government-of-change, we still do not have a new alternative political orientation. There is a total absence of public policy to accompany these proposed plans in education. What also worries me is the fact that after these four years, we also do not have an approved curriculum […] only some rough drafts*' (114:8). This has serious implications, not only for the way teachers feel about the unclear situation now, but also for the way they judge the new law. As explained by an urban teacher trainer who has been involved in the curriculum design process, '*for the design of the new law we work against the old law, but we are still paid by it…there is a lot of uncertainty and this leads us into a crisis*' (8:33). A MoE official added in the absence of a curriculum, '*everyone does what he wants. There is an institutional and academic chaos, but this is also because of the many societal conflicts*' (76). For many teachers, this situation of 'chaos', 'impasse' or 'crisis' has simply meant continuing with the last policy with which they were familiar – either that of 1994 or an earlier reform under which they were trained as a teacher. This justifiably frustrates many teachers, as they are in a state of limbo, unsure of what the future reform will bring and how to approach changing their curriculum.

Yet, some of the teachers in favour of ASEP are already starting to act on the new ideas in their classrooms. An urban teacher trainer for instance argued: '*I completely agree with the new law. It is true it has to be made more profound, and though there is resistance from others [other teacher trainers], I already work with these ideas*' (9:59). Moreover, one of the rural teacher training institutes that favours ASEP, for a while organised weekly meetings with its trainers to discuss strategies to implement the ideas brought forward in the policy plans (see chapter 7). Because of the above mentioned impasse, however, this is not the general trend. And while these exceptions do paint a somewhat more positive picture of what the future could bring with regard to implementation of the law, it is questionable whether these 'early' interpretations by educators, without having any training, clear (conceptual and practical) guidelines or educational material provided, will indeed contribute to the envisioned policy outcomes. Thus, for most of the teachers the simple lack of knowledge about the new reform is a pressing issue related to their opposition. As the concepts in ASEP are very theoretical, a strong understanding of it requires some kind of engagement with the subject matter. While teachers are generally aware of the new discourse, there is no clarity about the meaning of the concepts embedded in the reform. The definitions of ASEP's pillars remain vague, especially in regard to the classroom.

There is a lack of communication between the MoE and schools, allowing teachers to take issue with the law for the simple reason that it has not been clarified to them. Moreover, as the reform's opposition is quite passionate, it brings its reasoning to the teachers, as was exemplified for the case of the La Paz teachers' federation above. Therefore, some teachers have access only to oppositional sources of information and know very little about the full process or contrasting points of view. In conversations with La Paz teachers, this stark opposition to reform resulted in their participation in protests. However, once informed about the content of the law, one teacher explained her regret of attending the protests. While part of her opposition was resolved, in that she is now aware of the contents of ASEP, her experience emphasises what many teachers have gone through. Various other teachers reject the law for that same reason.

Another issue in debate is around the question whether ASEP fosters unity (as it is intended) or creates stronger social divisions. The ASEP law, in its (discursive) approach, aims to overcome any form of discrimination, considering the current goal of *vivir bien para todos* (to live well for everyone) without discrimination (Article 1 of the ASEP law, MoE, 2010b). According to the first Minister of Education under Morales, the new law aims to overcome the historical division between rural and urban education, by unifying, for example, all teacher unions and teacher training institutes rather than maintaining the urban-rural divide that has existed throughout Bolivia's educational history. A MoE official added to this, how *'the new law aims for a unifying education, yet with its particularities at the local, regional and departmental levels. This means that we should combine unity with diversity in our vision of maintaining the integration of the country'* (44:2). On the other hand, an urban teacher trainer expressed criticism that is shared by a group of other resisting actors, on how he thought the new law, instead of unifying the Andean and lowland region and rural and urban areas, actually reinforces regional divides. *'The law is very biased, because it carries the name Avelino Sinani, and he was an indigenous man who lived there [in the highlands]. So teachers from the east of Bolivia do not accept this. It is not a Bolivian law, but a law for the Andean world. But who supports it? The rural teacher, because they have been the principal actors in the creation of this reform.'* (10:5). These types of reactions that interpret some form of positive discrimination from the new law are both understandable and expected, and perhaps reflect the tensions between universalistic and particularist interpretations of whose approach is valid (Wallerstein, 2000), with the current government claiming validity of the decolonisation project based on historical structures of discrimination and exclusion for centuries in a row.

In line with the critique of the potential to create wider divisions, is a fear of a reverse form of discrimination. As with any type of essentialism – or simplification of the cultural and ethnic complexity – the current approach carries the danger of 'idealised indigenous-ness' and the demonisation of everything non-indigenous. Moreover, the strategic use and emphasis on Andean culture implies another serious danger, of what Postero calls *andinocentrismo*, or Andean-centrism (2007: 21). Instead of the historically marginalised position of indigenous groups, in turn some now fear exclusion and discrimination for those groups that do not necessarily feel part of the decolonising, communitarian and productive education plans: urban middle class citizens, people that do not identify as indigenous and people from outside the Andean region. The media play a critical role in criticising the new law as an *'ethno-centric and racist intent of the indigenous movements to impose ideologias indianistas [Indian ideologies] in the cities'* (Gamboa Rocabado, 2009:57). According to the opposition of the new ASEP law, it is too focused on rural areas. Communitarian education, in their view, is less relevant to the individualised environment of the cities. What follows is the question of whether this ASEP law is then as inclusive in its application as it – at least discursively – aims to be. Still, there is an urgent need to overcome the deep historical structures of discrimination against indigenous peoples in Bolivia. An indigenous movement presents his side of the story – or, his side of the tortilla: *'Evo, our president, uses a discourse saying that the moral base of Bolivia now lies with the indigenous groups, because we want to eradicate corruption, and all those bad things that have damaged us. You see, now the tortilla is turning upside down. Before, we were considered stupid, ignorant illiterates, but now, we are the strength of Bolivia'* (14:6).

Finally, one of the biggest challenges is the successful transformation of teacher education as part of the reform project. The Normales are widely perceived to be crucial for successful implementation of any reform, not excluding ASEP. However, the teacher training institutes are not easy to change, as I will discuss in the following chapters 6 and 7.

5.8 Concluding considerations: a bumpy road to decolonisation

Since 2006, the field of Bolivian education, and teacher education more specifically, is subject to various processes of (envisaged) transformation, as mentioned at the start of the chapter: firstly a radical, ideological and epistemological reorientation of Bolivian education under the header of 'decolonisation'; secondly, the continuous attempts to improve the quality and relevancy of education for all; and thirdly, a context of continuously shifting power relations and struggles between the government and other education actors, most importantly the teachers (urban) union. While ASEP's 'program mechanism' (Pawson 2002: 341-342) – being the various supportive and resistant interpretations of the ASEP law by a range of Bolivian actors in the education field – both works for and against Morales politics of change, the actual 'ASEP Programme' itself (Pawson, 2002: 342), is also significant as it defines a new and influential ideological discourse of decolonisation and *vivir bien*. In this sense, a new hegemonic government discourse is taking shape, while at the same time it is being interpreted, mediated and defied by those that have to move these ideals into an educational reality. The Bolivian (teacher) education sector has entered a process of *recontextualisation* (Fairclough, 2005: 931-932), as different strategies are developed by various actors and at different scales to enforce or resist the new discourse and related ASEP policy initiatives. Considering the amount of resistance to the ASEP law, it is unfair and perhaps too early to speak about a new hegemonic discourse of decolonising education. Nevertheless, the MoE and other proponents of the law are developing strategies to disseminate and implement parts of this new law. In terms of the *operationalisation* of these new discourses (Fairclough, 2005: 931-932), the indigenous discourse together with the decolonisation discourse has materialised in written policy texts of the National Development Plan, the new Plurinational constitution and the ASEP Reform.

ASEP engages new approaches to teaching and learning, as is exemplified by Saavedra's quote at the start of the chapter about education as something that should deal with 'the totality as human beings'. The main objectives of educational decolonisation in Bolivia are the opening up of different knowledges toward cultural/linguistic diversity and the creation of a critical awareness to function as an instrument of liberation of marginalised groups (Gamboa Rocabado, 2009). To some extent designed in cooperation with social movement actors, intellectuals and progressive political leaders, the reform agenda envisages to go against 'Western', 'European' or neoliberal ideas that, until present, dominate many education systems worldwide. The envisaged result is a transformative restructuring or deconstruction (Fraser, 1995) of the education system, together with the revaluation of 'original' or indigenous knowledges (Walsh, 2007a; 2007b) and values through education; an approach that shows similarities to the ideas of Freire when he was involved in decolonising the education system of Guinea-Bissau (1977).

The Normales come out as a complex arena – or strategic selective context – where different power relations are played out. This chapter has shown a mainly centralised system of teacher education with the MoE that primarily finances, guides and (only to some extent) controls the Normales. The interviews and actor maps reveal a central role for the power struggle between the MoE and the teachers unions, especially the urban federation of La Paz, placing the Normales at the frontline of socio-political struggles. The power of the MoE in the Normales is being limited, negotiated and mediated by the supportive or resistant influence of unions and social movements such as the CEPOs. At the same time, the relative power of the unions is also being 'attacked' through the processes of institutionalisation, which aim to strengthen the transparency in Normales. In summary, the Normales are important institutes in the wider education sector and many actors have a stake in what is taking place inside them.

Bolivia's recent decolonial approach is both unprecedented and contested. Perhaps not unexpectedly, considering the radical nature of the new ASEP reform, there is considerable resistance – from teachers, the urban teachers' union, from parents, from within the MoE, from the church, and the old elite including political leaders of the low lands and middle class citizens in urban areas. From a Neo-Gramscian perspective, while the MAS adopted a 'war of position' and a 'war of manoeuvre' itself in gaining state power in 2005, through social reforms such as ASEP, the current Bolivian government is currently aiming to create a counter-hegemonic 'culture of power'. However, in doing so, it seems to be caught up in again in a new 'war of manoeuvre', now defending its new decolonial position against the opposition to this 'revolutionary reform'.

It appears that the education sector in Bolivia is not only in an impasse, the system is also trapped in a prolonged crisis. A former teacher trainer and curriculum developer explained this as follows: *'when things are in crisis, you have to turn it around. It is like having fever: either you get well or you die. I do not think we [the education system] are dying, we are going to try to cure ourselves, but more open discussions will be inevitable'* (8:33). The chapter showed how the tense political situation and long process towards consensus on the specifics and practicalities of the new education reform results in a 'sense of waiting' for new policy directives to come, at a time when social tensions are rising. Moreover, there are concerns around the feasibility of the creation and implementation of the new inter-/intracultural and plurilingual curriculum. This impasse also relates to the growth of opposition due to a lack of communication and information sharing between the MoE and other educational actors, feeding into feelings of insecurity and resistance, particularly on the side of teachers who find themselves in a vacuum. While some teachers continue to work with the 'old' reform guidelines and curricula, others relapse into the traditional teaching practices adopted prior to 1990s. Moreover, many parents still see indigenous languages and cultural references in schools as unwanted aspects of the new governing approach, as they argue that their children need to learn the dominant language (Spanish) in order to reach upward social mobility. According to the government, ASEP has been designed with complete participation of civil society, but many actors – including many teachers – disagree. In addition, debates are ongoing as to whether the new law will foster unity or create deeper divisions in Bolivian society. Linked to this issue is the potential risk of a reverse form of discrimination and exclusion of non-indigenous societal groups.

For reasons like these, it is important to question whether ASEP is an imposition into the lives of the Bolivian population, and subsequently whether decolonisation can be considered legitimate as a new 'imposition', as it is perceived by some actors. Important for this study, is the recognition that the present decolonisation politics of Evo Morales do not necessarily reflect the lived experiences of more and more urban lower class and middle class indigenous groups, whose identities are very hybrid and complex (Albó in Kohl, 2010: 11). This wide range of tensions and critiques are triggered by the fundamental contradiction of a state led 'imposition' of Bolivia's decolonising and endogenous path to development, which is perhaps not perceived as legitimate or appropriate by the entire population. Or, as formulated by Postero (2007: 20), it might be a misleading utopia to portray the indigenous people, and Morales' project for decolonisation as the new answer to neoliberalism and global capitalism. Nevertheless, Postero argues, the idealist utopian visions based on Andean culture employed by Morales' government effectively negotiate spaces for socio-political transformation, as they derive from traditional (indigenous) narratives to create a widely accepted perception of appropriate and possible forms of social change. However, and as shown in this chapter, this effective strategic essentialist strategy carries the danger of reverse discrimination and Andean-centrism (Postero, 2007: 1) or rural-centrism. The opening up of these spaces or niches for change in the context of the Normales is further taken up in the following two chapters.

In conclusion, the road to Bolivia's 'imagined' decolonised education system *and* society is long and particularly bumpy, given the radical and transformatory nature of ASEP, the multiple interpretations and multiple interests involved in (any) education system, including an opposition from those that may support Morales' wider political project, yet are wary about a potential negative impact of the new education route on either their children's upward social mobility, or their own already overburdened tasks and routine matters in the classroom. Once again, Bolivian teachers are faced with a new reform framework. Yet, it remains to be seen how far teachers are able and willing to really function as 'soldiers of liberation and decolonisation' in a highly sensitive context of both old and newer socio-political divisions and tensions.

Bolivian Normales as a socio-political battle field – institutional opportunities and obstacles to transformation

The transformation of Bolivian education has to start with changing the Normales'
Ministry departmental director of Teacher Education (101:7), May 2010

6.1 Introduction

Photo 7. Protesting youngsters and parents in front of the MoE, La Paz

After a morning of meetings in the teacher education department and the financial department of the Ministry of Education (MoE) in May 2010, I walk down the stairs as I see a group of protesters in front of the gate (Photo 7). *'The police have arrived to make sure they do not enter the building'*, a staff member assures me, as he sees me taking this picture, *'for weeks in a row these applicants for the Normal are coming here to protest. They were not accepted, and now they even take their mothers to help them shout. But they do not understand we do not need everyone to become a teacher, we will have too many!'* I leave the MoE and convince the guards to let me through the gate. Suddenly, the group starts to move slowly towards a close-by square. As I am interested to hear about the reasons and opinions of these applicants and their mothers to keep on protesting, I decide to follow the crowd. While walking, one of the mothers explains *'these young people got very high marks for their entrance exams, senorita, they are struggling now for three months already'*. Dynamite explodes; we have to stop as we cannot hear each other for a few seconds. A young man continues, *'we are with 430 postulantes (applicants) here, who should have been accepted and allowed a position in the Normales. And it is the same situation at the national level. These demonstrations continue as well in Oruro, in Cochabamba, in Santa Cruz, all over the country'*. The crowd gathers in the square where a young woman starts to address the crowd: *'How long do we have to continue this struggle? When are they going to take us seriously? We were standing in front, and they have punched us in the stomach, and many of you did not come to help us. If you come here, you have to fight! We will stay the whole year if we need to!'* [123]

Since education is perceived as one of the few options to escape a life of economic insecurity, entering one of the Normales becomes the main driving force behind peoples' strategies of demonstration, protest and hunger strikes. Many of these young protestors are simultaneously in favour of Morales' political project, while they also fiercely protest against the measures taken in the education sector, in this case the limited spaces that are opened up in the teacher training institutes. This dual position is illustrative for the positions of many of Bolivia's educators, who face a very complex political situation in which various stakeholders play powerful roles. This tense socio-political state of affairs and political power plays are also reflected in Bolivia's Normales, constituting a socio-political 'battle field' where political affiliations, union strategies and historically embedded institutional cultures all influence the way new generations of teachers are trained, and the way policy initiatives are mediated and adopted.

Changing Bolivia's teacher training institutes as a first step in transforming and decolonising the education system is by no means an easy undertaking. While research on Bolivian (teacher) education tended to focus on the exclusionary nature of many Normales in terms of linguistic and cultural issues (see for instance Speiser, 2000: 228-229), this chapter tries to take this discussion a step further, by portraying both a detailed list of institutional challenges, yet also a changing political and societal context and possible niches for change at the level of the Normales. This chapter specifically aims to set out the contemporary issues of the institutional governance of teacher education in Bolivia, showing how the Normales constitute a tense socio-political battle field. Building on the historical overview presented in chapter 4, this chapter takes up the more recent and continuing issues and debates on Bolivia's Normales. First, I briefly highlight the picture of 'bad governance' of the Normales that is apparent in the few studies that have been conducted so far. I continue by exploring the micro-scale mechanisms of the institutional cultures of the two case studies. Following up on the demonstration at the beginning of this chapter, I continue to explain the reasons for the continuing struggles to enter the Normales. The following part reveals continuing institutional and beyond-institutional obstacles and opportunities to the transformation of these institutes, as part of Bolivia's wider politics of change. Consequently, the chapter pays specific attention to the most important, yet contested, attempts for change in Bolivian Normales from 2000 onwards, including the struggles around universities' administration of several Normales from 2000-2005, and the recent process of *'institucionalización'*, which has been initiated to reorganise the Normales and its staff. The chapter continues to discuss the potential niches for transformation of the ASEP reform. Finally, I use the case of the PDI (*Practica Docente e Investigación* – the internship and research practice) course to analyse in more detail the obstacles and potentials of a discursively, seemingly promising Social Justice Teacher Education (SJTE) device. As argued in the former chapter, on a discursive level many parts of the ASEP reform envision a unified, decolonised, high quality teacher education system that closely links to the international debates on SJTE. Yet, with this chapter I aim to illustrate how there is still a long way to travel to change the continuing old habits of the Normales and to put these new ideals of change into practice.

---

[123] Audio and video recordings, 4 May 2010.

The fragments below from my fieldwork notes (Box 5) illustrate how amidst a context of continuous institutional challenges, including insufficient buildings and materials, isolation from its surrounding community, forms of corruption, discrimination, traditional teaching styles and generally a rather conservative outlook – which are all discussed below – there are also initiatives that inspire change in the institutional context of the urban Normal, as is exemplified by Ramiro's and his new classmates' experiences in the newly started Aymara course.

Textbox 5. Aptapi in Ramiro's Aymara course

During the first week of my third visit to Bolivia I started to arrange several feedback discussions with students and trainers. In response, I received a text on my cell phone: *'Hola Mieke! Come to our Aymara course this Wednesday. Our 'profe' invites you to a discussion. And me and my 'compañeros' want to welcome you back with an Aptapi. You will let me know? Ramiro'.* We agreed that I would come the following Wednesday for the discussion and I curiously accepted the invitation to the 'Aptapi', a traditional indigenous communal meal.

During the first hour of the Aymara course I observed how the trainer made efforts to engage the students in active forms of participation. Still, he told me during the class, it is hard to have everyone engage at the same level, as some students had a more passive knowledge of the Aymara language than others, and they had to practice their pronunciation to become more confident in the discussion. In order to do so, the trainer demonstrated an Ayamara word, wrote it down on the blackboard and students, all seated in a big circle, would repeat the pronunciation one after the other. I was the last person in the row and with great anticipation the students awaited my turn, which received a good laugh. Ramiro seemed a different person in his new class. Compared to his rather shy attitude in the English classes I had seen him in so far, he had now developed into the class representative and one of the most well spoken Aymara students: *'Aymara is my language, and I am proud of it'.* During the second part of the class the trainer gave me the floor and excused himself, as he was very busy and would take advantage of me taking over the students so he could catch up with other work. During the feedback discussion, Ramiro and his classmates, as well as responding to some of the outcomes of my study, also reflected on the difference between their class and other courses in the Normal: *'We have a very special group, because we have all very consciously chosen to become Aymara teachers. We organise things together, like these Aptapi's, we do them more often. Also, we decorated our classroom, with 'Do not discriminate, we are all the same'* (see Photo 8).

When the sun started to set and the cold Andes wind entered through the thin classroom windows, one student put on some music and others started to unpack their contributions to the Aptapi (see Photo 10). In the middle of the classroom floor, a colourful carpet was filled with different types of yellow, white, pink and black dried potatoes, corn, dried fish from the Titicaca Lake, white cheese and boiled eggs. While we ate, the music varied from Bolivian folk songs to Hip Hop, reflecting the diverse cultural influences these future teachers identify with. However, it was only when *Los Kjarkas* started to play, that the students got up to dance the Bolivian *Tinku* dance.

Afterwards, Ramiro drove some of his colleagues and I back to the centre of the city in his taxi and, while managing the busy traffic effortlessly, he mentioned *'I am really happy I am now with my new colleagues in the Aymara course. It is still not easy, and we still feel isolated within the Normal. Most of our trainers, not the one of today, but many of them they do not even speak Aymara fluently. They do not give us the best trainers. And there is no culture of speaking Aymara in the Normal, so we also continue in Spanish most of the time. So it's hard, but at least we try'.*

Photo 8. Aymara course in Simón Bolívar   *Photo 9. Students preparing the Aptapi*

6.2 The story so far: bad governance in Normales

In general, and regardless of the huge numbers of candidates waiting to enter, Normales have quite a negative status in Bolivian society (e.g. 56:16) and literature. Interestingly, many of the observed and discussed problems in Normales nowadays are quite similar to the problems already mentioned by the Belgian Rouma, who founded the first Normal in Sucre at the beginning of the twentieth century, including: *'the scarce preparation of the postulantes, a lack of capacity of teacher trainers and a lack of teaching materials'* (Rouma 1931 in Del Granado Cosio, 2006: 5). Nowadays, the list of 'problems' is much longer. In this section I first discuss how these problems are portrayed in studies on Bolivia's teacher education institutes conducted so far.

A study of the quality of teacher education in 1999 showed a rather negative picture. There were cases of rural institutes where only 3% of the students performed 'satisfactory'. The Simón Bolívar came out best, but still with alarming results: the 'best performing' institute according to that report only had 28% of the students performing 'satisfactory' (Medicion de la Calidad 1999 in Lozada Pereira, 2004: 166). With regards to the urban institute Simón Bolívar, the MoE in that same year reported about a lack of maintenance of the buildings and sanitation, a gap between administrative and curricular developments, a lack of participation of students and trainers in institutional policy making or curriculum development, and a general lack of trust in the institute (Ministerio de Educación de Bolivia, 1999: 15-18, 21-22). A lack of institutional efficiency, time wasted by administrative staff because of lengthy reporting procedures and inadequate infrastructure of the Normales were also reported in 2002, in an external evaluation report of the Normales under the administration of Universities (Concha et al, 2002: 22, 27).

The 2004 UNESCO Report on Bolivian teacher education discussed the 'institutional weakness' of the Normales, which *'consists of a vertical and centralised administrative system, the continuation of traditional teaching practices, the lack of monitoring and the impossibility to access information on own resources. Besides, there is no regulated system of information processing, the system of acceptance of new students is not unified and not all trainers indeed have a Masters degree'* (Lozada Pereira, 2004: 122). Besides, as demonstrated by Lozada Pereira, the capacity to manage the institutes well was often very low. He reports on arbitrary decisions made on time tables and appointments of new (sometimes incompetent) staff. 'Efficiency', 'quality' and innovation are not core concerns in the institutes as per this author. He continues by describing a situation that could be called institutional bad governance: '*the administrative processes are bureaucratic, heavy, vulnerable to corruption and old-fashioned. [...] The conflicts in the country, particularly in the cities, result on the one hand in indifference and on the other hand a strong resistance [in the Normales]. As a result, traditionally the necessity of a rational and engaged organisation or the feeling of being part of a wider [national education] project have been ignored [...resulting in] strikes, demonstrations and mobilisations*' (Lozada Pereira, 2004: 147).

More recently, a MoE staff member responsible for the teacher education sector wrote how '*Pre-service teacher education is a concern of everyone, considering its impact on society. Despite this societal importance it is not transforming fast enough because of many and complex variables involved. [This includes] for example changes in public education policies of succeeding governments; the difficulty of in-service teachers to change their 'habitus' acquired in their profession into more innovative pedagogical processes; the economic costs; and the lack of synchrony between the urgency of political pressure to obtain short term results and the time needed to implement scientific and technological knowledge. Generally speaking, transformation is a long and arduous process*' (Del Granado, 2011). This last statement, that institutional and educational change takes time is more widely acknowledged in the literature, and is reflected for the case of Bolivian Normales in the overview of institutional obstacles to change discussed below.

6.3 Picturing the institutional culture in two Normales – hierarchical relations

Let me continue by elaborating on the '*micro-scale every day complexities of power relations*' (North, 2006: 524) in the two Normales this research focuses on. The 'institutional culture' of the Normales is defined by the Bolivian MoE (1999) as the '*shared values, beliefs and principles that guide the institution and define the conduct expected from its members, and is expressed in the institutional structure, management and functioning*'. The same 1999 MoE report, that evaluated the urban Normal Simón Bolívar, described a lack of participation of trainers and students in the formulation of the institute's main vision and mission, and in decision making processes. It reports a 'traditional, vertical' management style. The report also demonstrated a general lack of trust within the Normal, while personal interests played a role at the management level (Ministerio de Educación de Bolivia, 1999: 15). The report concludes by stating that Simón Bolívar '*continues to maintain itself in isolation with its internal problems*', and in isolation from its surrounding environment or other actors that could (or should) be involved in teacher education. A continuation of this vertical and non-democratic leadership style, and the institutional problems of mistrust and isolation, were confirmed by teacher trainers and (former) students (e.g. 8:34; 104:2; 108:7). Over the past four years I observed a relatively strong hierarchical system in both the urban and rural Normales, where relations between staff and students can be characterised as rather formal and vertical. However, I did notice some differences between the two institutes.

While people in the urban case come and go to the institute only during working hours, a large group of students and staff live at the rural Normal, at least during the working week. This campus life creates a closer sense of community. However, this is *only* a common feeling for those that live here. Both students and trainers that live elsewhere are excluded from the central eating room (*comedor*) and have to buy their food in local owned shops on the property. The architecture of the rural institute is more open than the urban one and stimulates more contact between students and staff. The rural institute does not have a fence that separates it from the surrounding farm houses. Neighbouring donkeys and sheep happily graze on the Normal's premises, adding interesting effects to some of my recorded conversations which were normally held outside. Not everyone is happy to have to share the school premises with neighbours and their cattle, as one student mentioned *'the village people use these grounds as if it is a public road, so we should have a wall here'* (30:25). There is one central and single floor building in which all administrative staff are placed. The director's door is only one step removed from the central sports ground in the middle of the premises. Interview data revealed there is indeed more direct communication between staff and students, but this did not mean students felt they were 'heard'. Many students complained about the state and crowdedness of dormitories, a lack of sanitary facilities and very little internet or computer facilities at the campus. Although I spent less time there, it was easier to get an understanding of *who is who* and *what is what* in the rural Normal, because of its size, open architecture and for the reason of the cooperative attitude of the directors at that time (August/September 2008).

The urban Normal, in contrast, is a massive concrete construction that is surrounded by a fence, which separates the premises from the street and the urban neighbourhood. To get in, you have to pass the main gate and the guards' house. Particularly during the period of new inscriptions, it is hard to get in without knowing the guards or having the right papers. Thus, the Normal is only accessible for a select group 'who belong there'. In terms of the architecture of the main building, the higher in the hierarchy the staff is positioned, the higher up they are located in the building. Thus, in order to see the general director one has to climb three flights of stairs and pass through the secretary's office – usually several times before an actual meeting is settled. It takes either a very serious issue or 'good connections' for students to get to speak to the director (103). In a feedback discussion with a class of urban teacher students, one student mentioned how he misses a form of *'civismo'* (a sense of civic responsibility): *'when we walk in the corridors often teacher trainers do not greet us. And then, when you greet them, they sometimes do not respond. This attitude, this energy is poisoning us'* (110: 6). This quote reflects the strong hierarchical relations in the Normal. The majority of students at the urban institute that live in El Alto have to travel for an hour or more in order to reach the Normal in time for the first class (starting at 7.30am). This often means having no breakfast, and students complained of too long and continuous planned classes which give them no time for a proper break to get something to eat (18:30; 19:40).

Perhaps because of this difference in scale, the urban institute seemed to have more troubles with organising the entrance bureaucracies of new students and making new timetables in time for the start of the new semester. In September 2008, students in the rural institute started their regular schedule three weeks earlier compared to the urban case (which by chance gave me the possibility to observe the final presentations of PDI by six-graders in both institutes). Students in the urban Normal complained of the classes they had missed. Coming to the institute and finding out there are no classes, is unfortunately not an exception in the weeks at the beginning and end of each term. This situation does not deter huge numbers of youngsters to enforce their way into the institutes.

6.4 The struggle to get in: rising numbers of applicants

'*Mister Minister, we are students [that] passed [the exam], we want justice!*', a banner says that is held by a group of protesting youngsters in La Paz (Photo 10, La Prensa, 18-03-2010a). The young man in the middle of the picture holds a sleeping-bag, as they are preparing a hunger strike in the residence of the retired teachers' organisation. According to the newspaper, another group of protesters in the week before sewed their lips together as a radical way of protest against not being accepted into the Normales. The number of applicants for the Normales is increasing fast. In 2007, a MoE official told that in 2005, about 17,000 people applied for Simón Bolívar, while there were only 500 positions available (76). In the beginning of March 2010, 56,000 people took the entrance exam, with only 7,500 available posts at the Normales. Through a series of demonstrations and protests students have demanded that everyone who scores 51% or higher should be admitted to a Normal. After a few days, the Minister of Education declared that there will be 1,500 more posts available, totalling 9,000, and that this was the absolute maximum. He also warned that the classrooms of the institutes might become overcrowded (La Prensa, 16-03-2010; La Prensa, 18-03-2010a). In 2011, the situation is growing even more tense, as the MoE brings out alarming figures, of around 20,000 unemployed graduates currently, with 7,000 *normalistas* graduating this year and 24,000 students currently enrolled. Bolivia will be confronted with huge unemployment rates among these new teachers. Still, this situation does not stop young people from taking part in the entrance exam over and over again, and when their scores are high enough but they do net get accepted, with a sense of desperation they take serious measures to enforce their 'right' to teacher education by crucifying themselves, or sewing together their lips (La Razón, 31-03-2011).

Photo 10. Protesting prospective students preparing a hunger strike

An important institutional change – initiated during the former reform and further carried out currently – is made with regard to the entrance regulations to the Normales. First of all, institutes are not allowed to take in students to their full capacity, but according to the demands for new teachers in that region, they ought to limit the number of spaces available for student teachers. Bolivia again makes an exception to the global rule here, since in most places teacher training institutes have to struggle to attract enough interested students. Secondly, Bolivian prospective students have to pass a (national level) entrance exam, as well as a personal interview at the respective institute in order to be accepted as a *'postulante'* (or 'teacher student candidate').[124]

The entrance exam is criticised by various trainers for not ensuring a better qualified, let alone vocationally motivated, teacher, since it is still based on memorising facts (e.g. 47:10). The names of those who scored high enough in the exams appear on a list that is published in the newspapers and disseminated at Normales a few weeks after the exam. Those with the highest scores are invited to an interview in the respective Normal. These interviews are designed not only to test students' skills, but particularly their motivation and vocation for becoming a teacher. Based on my observations of one afternoon of intake interviews for future English teacher students in the urban Normal, I concluded that the interview questions were both limited in time (sometimes an interview took less than five minutes), and limited in terms of the scope of the questions asked. Based on the interview guide of the institute, a wide range of issues had to be addressed during the interview, including: the *postulantes'* motivation to become a teacher; the reason for wanting to enter this particular Normal/specialisation/education level; knowledge of the education system and reforms; knowledge of the socio-cultural context; the home situation;a capacity to critically analyse and make decisions also under pressure; emotional balance; tolerance and intercultural skills, among others (Instituto Normal Superior Simón Bolívar, 2008). Although this list is not even complete yet, the length of it already shows the over-ambitious aim of an interview that is indicated to take 'about ten minutes' per candidate. During the observed interviews, only a few of these issues were taken up. Besides, the attitude of the interviewers made the candidates feel uncomfortable, while the interview guide states the opposite should be the case. A male candidate told me how he was refused entry to the morning interviews because he was not wearing a suit and how he had to go to the other side of town to borrow one in order to be interviewed. In sum, the entrance interviews I observed were narrow in scope, time and in general a demotivating experience for future candidates.

Up to today, this extended process has not stopped overwhelming numbers of people taking the entrance exams, to the extent that in some places, like La Paz or Paracaya, only about 10% of all exam takers get allowance to enter the Normal (17:42, 22:5, 47:8, 62:8, 76:15, 98:8, 103:1). This had led to serious conflicts and pressures on the MoE as well as the Normales from the sides of the *postulantes* and their families. Despite the fact that numerous people make great efforts to enter the Normales, these institutes are also notorious for a continuing lack of quality of the training they offer, a statement which is mostly confirmed by the data presented in the following section.

6.5 Continuity: an overview of current institutional problems

In this section I present a detailed overview of the main contemporary problems at the two institutes included in this study, based on respondents' perceptions and my own observations and analysis. To some extent, these correspond to the difficulties already observed by the reports of the MoE (1999), Lozada Pereira (2004) and Del Granado (2011), but my analysis also adds novel insights and issues. I discuss the following issues successively: insufficient institutional

---

[124] Students carry this name from when they take part in the entrance exams until they have completed the first semester of *nivelación*.

infrastructure; the Normales as islands; exclusivity of the profession; corruption; discrimination; traditional teaching styles and an attitude of apathy in the Normales.

Insufficient institutional infrastructure

One of the most often mentioned problems of the Normales, by both staff and students, are the inadequate facilities in both institutes. This includes a lack of maintenance and renovation of the existing buildings, too few adequate classrooms, no climate control inside the classrooms (*very* cold in the highlands in winter and *very* warm in lower regions in summer). A student in the urban Normal alleged that *'the majority of students are thinking more about the cold than paying attention to the class'* (18:25). Sanitation facilities are scarce both in the urban and rural institute (including the boarding school), sometimes not well kept, and in the case of the urban institute privately run, which means students have to pay to use the bathroom. However, students said the bathrooms have become a bit cleaner since this regulation. In some Normales there are day-care nurseries for the children of students. Nonetheless, spaces are limited and several students complained of the quality of the service, which made them decide to place their children elsewhere (in other nurseries or with family when possible). The rural Normal did not have such a service at the time of fieldwork and some students were forced to take their babies into classes. Students also complained about insufficient sporting/play ground facilities, as well as low equipped libraries. The student-trainer ratio fluctuates in both institutes, roughly between 10-35 students per trainer depending on the course.

According to Lozada Pereira (2004: 178) rural Normales need most attention and investment of the state. In the current context and based on the results of this research, I disagree on his point. I think all Normales need a similar investment in order to improve both their facilities, as well as to successfully reform the institutional governance and teaching in accordance with the new law. Considering the engaged attitude of the rural institute, the external support that has focused its investments mostly on rural institutes, and the resistance in parts of the urban case described here it would perhaps seem more valid to invest considerably in support to urban cases. A former Normal director now working in the MoE supported this observation: *'We have certain Normales who have accepted the new policy lines, but there are also some urban institutes that are not as open'* (115:8).

Similar to Lozada Pereira's observations (2004: 177), there is still a general lack of facilities at most Normales, including the boarding school spaces and ICT facilities. Various Normales received small scale external (donor) support to improve their facilities, whilst the MoE similarly aims to invest in improving the infrastructure of several Normales (La Prensa, 16-03-2010). Still, students in most institutes I visited complained of poor libraries, poor classrooms and little or no ICT facilities (including access to internet, but also a lack of projectors and computers in classrooms for power point presentations or video screening). While the urban institute has around 55 new computers (103:17), students did not have access to them. The current Minister, as his predecessors, has promised and made some efforts to improve this situation, as a complete infrastructure is generally accepted as a requirement for good quality (teacher) education. However, according to the director of the teacher education department at the MoE, *'the mere fact that the state cannot provide the basic material to it's teacher students, like text books and libraries, is another form of social injustice because this prevents an equitable access of all people to knowledge'*

145

(44:5). The insufficient state of infrastructure of Bolivia's Normales thus remains a pressing issue, also for this current government.

Normales as islands

Close cooperation between teacher education institutes and the wider (school) community is a key aspect for good quality teacher education, as perceived both within the ASEP Reform as in the literature on SJTE (see chapter 2). While the new ASEP law is focused on a communitarian and cooperative (teacher) education system, the reality in most Normales is quite different. There is little or no constructive contact between the institutional life inside the Normales and community life outside of that, as was confirmed by various trainers and students in the Normales. Of course we should not generalise about *all* Normales here, with clear exceptions such as the Normal of Warisata that has taken efforts to connect to the surrounding environment historically and is still doing so – for instance through inviting representatives of the community in democratic committees for decision-making at the institutional level. Nevertheless, the two Normales under study were characterised, and criticised, by many respondents as being 'islands'.

In line with earlier studies, there is an evident disassociation between the Normales and their local and departmental environment (Lozada Pereira, 2004: 122-123; Del Granado Cosio, 2006: 47; Von Gleich, 2008: 99). According to a MoE evaluation of the transformation of Normales to INS from 1997-1999, the environment and community to which the institutes belong is the most important variable in the 'institutional life' of a Normal. Various institutions and groups belong to this 'environment', such as the local community and community organisations, schools and school networks (*nucleos*), pedagogical advisors (who were still working at the time), school directors, school boards and parent committees. The report showed that Simón Bolívar did not have an analysis or a strategy to live up to the demands and needs of the local environment. There was a lack of a clear approach for permanent cooperation outside of the institute. Trainers identified that this was due to a lack of support from the MoE and students argued the curriculum did not engage enough with the local environment (Ministerio de Educación de Bolivia, 1999). A similar situation is still continuing today.

As a solution to this state of affairs, an urban teacher trainer proposed to organise more public events such as fairs at the Normal, so that the community members could see what is going on inside the walls of the institute: *'we have to present ourselves to the outside world. The most important thing would be to show we are involved in educational research, and to show how we are training a new type of teacher that corresponds to a new societal model'* (10:31). During two group discussions, various students also commented on the public events that some universities organise, for instance about the AH1N1 flu epidemic or as a public closure of the academic year, and how this would also be good to have in the Normales in order to *'respond to the societal needs and the educating function of the Normal'* (110:1; 120:4). In line with these arguments, ex-Vice Minister of Education and academic Saavedra argued how *'the Normales need to open up to the rest of society, and therefore we could use the new information and communication technologies.*[125] Often, the only contact between Normales and schools is through the contacts made because of students' PDI course. These observations are still relevant for the situation today. The established contacts between schools and Normales in the

---

[125] These quotes are based on fieldwork notes and the 'Memorandum of the International Seminar', that can be retrieved from http://educationanddevelopment.files.wordpress.com/2009/02/memorandum-del-encuentro-internacional-sobre-descolonizacion-y-educacion.pdf.

context of the PDI course are limited. Again, the urban Normal is an institute that isolates most of its practices on its own 'concrete island'. The contact between the 27 teacher training institutes is limited as well, while every institute '*does as it wants*' (65:3). Contacts are mostly limited to formal meetings between the management staff (the three directors) during national level reunions.

Finally, a MoE official that has been involved closely in the design of the new law, argued how the Normales have a '*military institutional attitude with no links at all with their environment. They are islands, and on the basis of this situation we propose an institutional transformation to an intercultural institutional attitude*' (96:4). Here, it is useful to build on the insights of Talavera (2011), who argues that the Bolivian union culture of resistance had its roots in the period of military dictatorships of the 1970s. Considering the close ties between the Normales and unions, it is not unthinkable that the current conservative attitude of teacher trainers, as well as the enclosed structure of Normales as islands, is also rooted in this same period.

Exclusive or 'fixed' teaching professions

In my view linked to the problem of institutional isolation, is the issue of 'fencing off' both the training positions within Normales, as well as the wider teaching profession, exclusively to Normal graduates. Many Bolivian educators, and especially their unions, strongly defend the *Codigo* and *escalafón*, in which teachers' labour rights and the 'fixed profession' – the teaching profession only being open to *normalistas* – was written down. A MoE official and several trainers (6; 94; 95) claimed that in order to change, teachers need to let go of this fixed profession idea that protects teachers and secures them of a job-for-life. In this regard, Tatto (2007: 14) speaks of 'untouched monopolies' of teacher training institutes in various contexts, while Lozada Pereira (2004: 44-45) refers to a kind of 'endogamy' of the Bolivian teacher training institutes. Lozada Pereira supports the idea that the 'non-removability' of trainers is a negative aspect, and writes about an 'inbreeding' that in the end reduces the quality of the Normales. '*This way, even the academic competencies of the trainers in Normales have become politicised. They lost their focus on quality but rather hire people on the basis of political recommendations. [...] An institute that does not admit any innovation, that rejects everything that is new and foreign, and applauds itself for imitating the old ways, results in an internal degeneration*' (Lozada Pereira, 2004: 70-71, 90).

The *escalafon* is still strongly defended by the teacher unions and the new ASEP law acknowledges the main principles of the document. However, parents have strong complaints against the *escalafon* and the almost automatic promotion to higher scales for teachers, because they think teachers are not evaluated and stimulated to improve their teaching (Gamboa Rocabado, 2009: 60). In line with parents' arguments, Yapu states how '*the 'inamovilidad docente' [fixed teaching profession] is often a factor that obstructs [educational] quality, because low performing teachers cannot be suspended, or taken out*' (2009: 32).

Here is it helpful to look at a study on the case of Mexico, in which Tatto et al (2007b) analyse the horizontal salary promotion system which is called '*Carrera Magistral*'. This *carrera* – a system of in-service training and examination – was designed to overcome the criticism to automatic promotion on the basis of years of experience instead of professional quality, a critique that I have described in the case of Bolivia in terms of its *escalafon*. The study of Tatto el al (2007b: 157-161) discusses how on the positive side, the *carrera* increased Mexican teachers' chances to increase their salary, while teachers were better informed about (a still limited body of) pedagogical literature and became more knowledgeable then their colleagues who did not follow in-service trainings. On the negative side, however, the authors describe several difficulties, including a lack of adequate measurement mechanisms for the impact on students' learning attainments, a focus on knowledge rather than skills, an urban bias in the access and content of in-service trainings, a negative effect on diminished time for team work and joint efforts to improve the school level, and the fact that the exams are very time consuming, leaving too little time for teachers to accomplish their teaching tasks. Even though these and other difficulties also count for Bolivia's attempts to create a successful in-service training system (chapter 5), I support the view of some of the critical academics mentioned above whom, in line with the concerns of Bolivian parents, argue for the need to rethink Bolivia's *escalafon* system of automatic promotion, and more closely link promotion scales to training opportunities (in urban and rural areas) to in-service teachers, as well as a system of evaluation and guidance.

Corruption

Corruption, or 'political favours', is another institutional problem that was confirmed in former studies and continues today. Lozada Pereira, for example, affirmed the existence of '*old practices of corruption and political and union discretional attitudes*' in the Normales (2004: 168). Besides, Concha et al observed a huge divergence in salaries of different posts in the Normales, not based on the qualifications of staff members but more on 'discretionary estimates' (2002: 60). Another way of presenting the issue is to talk about a lack of trust at the institutional level (Ministerio de Educación de Bolivia, 1999).[126] Currently, critical voices both inside and outside the Normales still complain about ongoing 'friendship politics' (100:16), or the veto power of the unions to keep certain candidate trainers out of the system (107:6). During my fieldwork periods, examples of corruption and political favours were mentioned mostly with respect to the ways in which students and staff obtained a position in the institute. Examples were not just limited to trainers that '*stayed in not because they are capable, but because of their connections*' (16:60). Students also showed how some of their peers had entered for 'political reasons', as they checked the list of students who passed the entrance exams that was published in the newspaper El Diario, and two of their classmates had not appeared on that list. There are always some that enter through the back door, the student explained, '*for one of them, we realised his mother works in the administration*' (19:6).

'Politics' are also influencing the (mal-)functioning of the student federations, according to a teacher student at the urban Normal. '*The Trotskyite teachers created their own political student party, like [trainer x]. [Trainer x] approached some of us, and I got involved. But I just listened and observed, I did not have a say ['ni voz ni voto']. And the director, he was creating another student party. When this party gets elected, the director can expect to have no troubles with them*' (103:18). The idea that student federations have ties with the management staff was also shared by other students during a group discussion at the Normal in the city of Santa Cruz: '*When a student 'front' [party] who is supported by the management staff wins the elections, its obvious that the director tells them what to do, and they do not consult the base*' (123:1). Another student explained this resulted in a low number of students actually voting during elections, or giving in 'neutral' votes, since '*it does not matter who wins. Whoever wins the elections will forget about the rest of us soon. I do not feel represented at all*' (123:1).

---

[126] Chapter 1 illustrated how a lack of trust in official institutions can be considered part of the fourth dimension of conflict in Bolivian society.

The institutionalisation process is part of a political recognition (48:13) and solution to this situation of 'politicking' in the Normales. In the words of a senior and obviously frustrated trainer at the urban Normal: *'The new constitution states that education is the highest function of the state...but this has not been proven to be true. It is a demagogic slogan, because we continue in this country with no more than politicking, corruption, lies and accusations between the left and the right, but with no concern at all for our education system'* (47:15). When reflecting on these issues with an academic and educational expert in the final fieldwork period, this frustrated view was confirmed again: *'These issues of corruption have to be opened to a public debate at some point. The corruption of the management of positions is totally irrational, it's really dramatic. It has almost become legalised, this system of corruption. Because people are in need of work, they have to follow this example of corruption to get in'* (114:2). While I was unable to gather comprehensive data on the level of corruption in Normales, the opinions of respondents expressed here are still alarming and worth further study and debate.

Discrimination

Another sensitive but incredibly relevant issue that came out of the interviews and observations were various stories of discrimination and exclusion. The 'second dimension of conflict', as this was termed in chapter 3, is a lived reality in the Normales: *'The system of teacher education in Bolivia is vertical, very individualistic, very racist and we want to change this'* (95:16, indigenous movement leader). To some extent, some things are changing slowly in the Normales. Whereas I did not see any student or trainer dressed in traditional 'indigenous' clothing in any of the institutes I visited during the first fieldwork period (2007), some started to openly dress *'the way they would do at home as well'* (32) in the years that followed. Nevertheless, structures of discrimination, exclusion and the tendency to 'homogenise' (73) students are still present. A rural teacher trainer, for instance, expressed how *'there is discrimination for sure, although you might not see or hear it. There is discrimination based on people's surname, their social status'* (31:19). Another trainer reminded how *'the vice-president Victor Hugo Cardenas [during the presidency of Sanchez de Lozada] because of our history he abandoned his Aymara surname and adopted another surname, so he would not be discriminated in university and in wider society'* (107:13, also 117:4). This is, however, in contrast to the more recent story of Ramiro, who changed his surname back to the original indigenous version, because he was proud of it and felt he could openly express this.

Most stories of discrimination and exclusion, either in Normales or in schools, were related to what could be termed ethnic and class discrimination. Female teacher students also complained about discrimination on the basis of gender. It was for instance mentioned how: *'in the [urban] institute we are discriminated as female students, and we also have to deal with all domestic problems because our men do not care'* (16:35). Another student in the same group discussion added that when they enter a new school as a young teacher, *'they discriminate you for being a woman, they might abuse you, and when we want to introduce something like sexual health, the parents will not let us, they do not want us to change anything'* (16:71). This shows both a fear to be treated badly as a young female teacher in a new environment, as well as the expectation not to be able to bring about innovations in their future teaching.

Finally, the divided rural and urban school system sometimes triggers people to think and speak in terms of 'they and us', creating a ground for separation instead of unification, as the new law aims for. The mere fact that there are still two unions, with obvious differing points of view, contributes to this segregated system (68:14). Clearly, I cannot present a complete story about all forms and levels of discrimination in the Normales, as this would need further study. However, the issue was raised often enough to include it here as a serious challenge that should be overcome, particularly considering the current goal of *vivir bien para todos* (to live well for everyone), without discrimination (Article 1 of the ASEP law, Ministerio de Educación de Bolivia, 2010b).

Traditional teaching styles

Already since the 1994 Reform project, the traditional teaching styles that are still adopted in Normales is an issue of great concern (Lozada Pereira, 2004: 147; Concha et al, 2002: 42). *'Most trainers were trained themselves long ago, with a very old curriculum. The oldest ones even come from the nationalistic and revolutionary tradition of the MNR'* (8:28), explains a teacher trainer. The following quotes from teacher students provide some evidence of the continuation of this situation. In a group interview with three students, one of them commented: *'what we need here is that our trainers are trained and updated, they are very conservative in their teaching and they do not motivate us to learn, which in turn makes us passive'*. Another student continues: *'this trainer is knowledgeable, he knows many things, but he does not know how to get it across, he is very disorganised and has no good teaching methods'* (16:51). A colleague student in an interview added that *'most trainers just complete their class hours and that's all'* (18:20). One of her classmates mentioned how he *'subscribed to learn something about teaching here, but really I have lost a year learning hardly anything'* (19:85). Finally, one of the urban students reflected how *'we need more activities in class, the classes of trainer Y make us fall asleep'* (21:37). Indeed, during various observations of the classes of this trainer, I hardly observed any other teaching technique than questioning and answering (with often the same students replying), and copying material from the blackboard, a situation that in reality made some students fall asleep. One urban student came up with the term *'anti-pedagogical'* (103:18) that helps to summarise these negative views on traditional and ineffective teaching techniques that were shared among most of the student interviewees.

Besides students' critiques, a MoE official confessed that there is *'not enough attention for the training of trainers, whose practices are traditional and conductivist'* (76:10). These conductivist teaching techniques had their roots in the times of the Reforms of the military regimes (1968-197). The attitude of resistance to change these 'traditional' practices since the newer reforms of the 1990s and the current one, can therefore be explained by both ideological, political and economic motivations, but certainly also by the working habits that these older generations of educators were trained with themselves (Talavera Simoni, 2011: 187). A teacher trainer, who is also a university teacher, shared his critical point of view on the *'curricular structure of this institute, it is based on the logic that we have to teach them how to teach in one way, we do not see them as planners or facilitators of learning processes. There is too much focus on the theoretical content base, and not enough on teaching strategies. They should be able to apply two, three, four different strategies depending on the social context of students, and their level'* (50:14). Another trainer worried that *'teacher students see the example of very mediocre trainers, and they leave the Normal with this unmotivated stereotype and example in mind* (13:53). An important solution to overcome these traditional and negatively viewed teaching styles is to train and support the trainers. While efforts in this area already took place in the context of the Normales EIB of the 1994 Reform (see also Lozada Pereira, 2004: 140-141), and are planned for under the ASEP law as well, this is still an area of concern. One of the teacher trainers rightly argued that what is needed is a system of support and evaluation, as now *'everyone works the way they like, there is no coherence, there is no central evaluation system. As a result, our students have a lot of limitations* (13:37).We should, however, avoid a simplistic 'blaming the trainer' argumentation, as there are neither small (economic) incentives nor enough in-service support for the already overburdened trainers to innovate (115, 114).

Apathy and institutional inertia

Finally, in response to the question 'if you would be the director of a Normal, what would you change?', a MoE official replied promptly with *'at this moment there is nothing I could change, because of the union influence and politicking, so I would not have the authority to change anything. [a sigh] Like here, I actually also do not have much authority to change...'* (6:10). This response reflects a sense of apathy or a 'bad attitude' (5:50) among trainers who feel they have little space for manoeuvre to actually change what could be called a form of 'institutional inertia'. This passive and resistant attitude of a group of trainers is further instigated by a lack of communication and engagement of trainers in decision-making matters, due to a centralised (Lozada Pereira, 2004: 147), hierarchical (Concha et al, 2002: 59), top-down and vertical management style of the Normales, in which there is little contact between the management staff and trainers.

One of the directors of the urban institute confirmed that *'the older teachers have not immersed themselves in the new teacher training techniques, so there is a part of us that really does not want to change, they rather stay passive and repeat the past, they are reluctant to learn new didactical methods.'* He continued to argue how all institutes should *'have a permanent system of training. Currently we are organising a programme with Andres Bello. But we also need the willingness of trainers to get involved. Unfortunately, there is nothing we can do about those that are not interested, and we have realised we have this deficit in our personnel'* (17:18; 17:24). As mentioned above, a reason that was mentioned to explain the unwillingness of trainers to change was related to the lack of economic incentives to change: *'nobody wants to work more for free'* (104:5). Another reason brought forward was a lack of trust in the politics both at a national and institutional level: *'I do not trust any of the laws in this country to begin with, because, as you can see, the Normales have always remained as they were'* (10:3). An NGO worker, involved in the Normales EIB in the 1990s, verified this by saying *'there is little creativity, diversity, originality and innovation. Like I said before: they want the status quo, that nobody changes, so that they do not have to change themselves. I do not think everyone in the Normales thinks this way, but certainly among the institutions' management they do'* (73:7). The non-transformatory character of the Normales was explained in various interviews in relation to the influence and often resistant attitude of teachers' unions. Regardless of the changing power relations because of the institutionalisation processes, the unions seem to remain in a relatively powerful position when it comes to (holding back) transformation of the Normales. According to a rural trainer, the federations create a *'barrier'* to change in the Normales and in the schools, as *'it is not in their interest to change the education system'* (39:15). Following from this logic, an urban teacher student thinks that real change in the Normales has to start with changing the attitude of those trainers that are closely linked to the union: *'they organise their marches because they want a higher salary, they do not care about the quality of the education. Some trainers here are better at motivating us to become a 'sindicalista' (unionist), than to become a dedicated teacher'* (20:17). This quote illustrates a more general supported idea of a trade-off between 'unionised educators' (e.g. actively struggling for salarial issues) as opposed to vocationally motivated educators.

Hence, the argumentation that follows from these interviews is that a relatively large part of the trainers have adopted an attitude of inertia for different reasons, including a top-down management style, a lack of incentives, a lack of trust and the influence of unions. From this section, it seems we have to conclude that '*Normales do not contribute to the processes of change* (114:9). This would, however, be far too one-sided, as I also encountered various reform initiatives that aim(ed) to open up potential niches for change, to which I now turn.

6.6 Attempts for change: contested reform initiatives in Bolivian Normales (2000-present)

Over the past decade, two major reform initiatives have attempted to bring transformation to the Bolivian teacher education field. Within the socio-political 'battle field' of Bolivian teacher education, both the external administration by Universities and the institutionalisation process have been met with varying degrees of resistance or ethusiasm, as is now elaborated.

The struggle against university administration of Normales: 2000-2005

Between 2000 and 2005 the monopoly of a number of the Normales was challenged through the administration by both public and private Universities.[127] Linking teacher training institutes with Universities is part of a wider global move, with exceptions such as the United Kingdom and Mexico (Tatto, 2007: 161). In Bolivia, this was something new and these universities had no prior experience with administrating Normales (Contreras and Talavera, 2003: 23). The Ministry envisaged strengthening the quality of these institutes by letting public and private universities manage them. The idea behind the initiative was that diplomas obtained would get a higher prestige, and teacher students would be given the opportunity to continue a university career (Contreras and Talavera, 2003: 22-23), while at the same time more cooperation between the institutes would be stimulated. Because of severe conflicts with unions and teacher trainers alike, the MoE decided to enforce a 'contract by exception' of four years of this external form of administration (Del Granado Cosio, 2006: 78-79). A teacher trainer at Simon Bolívar[128] (86:1) and one in Sucre (97:6) assured me this project was pushed through because it was a condition of the World Bank, one of the main financers of the reform process in the 1990s. Interested universities were asked by the MoE to send in their proposals, and a committee that included experts from GTZ evaluated these proposals (interview 25:4). The MoE did, however, not put in enough effort to ensure the quality, rigour and relevancy of these proposals (Del Granado Cosio, 2006: 80).

It was decided that the Universidad Mayor de San Andrés (UMSA) was allowed to administer Simón Bolívar, '*not so much because of the presented proposal by the UMSA, but more so because of pressures from the trainers and students at Simón Bolívar that were afraid of being linked to a private university*' (Del Granado Cosio, 2006: 81). As explained by a senior teacher trainer: '*Not only teacher trainers but the whole teacher force fought against this. We could not avoid the administration by Universities, but at least we managed to push for a participation with a public university*' (86:1). He continued his story by telling how internal struggles sustained, particularly within Simón Bolívar: '*In 2005 the university administration entered into a profound crisis. There was an anti-teacher [anti-normalista] attitude in the*

---

127 While Nucinkis wrote how '*4 public and 5 private universities were contracted to work with 11 Normales, 4 of them EIB, leaving 7 Normales under control of the Ministry*' (2004: 19), Del Granado (2006) mentioned only 10 institutes were administered by Universities.

128 Who is now working at the Ministry of Education, and was a former union leader as well.

university, leading to an anti-university attitude with teacher trainers'. Another teacher trainer (13) told how some school directors closed their doors for the internship students, because they thought students were only prepared theoretically, and they disturbed the teaching process too much because they did not know what to do when they entered a classroom.[129] There was also strong critique on the way the management staff were appointed, and particularly the fact that one of the Normal directors was an architect, *'who knew nothing about educational management'* (10:18, 49:30). An urban union leader concluded by saying that *'the administration of the UMSA was a disaster, nobody understood or cooperated with each other'* (49:7). Lozada Pereira (2004: 166) refered to a Ministry evaluation that showed not one university that administered a teacher training institute had managed to press for genuine transformative changes and to change the vertical and hierarchical character of the institutional governance.

Amidst these mostly negative experiences of a too academically oriented training, there were also positive recounts. According to a national level evaluation report of the respective Normales, *'the presence of Universities has generated an environment of professional development for trainers and the stimulation of educational research'* (Concha et al, 2002: 61). A former teacher student who studied during the University administration at the Simón Bolívar reflected on her studies in comparison to the way students now study at the Normal. In her view, the 'university teachers' brought different teaching styles and different *'personalities that would function as a model to us'* (100). In contrast, this ex-student perceives the current 'normalista-teachers' to *'put the same etiquette on all students, they will all leave the Normal exactly with the same attitude as their trainers and their peers'*. When I asked her about innovations during the University administration, compared to the Normales now, she made it clear there is little space left for innovation nowadays. She continued her argument by explaining that all students during the University administration had to conduct and present their action research oriented PIP (*Proyecto de Innovación Pedagogica* – Pedagogical Innovation Project) in their final semester, whereas now this is no longer obligatory (100:10, 100:11, see also chapter 7). An academic and staff member at Simón Bolívar during the period from 2000-2005 similarly presented a positive view: *'we are very proud of the publication of education research projects during the university administration...we also published numerous reports and an overview of the 5 years of administration'* (25). He continued to tell how the interaction between the University and the Normal became very tense because the urban teachers union thought differently and struggled against this external academic administration.

Thus, the university administration of several Normales between 2000 and 2005 became an increasing trigger for internal institutional tensions and battles. Eventually, in 2005, after a series of strong protests from teacher students and a group of (*normalista*) trainers (5:14, 49:34), the Simon Bolívar – and all other institutes – were placed under the authority of the MoE again. Three other contracts with Universities that administered Normales were already broken in 2003, after disappointing evaluations (Lozada Pereira, 2004: 111). In contrast to these widely supported separations, the class of the ex-student quoted above was fiercely against this closure of the University administration at the Simón Bolívar, since they thought the quality of their teaching was excellent. In order to let these 27 students finish their studies, a group of fired 'university-trainers' continued the last four weeks of classes on a clandestine basis in the university (100:14).

---

129 In contrast, Lozada Pereira (2004: 167) argued that school teachers were positive about the increased levels of the teacher students who completed their internships.

Thus, in retrospect, there are two rival camps in Bolivia on this issue; those that believe this was the best period for the Normales, and those that were opposed to this administration and in the end demonstrated until the Normales could go on by themselves again. The memories of this radical restructuring of the Simón Bolívar discussed during interviews varied from very positive (for instance two university lecturers who were involved in the process), to devastatingly negative (mostly union members and/or teacher trainers that were involved – or discharged – at that time). This opposition claimed the 'university people' were not at all prepared to teach about the reality in classrooms and about teaching styles and methods, because they lacked 'real teaching experience'. These advocating ideas for more vocational oriented training are also reflected in global debates, where there is a recent tendency to delink teacher training from universities for similar reasons (Tatto, 2007: 14).

Regardless of the major tensions and struggles the University administration of Bolivia's Normales generated, the UNESCO report of Lozada Pereira (2004: 153-154) still concluded this link with the university has been one of the most positive outcomes of recent Reform processes in the teacher education sector. Similarly, the report of Concha et al (2002: 62-63) called for a continuation and deepening of the (administrative) link between Normales and universities. Interestingly, things have changed rather drastically since these reports were published, as the administration of universities was forced down, and a reopening of these contacts seems unlikely in the near future. Considering the positive findings of both of these reports, yet without ignoring the valid arguments brought forward by the *normalistas*, I argue a different form of cooperation – not an administrative but a more independent one – between Normales and universities might be considered in the future, as this could help to create more opportunities for trainers' professional development and joint research projects between Normales and Universities.

Attempts to open a closed system: the process of 'institutionalisation' (2006-2010)

Some of the Normales were 'opened up' during the period of 2000-2005, in the sense that all university graduates could apply for a teacher training function. In this way the government tried to break through the exclusive right to become a trainer in a Normal only for those that graduated from a Normal, by opening these positions to other qualified university graduates as well. The historically established *escalafon* system of a 'fixed profession' was challenged, but only for a little while. It was estimated by a director general of a Normal that between 2000 and 2005, around 80% of all teacher trainers were *universitarios* and not *normalistas*.[130] According to another Bolivian researcher, during the University administration, many union leaders lost their positions in the Normales, yet they quickly returned after the Normales were 'autonomous' (administered by the MoE) again (78:3). Nowadays, again we see a closure of the institutes, exclusively inhabited by *normalista* trainers.

In an attempt to address the criticism of an 'exclusively *normalista*' and low-quality teacher training force, the Bolivian MoE initiated an 'institutionalisation process'. In 2006, when University administration as part of the Normales ended and the MoE took on its centralised role again for all institutes, the first steps towards an institutionalisation process were made (86:1). The ideas behind this 'process of institutionalisation' originated from the teacher education

---

[130] An AECID (Spanish cooperation) staff member estimated around 60% of the teacher trainers had a University degree only.

reform proposed in the 1990s, when it was established that all teacher trainers minimally had to have a *licenciatura* degree (comparable to a Bachelors degree) and, ideally, knowledge of at least two languages (Lozada Pereira, 2004: 75, 120). When the institutionalisation process began to be implemented in 2007, all management, teaching and administrative staff of the Normales had to go through a requalification process and apply anew for their positions. In contrast to what Lozada Pereira predicted in 2004, the 'taboo' of opening the Normales to non-*normalistas* still exists and the system is 'closed down' again exclusively to *normalistas*: only those graduated at a Normal as well as having a University degree (minimally *licenciado*) were accepted. According to the head of the teacher education sector at the MoE this process intends to appoint the best trainers on the basis of the number of points they have gained over the years (linked to their years of experience in the *escalafón*), and as a continuous evaluation system of the teacher training staff (44:1).

Opinions differ whether the quality of the trainers that have been institutionalised, and can therefore stay for at least three years, has actually improved. According to a Normal director, this process has both improved and worsened the quality of Bolivian teacher education: '*the institutionalisation process has been good, because the best trainers were chosen. [...] However the younger generations of trainers could not enter because they did not have enough qualifications points [based on the years of experience], and so the older generation was favoured. This creates big problems [...], for instance because the older professors cannot manage computer systems well*' (40:9). On the one hand, the fact that trainers are evaluated on the basis of their experience is already an improvement, according to some.

On the other hand, both students and trainers complained that the process of who is (not) appointed is still not transparent. A trainer at the urban Normal for instance, talked about the institutionalisation process as being something '*fictitious*', since '*what counts here is the political affiliation, where friends give each other positions based on their political taste*' (10:17). One final year rural student confirmed this point of view: '*you might know this country is facing a revolution now. There was one good teacher that was sacked, and she was not a member of a certain party. Most teacher trainers here are 'Masistas', of Evo Morales' party, and they came or stayed here because of that*' (41:9). Several other students also criticised the process to be based on political favours, instead of the professional qualifications and quality of trainers (37:28, 103:16, 123:4). Although these claims are hard to 'prove', they seem to be in line with what management staff in both the urban and rural institute called 'invited teachers', a relatively large group of trainers who entered (or stayed within) the system without having to pass the institutionalisation process requirements (36:1, 62:12). While in 2005 and 2006 students were one of the groups that pushed for an institutionalisation process – or at least a process of change – they are now generally quite negative about the effects of this process: '*it has gone from bad to worse, I am afraid*' (111:10) one student explains about the quality of the teaching they received before and after the process. Both trainers and students also complained about the direct effects, often meaning a loss of time or classes, of this institutionalisation process. The process of evaluating and changing the teaching staff and the job uncertainty for existing trainers have often led to days or weeks without classes for some subjects in both institutes (5:27, 36:1, 38:7).

It can be concluded that the institutionalisation process so far has been a far from smooth process. The intended improvement of the transparency of teacher placements as well as a better qualified teacher trainer force have only very partially been met, according to the critical views of both students, trainers and even management staff and a government official (71:2). Even though I have shown how this process is not always smooth or without politicking, according to some students the quality of a part of the new training staff is indeed better. In my view, the institutionalisation process does provide a potential space for improvement, as it aims to make the appointing of trainers more transparent and based on their years of experience. What seems to be absent in the actual implementation of this initiative is a selection process based on trainers' demonstrable qualifications, rather than political affiliations or the 'automatic' gained qualification points according to trainers' years in the profession.

6.7 ASEP's 'new teacher education' – potential niches for transformation

Although it is still too early to see clear and tangible results of the new teacher education system under the ASEP law, this study shows that the changing socio-political context, including Morales' politics of change and the ASEP reform project, do open up new spaces for change in the Normales, for instance as illustrated by the story of Ramiro's Aymara class (Box 5). An interesting outcome of this study is the difference between the urban and the rural institute in the acceptance and approach towards the ASEP reform plans. The majority of staff in the rural Normal already responded positively to these plans in 2007, and continued their engagement with this project through organising and participating in workshops and meetings both inside and outside the institute. This positive attitude towards an education reform, which is supported by the rural union, is a new and promising development in terms of more successful implementation prospects, as illustrated by the following comments of the director in the Normal of Warisata: '*we are struggling on a daily basis to follow the changes that our 'compañero' Evo is looking for*' (67:20). In contrast, the ASEP plans were received with less enthusiasm, particularly at first in 2007, in the urban Normal. This attitude, however, changed slowly over the past four years, as I encountered less open resistance to the new Reform plans. Critiques in 2010 were not so much directed at the content of the law anymore, but more on the lack of support for the fast introduction of the new teacher education curriculum.

Bearing in mind this more general distinction between the acceptance of the new law in the urban and rural institute, my study also shows how in both institutes there is quite some heterogeneity in the attitudes of individual trainers towards the (new) reform project. As a rural trainer outlined: '*Indeed these politics of change exist, but it depends very much on the commitment and background of each trainer, because each of us has different experiences. For instance, I have worked in indigenous contexts, in mining contexts, in urban and rural regions, with children, youngsters and adults, and parental committees. So I realise we need a new type of teacher that responds to all of this. But other trainers did not have so much experience, or stayed in one place for 15 years, and this will not help them in understanding why we need these politics of change*' (33:6). This interpretation might help to explain why a group of urban trainers with little knowledge of other contexts, and supported by their unions' position, assumes that the new law is made to fit these other contexts and is not suitable for the urban one. An indigenous social movement leader and former trainer argued how '*interculturality has been focused more on the rural areas, while actually we really need to work in urban areas where intolerance and racism are more serious*' (24:15). From his time as a teacher trainer, he remembered how '*the institutional management had a strong influence on us. I remember we would go to staff meetings, and we would all remain silent, I was alone, there was no support*'. In the end, this trainer left the Normal and joined one of the

CEPOs. In response to whether he sees an opportunity for change in the Normales, he argued much work needs to be done to re-train the trainers, to stop the cycles of reproduction. '*In the end, either the new teachers will leave as agents of change, or they will just continue to keep on reproducing all these negative things*' (24:15).

While especially the urban institute can be characterised as a rather conservative 'strategically selective context' (Hay 2002a), it is also subject to change. While in 1999 the MoE (1999: 20) reported on a general lack of willingness of trainers to improve their personal and professional development, over the last few years this situation is slowly changing. While bearing in mind the attitude of apathy of many of the trainers, in conversations with urban trainers and directors, it also became clear how some of the trainers do follow extra courses, or are engaged in collective or individual research projects, being stimulated to do so by the team of directors. The urban academic director hopes that '*the new law will hopefully finally give us the resources to create and generate the knowledge we get from research we undertake. We should publish in a participatory way our new knowledge, students and trainers together*' (17:32, 17:37). The 2002 evaluation of the University-administered-Normales also showed a growing interest of trainers to engage in permanent training activities and exchanges with colleagues (Concha et al, 2002: 81). On the whole, trainers responded positively to the opportunity of the feedback discussions I organised which led to an exchange of ideas and opinions between trainers. Such peer-to-peer events could potentially be a promising way of stimulating engagement of and information sharing between trainers (5:50, 15:4). Another interesting initiative is a journal that has been produced by trainers and staff of the primary teacher education career at the Normal Mariscal Sucre (or 'the Pedagogical University'), in which trainers published articles on innovative developments, organisational issues in the Normal, or reports on activities undertaken.

Finally, in accordance with the studies of Lozada Pereira (2004) and Concha et al (2002), yet without ignoring the *normalista* arguments *against* external administration by Universities, I argue that a closer cooperation between Normales (still as independent institutions) and Universities could be a potential way to improve both teaching and research/evaluation in the Normales. The fact that several trainers are currently involved in further studies and research projects, with either the Universities or other training institutes, is therefore a welcome development and could perhaps open ways to further cooperation, joint research and dissemination between Normales and research institutes or Universities.

There is, in short, still a dire need for change, innovation and '*a more positive, non-violent, but creative and open experience of teacher education*', as nicely put by the sociologist Saavedra (61:32). In the new curriculum, there will be more attention for research and innovation, and not just in the PDI course. The new prevelant teaching technique in the Normales will be focused on research projects, with the aim to develop new knowledge (102:3). From a positive point of view, the new '*curriculum in the hands of a good teacher can be a hotbed for innovation, that will be created and recreated by the teacher-investigators, because the Normales will become research institutes as well*' (Del Granado, 2011). In this sense, the rationale of the PDI course, including the renewed focus on teacher-investigators and the production of knowledges (productive education) in the new ASEP curriculum, are linked to the SJTE criteria of an action research method that stimulates active reflection and critical thinking (and action). I will now turn to analyse if and how these SJTE criteria are met in reality.

6.8 A missed opportunity – the challenges and potentials of the PDI course

As stated in chapter 2, action research as part of a teacher education curriculum can ideally enable future teachers to produce and control knowledge in order to act upon desired educational and societal changes. However, it depends on the quality of the practical experience and the level of support teacher students receive whether these actually help to build a social justice awareness and understanding, or if it will function as a reproduction of the status quo, merely reinforcing rather than challenging negative stereotypes (McDonald and Zeichner, 2009: 604; Sleeter, 2009: 619-620). One of the directors at the rural Normal shared a reflection that links to the critical pedagogical approach to teacher education. He argued that the PDI course within teacher education has three important goals to develop including teaching skills, research and 'cultural dissemination'. PDI should *'create new knowledge to reflect on our practice, and systematise and socialise this new knowledge into real spaces such as the institute and wider society, with the desire to change, to develop, to progress as human beings.'* When I asked whether the PDI course is currently stimulating this, he responded with '*I think PDI now neglects this, as it only includes the first two functions of teaching skills and research. There is no dissemination yet*' (43:22). Actually, his view is still too positive if compared to the experiences of students, which have convinced me that the PDI course is yet another missed opportunity in Bolivian teacher education.

Still, students are generally positive about the fact that they get the opportunity to observe and practice in schools. *'The most incredible thing is to get to know the children, their way of being and thinking, what they want to become. Through PDI I gained more confidence and I learned new things about ethnographic and participatory research and collecting data'* (34:1). Moreover, students' internship periods have the potential to build a bridge between the theoretical preparation and the practical experience. *'One of the best things of the Normal is that we go out to the schools every semester. If we would not have had this experience, we would be 'fried' [fritos]. Because the training here is just basic, and it is in the schools that we really learn and strengthen ourselves'* (123:10). Furthermore, internships can potentially open up the connection between the Normales, schools and the departmental education sections (*SEDUCA's*). From a critical perspective, a teacher trainer in the Normal Mariscal Sucre explained how *'only because of PDI the Normales are forced to create contacts with the SEDUCA's to find schools where students can do their internships. But afterwards, to bring about important transformations in the education system....no. This is one of the biggest challenges that we need to overcome, we have to find more integration'* (107:1). One of the reasons to pay close attention during fieldwork to the PDI courses within the larger teacher education programme was exactly this assumption; that PDI could build a bridge between the isolated Normales and the 'educational mainland'. Regardless of the potential of the action-research methodology of the PDI course (see for instance Liston and Zeichner, 1990; Price, 2001; Zeichner, 2009), I also encountered a number of challenges.

Investigation and internships were already part of Bolivian teacher education for about four decades, but developed into a more systematic and continuous course throughout the training programme since the Reform of the 1990s (5:2). In the first semester the internship period is normally one week, followed by two weeks in the second semester and up to one and a half moths in the sixth semester (yet this will probably change with the new five year system). The placements of all these teacher students in primary and secondary schools each semester is a huge organisational challenge. Especially in the urban institute, this led to some delays and confusion with students as to where they had to go. Students in the rural Normal complained that because of the institutionalisation process, there was a lack of newly hired PDI staff that would arrange the contact with schools. In both institutes, students expressed their concerns of an insufficient preparation before they set of for their observations and teaching practices at schools (18:32). '*Many of us were confused even though we only had to do the observations; this was still difficult because we had no idea what we had to do. And our trainer did not join us, she left us there inexperienced*', a second semester student told me (19:83). Usually, the PDI mentors from the Normal would visit the school only a few times during the internship period of the fifth and sixth semester teacher students. Moreover, when they were there, in many cases the visit had a more formal character of meeting the principal, checking for troubles and signing off some forms (58:4; 59:10). These trainers, in turn, criticised the institute for giving them too many students to supervise in different schools that take a long time to get to. Often, these visits had to be done on top of other classes.

As a result, students complained that they felt left alone. When lucky, the students would encounter a enthusiastic guiding teacher in the classroom where they were doing their practical work, or a dedicated parental committee or school director, as was the case in one of the 'internship-schools' I got to know. Some guiding teachers I interviewed were genuinely motivated to help the teacher students to develop their teaching skills. Others complained about the extra burden, or did not show up and left the children in the hands of the interns. A former teacher trainer who now works in a social movement argued how in the final defence, the guiding teacher should form part of the committee, which would also help to create closer links and better understanding between school teachers and Normal trainers (72:21).

Another issue that struck me was the fact that urban teacher students *only* have their practice in urban schools, while they are supposed to teach the first two years of their career in a rural school. Similarly, rural teacher students do their internships in rural schools, but a group of them later on ends up working in urban schools. With regard to this difficult situation, a trainer at the rural institute responded, from a rather narrow perspective, how '*some students have never been to the countryside. They come from the city but they, sometimes by mistake, decide to study here to become a rural teacher. So, when they leave this place they have to work in a rural context, out of their vocation to be a teacher, they have to adapt to this* (36:15). It is then no surprise that future teachers' expressed feelings of 'isolation' and feeling unprepared for 'the educational reality' when they entered a new school community for one of their internship periods, which is a more common phenomena globally (Achinstein and Ogawa, 2006).

Following an action research approach, students are asked to subsequently conduct observations, define an educational problem, design and implement a solution to the problem and to report on this process in a final Pedagogical Innovation Project (PIP) paper and final defence.[131] However, there are two ways students can avoid a PIP. On the one hand, students with excellent results throughout their studies can graduate without the final defence. On the other hand, students are given the choice to, instead of a PIP, write a 'monograph' on a theme of their choice which is not linked to the action research approach. At least in the urban Normal, most students ended up writing a monograph. This way, in my view many students do not enter

---

[131] In the literature, these action-research papers are represented as 'significant snapshot' of the pre-service teachers' study of their teaching (Price, 2001).

the entire process of reflection that occurs when one reports on and writes about their experiences of their internship and PIP. Hatton and Smith (1995: 39), for instance, emphasise the importance of stimulating linkages between 'meta-cognition and critical reflection' in teacher education, since it often fails to do so and reinforces a cultural view of teaching which calls for teacher rationality and individualism, failing to establish the political or problematic nature of schooling. They argue for the development of *'a developmental sequence, starting the beginner with the relatively simplistic or partial technical type [of reflection in TE], then working through different forms of reflection-on-action to the desired end-point of a professional able to undertake reflection-in-action'* (Hatton and Smith, 1995: 45). In this sense, the Normales have been unable to fully use the SJTE potential of the PDI course to *'develop skills as a reflexive practitioner'* (Greenman and Dieckmann, 2004: 240), and *'the goal of action research as a vehicle for educational change'* (Price, 2001: 43).

In addition to the need for good supervision and stimulation during students' internships, the success of PDI as SJTE instrument also depends on teacher students' dedication and motivation. There is an interesting example of one of the students who was involved in the photo-workshop. With the photos he took during his final internship period, he showed me the main educational, and – in his words – also societal problem he encountered and focused his project on: human relationships. In the photos he showed how children were sitting in rows and the teacher was only directing questions at students in the front rows, *'while many children were not participating'* (illustrated in Photo 11). As a solution, during his classes he asked the teacher if he could rearrange the setting of the tables together in small groups. Having done so, he stimulated the children to work in groups and to share their pencils and other materials (which were scarce). He proudly showed pictures of children's drawings he had put on the unpainted walls. The children made these drawings using the letters and numbers he had just practiced with them. *'Then I realised the difference between my class, with children all working with attention, and the class of the teacher when she had to shout all the time, 'sit down!', 'be quiet!', and 'what are you doing? The next week the teacher continued with some of my techniques, and I loved it. Always, human relations are very important; these photos of my project show how we can be partners and work together, not just the students but also we as teachers'* (66).

Photo's 11, 12 and 13, illustrations of the photo workshop with final year teacher students

In line with Bartlett's (2005: 355) point, it remains a challenge to put into practice such 'Freirean' progressive pedagogies of critical reflection-and-action in teacher education colleges. The quality of future teachers' practical and research experience is very dependent on guidance they receive, both within the Normal and in the school, where active forms of reflection (such as diary writing or peer-to-peer observations) need to be actively provoked (Vaillant, 2010: 124). While in some schools and classrooms included in this study, the guiding teachers were open to getting to know new teaching techniques and to support the application of students' solutions to educational problems for their PIPs (55:1), in other cases students ended up copying the rather traditional teaching style of the guiding teacher. Coming back to Yogey and Michaeli's statement (chapter 2), in order to bring about transformations in a difficult socio-political reality such as Bolivia, a teacher training model should indeed be directed at encouraging teachers as 'active intellectuals', who are equipped with social and political awareness, through on the one hand deepening future teachers' understanding of society, while at the same time having them engage in (accredited) *experiential service learning* (2011: 317-318), such as the PDI course. In its policy design and discourse the new Bolivian government seems to respond to this transformative approach to teacher education, yet, in reality, the revolutionary curriculum and other reform documents as products of the governments' 'political symbolism' (Jansen 2001b) do not necessarily translate directly into changed practices. In this regard, Yogey and Michaeli observed how turbulent social and political contexts paradoxically lead many teacher education institutes to stick to rather conservative models providing *'an illusion of security'*, hindering the necessary processes of *'dynamic, productive pedagogic thinking'* (2011: 315). The earlier discusses institutional inertia in Bolivian Normales seems to reflect this tendency to 'stick to the old', which negatively affects the potentially transformative initiatives such as the PDI course.

6.9 Towards a Bolivian Social Justice Teacher Education?

As was set out in chapter 2, the literature distinguishes three agendas for teacher education: the professionalisation; deregulation; and the social justice agenda (Cochran-Smith, 2004; Sleeter, 2009; Zeichner, 2009). The 1994 Reform primarily fitted the professionalisation agenda, while Bolivia's new policy lines – next to a professionalisation focus – also pursue a social justice and critical inter-/intracultural rationale. Considering the recent installation of a longer and more intensive teacher education programme, Bolivia clearly follows its own and exceptional route that is diametrically opposed to the general global trends of the deregulation and deprofessionalisation of teacher education. Bolivian teacher education as presented in the ASEP law responds to Torres del Castillo's (2007: 9) argument that Latin American teacher education programes should not solely focus on the 'teaching role', based in a singular context – the educational institutions – but include other possible areas in which teachers can develop. This includes training outside the school – in Bolivia through the PDI course – as well as cooperative learning with(in) communities and awareness raising on socio-political issues, which both form part of the new teacher education curriculum-in-development. It therefore aims to respond to a form of SJTE as described by Cochran-Smith (2004: 205), being *'an expanded view that includes teachers' roles as members of school communities, as activists, school leaders and theorizers of practice'*; it also aligns with Sleeters' interpretation in which teacher education *'should build collaborative relationships with historically underserved communities'* (Sleeter 2009: 611). Nevertheless, Bolivia's revolutionary goals of training the new and existing teaching force as creative, reflective and critical agents of change, that are in line with the way SJTE is interpreted in critical literature, is anything but a simple undertaking.

I apply Sleeter's (2009) framework to analyse if and in how far Bolivian teacher education policy and practices live up to some of the features of SJTE. Briefly recalling this categorisation mentioned in chapter 2, Sleeter discusses three key strands of SJTE, including: 1) equitable access to high-quality, intellectually rich & culturally affirming teaching, 2) prepare teachers to foster democratic engagement and dialogue; and 3) prepare teachers as equity advocates for children and youth, challenging a dominant 'culture of power'. Sleeter explains how in the first strand, teachers must be able to teach all children effectively so that the historically subordinated groups can also gain access to the dominant 'culture of power'. What is interesting in the case of Bolivia, which is obviously very different from the US context where Sleeter's work is focused, is that there are various ideas on what this 'culture of power' nowadays entails. While the new government and its sympathisers aim to install an new hegemonic 'decolonial culture of power', on the other hand antagonist groups, and even MAS-voting parents, are not entirely convinced of the benefits of changing the 'old', Spanish-oriented and 'modern' culture of power, particularly considering the global context of intensifying worldwide connections and tendencies of homogenising cultures.

This is where the other two 'strands' of SJTE described by Sleeter come into play, as they aim to foster democratic engagement and dialogue (the second strand) and stimulate a critical attitude towards the dominant culture (the third strand). Chapter 5 showed us how, with regard to democratic organisation of institutions (strand 2), most Normales do have some system of representation of students, but these are often not functioning well and exist more on paper than in reality. Furthermore, various trainers complained of vertical and exclusionary decision-making procedures in the Normales. The third strand, to prepare future teachers as 'equity advocates' for children and youth, can perhaps be best connected to ASEP's attempts to, through schooling, revalue the historically marginalised socio-political and cultural position of the many indigenous students.[132] Sleeter continues to present three key areas of action of SJTE, including recruitment, professional coursework and guided fieldwork, and Table 6 accordingly shows a list including both 'contributing' (+) factors of Bolivian teacher education to Sleeters' SJTE, as well as Bolivian teacher education practices that do not promote SJTE (-).

In relation to the recruitment of future teachers, Cochran-Smith et al (2009: 630) discuss (and counter-speak) the 'ideology critique' of more conservative studies, arguing students should not be screened on their disposition for social justice, as this is a misuse of gate-keeping powers. In contrast, the authors claim that we should not only recognise that education is inherently political, but also that knowledge transmission is never a neutral job and recruitment on the basis of one's values and beliefs is therefore not necessarily illegitimate. From a social justice perspective, and in contrast to a market driven and deregulated interpretation of democracy, freedom couples individual rights with social responsibility for the public good and equal opportunities (Cochran-Smith et al, 2009: 637). In Bolivia we can observe two developments in this regard. Firstly, *postulantes* who pass the entry exam are interviewed by the Normal they

---

[132] Chapter 7 elaborates on the current changing identity formation processes of (future) teachers themselves, which potentially also affects their functioning as 'equity advocates' and facilitators of critical engagements with dominant and alternative 'cultures of power'.

applied for, in which they should be asked about their motivations to enter the teaching profession, however, these interviews are quite limited in their length and depth. Secondly, the standardised entry exams are – according to the students who passed them – very much focused on the memorisation of facts. This results in the better performing – and often older, more experienced and second-career – students passing these exams.

Sleeters' Social Justice Teacher Education framework applied to Bolivia	THREE SJTE STRANDS		
	1. Equitable access to high-quality, intellectually rich & culturally affirming teaching	2. Prepare teachers to foster democratic engagement and dialogue	3. Prepare teachers as equity advocates, challenging dominant 'cultures of power'
AREAS OF ACTION **Recruitment**	+ Older and second-career professionals entering + Majority of students of indigenous background (see chapter 7) - Standardised entry exams testing memorisation	+ Legal framework for inclusion of all citizens	+ Entry interviews including questions on vocation - Entry interviews in reality limited in time and scope
Professional coursework	+ Socio-political focus in subject matters of new curriculum design - Little attention for identity-reflection	+ Inter-intracultural education (But only partly implemented) + Multilingual education (But only partly implemented) - Hierarchical institutional relations, political 'favourism' - Little 'democratic decision-making' at institutional/classroom levels in Normales	+ ASEP Reform stimulates engagement with 'alternative' and indigenous knowledges - Research on 1994 Reform shows simplistic/folkloristic interpretation of intercultural education (chapter 4)
Guided fieldwork	+ PDI course provides promising framework for continuous guided fieldwork experiences in local school communities - Little *guidance* in PDI course, leading to little critical reflection - Teacher students are not obliged to engage in an action research final project	- Although PDI provides a niche for cooperation between Normales and the wider (school) community, there is little actual collaboration	+ Feedback meetings organised for students to share and reflect on teaching experiences - Reflections mostly focused on practical and pedagogical issues, not so much on students' future socio-political role/responsibilities

Table 6, Sleeters' SJTE Framework applied to Bolivia, adapted from Sleeter 2009: 617

6.10 Concluding reflections: old habits meet new ideals

The Morales government aims for a radical restructuring in terms of the governance mechanisms for the teacher education sector, as well as a socio-political redirection of its curriculum. This new political direction seems to mirror a growing acknowledgement and pressure for a genuine transformation of the teacher education system. A teacher trainer for instance mentioned how he thinks this 'new teacher education' should ensure that *'young teachers that will leave the institute are going to identify themselves with their context, they are going to participate, to integrate in the communities problems. They will not only leave this institute as ordinary teachers, but as active teachers, who are concerned with the social and political problems of the community'* (5:16). An indigenous movement leader similarly sees an important role for the 'new' teacher education in *'strengthening the intra-, intercultural and plurilingual education through the Normales, we will change the way of thinking. What we as indigenous could not do before, now we can change, through the Normales. [...] Because those future teachers will eventually really change the reality in schools. If we do not change teacher education, we will keep on sliding'* (14:7). Some initial changes in this direction – such as the newly-started Aymara course of Ramiro – are already visible.

However, this chapter has shown how historically embedded institutional cultures and political strategies of the different stakeholders involved are not necessarily creating an enabling environment for these political transformations to take place. The Normales, as *'complex and emergent sites of struggle and contestation'* (Jessop, 2005: 28), consequently mediate these sometimes opposing power relations, as the institutes are positioned on the verge of ASEP's transformation from a ideological policy into an educational reality. What has become clear, is that similar to the 'jammed' or 'broken' government mechanisms that the Morales government encountered at the national level, the same thing could be said for the Normales: they have inherited some of the continuing mechanisms of corruption and lethargy, forming potential barriers for processes of transformation (e.g. decolonisation, liberation, innovation) to take place.

Drawing from Fairclough's theoretical consideration on institutional change through the lens of critical discourse analysis (Fairclough, 2005: 935), this hierarchical and top-down management style, together with centralised authority and a powerful interference of the teachers unions in Bolivian Normales, is part of a historically developed 'fix' for Bolivia's teacher education arena. The 'neoliberal' and 'intercultural-bilingual'-fix of the (teacher) education system, originating from the 1994 reform narrative, is no longer seen as viable by various groups, particularly since Morales came to office. Bolivia faces real changes, both in the political arena as well as developing changes in the socio-cultural realm, where being indigenous is no longer un-done. These wider socio-cultural and political changes affect the teacher training 'fix'. According to Fairclough (2005: 935), *'the implementation of a successful strategy is a matter of the operationalisation of new representations and imaginaries – new discourses and narratives – in new ways of acting and being and new material arrangements'*. A niche for change has opened up through the willingness of the rural teachers unions, and linked to that the rural Normal included in this study, to open dialogue and to contribute to the new plans for a decolonised education system. The relative rural 'open' versus the urban 'closed' attitude towards the new ASEP reform are congruent with the architectural style of both institutes: the rural Normal having an open and more or less public terrain and building structure, while the urban Normal is a concrete bunker surrounded by a guarded fence. Yet, recalling Tatto's (2007) assertion, we cannot view Normales as homogenous nor passive agents. It is therefore important to acknowledge the internal diversity of opinions both within and around the urban and the rural institute, as well as the management staff's supportive (in the rural case) or critical attitude (in the case of the urban Normal) towards the ASEP reform project. Hence, a new ASEP *hegemonic* fix has not emerged and has certainly not been institutionalised yet. It is still too early to observe deep transforming effects in the organisational structures of the Normal and the inertia of many Normales is a serious obstacle.

The main institutional challenges I distinguished include: an insufficient institutional infrastructure; the Normales as islands; an exclusive profession; discrimination; corruption; traditional teaching styles; and an attitude of apathy in the Normales. Regardless of this troublesome institutional environment, for many youngsters the struggle to enter the Normales – and thus a life long system of relative security – continues and has even intensified. At the same time, trainers and staff members fiercely defend their positions to stay as they are. Once inside, students are often disappointed by the quality of the education they receive. Over the past decade, several reform initiatives targeted this lack of quality, with temporary administration of several Normales by universities in the period between 2000-2005, which was followed up by the recent process of '*institucionalización*' to reorganise the Normales and its staff. Bearing in mind the tensions around these projects, I also see possible niches for change in them, as both national and institutional politics have (re)focused their attention to opening opportunities and stimulation for trainers to upgrade their knowledge and techniques. I also identified ASEP's stronger emphasis on research as a transversal training element as beneficial development, which could potentially open up opportunities for new forms of collaboration between Normales and Universities or research institutes.

In order to improve the quality and alignment with the new reform, the current system of teacher education requires a system of continuous evaluation, dialogue *and* support. Potentially, the PDI course – but so far mostly on paper – carries elements of a SJTE instrument, that could stimulate students understanding, critical reflection and creative practical responses to educational and societal problems, provided that they receive a proper support from the Normal and the school, and are guided in critical reflection processes throughout their training programme.

In short, this chapter has shown how 'old habits' – or barriers to institutional change – are being challenged with 'new ideals' that open up possible niches for transformation. Since the strategically selective context of Normales is influenced by, and in turn influences, the people involved, we now turn to understand the perspectives and characteristics of these agents.

PART IV

AGENTIAL FACTORS:

TEACHER IDENTITIES, MOTIVATIONS & ROLES

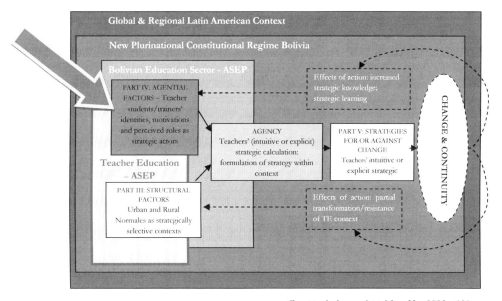

Conceptual scheme, adapted from Hay 2002a: 131

As illustrated in the conceptual scheme above, this fourth part of the book analyses the so-called 'agential factors', defined here as teachers' identities, perceived roles and motivations in relation to the contemporary socio-political discursive context of change. From a SJTE perspective (see chapter 2), in order to teach for social justice, teachers need a 'positional identity' (Moore, 2008: 593), meaning a close understanding of their own 'cultural being' as well as the influence of race, ethnicity, social class and gender on their worldview (McDonald and Zeichner, 2009: 604). Reflexive processes of identity construction, which are linked to teachers' critical social awareness and agency, should therefore be a key element of teacher education programmes (Clarke, 2009: 191, 195; Price, 2001: 48; Beauchamp and Thomas, 2009: 182).

While Mayer (1999 in Walkington, 2005: 54) argues for an explicit focus on teacher identity (as something 'personal') as distinct from teachers' functional roles, this thesis aligns with insights that see the concepts of teachers' identities, motivations, roles and agency as interlinked and influenced by various internal and external aspects (Moore, 2008: 590; Clarke 2009; Walkington 2005). The international journal on Teachers and Teacher Education identified teachers' identities as one of the key focus areas that help to understand this field (Hamilton and Clandinin, 2011).[133] Jansen rightly warns for theoretical considerations on teacher identity that are not connected to 'developing contexts' (2001a: 243-244). In order to understand teachers' 'agencial factors', I therefore draw from studies that either focus on the Global South, or that are particularly relevant to the case of Bolivia and the purposes of this study. Teacher identity is both dynamic and contested, and differs across countries, regions and communities. Torres del Castillo rightly argues that '*teachers are not just teachers*' (2007: 9), they are also men and women, sons and daughters, fathers and mothers, ex-students, workers, community members, voters and neighbours. Instead of a viewing identity as something teachers *have*, MacLure states it is rather something teachers *use*, to justify, explain and make sense of themselves in relation to the wider context (MacLure, 1993: 312). Clarke talks about the '*unfinalizability*' of teacher identity. Without claiming to define the concept, he discusses it as '*a paradoxical complex matter of the social and the individual, of discourse and practice, of reification and participation, of similarity and difference, of agency and structure, of fixity and transgression, of the singular and the multiple*' (Clarke, 2009). Ideally, teachers critically reflect upon all of their multiple identities and in a process of continuous reflection they form new kinds of 'hybrid identities' out of these. This is needed in order to discuss and work with different aspects of diversity and change in their classrooms (Davies, 2006a; Davies, 2008).

The work of Beauchamp and Thomas (2009) brings together the various debates on teacher identity. Although there is no clear and comprehensive definition of what a teacher identity is, there is consensus in the literature on the importance of both internal and external influences (Beauchamp and Thomas, 2009: 177). Teacher identity relates to personal perceptions and experiences, the role of teachers in a given society and the way others view them, which is often linked to or fuelled by competing interests and ideologies, as well as changing circumstances (Welmond, 2002: 42). Following this line of argument, I have developed the analytical concepts of the *internal* and *external landscapes* that help to understand the changing contextual, structural, external and internal factors – including discursive as well as material dimensions – that influence teachers' identities, beliefs and strategies.

The personal dimension of teachers' identities – or the *internal landscape* – has been studied through biographies, life histories and narratives and has gained more attention in research since the 1990s (MacLure, 1993: 311; Palmer, 1997; Clandinin et al, 2009). The *internal landscape* includes both the 'self' or 'personal identities' of teachers, together with their 'professional identities' (Beauchamp and Thomas, 2009: 179). The professional identity of teachers is constituted by their educational experiences and beliefs on the one hand, and career experiences on the other. In chapter 7, the *internal landscape* is further analysed through a number of teacher students' and

---

[133] For studies (including this one) that analyse the identities of teacher students, who often have only limited experiences of what it means to be a teacher yet, it is useful to think of students' 'developing identities' (Moore, 2008: 590; Beauchamp and Thomas, 2009).

trainers' 'profile-indicators' including: age; gender; class; cultural/ethnic self identification; language; urban/rural descent and preference; and educational/work experiences.

With regard to the *external landscapes*, due to the complexities of social changes, the life and work of teachers is situated in constantly *shifting past and present landscapes*. Particularly in rapidly changing contexts such as Bolivia, teachers need 'flexible' identities in order to deal with these changing landscapes (Welmond, 2002: 24-26; Clandinin et al, 2009: 141-142). Building on the work of Beauchamp and Thomas (2009) on external contextual factors of teachers' identities in the education sphere – the school environment, the nature of the learner population, the impact of colleagues and school administrators – for this thesis I add the wider socio-political and economic factors at the local, national, regional and global scales that influence the present changing identities and beliefs of Bolivian teacher students.

The notion of 'the ideal teacher' relates to both the *external* and *internal landscapes* of teachers' identities – or the external and personal perceptions of 'the ideal teacher'. Teachers have to somehow merge their own aspirations and wishes with claims coming from the state and other levels (Welmond: 2002: 24-26, 43, 55), including wider society. (Beauchamp and Thomas, 2009: 181; Clarke, 2009: 185). The 'policy images' of an ideal teacher can conflict with teachers' own (personal and professional) identities. This 'identity conflict' lies at the heart of the implementation problem of educational reform in most developing countries' (Jansen, 2001a: 242). Teachers' personal perceptions of '**the ideal teacher**' relate to **professional, socio-political** and **ethical-emotional dimensions** of their identity. I am inspired here by Jansen's (2001a: 242-243) three-fold conceptualisation of teacher identity in the context of developing countries. Firstly, Jansen's *professional basis* includes ways in which teachers understand their capacity to teach as a result of their subject matter competence; their levels of training and performance and former qualifications. Secondly, the *political basis* contains ways in which teachers understand and act on their value commitments, personal backgrounds, political views and professional interests in the context of changing demands and how teachers understand their authority to act or withhold action (for instance in response to reforms). Thirdly, the *emotional basis* consists of ways in which teachers understand their capacity to handle the emotional demands of a new policy in the context of existing stress and pressures (being demands from parents, large numbers of students, lacking facilities, traumas and conflict). I also draw from Palmer's (1997) work, who writes about the need to better understand the '*inner landscape of teachers' life*' through their intellectual, emotional and spiritual characteristics, relating to teachers' identity and integrity. My professional category can be linked to Jansen's professional and Palmer's intellectual dimensions; the socio-political category relates to Jansen's political basis; and the ethical and emotional category can be associated to Jansen's emotional and Palmer's emotional and spiritual dimensions. These analytical categories are applied in chapter 8.

Internal and external perceptions of *who an ideal teacher should be* and *what her/his roles are* are intrinsically linked to teachers' **motivations**. Welmond (2002: 28-30, 43), inspired by Woods, elucidates three different forms of motivations of teachers. Firstly, teachers are defined as individuals who choose teaching out of the absence of viable alternatives, '*or in order to decide not to decide what to do with their lives (career continuance)*'; secondly, teachers can have a professional commitment, being subject specialists with an interest in a career within the education system; and thirdly, teachers can have a vocational commitment to teaching, '*when they care for pupils and* *encourage growth and learning*. For the analysis of Bolivian students' motivations, I slightly adapted Welmond's categorisation and constructed a tripartite typology of teacher motivations that are particularly relevant to the Bolivian context, including: 1) **economic**; 2) **pedagogical-vocational**; and 3) **socio-political motivations**. My first and second categories correspond with Welmond's first and second-plus-third categories, and I added the socio-political category because of its relevance when analysing Bolivia's current envisaged role for teachers as agents of change. The specifics of this typology and its application to the data are taken up in chapter 8.

Identifying with the old and the new
– changing identities of teacher students and trainers

'To acknowledge the differences that make up teacher identity is to be aware of the potential for enhancement'
(Walkington, 2005: 54)

7.1 Introduction

After the morning classes have ended at the urban teacher training institute Simón Bolívar, groups of students leave their cold classrooms to warm up in the sunny spots of the court yard. Some cross the square to join a quick match of soccer, others buy an early lunch at one of the privately run *comedores*. I sit down in a quiet and sunny corner with Cecilia, aged 37, a student in the English teachers' course. Cecilia previously studied tourism, and has already worked as an untrained teacher in a rural community in the Yungas, the tropical region of the La Paz department. *'When I was in the Yungas, there was a sense of reciprocity. I respected the students, regardless of their age, and they respected me, and they [the community] took care of me as well. We worked to open a bit the vision of these students, to show there is more to do than stay and work in the coca planting sector. I told them they could achieve more. And, thanks to God, some of them even received a scholarship to study in Cuba, and some others left for the cities to study engineering, or to enter the Normal. I am really content they chose these new routes, as at some point, we all return to where we come from. And when they will return one day, I am sure they will bring something, and they will make a change'.* Now, she is in her second year of the Normal and cannot wait to continue teaching as a trained teacher. She also works as a telephone operator in the afternoons, since *'my mother depends on my income'.* When I asked Cecilia to describe her idea of an ideal teacher, she responded *'this is like describing myself, or what I aspire to be like. For me, a teacher needs to be an integral educator, not only focusing on students' knowledge, but also on their habits, their personalities. For me, being a teacher is a huge responsibility. We have the possibility to change someone's mind, someone's decisions in future life. Being a teacher is not something for one day, it is a long term commitment'* (18). Cecilia's story illustrates the multiple aspects and influences that made her decide to become a teacher in the first place, yet also her personal reflections on her identity and role as a teacher.

Part of a teachers' job as a potential change agent is to understand their own identities and positionality in this world. Being a teacher in Bolivia nowadays means being confronted with *change* in all corners of daily life, including a changing socio-political environment that affects families, schools and communities, and with upcoming new policy guidelines and curricula arriving at schools and Normales. Educators at all levels thus, willingly or unwillingly, have to face and position themselves in response to these politics of change. In order to understand teachers' strategies (in chapter 9), we first need to explore teachers' identities, motivations and beliefs. First, this chapter explores the changing identities of student teachers and teacher trainers, while the next chapter discusses teachers' perceived (educational and societal) roles, perceptions of the 'ideal teacher' and student teachers' motivations. Understanding the identities and motivations of these two groups of actors is essential to comprehend the possibilities for and obstacles to educational change (Robinson and McMillan 2006: 189), and to answer the question whether (future) teachers can be agents of change.

The chapter first discusses and challenges the rather homogenising and passive conceptualisations of Bolivia's teachers in part of the literature so far, and argues for an agency oriented approach to understanding teachers' various strategies – for *or* against change. I argue that there is a need to rethink the traditional roles of teachers as mere 'messengers of the system', particularly because the 'old system' has changed radically since the installation of Morales. Indigenous and non-indigenous, urban and rural, old and young Bolivian (future) teachers' are faced with a changing context of a Latin American 'indigenous awakening' and a continuing unequal society and economy. These changing landscapes – including a new education reform – force teachers of all kinds to re-imagine their identities, roles and even motivations. The chapter shows the specifics of this changing profile of the current group of students based on two important developments. Firstly, I observe an increased age and often wider experiences of students who enter the Normal, such as Cecilia. Secondly, there is a growing recognition of indigenous culture and languages through personal and collective identity formation processes, illustrated by Ramiro's story in chapter 1. I conclude by arguing how I see a largely unused potential in a changing profile of the future teacher force, in a changing and possibly more enabling – yet very tense – societal and institutional context.

7.2 Challenging homogenising views on Bolivian teachers' identities and roles

Studies conducted before 2006 (and the presidency of Morales) write about the ambiguous role of teachers and forms of teacher training in reproducing the structures of the hidden curriculum, strengthening instead of withstanding the ongoing homogenisation of Bolivian education. In this view, the teacher often represents an *'alien power and knowledge'* in local communities (Regalsky and Laurie, 2007). In addition, Bolivian teachers are often seen as important figures within rural communities, since they embody 'the way out of poverty'. These teachers sometimes come from the same rural community, but chose the teacher profession and in the words of Canessa, *'are great proponents of the Bolivian Dream whereby through hard work and study one can 'whiten', 'progress' and become mestizos'* (2004: 190). Canessa argued that despite the education policies for intercultural and bilingual education, schoolteachers are in fact still *'a major source of assimilationist cultural ideology and [that they] are principal agents in reproducing hegemonic racism in indian communities'* (2004: 185). This author rejects the 'essentialist' assumption that teachers should share the same cultural and linguistic background as their students (being indigenous). He argues that teachers had to take a decision to become a teacher, and thus to leave 'traditional' (rural) life and to obtain a level of social mobility through formal study. In his point of view, it is very unlikely that those who distanced themselves from 'being indian', would later on valorise and promote this same culture in the classroom (Canessa, 2004: 187-189, 197-199). Children from peasant families who enter the Normales would then change from *indios* to *mestizos* (Regalsky and Laurie, 2007: 238).[134] Even though Luykx (1999 in Regalsky and Laurie, 2007) demonstrates that student teachers do show resistance against the creation of this dominant *criollo* culture, Regalsky and Laurie remain committed to their statement that teacher education is creating a submission to state authority under which teachers have to work, even in communities where they originally came from (2007: 239). In 2000, Speiser presented a similar view by arguing that '*schooling has always been oriented towards the so-called 'national community', which is ideally white, modern, urban and non-indigenous*' (2000: 228-229). The trained teacher is thus viewed as an ambiguous link between the community (to which they do or do not belong) and the school (D'Emilio, 1996: 9, 21), and between local and regional power networks.

In the current context of Bolivian society, we need to rethink the idea presented in some of the literature up to now, of Bolivian teachers as poor and marginalised peasants that will become '*mestizos*' and work towards a homogenising 'national community'. In addition, it would be inaccurate to state that teachers operate as 'unilateral agents of the state', as teachers operate both as state employed officers, but are also engaged with local communities, parents, social and indigenous movements and teachers' unions. Bolivian schools and Normales alike can be characterised as spaces in which power relations are mediated, potentially challenging the historical exclusionary and essentialist forms of education. This homogenising and reproducing idea of the Bolivian teacher does not hold, even more so when considering Bolivia's current changing socio-political context. When following a Gramscian and critical pedagogical perspective in which education is *not* a mere apparatus of the state and educators are strategic subjects, we should rethink Bolivian teachers' roles in relation to their agency – either for or against the current governmental policies. Careful considerations of what it means to become a 'decolonised' teacher that is perhaps more aware (or even proud of) her/his indigenous background and identity, or reversely feels unrepresented and in resistance to the decolonial reform (chapters 5, 6), needs future attention in research and policy.

7.3 Identities in the Normales: a student teachers' and teacher trainers' profile

Relating back to the discussion in the introduction to part IV, both the *internal landscape* as well as the *external landscape* are important when attempting to understand teachers' identities. This section first presents a teacher students' and teacher trainers' profile, based on data from different groups of respondents, representing the *internal landscape*. When constructing these students' and trainers' profiles, I focus on several elements of this complex framework that are particularly relevant for the context of Bolivian teachers, namely their: 1) **age**; 2) **gender**; 3) **class**; 4) **cultural/ethnic self identification**; 5) **language**; 6) **urban/rural descent and preference**; and 7) **educational/work experiences**. Through critical discourse analysis of these aspects, I suggest a new and changing *internal landscape* of the identities of students, based on perceptions of respondents from interview and survey data.

---

134 See also 'the citizen factory (Luykx 1999).

Student Teachers' Profile

Age

One of the elements that illustrates a changing students profile is the increasing age of students that enter the Normales, like Cecilia who started her teacher training at the age of 35, after having worked for some time. The average age of the group of 164 students included in the survey at the urban institute is 25 years-of-age, and for the 158 students at the rural institute the average age is 22.[135] Formerly, as was explained to me by various teacher trainers, most students entered the Normal immediately after their secondary education, around the age of 18. Now we see a rise in age, because a large part of the students have already followed and/or completed another course of study, and some have previously worked for a number of years. Thus, instead of a group of fairly inexperienced youngsters, we now see the Normales inhabited by a mixed group of young school leavers, somewhat older students with a full or partially completed university study and more experienced professionals. In the urban institute, around 40% of the students that took part in the survey entered the Normal after finishing their secondary education. Of those, 7% indicated to also have gained extra job experience (in different sectors) before starting at the Normal. In contrast, 60% of the students have already completed a higher education study before entering the teaching profession. The rural situation is rather different. Here, 92% of the survey participants entered the Normal after finishing secondary education. Of those, 20% have work experience (in different sectors) and only 8% have finished a higher education study. This can be explained, at least partly, by a smaller range of opportunities for rural students to follow a higher education in comparison to their urban colleagues.

Gender

A female dominance of the profession also remains.[136] The survey results among 322 students showed how, at both institutes, the majority of respondents were female.[137] In an interview with three female second year students at the urban institute, it was outlined how gender inequalities still exist. They spoke about difficulties to (obtain) work as a woman, about male dominance in higher positions, about male neglect of domestic work and about discrimination and abuse of women, both in the work place as well as in the home or in the community (16:35; 16:70; 22:18). In the rural institute of Warisata, one student firmly argued how *'one day it should be completely normal to have a Cholita as president!'* (69:27). [138] She not only argued for gender equality, but also for equal rights of indigenous women. Both younger teenage-mothers as well as older women with children complained of the difficulties they had with finding good child care. Their stories revealed how in some cases, older family members would take care of their children during class hours. However, single mothers or those living apart from their (extended) families complained of a lack of child care facilities at the Normales. At the urban institute, there is a limited and somewhat irregular child care service. On the other hand, female students also told me that they

---

135 The government considered introducing an age-limit for subscriptions to the Normales, but protests have so far hindered this (personal communication Education Expert of the Dutch Embassy, La Paz, 17-02-2011). Survey respondents were students in their first and third year of study.

136 UNESCO's Institute for Statistics show that two thirds of all (primary and lower secondary) teachers were female in the period between 2000-2004, and a similar situation continues to exist (http://stats.uis.unesco.org).

137 At the urban institute, 68.3% of the survey respondents are female, with 31.7% male students. In the rural institute, a similar picture arises, with 72.3% female respondents and 28.9% male respondents.

138 Cholita for young girls or Chola for married women in common Bolivian speech refers to a traditionally dressed woman from an indigenous background.

chose a teaching career because of the flexible and limited number of working hours a day that permits them to combine their work as a teacher and their family.

Class

Some of the life histories of students reveal their difficult and often marginalised family backgrounds. Most students come from low or low-middle class families (90:5) because, as will be illustrated in chapter 8, becoming a teacher is a possibility for 'upward' social mobilisation. A female rural student told her story: *'I graduated from high school in 1999. But because we are with six brothers and sisters at home, and I am the youngest, I started to work. Our economic situation did not permit me to start studying at the Normal then. But I kept on dreaming about becoming a teacher, I really only wanted to be a teacher. Later on I studied 'auxiliar de educación' [classroom assistant] so I could work with young children. But then there was the opportunity to take part in the entrance exam of the Normal, and I finally succeeded'* (29:32). On another occasion, I was sitting with a young male student in the rural institutes' library, discussing his irregular Normal-trajectory. *'I was in third grade, but I had to stop because of a problem in our family. My mother was ill, and there was nobody to take care of her. My brother wanted to leave high school, but I did not want him to. So I left the Normal in 2006 and sacrificed myself for my brother. But, when I returned here, there was no fourth grade [because for some time students were not admitted for specific subjects]. The only thing I could do is start all over again in first grade, with the new group of students. So I lost 12 years all together. But I do not think about that anymore, for a mother, you do everything.'* (41:14). These stories paint a picture of the often problematic family situations that these future teachers come from and show how becoming a teacher is seen as a way to overcome poor families' material conditions. Thus, particularly for working and middle class women, entering the Normal is an often devised path to social mobility (Robertson 2000; Weiner 2008).

Cultural and ethnic self identification

Teachers' understanding of social markers such as gender, class, religion and ethnicity is important for their so called 'positional identity' (Moore, 2008: 593). Recent processes of 're-ethnisation' and 're-identification' – as was explained to me by a former Normal director now working in the MoE (107:11) – stimulate students to have a greater awareness, acceptance and self esteem in relation to their cultural-ethnic background. According to an indigenous educator, Bolivian future teachers find themselves in a historical moment of reconfiguration of identities: *'If I was asked if I was Quechua or Aymara when I studied at the Normal, I would have denied either option.[...] Now, it is important to see how understanding one's own identity has changed'* (107:11).

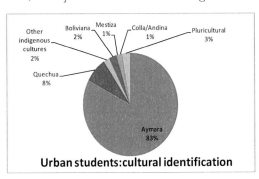

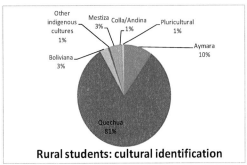

Figures 2 and 3, students' cultural self identification

With regards to students' cultural and ethnic self identification, in the surveys for student teachers I included the question '*with what culture do you identify?*'. Figure 2 illustrates how students in the urban institute primarily identify themselves with the Aymara culture and thus with having an indigenous ethnic origin. It is however necessary to take into account that these self identifications might be influenced by the context in which the question was posed: these answers are thus time, place and context dependent, but nevertheless show a (changing) picture of students' growing indigenous awareness/recognition, at least in the institutes included in this research.

Figure 3 on rural students' cultural identifications illustrates how most students in the rural institute identified with the Quechua culture. Taking into account the dominance of the Aymara culture in the urban research location, and Quechua in the rural location, this outcome is not very surprising. However, what *is* interesting is the fact that in both cases, a large majority of students 'dare' to link themselves to an indigenous culture. These data contrast the view of the authors mentioned in the beginning of this chapter, who argued that students in the Normales leave their indigenous identity 'behind' and adopt the 'modern *mestizo*' way of life. What I saw in the Normales of today might be explained as a transition-phase, between this dual 'indian-*mestizo*' switch that students used to make when they decided to become a teacher, to a identity-construction process in which both elements of old and new ways of living, old and new forms of teaching, and old and new socio-political views are combined. For instance, identifying as being indigenous does not preclude the possibility of being a member of a 'western-inspired' music performance group. This is linked to a simultaneous socio-political transition discussed in the chapter 1. We have to take into account that due to the socio-political and cultural diversities of the different geographic regions, this transition-phase might have different natures and implications in different Bolivian contexts.

Languages
It is interesting to see how there is a discrepancy between a majority of students choosing Aymara or Quechua when asked about their cultural self identification, while smaller numbers of students indicated that they have an indigenous language as their mother tongue. These results resonate with Canessa's (2006: 256) statement, that language is a very poor indicator of indigenous identity and the fact that until 1994, but in many cases even until today, Spanish is the main (or only) language of instruction in schools. Similarly, Howard (2010: 181) in an analysis of present day Bolivia under Morales, writes how it is not incongruous for Bolivia's president to claim Aymara identity while making little active use of that language. While language might be considered a poor indicator of 'being indigenous', it is nevertheless a relevant characteristic of Bolivia's future teachers' profile, considering ASEP's envisaged plurilingual education system. The two figures below (4 and 5) illustrate how the majority of both urban and rural students indicated to have Spanish (*Castellano*) as their mother tongue, with Aymara being the second largest language in the urban institute and Quechua in the urban one.

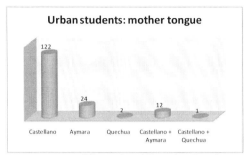
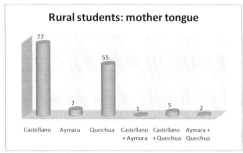

Figures 4 and 5, students' mother tongue in numbers of student survey participants

In the urban institute, 122 out of 161 (76%) students indicated to only speak Spanish, while the rest considered themselves bilingual (see Figure 4). In the rural institute a small majority of around 52% (77 out of 147 respondents) have Spanish as their mother tongue, while 38% of the 'rural students' indicated to being raised with either Quechua or Aymara (5%) as their mother tongue. However, being raised bilingually does not mean these students still speak both languages. A female teacher student who was born in a rural area and who is now living in the city explained: '*I have lived for 5 years in the countryside. I remember that when I came here, I spoke Aymara. But because then in the education system they discriminated against you, I forgot to speak it. I understand and speak just a little bit now*' [16:74]. It can be concluded that there lies an enormous challenge for the Normales – and in essence the whole education system – to ensure a teacher force that can genuinely provide bilingual or even trilingual education, as is written down in policy.

Urban/Rural descent and working location preference

In terms of students' rural/urban descent, evidence shows how in the urban context 95% of the survey participants were born in an urban area, and continue to live there. In the rural institute 45% of the students were born in an urban area and 55% in a rural context. At this moment, 40% still live in a city and 60% live in the country side. However, the categories 'urban' and 'rural' have no clear boundaries and are interpreted in various ways. Some students from the outskirts of El Alto, an urban area on the highlands close to La Paz, for instance claimed to have a rural descent. This data thus has to be viewed as indicative. Students' choice for a rural or urban Normal is mostly based on proximity of the institute: '*I choose not to go to Warisata [a rural Normal] because my family is poor, and I would have to pay rent for a house there. Here, I have an extra job at five in the morning, and then I go to classes afterwards*' (103:2). This male urban student also explains that economic and family reasons often play a role in one's decision for an institute. In some cases, students fail to enter in one institute and then try another one.

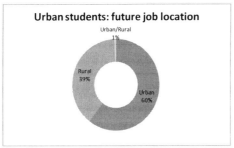
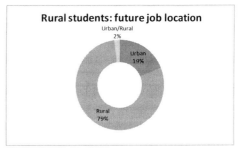

Figures 6 and 7, students' preferred future job location

Interestingly, not all urban students prefered to work as a teacher in a city school later on: 39% of urban students stated they wanted to leave the city to work in a rural context (see Figure 6). In terms of gender differences, the urban male students included in the survey evenly preferred an urban or a rural future job location, whereas the majority of female students prefer to stay in the cities. This outcome fits with the reality of a lack of female teachers in Bolivian remote areas. As for the rural students, a large majority (79%) prefer to work in a rural location (see Figure 7). Here, a majority of rural male students and a large majority of female students all state to prefer working in a rural school. How then to explain the existing problem of a lack of teachers, and particularly female teachers, in rural areas? This can be partly explained by the fact that students choose to live in urban areas after their two years 'in the province', because life circumstances are more difficult than expected. Besides, it should be taken into account that the definitions of what counts as urban and what as rural are not always clear; areas in the proximity of cities are still seen as urban areas by some, and as rural by others. Therefore, these answers are only rough indications of students' preferred future working location. Chapter 8 discusses teachers' different (perceived) roles in rural and urban contexts and elaborates further on the reasons behind students' preferred job locations.

Education and work experience

I have spoken to and heard from a wide array of professionals entering the Normal to become teachers, including doctors, lawyers, architects, musicians, IT- and financial workers, untrained teachers, NGO-workers, as well as people coming from the tourism sector, like Cecilia. A structural lack of job opportunities in other sectors in the last few years has contributed to a changing profile of the students that study to become teachers. Many of them have already finished another study, failed to get a job and so turn to becoming a teacher as a second career move. Some have already been working as untrained teachers and now follow the Normal courses to be able to subscribe to the *escalafon* and according salary arrangements (see chapter 6). Others are simultaneously pursuing a university career at a teacher training institute to widen their job opportunities in the future: '*I think most of us choose the Normal as a second option*' (female urban student, 16:44c). However, students do not talk about their former studies or career openly in the Normal, as became clear from this group interview with a female and a male urban student: '*A: I think 50% of the students already have a profession. C: Or they have studied somewhere else, or they study at the same time, I think it is even more than 50%. A: But they don't tell. [Why don't they tell?] C: It is not allowed to have a university degree. So they don't tell this, I think in this first parallel class of English teachers about 90% of the students already has another profession*' (19:91a+c).

As explained before, the teaching profession is seen as a way to obtain a secure job position and salary, and welfare arrangements. Perceptions vary on the relationship between this increased age and educational/working experience and students' motivations and/or vocation to enter the job. Some argue that due to the financial reasons to enter the Normal at a later age, motivations are mostly economic and often not vocational (e.g. 89). Yet, others believe that the (life and working) experience brought into the institute by these older students can also be beneficial for their vocation and teaching skills, and in addition a higher educated student population could stimulate trainers to improve their preparation and quality of their classes (122:14). These observations challenge the majority opinion that these older students are 'a problem' or, as perceived by some trainers, that they 'steal away' the opportunities for younger students to enter the Normal. We now turn to understand the main characteristics of the teacher trainers.

Teacher Trainers' Profile

There has been an international lack of attention to research teacher trainers (Robinson and McMillan, 2006). By understanding who the trainers of the students are, we might gain insights into what role models are available to the student teachers and to what effect the profiles of the trainers might have on students. As argued by Clandinin et al (2009), students and trainers develop interwoven identities and there is thus a need to understand identity formation processes of both groups. It is important to create a teacher trainers' profile, similar to the student profile. I will again look into the following aspects of the *internal landscape* of trainers' identities: 1) **age**; 2) **gender**; 3) **class**; 4) **cultural/ethnic self identification**; 5) **language**; 6) **urban/rural descent**; and 7) considering their role as educators of future teachers I specifically elaborate on their educational **and work experiences**.

Age

While an older age in itself is not necessarily an indicator of a lower quality of trainers, it was relatively often referred to in interviews as an issue of concern. In the urban Normal, the twenty teacher trainers included in the survey had an average age of 51 years old and an average of 27 years in the teaching profession. Regardless of the benefits of their long term experience, students complained of trainers' relatively old age, relating it to a lack of updated knowledge of innovative teaching methods and techniques. This argument was often related to trainers' age, or to a lack of motivation to innovate because of continuing job security based on political favours for a group of older trainers. Chapter 6 shows how an older generation was indeed still 'kept' inside the institutions, regardless of their qualifications according to some. Younger and middle-aged trainers at the urban institute were also critical of their older colleagues who had little impetus to change (17:8, 17:22, see also chapter 6). A male staff member reflected: *'We have professors who already passed the age of 60 but continue working. So, they are already in the teaching profession for 30 or 35 years. They do not update their knowledge or teaching techniques anymore. We know that these older teachers use traditional teaching methods, and they cannot live up to the needs of the younger students, for instance related to technological skills. It is a huge problem'* (48:8). A foreign NGO-worker, who has been involved in the reform of Normales since the 1990s and is still active in the field of educational politics in Bolivia, argued that when the Normales cut most ties with the universities (and 'university trainers') in 2005 (see chapter 6), *'they have thrown the old people in again, completely outdated ['desactualizada'], but with a political 'weight'. They control the Normales. Now, the institutes do not want to innovate, nor improve or change.'*(73:5)

A counter-voice to this pessimistic view is given by a senior rural male teacher and staff member, who has been involved in the teaching profession for almost four decades himself. *'In these 38 years I have seen the reality of changing human resources, changing strengths and weaknesses, and so I have come to realise I have to be a reflexive trainer, in order to train reflexive future teachers. At the same time, my students who will be the future teachers, they have to understand they have to become the new human resources, based on a new ideological system'* (33:6). This teacher thus argues that for a teacher trainer to 'survive' as a human resource – a trainer – in the Normales, you have to be flexible and adapt yourself to changing circumstances.

Gender and class

While the majority of students are female, a small majority of teacher trainers are male. This finding is in line with outcomes of earlier studies, such as a MoE evaluation (1999) and Delany-Barmann's study on three EIB Normales (2010), which also show a majority of male trainers. A possible explanation is given by a rural indigenous female teacher who explained the difficulty to make a choice between being a mother and having a career as a teacher trainer. Because she comes from a remote rural indigenous community in the South of Bolivia, she has to live separately from her husband and two children if she wishes to continue her career and she only travels to see her family during the holidays. *'My husband lives with the children; he has the role of being a mother to them. 'I feel bad', I have told him, 'I want to dedicate myself to my children, and to being a house wife'. 'No sweetheart', my husband said, 'you have to continue, also for the sake of our family'. So I have all the support from my husband, and this stimulates me even more. I have to continue the struggle for the indigenous claims'.* Pausing for a moment, she continued: *'When I will be old I can rest and feel peaceful after having done something, that is how I think, that is how I can live with this situation, of the responsibility of being a mother and having sleepless nights of all the work'* (32:22). This quote reveals how female trainers face barriers in terms of gender and at the same time their ethnicity (being indigenous). In addition, this example indicates that, like the majority of students, teacher trainers have a marginalised background. Like their younger future colleagues, the majority of trainers come from lower and middle classes and they often also entered the teaching profession some decades ago as a way to improve their living conditions.

Cultural/ethnic self identification

Only one of teacher trainers included in the survey in the urban institute still identified with being *mestizo*. Similar to the characteristics seen in the student population, most trainers also claimed to have an indigenous connection in some way. Figure 8 shows how a large majority of the urban trainers identified themselves with being either Quechua or Aymara.

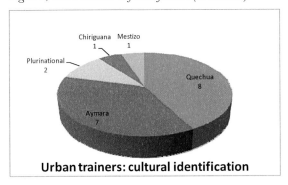

However, this picture does not mean that 'diversity' or being indigenous is accepted in all institutions. This is shown significantly through the lack of acceptance of traditional/indigenous ways of dressing of teacher trainers. According to Howard (2010: 183), in the Andean region clothing styles are as important as languages with regard to symbolic struggles for power and identity formation. In 2003, Albó and Anaya described how the wearing of the *pollera* – the traditional multilayered skirt worn in various styles by indigenous women – was prohibited in many (urban) Normales (Albó & Anaya 2003: 205). Now, there are no official regulations that prohibit this way of dressing. Nevertheless, I have seen very few trainers dressed in traditional clothes; this was only the case in some of the rural institutes. In an interview, a rural female trainer explained how it is a continuous struggle for her to be accepted when dressed in her 'own way'. '*The director has proposed to all teacher trainers to come 'uniformed' [meaning 'western style' jacket and tie for men and 'western style' clothing for women] on Mondays [when teachers have a weekly meeting after the classes]. But I kept on coming in my traditional clothes, and there was some critique on that. But I am sure of my identity, of who I am, and I do not want to change that. Also, I do not feel comfortable in other clothes. But I think that when this institute is serious about interculturality, we should not homogenise people through wearing uniforms. I want everyone to be treated equal; I want to be treated like that as well. Some teachers complained, that there is a danger we would all show up unclean, unprepared and without jacket and tie. It makes me sad. I am not unhygienic just because I wear traditional clothes. At some point they will have to reflect. I have an academic career as well. And I can communicate from the point of view of the communities*' (32:19). This story illustrates the deep structures of discrimination (see also chapters 3 and 7) that remain to exist, even in the rural institute where a strong inter- and intracultural discourse is introduced by the management staff.

Language

With regards to trainers' languages, similar to the picture of the students, there seems to be a divergence in trainers' mother tongue and cultural self identification. For example, identifying oneself with the Aymara culture does not necessarily mean this person also has Aymara as their mother tongue, or even speaks Aymara. From a small group of 20 urban teacher trainers included in the survey, approximately half of them have Spanish as their mother tongue, around 25% Quechua and 25% Aymara. Yet, as my conversations with both students and trainers revealed, the skills to actively use an indigenous language sometimes have vanished. Thus, if indigenous languages are to become part of the obligatory curriculum for all students, extra training for the trainers will be necessary.

Urban/rural descent

In the urban institute, there was a balance in teacher trainers coming from urban and rural backgrounds. In the rural institute, a larger part of the teacher force originated from a rural context. Because of migration flows, as well as the nature of the teaching profession in Bolivia, many teachers have been working in different contexts. Being born or even trained in a rural or urban place does not necessarily mean that trainers have only worked in that same context. A senior male trainer now working in the city, mentioned in his survey that he was raised in a rural and an urban context, because he lived with a miners-family (who often migrated). During his working life he also worked in many different places, *'because I have been travelling a lot, I know many different cultures'* (47:17). Nevertheless, there is also a group of trainers that have been working in a singular context for a long time, which according to the travelling teacher is negatively impacting their attitudes: *'This is what is lacking in our understanding of each other, we don't know each other, not here [in the highlands] or there [in the East]'* (47).

Educational and working experience

All trainers included in the survey graduated in a Normal. In the urban Normal, a majority of trainers employed also graduated from that same institute. A majority of the teacher trainers also have a University degree in Educational Sciences (*Licenciatura* – similar to a Bachelors degree) and around half of the trainers have also completed a Masters or PhD. More than half of the trainers are currently involved in a study to obtain an extra degree (*Diplomado, Maestria,* or *Doctorado*). Yet, not all trainers want to be open about their studies and personal development to their colleagues. One urban trainer told me about his almost finished PhD thesis. However, he insisted I kept this information to myself for the time being: *'we can share our work together, but it is a secret to the rest. A surprise it has to be, when it is finished'* (48:29). On why this was a secret, he responded that it was very problematic to make it to the end of the PhD, due to regulations in the University and he did not want to raise false expectations. The director of the institute did tell me later about four trainers who were working on a PhD and this trainer was known to be working on one as well (62:6). The director also mentioned how currently around 80 trainers (including the director himself) were involved in the training (for a *diplomado en educación*) at the Interregional Institute Andres Bello (organised by Cubans).

A female urban trainer shared with me how she initially found it difficult to go to the university again for her next degree and to cooperate (or compete) with younger students. *'The younger students think I do not know more then them, but I say that professors at any age can develop and adapt themselves. Actually, I have adapted so well that now all students want to be in my group when we do assignments'* (5:46). Several female urban trainers spoke to me about their joint efforts for a qualitative research project aimed at 'improving the quality of teacher training'. The academic director explained she wanted the trainers to 'share their knowledge' through publication and dissemination in seminars. Yet, while she mentioned how *'in the 1960s and 1970s, the Ministry of Education provided a service to publish studies'* (17:35), this is not the case anymore, as there is currently a lack of sufficient resources.

Approximately half of the trainers admitted to having another job alongside their duties at the Normal. For example, I have spoken to teachers who are also University lecturers, thesis supervisors (at the University), consultants or lawyers. Even the director of the urban institute is working part time as a university teacher in civil engineering, *'in the afternoons and evenings, so it does not affect my activities here in the Normal'* (62:13). These extra jobs are often considered necessary, but also as negatively influencing the work of teacher trainers. During a group discussion related to these findings with a group of urban teacher trainers (May 2010), some opposing ideas on having extra jobs were debated. It was mostly the active union members who criticised other trainers for working 'extra jobs', such as lecturing in a university, saying *'they never have time to invest in working together with colleague trainers'*. In contrast to these critiques, it is exactly those trainers who could bridge the existing gap between the Normales and universities. As elaborated in chapter 6, various studies concluded how 'independent' links between universities and Normales could have beneficial effects on the quality of the Normales (Lozada Pereira 2004: 153-154; Concha et al 2002: 62-63). In addition, some of these multi-tasking trainers also argued that because of their wide experiences inside and outside the Normales, they could bring something extra, something valuable to the classrooms of the training institutes. Several trainers told me the stories of their lives, like this very passionate 58 year old male teacher who has been teaching for 41 years. He was born in a rural area and identifies himself with a 'plurinational' cultural identity: *'I have been working as a teacher for a long time. But I have also worked in international projects, with USAID, on mathematics for radio teaching, and with UNICE, on curriculum development for multigrade schools. I also worked for the United Nations on the 'Literacy Plan', and in a programme for distance learning in the highlands [Altiplano]. Then I worked with the European Union as a consultant for an adult education programme in El Alto. We created 12 pedagogical centres, like they exist in Spain and Italy. And finally, I worked in the Cuban literacy programme* Yo Si Puedo' (9:1). Several students confirmed my positive image of this man who stands out in the group of trainers. He works passionately with his students, motivating them, organising thematic working groups and so on. Trainers like this one can be seen as part of the 'exception to the (conservative) rule', as discussed in chapter 7.

7.4 Reflecting on student teachers' and teacher trainers' profiles

The information above can help to identify the complexities of the internal landscape of teachers' identities or, in the case of students, of their developing or imagined teacher identities. As a reflection of the complex reality, the heterogeneity of the answers of the respondents mirrors the heterogeneity of these groups of trainers and students, and is inherent to the mostly qualitative methods used in this research. I try to show a varied picture, a picture of the multiplicity of the characteristics of both students and trainers within the institutes, and between the urban and rural institute. I believe that there is a need to rethink the common negative views of students and their trainers, and to accept a more nuanced picture of both students and trainers at the Normales, as there are two main developments that lead to a changed profile of students.

Firstly, we can see how a lack of job opportunities has been an incentive for somewhat older people and professionals to enter the Normal, instead of the former majority of young secondary school leavers. On the one hand, this might lead to higher educated teacher corps. An urban female student argued that she has faith in this new generation of future teachers, because they 'know more', and *'they are going to change something in the education system, they look forward to being a teacher. Part of the students is here to learn, but they already also know, they are the ones that are needed in our society, for instance the mathematics students most of them are 'universitarios' [graduated from or studying in University]. This is what our society now needs, people who know, it is a good thing we have engineers coming here to study to become teachers'* (19:97). On the other hand, it also has a potential impact on the kind of motivations and dedication of teachers, which is discussed below. Somewhat older teachers who begin teaching might receive more respect from parents and the community, but their former career and own family life might also form a barrier to genuinely integrating in a (remote) community, which is seen by many respondents as a crucial development for an ideal teacher (see the section below).

Teacher trainers see themselves faced with challenges regarding the increased age of their students: '*The problem is that the ones we select to enter the 800 places, out of 20,000 'postulantes', we choose the professionals, because they perform better in the exams. The young people who just left school feel disadvantaged. There is a very strong crisis now in our institute, because sometimes the professional-students know more than our own trainers. [...] Also, the majority is not interested in the quality aspects [of education], they just want to pass the career with as few hours as possible. Around 20 years ago, students were between the ages of 19 and 22 years old, now students are much older, even about 50 years old.*' Although I have not met the 50 year old student, and I am sure this was an exception to the rule, there is indeed a strong tendency of professionals – outside or inside the education sector – with University degrees entering the Normal. Viewed from another perspective, this might also become a trigger for a quality improvement of teacher education, so that trainers still feel competent enough to train all students. Also, as was described in chapter 6, the changed policies for '*postulantes*' to enter the Normal might lead to an increased (academic) level of students in the Normales, now 'those who performed best' will be accepted (La Prensa, 18-03-2010a). Such policies aimed at recruiting 'better candidates' are not exclusive to the Bolivian case, as Tattoo describes how generally better teacher candidates are perceived by policy makers world-wide to have a stronger content knowledge and the ability to gain pedagogical knowledge 'on the job' (Tatto, 2007: 272-273).

Secondly, the *internal* and *external landscapes* of teachers' identities meet each other in the sense that there is a growing recognition of indigenous culture and languages at the societal level which affects the identities of students and to some extent also those of trainers. The data shows how newly trained teachers in both studied institutes seem to be more aware and also more proud of their indigenous backgrounds then was assumed before. One teacher student from El Alto proudly told me he now openly uses his Aymara surname, while his mother told him when he was young that he always had to try to stay away from using it to avoid being discriminated. This changing attitude might promote a more open dialogue about different identities and possibly counteract the reproduction of the historical *castellanisación* of Bolivian education. The other way around a space for dialogue about diverse identities might change teachers' beliefs and attitudes. In relation to these developments, the new education law seems to promote a somewhat more enabling context for teachers to openly announce and discuss their, and their students', multiple identities. The new ASEP reform aims to (re)value indigenous or 'original' knowledge and culture. Chapter 5 explained how this new ASEP law is received in an atmosphere of both receptiveness and resistance to 'reverse forms of discrimination'. Still, some effects of these developments can already be observed. For example, an urban teacher trainer recently started to stimulate his own children to learn Quechua, the language he himself was raised with: '*every Sunday afternoon after lunch until 6pm, we only speak Quechua, and I do not answer my children if they speak in Spanish. My children became very interested, and at school started to discuss what languages their classmates speak*' (117:6).

An important challenge for policy makers and teacher training institutes becomes clear when comparing the policy ideals of a bi- or trilingual system with the reality in the Normales. The majority of students in the urban institute have Spanish as their mother tongue, and most student teachers' are not bi- (or tri-) lingual. Even in the rural institutes, where they are supposed to mainly train rural future teachers, not all students speak another language besides Spanish. This has major consequences for the aim of genuine bilingual – and intra/intercultural – education. Similarly, many teacher trainers also often lack the skills to speak – let alone teach in – indigenous languages. In a focus group discussion with eight urban trainers, where I presented these outcomes, a female trainer reflected that: *'When most students do not speak Aymara, Quechua or Guaraní, but they do identify themselves with those [cultures], the implementation of their training is what worries me. Maybe I am trying to implement a process of teacher formation that is different to what they actually need. And this is also not mentioned in the ASEP law'* (117:8). At the end of the meeting, she said she enjoyed the conversation with her colleagues. As a result, she proposed to her colleagues to organise such discussions more often. I do not know whether this has actually happened, but the intention to engage in a collective reflection seemed to fit into my earlier discussed 'opportunities for institutional change' in chapter 7.

In chapter 6, I discussed different 'institutional cultures' in the rural institute where everyone (during the week) lives inside the Normal and in the urban institute where people only come during the day. These different institutional cultures affect the relationships between students and teachers, even if it was only related to the time teachers have available when they live at the institute, eat together, walk around during the evening and can have a chat with students. Still, most students in both institutes criticised their trainers for being too authoritarian and often unavailable, with a few exceptions. Often, these complaints related to their trainers being 'too old', 'too traditional' or 'not open for change and innovation'. The majority of teachers are indeed in the last phase of their working career. It is, however, important to stress that these senior educators also carry with them a wealth of experience. In general, 'younger' and 'older' trainers alike, see themselves faced with an enormous pressure, since they have to keep up with continuous policy reforms. Because of changing reform programmes, they have to train future teachers for school environments that are very different from the ones they experienced themselves as students or younger teachers (Robinson and McMillan, 2006). The MoE is still in the process of developing support systems for in-service teachers *and* teacher trainers, but this remains in its early phases.

When students were asked to reflect on the quality of their trainers, it became clear that in their eyes there is only a minority of trainers – in both institutes – that have the genuine dedication, motivation and knowledge required to provide the quality training that students would like to have. However, after a while, when having more informal conversations with the urban students, I found that their opinions also changed over time. Interestingly, in the rural institute various students told me how the 'institutionalisation process' has brought in some good quality new trainers. *'From the first trainers I had, for me about 30% has a vocation, and 70% come here just to complete their working hours. But now they changed the teacher trainers, I think it is almost a 50-50 division.'* (41:8) Another student agreed, and stated how *'the new teachers have some good ideas, they came to this institute after being school directors, so they know.[…] For example the teacher we had for PDI last semester, he had some good ideas, […] he did not base all what he said on theory, he did not just examine us on what is in the books, but on what we understood and learned'* (30:29). A number of students were very positive about certain trainers, while other students commented negatively about those same trainers, which makes it hard to generalise these views and their relative value.

The data thus shows a rather heterogeneous image of the quality of teacher education by trainers, with both positive and negative accounts of both students and trainers themselves. Nevertheless, the negative images from student teachers of their trainers in most of the interviews endorse the dominant societal view on the Normales as low-performing institutes. Moreover, while some of the quotes above do show a genuine initiative together with valuable working experiences of some of the trainers, most respondents were relatively negative of the overall quality of teaching by the staff. So, even with a qualified teacher training force, students (and staff members) still complain of the low quality of teacher training and a lack of enthusiasm for change. This might be explained by the many structural challenges, such as: time constraints; institutional (mis-) management; low status; insufficient training and support for trainers; and a sometimes counterproductive conservative influence of teacher unions. Could this minority of motivated teacher trainers have an effect on the quality of teacher education when structural obstacles are overcome? These issues are further analysed in chapter 9.

7.5 In conclusion – A mis(sed) understood opportunity

During one of the focus groups with trainers in which we discussed preliminary outcomes of this study, the issue of changing and complex identities was linked to the idea of diversity. Similar to international debates in the literature, the discussion turned to the dilemma of supporting diversities whilst at the same time trying to overcome segregation. Whenever this issue came to the table, most respondents supported the idea of 'unity in diversity'. In line with the ASEP law, a group of rural trainers argued that in order to create this sense of unity in diversity, teacher education should aim to create 'one type of teacher', without discrimination or distinction between the 'urban' and 'rural' stigmatisations. In addition, they argued the separated union system with an urban and a rural federation should be changed into one representative body for all teachers (121:10). In another feedback conversation on the outcomes of this study a Bolivian researcher and lecturer told me: '*Your research signals something important, and coincidentally I discussed similar issues this morning [in the MoE]. The repertoire of ancestral knowledges, rituals and communitarian learning of all these youngsters with an indigenous background, these are absolutely unknown to the Normales and Universities. So, this potential of a wide diversity of knowledges and experiences is not developed at all*' (114:16). In other words, it is an unused opportunity for change.

The following quote by a Bolivian ex-teacher who now works for UNICEF confirms the importance of dealing with teachers' identities in Normales: '*Unfortunately, I went to a Normal where nobody spoke of identity, no one spoke of my culture – Quechua – either. Many teachers now live with an internal conflict related to their identity. This destabilises teachers psychologically, so that they cannot express their intentions, their desires to the children, and then the teacher becomes an uncritical instrument of knowledge transfer, without a critical vision. [...] To me it seems fundamental that as a teacher I know the horizon of my identity, and then also to know what we want with education in our country*' (3:13). Understanding teacher students' and their trainers' complex identities is by no means an easy task. Like Walkington's quote at the beginning of this chapter shows, it is exactly the changing nature of Bolivian teacher students' identities that open up a potential 'for enhancement' of their educational and societal ethical-political agency.

In the case of the two Bolivian Normales I perceived the complex and changing nature of student teachers' and trainers' profiles as a missed and misunderstood opportunity. Teachers' identities receive a lack of attention and understanding in Bolivian teacher education practices and policy, while the literature show that in order to teach for social justice, teachers need a close understanding of their own 'cultural being', as well as the influence of race, ethnicity, social class and gender on one's worldview (McDonald and Zeichner, 2009: 604). Reflexive processes of identity construction, which are linked to teachers' critical social awareness and agency, should therefore be a key element of teacher education programmes (Clarke, 2009: 191, 195; Price, 2001: 48; Beauchamp and Thomas, 2009: 182). Consequently, this chapter aimed to contribute to an understanding of the complex and changing identities of Bolivian teacher students and trainers. The *'internal'* 'stories to live by' and material life conditions of Bolivia's teacher students and trainers – constituting their profiles – are often characterised by marginalisation, discrimination, struggles on identities, insecurity about basic human needs and thus extra jobs. With regard to the *external landscape* of teachers' identities, they are faced with a rapidly changing context of a Latin American 'indigenous awakening', a continuous unequal society and economy and an upcoming new education reform. Considering the rapidly changing contexts of Bolivia, teachers of all kinds (including students and trainers) therefore need 'flexible' identities in order to deal with these changing landscapes (Clandinin et al, 2009: 142; Welmond, 2002: 24-26), while they receive little support in terms of pre-service and in-service training.

This chapter discovered that there is a changing profile of the students that is influenced by two contextual developments: firstly a lack of job opportunities leads to an increased age and, in many cases, wider experiences of students who enter the Normal; and secondly, a growing societal and political recognition of indigenous culture and languages stimulates students to develop a growing awareness and acceptance of their own ethno-cultural and linguistic background. Teacher education institutions seem to miss and misunderstand the opportunity behind these developments. I argue that, on the one hand, there lies a potential benefit with regards to training a group of older, higher skilled and more experienced students. In teacher training institutes, often the detrimental side is emphasised: trainers face a more difficult job training these older and higher educated students, and younger students feel that there is an unfair competition between them (secondary school leavers) and the somewhat older generation of students. When I discussed these findings in April and May 2010, an urban Normal director confirmed the possible positive effects of having to train 'qualified psychologists, pedagogues, lawyers' and so on because it would *'push for more quality of our trainers, so they prepare themselves properly'* (122:14).

On the other hand, due to processes of 're-ethnisation' and 're-identification' students develop a greater awareness, acceptance and self esteem in relation to their formerly, often discriminated, cultural-ethnic background. Whilst the literature describes pre-service training as an ideal starting point to create awareness of the need to develop future teachers' complex and changing identities (Beauchamp and Thomas, 2009: 176, 186), the Normales do not sufficiently reflect on, and work with, the changing profile and identities of students. The next chapter discusses perceptions of the ideal teacher and future teachers' actual motivations to become teachers, confirming the weight of economic motivations, but also questioning the general assumption that Bolivian students lack the motivation and dedication to become good teachers.

8

Profesores '*de vocación; de equivocación o de ocasión*'? The unused potential of Bolivia's future teachers' aspirations

'There are people who actually want to become a dentist, but out of opportunistic reasons they enter the Normal,
because this gives a secure salary. But these teachers with a 'mistaken vocation' (equivocación) do not work with
enthusiasm; they are not excited when their students have achieved and learned something. I think these are
teachers by mistake, because they do not care if students learn or not'
(First year rural student teacher in Paracaya, 29:17)

8.1 Introduction

The above observation from a first year student in the rural institute points at the thin lines between a teacher students' 'real vocation', a 'mistaken vocation' (*equivocación*) or an 'opportunistic opportunity' (*ocasión*) – the latter being a purely economic motivation. At the Normal of Warisata, in a group interview with three second year students, one student similarly commented how '*we say 'maestros de ocasión' (opportunistic teachers) to those that only come here to later on receive a secure salary, and a secure job*'. His classmate continued with '*vocation is actually a really important factor, you are born with it, it makes you want to change the future; which is why you have to prepare yourself*' (69:13). These discussions all relate to the societal, political and personal perceptions of what an 'ideal teacher' in the Bolivian context should look like, what her/his roles should be (both in urban and rural contexts), as well as future teachers' motivations as teachers – '*de vocación, de equivocación, o de ocasión*'.

Considering Bolivian teachers' crucial role in promoting, mediating or resisting processes of educational, societal and political transformation, as well as their heavy responsibilities, there is a need to understand these roles and perceived responsibilities. The chapter therefore starts by providing an overview of the multiple expected roles of teachers in Bolivia, in both rural and urban contexts. Due to the continuing divide between urban and rural Bolivian education and the differing roles for teachers in both contexts, students' preferences to work in an urban or rural context are analysed. The chapter continues by describing the various perspectives of what constitutes 'an ideal Bolivian teacher' by various educational actors, which links to both *internal* and *external* aspects of the teachers' identity (see introduction to Part IV). An understanding of *what* teachers are supposed to do and what an ideal teacher looks like, provides a necessary foundation for the following discussion on *why* students want to become teachers. Consequently, the chapter continues to develop an understanding of the more general motivations to enter the teaching profession. The perceptions of different actors are discussed and analysed according to a typology of future teachers' motivations and illustrates how students' own motivations differ significantly from the common view of teachers' motivations by other key actors in the field. This chapter suggests that the teacher education system, as it functions now, largely ignores, and often fails to stimulate, a vocational attitude and social responsibility among students, which is commonly viewed as one of the key characteristics of the 'ideal Bolivian teacher'.

8.2 Teaching in rural and urban communities – roles and preferred locations

According to the ETARE pre-project for the 1994 Reform, the 'new teacher' had many roles, including *'the capacity to carry out educational research, to implement the outcomes in the classroom, with intelligence and creativity, own innovations and styles of teaching and optimizing its role as a trainer/guide [formador]*' (Lozada Pereira, 2004: 74). This perception of 'teachers as researchers and innovators' in the classroom is again reflected in the recently developed education plans for decolonising education and is taken a step further to the socio-political level. The ASEP policy discourse expands teachers' agency – in terms of their obligations, authority and autonomy (Vongalis-Macrow 2007, see chapter 2). In contrast to global tendencies that 'reterritorialise' teachers' agency to a limited teaching-for-the-test role, the Bolivian government emphasises their social and political responsibilities as a *'soldier of liberation and transformation'*.

As was shown in chapters 2 and 5, there are other trends that were initiated in the 1994 Reform that are still carried out, such as participation of the wider community in school management and a certain degree of decentralisation (the level of decentralisation is relatively limited in the final document of the law). Drange (2007: 5) points out that what this potentially means for the role of a teacher, is that they are no longer the only person influencing the school. Parents and community-based grass-root organisations, liaison committees and school management boards are all supposed to take part in the development of schooling and to analyse the needs of the school community in order to find solutions to any emerging problem. This includes both the decentralisation of decision-making and a shift of responsibility for infrastructure and the daily organisation of the school toward the municipal level. The municipality therefore receives resources from the national budget according to the size of its population. The urban teacher confederation in La Paz strongly resists the former and present decentralisation plans, as well as the influence given to parents and local organisations (see chapter 5). In an interview with members of the rural union at their headquarters in La Paz, a more favourable attitude towards the ASEP policy plans was expressed, as they consider a certain amount of decentralisation and community involvement as beneficial to teachers' work (83). It is too early to make any consistent statements about the actual implications of the ASEP policy for teachers' roles as mediators between the state and the community, yet it seems that decentralisation will, in some form, remain part of the Bolivian education system.

Although the new ASEP law aims to bridge the historical division between rural and urban education in Bolivia, in reality this divide is still very relevant and influential within the lives and work of teachers. The director of one of the rural Normales, for instance, elaborated on the different roles urban and rural teachers need to be prepared for: *'The urban teacher is simply made for the classroom. We [rural teachers] integrate more with the community, with civil society. In some cases the teacher is a judge, an official of the civil registration office, a teacher can have the function of a nurse, so we train these types of teachers, not just for the classroom, but so she/he can help the community where she/he will work'* (67:12). In contrast, an urban academic director thinks that not only rural teachers, but also urban teachers need to be aware of, and engaged in, society and the wider school community. She continued to say how *'we for instance pay attention to the environment, which is a universal problem, and other values that have to be strengthened within the future teachers. This is needed for the youth to improve their self esteem, their identity'* (17:8). In the interview, she explained how a strong teacher identity – based on principal values (such as care for the environment, respect for each other and elders) – is a necessary prerequisite for any teacher in order to fulfil their roles. Although new policy lines aim to overcome the rural-urban divide and unify teacher education in all Normales, there is no consensus on how this dual education system could be addressed. It is, therefore, still a reality for those who enter the teaching profession. Hence, we now turn to discuss students' preferences for their future job locations.

Understanding the multiple and changing roles of teachers in various contexts will help to comprehend students' preferences for future job locations and motivations discussed below. With the aim to map students' preferences to work in urban or rural schools, the survey included the open question *'please describe the three main reasons why you would want to work in a rural or urban context'*? These answers, together with data from interviews in which I asked similar questions, help to understand students' main motivations for their choices about future job locations. As explained before, being a teacher in Bolivia is one of the most popular careers for young people, because of the *relative* good working arrangements. I now discuss the different roles and conditions for teachers working in rural or urban contexts and link to that the preferences of student teachers for urban or rural future job locations.

Teaching in a rural community
Teachers in rural areas face specific difficulties. As in many other countries, in the so-called rural 'multigrade' schools just one or two teachers have the responsibility to teach all grades (72:26; 111:3). Moreover, as was mentioned by the rural Normal director above, teachers in Bolivian rural areas are often considered as important community members, having multiple additional social roles such as (local) lawyers, conflict-solvers and even as doctors. While teachers face enormous responsibilities, it is questionable whether they are fully prepared for these tasks through their training. Several students explained to me how they saw language as a barrier between the teacher and the students, especially when, as a teacher, you are not familiar with the local language spoken (see chapter 7). However, not all students agreed that in rural schools, all children speak Spanish. Some students argued that in some cases children only speak Aymara (in the highland area). One urban teacher student told of how she had visited a rural school, where the children spoke in Aymara, while the teacher did not understand them. *'They laughed at him. There was not much trust, and they accept a teacher who speaks Aymara better'* (19:51).

In addition, working and living conditions in remote areas are relatively more difficult than in cities, because of a lack of (clean) water, electricity and communication and travel services. Still, a significant number of the urban students included in the survey (39%) explained that they preferred working under such conditions. In their eyes, being a teacher in a rural area creates real opportunities to teach something valuable to children and to live closer to the environment (often referred to as *la Pachamama* or Mother Nature), because of the relative tranquillity of rural life and/or because education *'is much more needed'* in rural areas. For example

Cecilia (the urban female student teacher introduced in the former chapter, whom already worked as an *interina* – or untrained teacher – in a rural school) values the fact that there is '*much more to do*', and '*much more to change*' in rural areas (18:6). Indeed, there is a lack of (qualified) teachers in remote rural areas.

For 79% of the rural students included in the survey, working in a rural area seems more attractive than working in a city. Some rural students mentioned that they preferred the small scale community life to the individualistic and hurried urban lifestyle. Also, whilst urban students stated to prefer working in a city because of being used to the urban way of life, many rural students want to continue living in rural communities, because of more tranquillity, cleaner air, living closer to nature and 'friendlier communities'. Interestingly, rural students' ability to speak an indigenous language was brought forward as a reason to later on work in rural schools. Similar to their urban colleagues, several rural students argued how being a teacher in a rural school is more needed and more important. The survey answers of rural students also showed how some students liked the better status of the teaching profession and teachers' key role in rural communities. A few students also mentioned a higher salary – in the form of bonuses – as a reason to become a rural teacher.

The following part of an interview with two rural young female teacher students (TS), who had just started their first week at the rural Normal, reveals some interesting views on their future job preferences, as well as their personal situations and motivations (29:26 a+b):

Interviewer:	*Would you prefer working in a rural or urban school later on?*
TS A:	Here at the |rural| Normal, most people who subscribe come from a rural place themselves. For us, it would be all right to work in rural place, or even in a very remote area, because we are used to this, and we like it. For us, to go to a city would be uncomfortable, we would feel a bit saturated, without enthusiasm. There are so many things that would affect us. [...]
Interviewer:	*And what about you?*
TS B:	For me, it would not matter; I would adjust myself to living in a city or in a rural place. But I think that here in the Normal they prepare us more for the rural areas [...] and the most humble people who most need it live in the rural areas. There people need it most, there you can really do something, you can talk about sex education, there are so many things they need. I would prefer to work in the rural context where people really need it.
TS A:	And also, that they value your work as a teacher more, when you go to the rural area [...].
Interviewer:	*And do you already have a specific place where you would prefer to work? Maybe in this area, or in another part of Bolivia?*
TS A:	I want to go to the tropics (*el trópico*).
TS B:	I would prefer to go to a remote place, for instance at the border somewhere, my wish is to get to know and work in Beni, Guayaramerín, Riberalta.
TS A:	My wish is to go far away as well, to places I don't know, because a better opportunity for this you will not get. I do not know the tropics; therefore I want to go there. Then I can go fishing with my students.
Interviewer:	*And working in those places would also imply living there, right? What do you think about that?*
	I will adapt myself to every place. I would take my son with me. And my husband, I would leave him behind.
TS B:	I think it hurts to leave behind your family, in reality it will hurt, but if you have these 'life opportunities', it is all right, to get to know these places.
Interviewer:	*Yes, I understand, for me it is also a great opportunity to be here in Bolivia, but I also miss my family sometimes.*
TS A:	You suffer, but you also learn. Because you have more time, you think a lot. And if you cannot sleep, you are left with your thoughts. When you are far away, you value more what you have.'

This extract seems to shows various reasons for preferring to work in rural, or even very remote, places. The reasons included are familiarity with the rural context, wanting to help those students who 'need it most', but also wanting to get to know other parts of the country and, possibly, even to get away from a difficult family situation and husband.

However, various rural students also raised concerns with regard to working in a rural area. A third year student at the rural Normal Warisata mentioned how preferring to work in a rural context does not necessarily mean staying there forever: '*We also have this idea to excel more, because in the most remote rural areas the education is not like in the cities. For example, in the city you can give your classes and at the same time prepare yourself scientifically at the University, but in rural places it is not like that. You spend all your time there, dedicated to your job, to your house, to the work you have to do the following day, the students, all that. We do not have so much accessibility*' (68:18). Several urban students similarly expressed their doubts and fears about the (obligatory) two years 'in province': they fear a lack of materials; a lack of communication; missing their family and friends; and difficult living conditions, having grown accustomed to living in the city.

Others told how they see these two years as a valuable experience, yet they wish to return to working in a city afterwards. This argument is backed up by the survey answers of urban students explaining they want to live and work in a city for various reasons, including: to stay close to their family; to keep on studying; other career/work opportunities; better access to internet and libraries, and educational material; and because of being used to the 'urban way of life'. Various students also disclosed that they did not want to work in a rural area because of a lack of knowledge of local languages and a number of female students mentioned having children and not wanting to leave the city (and family) because of that. Thus, the majority of students with a rural background themselves recognise the difficulties of a future job in a rural school, but they, nevertheless, still see it as their preffered job location.

Teaching in an urban area
It would be unfair to state that the work of urban teachers, on the other hand, is easy. Teachers working in urban contexts also face difficulties. Urban teachers see themselves forced to work in two or three '*turnos*' (morning, afternoon and evening shifts) in order to pay for the expenses of their families. A teacher working at a school in a 'poor' neighbourhood in La Paz explained some of the other problems of the urban students. She was used to teaching children in the centre of town, where they would '*listen and learn much better*'. She related her current students' '*disobedience and laziness*' to the lack of support from parents in poorer neighbourhoods. Another teacher similarly explained how numerous parents have to work all the time, or even live abroad, to gain money. Teachers complained about homework that '*is never done*' and expressed their worries about children being left alone by parents.

In contrast to the motivations to go 'far away' of the two girls from the interview presented above, their urban colleagues more often referred to the difficulties of raising their children alone, without their family (who often live in the city) to help them out. Also, in relation to the transcribed conversation above, I often heard variations of the 'noble' argument to 'bring good quality education to the rural and humble poor', like in the conversation with the two students A and B above. Although this seems like a noble stance at first sight, one might question the patronising or even discriminatory ideas behind that view in some cases. Like this urban student who mentioned in his survey that he wanted '*to help the poorest rural people to escape ignorance*'

(U-134). Perhaps these patronising ideas still come from an education system in which teachers function as reproducers of hegemonic racism (Canessa, 2004). From a SJTE point of view (see chapter 2), training institutes should stimulate students to critically reflect on their motivations behind future choices and to make future teachers aware of potential patronising and discriminatory attitudes, as will be elaborated in the following chapter 9.

8.3 Views on the ideal Bolivian teacher

As set out in the introduction to part IV, various actors' perceptions are part of the *external landscape* of teachers' identities. In addition, following from Tatto's interpretation of Cummings, teacher education institutes are driven by their idea of the ideal teacher. Yet, there is little written about the various perceptions of what an 'ideal Bolivian teacher' is, nor how this is perceived in the Normales. In the surveys and interviews I conducted with students, teacher trainers and other education actors, I included the open question '*what are the three most important characteristics of an ideal teacher*'. As explained in the introduction to Part IV, based on relevant literature (e.g. Jansen, 2001a; Palmer, 1997) and the data I gathered on Bolivian perceptions of the 'ideal teacher', I designed three related analytical 'ideal' characteristics, including: A) *professional*; B) *socio-political*; and C) *ethical-emotional*.

Bolivian policy views on the ideal teacher

At the beginning of the twentieth century, the first Belgian-led teacher training institute in Sucre had an ideal image of the Bolivian teacher as being an 'apostle' of education, with a great sense of vocation and service to the community (Lozada Pereira, 2004: 67). This notion of the teacher as an apostle is still visible in the discourse of both students and trainers today. However, the old education paradigm of 'exposition-assimilation-repetition' was replaced by the 1994 Reform with an alternative education paradigm of 'experience-reflection-action'. The 1994 reform envisioned a new, and more comprehensive, idea of an ideal educator. Normales had to prepare teachers not only for the transmission of knowledge, but for a wider societal task of stimulating the construction of knowledge, values and attitudes in their students (Ipiña in Lozada Pereira, 2004: 71). In many countries formal teacher training and teacher development solely focuses on the 'teaching role', based on one particular context – the educational institutions – leaving aside other possible areas in which teachers can develop, such as training outside the school, cooperative learning within communities, awareness raising on socio-political issues and so forth (Torres del Castillo, 2007: 9). Particularly in the Bolivian context of a rapidly changing socio-political context, and a strong civic engagement in politics and societal issues, teachers can potentially be influential elements in reproducing, resisting or promoting educational as well as societal processes of change. Currently, the ASEP law employs a rather extended idea of the 'ideal teacher', as it continues and further reinforces the 1994 Reform principle of teachers-as-reflective researchers, while seeing teachers as crucial agents in the wider socio-political project of 'liberation and decolonisation'. The new law envisages an active pedagogical *and* socio-political role for teachers as agents of change. As such, the new curriculum for teacher education for instance includes new subject areas such as '*State, ideology, politics and education*', and '*Education for eco-ethics, eco-justice and socio-communitarian-ethics*' in the first year (see Photo 5 in chapter 5).

Before a consensus was created on the final approved version of the ASEP law in December 2010, interviews with various MoE officials showed a range of ideas on the ideal teacher. Historically the MoE has been famous for its rapidly changing staff and this tradition has continued over the past years, recently with an influx of MAS politicians, as well as former social movement members, into governmental institutions. An often made joke when I mentioned I had interviewed the Minister of Education was '*did you get to speak the minister of yesterday, of today or of tomorrow?*'. A result of a mixture of 'old' and 'new' governmental officials inside the MoE, and the fact that the new 'ASEP discourse' was slowly becoming institutionalised in the MoE, I realised that there is a somewhat vague image of an ideal teacher among policy-makers. The emerging discourse related to the ASEP law is starting to become stronger, but still exists next to the prevalent views from staff that were there before Morales, aligning with the 1994 Reform images of an ideal 'professional' teacher, rather than ASEP's ideal image of both a professionally and socio-politically committed teacher. The last ethical-emotional dimension of an ideal teacher can perhaps be best connected to the ASEP law's references to the need for education to foster '*ethical-moral, spiritual and affective capacities*' (Articles 5 and 13, ASEP law 2010), but receives less emphasis than the socio-political dimension.

A government officer who has been working for years in the teacher department of the MoE provided me with many rich details on processes inside the MoE and within the Normales. In line with the 1994 Reform idea of a professional-vocational Bolivian teacher, she explained how: '*a good teacher has always been characterised as an apostle of education. While his salary does not count, she/he has to be a dedicated teacher, a teacher who knows its subject. A teacher has to be a person in the school, someone who writes texts, who has been in the teaching profession for many years. Another important aspect is that a teacher should dedicate her/his time to the youngsters, not only to the school but also to other types of activities. So that is an ideal teacher, like I said, an apostle, a well prepared teacher, a reflexive teacher, but also someone who takes time for extra curricular activities, and with much time available to young people*'(6:8). In my conversations with this policy-maker, it became clear she was clearly frustrated with the decades of demonstrations on the need to increase teachers' salaries.

While many actors agree on the fact that teachers should not (only) fight about their salaries, this primarily professional perspective on a good teacher is contrasted by a former Minister and prominent developer of the new ASEP law. He brings the decolonisation ideology into the ideal teacher-discussion and represents many of the new officers that joined the MoE after 2006. '*A decolonial teacher [...] is skilled for a multicultural population, a teacher needs to speak three languages, he needs to be aware of other conceptualisations, other knowledges, and indigenous communities. And, we need teachers particularly for secondary education, focused on productive areas, which implement an ideology that is neither bureaucratic nor focused on increasing wages only. This is a huge defect, we have to break down this system, we need people that are politically informed, that have a non-salary oriented, non-colonial and productive attitude, that is really important*' (12:21). These ideas are reflected in policy documents, which seem to focus on both teachers' professional and socio-political responsibilities. In an official presentation by a MoE official in October 2007 (Medinaceli, 2007), an ideal teacher was for instance portrayed as: 1) having profound content and didactical knowledge and skills; 2) being a researcher and producer of knowledge; 3) being reflexive and to show solidarity; and 4) being respectful to all students and the pluricultural society. These views seem to incorporate the image of an ideal teacher by social movements that also emphasise teachers' socio-political role.

Social movement and union ideas of the ideal teacher

An interesting view on the ideal Bolivian teacher can be distilled from the demands coming from a range of social movements and institutions that were consulted in the context of the educational commission of the Constitutional Assembly from August 2006-December 2007. According to these demands, teachers need to show a *'greater social commitment'* and a new reform should encourage the formation of *'patriotic teachers that would work eight hours a day'* (Gamboa Rocabado, 2009: 66-67).[139] An indigenous movement leader who was connected to various CEPOs organisations and now works inside the MoE, defined the socio-political characteristics of an ideal teacher; he/she needs to have a *'political profile'*, a *'political clarity'* and is *'contextualised in reality'*. He continued by stating that: *'a teacher needs to be competent as well, I mean that he needs an integral training, he should not just be a mathematics teacher, but he also should be well aware of other situations that are relevant to our lives, he has to understand that in Bolivia we do not only have nine departments, but that we have 36 indigenous groups, and a teacher should also understand that diversity is a potential. So, we want a teacher who is contextualised with his/her diversity, a plurilingual teacher; we no longer want to have monolingual teachers. We also want teachers who are constantly connected to scientific research, and that she/he also knows how to work with new technologies. How can a teacher who does not know how to work with internet be helpful, when this is the reality of its students?'* (14:13). This quote is important, as it reflects very well the new policy image of the ideal Bolivian teacher who is not only aware of the local reality and needs of the community, but who is also knowledgeable in her/his subject and at the same time politically informed and committed to the job.

In former chapters it became clear how unions have quite some influence on what goes on in the Normales, while at the same time unions' perceptions of an ideal teacher have an influence on teachers' identity formation process. In other words, the unions' idea of a good teacher counts, yet it does not affect every teachers' multiple identities in a similar way. While all teachers are paying a contribution to the unions, they do not necessarily also identify directly with the ideology of the unions (see also chapter 5). I heard very different responses from teachers to the urban unions' points of view. In addition, and similar to the influx of social movement leaders into the MoE, I also met former union leaders now working within the MoE. In the Bolivia since Evo Morales, the clear boundaries between social movement/union ideals and government standpoints have somewhat faded, or at least created internal tensions over what an ideal teacher should be.

Nevertheless, particularly within the urban teachers' federation of the city of La Paz, a strong sense of distance and dissatisfaction with government ideals is felt. A female urban union leader told me how teachers in Bolivia need to survive with a low salary, bad working conditions and low status. It is therefore very difficult for them to fulfil their duties in an ideal manner. *'The government only provides the necessary, and our vocation as teachers needs to prevail, we need to be apostles, but we are human apostles, we have to eat, to dress ourselves and live as well'* (79). This union leader clearly feels she is treated unfairly by the government. In contrast, in my conversations with the rural union leaders, there was sympathy with the ideal teacher as represented in the ASEP reform, since *'teachers need to be immersed in the political, social and cultural context of our populations.'* Another rural

---

[139] The general idea behind a longer working day for teachers was to extend their work from the five hours in the classroom to another three hours, which could be used for preparation, training and peer reflection. However, this should be accompanied by higher salaries, because as long as teachers see themselves as forced into having multiple jobs to support their families it remains unrealistic to expect even longer working hours.

union member agreed and stated how one of the biggest challenges for teachers now is to work with the multicultural society of 36 different indigenous groups, and that teachers need to be trained in different languages. Pointing to teachers' professional development, they also highlighted the need for permanent training for in-service teachers in various locations, as rural teachers often have to travel a long way to locations where that training is provided (83). In summary, the rural unions align more closely with the policy image of the ideal teacher than the urban union.

Student teachers' perceptions of the ideal teacher

Both in interviews and surveys, the teacher students in the Normales most often referred to *professional* characteristics of an ideal teacher, followed by the *ethical and emotional* characteristics and finally, the *socio-political* characteristics were mentioned less. In this section I will highlight some interesting variations between the survey and interview answers. Firstly, a wider variety of answers are given in the surveys, which can be explained by the larger number of students included in the surveys as opposed to the interviews. In the interviews there was the opportunity to ask for clarification or further elaboration of the answers, which was not the case in the survey responses.

Firstly, with regards to the professional characteristics, the surveys and interviews show a similar picture. In both institutes, the following characteristics were seen as crucial ones for an ideal 'professional' teacher: being an expert in the subject/theme; being '*actualizado*' [up to date]; being patient; being responsible; having an attitude toward innovation/research; being punctual, dynamic, pedagogically capable/innovative; and finally having a vocation, which was mentioned relatively often. Secondly, concerning the ethical and emotional characteristics, we can see how there is a consensus among students on the importance of good interpersonal relationships (*relaciones humanas*). In the interviews this was most often explained as a good relationship between teacher and student (non-authoritarian, loving, caring, affective), but it was also related to the relationship between teachers and the wider community, teacher-colleagues and parents.

Finally, in relation to the (less often) mentioned socio-political characteristics, we see that most students mentioned a social commitment (*compromiso social*) as being an important quality (both in surveys and interviews). In addition, students commented on the need for an ideal teacher to have a 'realistic' awareness and understanding of society. Rural students often added to this that a teacher should be able to have a commitment to, and relationship with, the community she/he works in.

Nevertheless, this study shows how Bolivian teacher training often fails to develop these three dimensions. Various students shared their concerns about '*very basic subject matter training*' (132). Besides, there were complaints about trainers not being up-to-date, while in-service teachers have very little opportunities to stay '*actualizado*'. In relation to the second category, this chapter will argue how teacher training fails to stimulate a latent pedagogical-vocation and societal commitment of a group of students. And thirdly, students in their internship periods, as well as recently qualified teachers, expressed how they felt unprepared to emotionally deal with the various family problems that children are faced with (absent parents, alcoholism, abuse). In-service teachers also show resistance to new reforms, because of the emotional hardship of having to deal with new policy lines without sufficient training and support. Thus, there is somewhat of a divergence between the policy image of a professional and socio-political committed teacher and students' image of an ideal teacher primarily being a professional, but very importantly also fulfilling ethical-emotional capacities, and to a lesser extent a socio-political commitment.

Teacher trainers views on the ideal teacher

The answers given by the trainers in interviews on the three main characteristics of an ideal teacher show many similarities with students' views. This outcome is supported by what Clandinin et al (2009) call the 'interwoven identities of teacher students and teacher trainers.' When we compare the answers of students and trainers we can see how they seem to use similar terminology to describe the professional characteristics of an 'ideal teacher'. Due to the use of comparable wordings, it is possible to argue that 'having a vocation' and a 'social commitment' is part of a larger discourse on an 'ideal teacher' used in the Normales. More or less in accordance with the current policy image, firstly relative importance was given by trainers to the professional characteristics and secondly to the socio-political characteristics of the ideal teacher. In contrast to the students, less attention was paid to the ethical-emotional part.

To illustrate this, a female rural teacher told me about the enormously heavy and important tasks of rural teachers, for whom a social commitment is a requirement: *'The future teacher has to play an important role of a cultural, political and economic leader in the communities. He/she has to solve problems, be a doctor or even a lawyer sometimes. [...] In the community where I come from, for my uncles, my grandparents and my parents, they feel very good when the teacher takes up the role of having a genuine leadership in the community. But when a teacher comes with an authoritarian attitude, you do not have this possibility, there is no democratic space opening up then. [...] Also, a teacher needs to be a critical individual who is informed about all realities of the education system, from the macro to the micro level and the institutional level. How else is he going to analyse these realities?'* (32:14). In both rural and urban contexts it is very important for a future teacher to know how to 'live together', according to this male urban trainer: *'For me the most important thing is that a teacher learns to be, to know and to live together. We have not understood well enough what the meaning of community is, like Paulo Freire says. Do you know Freire? [Yes, I do] OK, so he says in his book Pedagogy of the Oppressed, that [...] we all have to unite to find something common, that is where the word community comes from. When a teacher does not understand the meaning of 'living together', when he does not learn to live in a community, he will never become a [ideal] teacher. We cannot think that a teacher lives in the stratosphere, or like a satellite in another place, while his work is here, he cannot be in another place. Therefore, a teacher is the only professional that has to be immersed in society, particularly his home, he sometimes has to move this, or even place it at a second or third level, because his first level of work should be with the community'* (47:33). This idea of a sincere community engagement of teachers was often expressed by trainers, and particularly in the rural Normal.

Relatively few trainers talked about the ethical and emotional sides of an ideal teacher. Compared to the importance given to human relations by students, in interviews with trainers this issue was mentioned only twice. In addition, students often argued how teachers should work against discrimination or work toward equal treatment and respect. This issue was less discussed by the trainers, but also not totally ignored. One rural male trainer and academic director explained how he interprets the issue of interculturality in this respect: *'We have students here from the cities, from the interior, from the Valle Alto, of all places, and people speaking Quechua. But interculturality first of all means that they have to identify themselves, and to value who they are, but with respect and tolerance toward the other. They should be sensitive and humble, but always with a spirit of personal growth. If you are Quechua that is fine, if you are an urban citizen or from the provinces, that is also fine, but you should not stay there. Personal growth, what does this mean? To continue studying based on the realities we live in, that teachers form teams to work together, to get a 'licenciatura' or 'maestria' or 'doctorado' degree. Interculturality is large, it is wide, and this is what future teachers should have. Intercultural means to have relationships with all people around you, with parents, other teachers, directors, authorities and students'.* (36:12). This quote, although not representing a majority perspective, links closely to the new ASEP Reform ideal, that is strongly supported by the directors of the rural institute (chapter 6, 7).

Other educators' perceptions of the ideal teacher

To continue with 'all people around you' mentioned in the quote above, what do other (educational) actors say about the characteristics of an ideal teacher? The responses of primary level in-service teachers' again focused on professional and social characteristics of the ideal teacher, paying little attention to teachers' ethical-emotional sides. A female urban principal told me: '*What we look for in a teacher is that he is innovative, permanently up to date and a leader*'. When asked what she meant with 'being a leader', she replied: '*A leader in all aspects, that a teacher knows how to lead a group, how to introduce a subject, how to delegate tasks, how to develop various types of competencies of students, these types of leadership is what we are looking for. That a teacher is democratic, participative, pro-active, that she/he uses different learning strategies that are adequate*' (13:74). Another urban female director emphasised the societal role of teachers: '*Teacher training has to deal with values a lot, because we teachers are a mirror of society, and students mirror us*'. I asked what types of values she was thinking of: '*Responsibility and ethics are very important, [the teachers] have to be very well prepared because, like I said, the Normal only gives the minimal part. Teachers leave the Normal unprepared. [...] Today we do not have the well prepared teachers of the old days anymore. I graduated from the Normal in Sucre, that was an institution, and I don't know if today there are still the same strict teachers. Thanks to them they trained us with much responsibility and ethics, to teach human beings. But now youngsters do not take it as serious as before, with the same responsibility that they have. [...] Teaching means a lot, and we are not just teachers anymore, we are also counsellors*' (60:2-60:4). These quotes lead us to believe that school principals are in favour of a 'strict' and somewhat 'traditional' ideal teacher. Linked to the earlier described negative image of teachers' training in the Normales, is the idea that 'education used to be better in the old days'. This societal stereotypical idea of an unprepared teacher who cares more about salary issues than the educational quality of an ideal teacher, relates to this negative and to some extent nostalgic viewpoint, and was confirmed in my conversations with parents, market sellers, taxi drivers and others.

An urban father and member of a parents association explains why he thinks teachers should be stimulated to do a better job: '*Within society, a teachers needs to show more interest, to really get to know the different issues at the level of the families, to understand the children and what their domestic problems are; and to create more confidence between teachers and students. I think that is the biggest problem in society, it is a vicious circle in which teachers, parents and all other members of the society need to have better communication, but that is not the case now. [...] A teacher needs to be dynamic, and well prepared. During the classes teachers go out to make photocopies, and that is a shame. In the meantime the students loose all their attention and start to play. I tell the teachers they have all afternoon and all night to prepare the classes. [...] They also should be at the school at 8 in the morning or earlier, many teachers are too late.*' (57:10, 57:22) This father's view echoes the professional image of an ideal teacher being engaged with the direct community, being fully prepared and up-to-date with the latest training and innovations, and punctual.

There is, thus, consensus on the importance of the professional characteristics of an image of an 'ideal Bolivian teacher'. In addition, current policy-makers and social movements especially emphasise the socio-political roles and trainers seem to follow that line of thought while students emphasise the importance of ethical-emotional aspects of a good teacher. Similarities in the use of words and concepts by students and trainers appear to point toward a common discourse in Normales on what an ideal teacher should look like. It seems that the current decolonising education discourse of ASEP has been influential in the narratives on teachers' socio-political characteristics, as agents of change, particularly in the rural Normal and rural teachers union, and for the new staff of the MoE. The ASEP 'policy image' of a teacher that is capable in all three dimensions of 'the ideal teacher' seems to partly conflict with student teachers' own (personal and professional) identities, that do not so much emphasise the socio-political roles. As stated in chapter 4, this 'identity conflict' lies at the heart of the implementation problem of educational reform in most developing countries' (Jansen, 2001a: 242), in Bolivia having resulted in a partial implementation of the 1994 Reform (see chapter 2) and an envisaged troublesome implementation of the ASEP law (see also chapter 5).

8.4 A categorisation of teacher's motivations

Internal and external perceptions of *the ideal teacher* and *her/his roles* are intrinsically linked to teachers' motivations for choosing their profession. Both in the surveys and in the interviews I included an open question on '*why do you want to become a teacher?*' Drawing from the outcomes of the data on Bolivian students' motivations, I slightly adapted Welmond's categorisation (see introduction Part IV) and constructed a tripartite typology of teacher motivations that are particularly relevant to the Bolivian context, including: 1) **economic**; 2) **pedagogical-vocational**; and 3) **socio-political motivations**.[140] Figure 9 illustrates how the different codes I used in Atlas Ti, to analyse interview transcripts, were grouped together into this typology. In a similar manner, I categorised the answers given in surveys.

Under economic motivations, I purposefully placed 'learning the English language'. Reasons mentioned for this motivation included, for instance, a better chance to get a good teaching position, as there are few (trained) English teachers. In addition, students also referred to the need for English teachers in private institutes and better opportunities to study or migrate abroad (to the US). Similar reasons were mentioned by this urban English teacher student: '*The quality of education is very low. I want to escape this country; therefore I want to study something in tourism, to go to another place. But in the meantime, they are not going to accept me in a University over there [abroad], or I would have to be an endowed person, because only they can go, students from the higher class, children from businessman or corrupt people, only they can get the scholarships*' (21:19). Parents' stimulation to send their youngsters to a Normal is also related to the economic security and welfare benefits of the teaching job. This chapter will show how these and the other economic and material motivations although prevalent, are not the sole motivations of students to become a teacher. In contrast to what would be expected from the existing literature on Bolivian teachers, most students also expressed to have more ideologically based pedagogical and socio-political motivations. Figure 9 illustrates how pedagogical types of motivations are linked to having a 'pedagogical-vocational

---

[140] My first and second categories correspond with Welmond's first and second-plus-third categories, and I added the socio-political category because of its relevance to analyse Bolivia's current envisaged role for teachers as agents of change. See also the introduction to Part IV.

motivation', while the socio-political motivations includes what many respondents called a *'compromiso social'* – a societal commitment. Both a pedagogical-vocational motivation, as well as a socio-political commitment was mentioned by different actors to be crucial characteristics of an ideal teacher. People's motivations, like their hybrid identities, are not static and can change according to their understanding of society. Considering Bolivia's changing socio-political situation, this chapter aims to understand future teachers' motivations at this point in time.

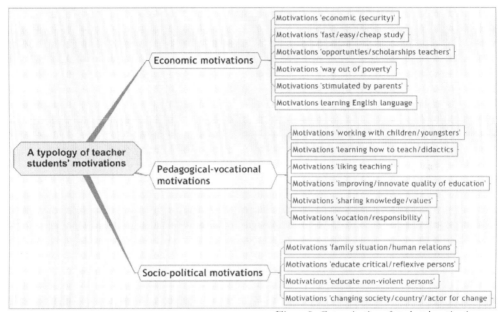

Figure 9: Categorisation of students' motivations

8.5 Perceptions of future teachers' motivations

According to the general public opinion, as well as several authors, in Bolivia a particular desire to teach is frequently not a motivation to start the teaching career (Canessa, 2004: 190; Contreras and Talavera, 2004a; Speiser, 2000: 228-229; Torres del Castillo, 2007: 13; Urquiola et al, 2000). A secure job position, salary and welfare arrangements are important – and understandable – reasons to enter the profession in the Bolivian context of low economic growth and opportunities. However, this is not the complete picture. The following section aims to provide a more nuanced view on future teachers' motivations to become a teacher.

Student's motivations – more than economics!

Figure 10 provides an illustration and an indication of the types of answers given in interviews with student teachers and the proportions of each type, based on my analysis and interpretations of these answers. Interestingly, these outcomes contrast the general negative view in Bolivian society and literature that students are only driven by economic motivations. Students claim to also have pedagogical-vocational or socio-political motivations and, similar to students' perceptions of the 'ideal teacher', with somewhat less weight given to the socio-political dimension. Responding to interview questions can have the effect of answering with 'politically correct' answers.

Figure 10, students' motivations (interview data)

So, while this figure might represent a too positive picture about students' level of vocation and societal commitment, it still helps to demonstrate that students do not *only* have economic motives. The difference between students' latent educational and socio-political motives and the perceived lack of vocation in dominant discourses, is what I call the unused potential of Bolivian future teachers as actors of change.

Figure 10 illustrates how the majority of students gave a pretty balanced answer when talking about their own motivations, as they included pedagogical-vocational, economic and socio-political reasons in their replies. With regard to the economic or 'opportunity' motivations, a young male urban student mentioned that besides his future work as a teacher *'which is only for a couple of hours per day'*, he also wants to work in commercial publicity, *'which I can also do in just a few hours'* (20:7). In contrast to the more material motivations, many students also used terms such as 'development', 'progress', 'innovations' and 'improvement' in their answers, related more to the pedagogical and socio-political categories. The quote of a rural student, for example, shows a strong social commitment: *'We have had so many years of discrimination, also within education, and therefore I have chosen to become a teacher, to improve Bolivia, technologically, culturally. Especially because we are here in Warisata, we deal with intercultural and bilingual education. I speak two languages, both Castellano and Aymara'* (68:1).

I found an interesting difference between the answers in interviews (see Figure 10) and surveys outcomes. In the interviews I did not only ask for people's personal motivations to become a teacher (as in the surveys); I also asked about the motivations of the majority of students in their Normal. When the questions were depersonalised, students almost always referred to the majority of students having economic motivations – a secure salary, fixed job positions, welfare arrangements (18:9, 28, 10) – to become a teacher. In several interviews, students came up with an estimation of how many students entered 'with vocation' – this was mostly estimated between 10 % and 30% – and a majority of students who entered for other (economic) reasons (e.g. 21: 14). However, from the surveys a rather different picture emerged, because only a small minority mentioned economic motivations as their reason to become a teacher. When writing things down black-on-white, students were perhaps tempted to give even more 'politically correct' answers. Besides, it should be considered that students' perceptions are not only based on their own experiences in the Normal, but that their images of economically motivated colleague students might also be strengthened and influenced by a national discourse of a negative image of teachers.

Other actors' perceptions of motivations of students
Most teacher trainers' believe that the majority of students enter the teaching profession because of economic motivations (including job security; a way out of poverty; short and easy study; having status in a community) and just a minority because of pedagogical-vocational or socio-

political reasons (for instance working with children; improving educational quality; or to change society). A rural trainer for instance mentioned: '*There are very few students who come here because of their vocation. That is what I have observed. [...] Perhaps because of economic motives, they go to the Normal*' (32:2, 32:5). Another urban trainer added: '*I recognise with much clarity those students that have a vocation to become a teacher, and those that arrived here because of opportunity. I estimate that this [the division] is more or less fifty-fifty. You notice their level of profoundness of the theme, the interest to get to know their theme. But I will do some research on this, and I will have a better judgement at the end of the semester*' (50:13/14). Likewise, an urban school director explained how: '*in our country being a teacher is easy, because we have a fixed salary. So they have a job, a salary, but when they start teaching I noticed that in some cases teachers do not implement changes. In contrary, they turn to use more and more traditional teaching, and here you can see that there is a lack of vocation to change. [...] From my experience with students coming here for their practical training, in general terms I think that 40% do have a vocation to be a teacher, and the others become teachers because of the secure work*' (55:4). A researcher, indigenous movement member and former teacher trainer argued that most students who want to become teachers are sons and daughters of peasants, and only few have parents that are middle class workers or politicians. '*Therefore, we came to understand that education is one of the building stones of colonisation. Why? Because at least you have to become something in life, meaning to leave life as a farmer, and because of this conviction, even out of inertia, people try to enter the Normal*'(24). Although similar estimates of other respondents vary quite a bit, they all indicate a consensus on the idea that most student teachers have a lack of vocation for their future job.

Another rural trainer voiced a more positive view and explained his strategy to 'develop vocation': '*To find out about students motivations, I share with them my own trajectory when I meet them for the first time, my life testimony as a teacher in different parts of the country, and I provoke them to explain what their motivations are, and most of them say yes, they have an interest, a vocation*' (33:7). When asked about their own motivations as trainers, they often referred to vocation being their main reason to work as a teacher (trainer). An interesting finding from the perceptions of teacher trainers is that although vocation is maybe seen as a crucial characteristic of an ideal Bolivian teacher, it can actually be 'learned' or developed. This means that, if stimulated by teacher training, those who decide to become teachers out of necessity can also gain a sense of vocation from their job. A former teacher trainer explained how he saw his role in stimulating a vocation among his students, revealing an exceptional but promising example: '*I started to show them a feeling for the teaching profession, I tried to generate more interest and value for this profession [...] I even exaggerated to them saying that the job of a teacher is more important than that of a doctor. A doctor saves lives, and cures diseases, but a teacher can also save lives! [...] when I resigned from the Normal it was heart-warming, many students came to say goodbye and one told me 'you have helped us to love our profession, I did not want to become a teacher, but now I love the job*'. He told me this was one of the best things he experienced as a trainer. He continued in a more serious tone, stating that '*I see that many of my colleagues do not do anything like this. But,* he added more positively, '*I think students are flexible, they can generate real spaces of change, of compromises, of educational transformations*' (24). The following transcription from a feedback-discussion, with a group of rural teachers on the preliminary outcomes of this research in April 2010, provides further insights into how 'vocation' can be 'learned' (121):

Fem TT A: A lot of the students are here out of necessity, or because their parents want them to. Many youngsters do not have a cause in life; they just want a secure job. But, we have to work with them; we have to engage with our societal values. The majority now recognises where they come from, we all start to recognise our identities. And for me...my vocation only came with time...

Fem TT B: But, we also have young people that really want to become teachers, they come here after having committed some mistakes in life, and they turn out to be the best students.

Male TT A: Having a vocation is not necessary, because you can 'catch' (*grabar*) it later on, you have to become aware of what you are doing and the things around you, a teacher needs to continue to innovate.

Male TT B: I feel a bit uncomfortable when I hear my colleagues ask why students come here if they have no vocation. Because... I never had a vocation myself when I started. I never thought I would become a teacher. But we have to develop, a teacher can never be the same as its students, he/she always has to be better. A teacher always needs to innovate.

Male TT C: There are two criteria with regard to teachers' vocation: '*hay maestros que nacen y maestros que se hacen*': there are those that are born with it, and those that have to learn it.

While most trainers agree that 'having a vocation' actually matters, either from the start or later on, being a good teacher is not necessarily the same as having a vocation, as good quality teachers also require a proper training, sufficient (pedagogical and financial) support and opportunities for peer reflection and professional and personal development. In contrast to trainers' discursive emphasis on the importance of helping to develop student' vocational commitment, this is only put into practice by a small minority of trainers.

Thus, while vocation is considered as something that can be developed, my research shows that often this stimulation does not lie at the core of teacher training practices. Teacher education fails to cover a potentially important part of future teachers' development. This idea of an unused potential was confirmed when I discussed it with a Director of an institute in Santa Cruz: '*a good proportion of the students indeed have a vocational tendency. Maybe our training is too formal now, too technical. Until now we have focused the training on the processes of teaching and learning, which made us ignore the other affective and personal part. Actually, I think that in order to encourage a vocational attitude we should continuously strengthen their enthusiasm and affection* (122:17). In contrast to these views of the Bolivian teacher trainers that vocation is something that can be developed 'from the outside', Palmer (1997) claims how vocation should not be imposed, as it should come from within. I consider both points of view as valid and a possible solution to combine these insights would be to pay more attention within teacher education to the self reflection of student teachers on their own motivations and roles. Or, in Palmers' words, there is a necessity of an 'inward connection' during teaching, to the 'teacher within', in other words an acknowledgement and awareness of the complex *internal* identities of a teacher. From the literature on critical and social justice oriented teacher education approaches (including Clandinin et al, 2009; Palmer, 1997; Walkington, 2005; and Zeichner, 2009) we can also learn that there is a need to create (safe) spaces within teacher training for student teachers to reflect, actively challenge and discuss amongst themselves their personal identities, motivations, their practical experiences (in the framework of the PDI course – see chapter 7) and their future roles.

A young female teacher who graduated ten years ago from the urban Normal, talks about her ideas of vocational teaching: '*it depends, some teacher dedicate their life and soul to teaching, and others not, maybe because they are tired. Some teachers are very old and they cannot stop working because their pension is not arranged well. Also, teachers who follow courses and update their knowledge should be rewarded for that. My friends make fun of me, because I always follow extra courses in my spare time, they tell me to stop spending my money on it. But I tell them I do it out of love for my work'* (119:21). This extraordinarily motivated teacher is an exception to the rule, yet she highlights certain structural issues that hinder teachers' continuous vocation, including a lack of pension arrangements for older teachers and an absence of structural teacher support and in-service training (as highlighted in chapters 6 and 7).

In relation to the last type of socio-political motivations, a former teacher now working in an international organisation argued that the main problem with students' limited pedagogical-vocational and socio-political motivations, is the absence of discussing Bolivia's reality in the training and the lack of a stimulating/evaluating environment for teachers when they have entered the 'security of the profession' (see also chapter 6). *'Students aspirations just stop when they receive their title, and they are assured of a job by the government. There is no political orientation. For trainers it's similar, their ultimate aspiration is becoming a trainer at the Normal, and then that's enough, then they only have to wait until retirement.* (3:14) This also links to what I call the missed potential, which so far is not taken up properly in the training structures for teachers.

Finally, and contrary to an attitude of apathy of a large group of teacher trainers (see chapter 6), I would like to end this section by showing the existence of the aspirations of a trainer and a student teacher to be(come) an actor of change. An urban trainer told me a teacher *'needs to be an actor of social change, a teacher has to stimulate changes in the societal context, and from their search for a change in an associated community which relates to the thought of the children and the youth. And from here also promote learning situations, and this way the community we work in can also develop, gain new knowledge, new technologies. In order to do so, I am looking for a new teacher profile, based on these characteristics; maybe a teacher should be like a mediator'* (43:13). The following quote from an urban teacher student similarly illustrates my point: *'A teacher has to open up panoramas. In our society, I think we need teachers who teach children to reflect, who can think for themselves, who do not reproduce, who know how to enter a discussion also with their teacher. That is my dream, that they do not accept just how things are. It is like...since we were children we have been taught to be passive, and many children think like that: 'I cannot succeed'. We have to motivate them more, and to help them and show them that they can, that what you start you also have to finish, that you are perseverant, that you can change your own reality, and by doing so also your surroundings. An educated population is a population that thinks. And they will be critical about their reality and transform it'* (19:34). Conversations like these made me realise the issue of 'future teachers as agents of change' is not something that exists only in discourse and literature, but is also recognised as a potential reality by educators in the field and is therefore the topic of the next chapter.

8.6 Concluding reflections – An unused potential

The ASEP law aims to bridge the historical division between rural and urban education in Bolivia. However, in reality this divide is still very relevant and influential in the lives and work of teachers in either rural or urban contexts. In the Bolivian context of inequality and poverty, particularly in rural communities, teachers have an huge responsibility as they often fulfill multiple pedagogical and social roles as varied as being a classroom teacher for multiple grades, a conflict broker in the community or someone who gives medical or judicial advice to less educated community members. Teachers in rural areas thus face specific difficulties of having to fulfill these multiple additional social roles, as well as coping with more difficult living conditions due to a lack of (clean) water, electricity and long travel distances between both family and training opportunities. Urban teachers', on the other hand, also face various difficulties. They see themselves forced to work in two or three shifts in order to pay their bills, while they also consider their job more difficult because of a lack of parental and community engagement in children's education.

Bolivia's political discourse on the ideal teacher (for the ideal citizen) has shifted from a more professional teacher image (in accordance with the 1994 Reform), to an image of a teacher who is professionally capable, emotionally prepared and ethically committed, while also taking her/his socio-political responsibilities seriously. But, is it realistic to expect all teachers – urban and rural – to be professionally and emotionally fully prepared and dedicated to their job, while at the same time functioning as active *'soldiers of Bolivia's liberation and decolonisation'*, as Evo Morales would like to see (Ministerio de Educación de Bolivia, 2010d)? Bearing in mind the difficulties of both rural and urban teachers' jobs mentioned above, this is perhaps a utopia if similar stuctural obstacles remain to exist. In email conversations with Ramiro, he reflected that Evo Morales often uses *'radical expressions and a bit shocking metaphors'*, but he often gets misinterpreted by Bolivian media. According to Ramiro, it is in the personality of Morales to want to break through existing *'schemes and structures'* of *'ignorance and marginalisation'*. Hence, by calling teachers Bolivia's 'soldiers of change', *'he does not so much refer to taking up arms or defending ourselves with arms, but the fight [he refers to] is about looking forward, and to do everything we can from within our position [as teachers]'.*[141] In a historical analysis of South African policy images of *'teachers as liberators'* at the end of Apartheid (1980s), Jansen argues how we could draw the policy lesson that *'new images of teachers, however compelling in political terms, do not translate into new ways of teaching and learning'*. He continues to explain how *'the image of teachers as liberators was perhaps an effective tool for mobilising teachers and students politically but it certainly did not change the ways in which the system functioned educationally'* (2001a: 243). Though the data of this study similarly shows how most of Bolivia's future teachers and their trainers have not adopted the new 'extended' policy image yet, this study also illustrates how the changing Bolivian socio-political context enables changing profiles and identities that might have a transformative impact on teacher students' future practices, as it already does for some of the exceptional decolonising and inter-/intracultural oriented trainers, including Ramiro.

Why, if being a teacher in Bolivia seems such a challenging job are so many young students and professionals so determined in wanting to enter the teaching profession? The common thought about Bolivia's teachers motivations in Bolivian society are shaped along the lines of an absence of alternatives and a way out of poverty. My research shows that indeed many students opt for the teaching profession because of material and economic motivations, which is, considering the socio-economic status of the majority of the Bolivian population, a logical and valid motive. Nevertheless, the general negative view in Bolivia of students *only* entering the Normales because of financial reasons should be nuanced as both interviews and survey results revealed how both urban and rural students also expressed various kinds of pedagogical and socio-political related reasons for entering the teaching profession.

This chapter demonstrated that there is a potential – yet unused – pedagogical-vocational and socio-political aspiration among the students at the Normales. Instead of blaming the

---

[141] Personal communication with Ramiro (introduced in chapter 1) in May 2011.

majority of (future) teachers themselves for a lack of commitment and vocation to the teaching profession and socio-political transformation, which is a commonly used argument, I argue that the structural constraints of the (pre-service and in-service) teacher training system fail to address and stimulate teachers' motivations to provide good education and become actors of change; Bolivian teachers miss a permanent source of support to help them stay motivated and updated, while they face low social status, a deficient pre-service training and the challenge to combine multiple jobs at the same time. Building on the SJTE debates, *ideally* teacher education programmes would stimulate students to become motivated, reflexive and critical teachers by creating spaces within teacher training to reflect, actively challenge and discuss amongst themselves their personal identities, motivations, practical experiences (in PDI – see chapter 7) and future roles (including Clandinin et al, 2009; Palmer, 1997; Walkington, 2005; Zeichner, 2009). Relating back to the SRA and critical education theorists, this active challenge and reflection will help students to avoid merely fitting in to the existing structures and uncritically following the beliefs and attitudes of their trainers. The current ASEP law, and particularly the PDI-course as discussed in chapter 7, brings a (still largely unused) potential for this type of reflection.

As a conclusion to this chapter, I would like to emphasise that – in contrast to the existing negative views of Bolivian teachers' lack of aspirations – we should not forget about those who have a (latent) motivation to be (come) a good teacher and actor of change. In Part V we will turn to look at the possibilities and constraints for teachers' agency, bearing in mind this strategic selective context (Part III) and the complexities of teachers' identities, motivations and roles (Part IV).

PART V

AGENCY, CHANGE & CONTINUITY

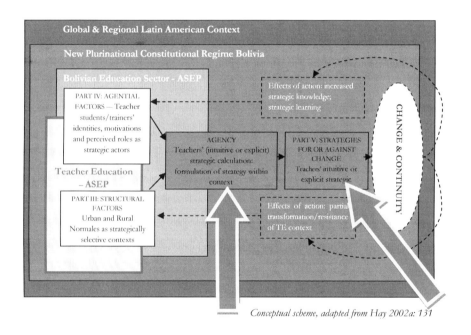

Conceptual scheme, adapted from Hay 2002a: 131

The final part of the thesis particularly aims to shed light on teachers' strategic actions as potential actors for or against change. The strategic function of education in processes of social change has historically been recognised and used (or even abused) for (geo)political strategies all over the globe: during colonial times in divide and rule tactics; in new independent countries, as an instrument for national integration and homogenisation; as an instrument of modernisation – and later marketisation; and more recently as a breeding ground for massive political revolutions in the Arab world. Tabulawa's (2003) work illustrates how the idea of educators as change agents has also been adopted in ideologically different debates. Education sectors in 'peripherical' states received massive flows of foreign aid, as part of a widespread modernisation and later on a democratisation project. In many countries in the Global South, a Western type of education was expected to bring about the necessary transformation into modern states based on '*Western values and entrepenuerial attitudes*' (Tabulawa 2003: 22). From a completely different perspective, the idea of teachers as change agents has also been adopted in critical pedagogical debates about SJTE, as elaborated in chapter 2. Drawing from Gramscian thinking, in order to bring about change, teacher trainers and teachers alike therefore '*must abandon their role as lackeys of the ruling hegemony and take upon themselves the responsibility to act as 'organic intellectuals*' (Yogev and Michaeli, 2011: 316).

Teachers are, as Giddens stated, 'actors with agency' (Giddens 1995 in Talavera Simoni, 2011: 22). Teachers' material conditions as well as their ideas, discourses and perceptions are reflected in their identites, motivations and strategies. We can thus speak of an interlinked relationship between teachers' identities and their agency (Moore 2008: 595). Teachers' agency has been defined in various ways, including as '*gaining control over ones behaviour*', '*the power to act purposively and reflectively*', or as '*the conscious role people play to bring about social change*' (Moore, 2008: 589). Some authors use the term 'voice' instead of 'agency', referring to how teachers '*make specific choices based on their own histories and their evolving professional lives*', while they are being '*constrained*' or '*shaped*' to some extent by their surrounding contexts (Delany-Barmann, 2010: 184). The importance of teachers' agency in relation to broader socio-political processes of change is discussed by Vongalis-Macrow. She argues how teachers '*are not only engaging in the reproduction of structural change aligning to globalization-driven reforms to their work and practice, but also, in adapting and reacting to new structural conditions, they are transformed through their actions*' (Vongalis-Macrow, 2007: 425). Teachers' strategies are hence fluid rather than static and closely linked to their changing perceptions of society and their role within it. Moore argues that SJTE should encourage teacher students' identity formation and 'critical agency', meaning the '*degree to which pre-service teachers adopted an identity as agents of change [...] to promote social justice*' (Moore, 2008: 594). Teachers' identities and their agency can thus be viewed as complementary 'co-constructions', eventually affecting processes of social change' (2008: 607).

Studying teachers' resistance to reform implementation is a pressing issue globally (Achinstein and Ogawa, 2006; Tatto, 2007). In order to overcome teachers' resistance to change, genuine participation of (future) teachers in policy-making processes is indispensable (Auala, 2005; Kosar Altinyelken, 2010). Collectively organised in unions, teachers can act in response to educational changes (such as reforms) and societal changes.[142] Vongalis-Macrow (2007) signals how, in light of the the crisis in the teaching profession (see also chapter 1), teacher agency is being narrowed down – or 'reterritorialised' – in many parts of the world. In addition, teachers' individual roles and responsibilities are promoted at the expense of collective teacher action and voice, hence downplaying the power of teacher unions (Vongalis-Macrow, 2007: 428-432). Consequently, it is important not to exaggerate the role of teachers in these processes of (social and educational) change, since their agency and strategies are often constrained by the strategic selective and multiscalar context they live and work in. Feminist and post-structuralist scholars in the field of education similarly emphasise the limits to agency; they challenge the idea that actors have access to power as a kind of commodity. In this perspective, empowered individuals or groups indeed have the ability to disrupt oppressive policies, practices and perspectives. They

---

[142] Education International, the international organisation representing teacher unions worldwide, struggles for the right to collective forms of teacher autonomy and teacher agency. Teacher unions, and in Bolivia especially the urban one, often focus more on issues of redistribution, and a fair rewarding system and status, than on recognition and the socio-cultural aspects of education.

cannot, however, completely and continuously overcome unequal power relations, nor escape from their position in a social order (North, 2008: 1192). Besides, it depends very much on (future) teachers' own motivations to become a teacher (McDonald and Zeichner, 2009: 603), teachers' (future) material conditions and the way teacher training stimulates or prescribes the future tasks of a (n ideal) teacher, in how far teachers can and will be engaged in struggles for social justice (Grant, 2009: 655).

Teachers, thus, can potentially act as agents in processes of change, be it as progressive, conservative or oppositional agents for/against change. The last part of this book aims to contribute to analysing and explaining how, and why, Bolivian teacher training institutions, policy makers, teacher trainers and (future) teachers – purposefully or unintendedly – design their strategies to *actively support*, *passively follow*, *passively resist* or *actively oppose* the broader goals of Morales' new regime.

9

Marches or maths:
Bolivia's future teachers as soldiers of change?

'We should be the change we wish to see in the world'
(Mahatma Gandhi, in Grant, 2009: 655)

9.1 Introduction

After weeks of unrest, road blocks and protests, Bolivia's social tensions reached a peak on 11 September 2008. A privately hired militia, funded by the local opposition, opened fire on MAS supporters in the rural regions of the department of Pando (Dangl, 2010). This violent encounter left eleven dead, and numerous supporters wounded (La Razon, 09-09-13). The following day, the horrific stories were on the tips of the tongues of students and trainers in the Simón Bolívar. Through cell phone contact with relatives and friends in the region, students heard that their fellow students at the Normal 'Puerto Rico' in Filadelfia, Pando, were among the victims of the conflict. A few days later, the newspaper La Razon reported that the director of this Normal, presumably a MAS supporter, had obliged all students and trainers to take part in the demonstration, obviously without foreseeing these tragic consequences (La Razon, 09-09-17).[143]

Photos 14 and 15, students and trainers protesting against violence in Pando, 16 September 2008

About a week after that day, on Tuesday 16 September, three Normales located in the cities of La Paz and El Alto suspended all classes while they organised a mass demonstration in support of

---

[143] The newspaper quoted a mother of one of the victims who lost their life, the mother stated the Director had pressured his students and staff with a fine of 1.500 Bolivianos (or about a month of salary for a senior teacher) if they did not show up during the march.

their fallen colleagues. Students and trainers of the Simón Bolívar gathered along with urban unionsts (e.g the COB, CONMERB, and the Retired Teachers organisation). One of the students I got to know in Simón Bolívar told me *'we are here to support our 'compañeros' from Pando. But you know'*, he continued, *'the Santa Cruz owned newspapers will tell you we are here to support the MAS, but I am not voting for Evo's MAS. I am here to demand justice for those in Pando'*. The student and his colleagues assured me that they were not obliged to come. The trainers, in contrast, were taking it in turns to sign an attendence list that was brought by the director.

Whilst most banners and slogans demanded 'justice' and 'solidarity', some of the participants also shared other motivations for marching in the streets. While an active union member recalled the necessity for a just retirement system, one of the trainers of Aymara language argued that the march was organised *'also because, as indigenous teacher trainers, we want to be respected, we want equality'*.[144] Apart from these different motives, and despite the felt obligations of trainers and perhaps students alike to be present that afternoon, they shared a common concern; being a teacher in Bolivia means being caught up in a context of social and political conflicts. These events, the violent encounter in Pando and the following peaceful demontration in La Paz, illustrate how Bolivia's teachers find themselves located in, and influenced by, a tense and multifaceted 'strategically selective context', in which they (un)intendedly design their strategies that, in turn, have an effect on this context. The fact that, in both Pando and La Paz, trainers and students were pressured to take part in the collective action on the street illustrates how the choice between 'marches' or 'maths' is not a totally free choice, but rather a strongly politicised one.

These and other types of demonstrations are occuring on a weekly basis all over the country, showing a continuous dissatisfaction with Bolivia's politics. It is in this context, that Bolivian teachers develop their professional and political strategies for, or against, Evo's politics of change. For Bolivia's teachers there is the rural/urban divide of the system, the unions' positions that teachers do or do not agree with, their personal socio-economic situation and opportunities to climb the social ladder, family pressures, the desire to remain faithful to political affiliations (either pro- or contra-Morales) and a lack of democratic alternatives; Evo is perhaps not the best, but for many certainly the only option. Based on the work of Gramsci, Baud and Rutten rightly emphasise the important role of individuals in processes of social change: *'The history of the Zapatistas or al-Qaeda would have been different without Sub-comandante Marcos or Osama bin Laden'* (Baud and Rutten 2004:6). Similarly, Bolivia's recent historical developments would have probably looked different without Evo Morales. On a lower scale, the classrooms and streets of Bolivia would look differently without the strategies of Elisa, Benardo and Dilma, three Bolivian educators who are introduced in Textbox 6. Their respective (absence of) strategies with regard to the current socio-political state of affairs are inherently interrelated to the strategic selective context.

---

[144] All quotes are derived from transcription no. 45, a collection of recorded conversations before and during the march of 16 September 2008.

Box 6. Three Bolivian educators and their strategies

Elisa* – is a 32 year old female student teacher at the Simón Bolívar studying to become an English teacher, because on the one hand she *'wants to teach children to become good and useful citizens for the country'*, while on the other hand she perceives learning English as an opportunity *'to travel and communicate in other countries'*. She was born and raised in the city, has Spanish as her mother tongue and identifies herself with the Aymara culture. She was formerly trained in linguistics and has worked as a management assistant. She is also a mother of a daughter (6) and a son (4), and she currently works as a private English language teacher after her busy schedule of classes in the Normal. She struggles to combine her family with her study and work, and depends on her mother for child care, as her husband works long days as well. She is not well informed about the new ASEP law, but she thinks it is crucial that teachers *'do not discriminate on the basis of colour or culture'*. Because she has little knowledge on the ins and outs of ASEP, she feels concerned about the implications of the new policies for her future job, but she has no clear stance for or against it.

Benardo* – is a 60 year old teacher trainer in Pedagogy at Simón Bolívar. He was born in a rural village where he learned to speak both Quechua and Aymara. As a strong supporter of Morales' new policy lines, he identifies himself with the 'Plurinational culture'. He graduated from the René Barrientos Normal in Oruro in 1968 and has served as an educator for more than 40 years, in different parts of the country. He formerly also worked as a consultant for international organisations such as UNICEF, and he currently is lecturing both in the Simón Bolívar, at a University in El Alto and at the UMSSA in La Paz. Guided by the ideology of the new ASEP law, in the Normal he follows an individual strategy to change and improve teacher education *'ideally into a scientific community of teacher education'*. He feels restricted by the institutional environment, which only partly supports the new policy ideals. Also, he has a critical attitude towards the unions' position of resistance. He explained: *'Education does not belong to God, nor to Aristotle or Karl Marx. Education belongs to the population, it is a social issue, an issue of social change, against discrimination and racism. Education is like oxygen. It allows me to live well (vivir bien)'*.

Dilma* – is a female primary school teacher, union activist and ex-leader of the La Paz federation, and a University student in her fifties. She clearly supports a collective strategy of resistance to the government policies, including ASEP, and continuingly battles in defense of teachers' rights to *'increase teachers' salaries and their retirement conditions'*. From a Trotskyist perspective, she believes that until radical structural socio-economic transformation has taken place, changes in the classroom will only be of a very minor significance, as it needs to be part of a 'total transformation'. *'Change'*, Dilma said, *'needs to start at the basis, and we, as a union, need to guide this popular basis'*. I observed, however, an interesting divergence between Dilma-as-union-leader and Dilma-as-school-teacher: one afternoon she loudly escorted a massive crowd of teachers through the city centre, resisting tear gas attacks as she continued to shout slogans in the megaphone; the next morning I saw her rubbing hand cream into the hands of the children in her classroom, while gently stimulating them to present their work in front of the class. Reflecting herself on her role as a teacher, she said *'in this chaotic situation we find ourselves in, which also affects the children and their families, we as teachers have to be the first soldiers in the process of social transformation'*. Unintendedly, she used the same terminology to talk about teachers as 'soldiers of change' that Evo Morales would use a few years later, during the inauguration of the new ASEP law.

* The names of these respondents have been changed to ensure their anonymity.

This chapter is dedicated to Bolivia's (future) teachers' agency – their space to manoeuvre – and the consequent strategies they adopt. Teachers are key actors when it comes to social transformation, as they constitute a group of actors that can work to enhance educational innovation and affect socio-political change, or resist against such processes. Drawing on insights from the SRA (Hay, 2002a) and critical education theories, the chapter analyses the possibilities and challenges Bolivian teachers face in their work in Bolivia's challenging context of continuing tensions, discrimination and instability. While bearing in mind the obstacles and possibilities for institutional change (described in part III of the book) and the misunderstood, and largely ignored, agential potential among student teachers (Part IV), this chapter aims to show what space for manoeuvre – or agency – is left for (future) teachers in order to adopt strategies that work for or against educational *and* societal change. The chapter starts by analysing Bolivian discourses around Bolivian (future) teachers as actors of change. I then provide an analysis of teachers' individual and collective strategies for change or continuity in the Bolivian context, and conclude with a discussion of possible steps to be taken in the area of teacher training.

9.2 Teachers' agency – Bolivian discourses on teachers as actors of change

According to Article 33.1 of the new ASEP law (2010, 'Objectives of Teacher Education'), within the state's new vision teachers are essential actors in transforming Bolivian society. The law stipulates how teachers should be trained to become '*critical, auto-critical, reflexive, proactive, innovative professionals and researchers, who are dedicated to democracy, social transformation and the integral inclusion of all Bolivians*'. The data of this study indeed confirms that many actors in the education field, including policy makers, teacher trainers, student teachers and teachers themselves, *perceive* educators to be potential or actual agents of change. These perceptions, however, also show that not all teachers are able or willing to be(come) change agents. The ideas of what a Bolivian 'teacher-for-change' looks like are discussed in this section.

Benardo, the senior trainer at Simón Bolívar, explains how current forms of teacher education have to change drastically: '*Currently teachers are prepared to become conservative actors, they are prepared only for their work within the four walls of the classroom*' (9:32). Benardo also sees the low level of education of those students that enter the Normal as a result of the reproduction of a '*system that has represented a certain model of the state for a long time. But now, reality is different. A wound is bleeding now, and we need a different type of teachers, and different trainers*' (108:10). Another pro-ASEP teacher trainer, working in the rural institute, also sees a momentum for change in the Normales, as there is '*a dire need to train new societal leaders. Teacher education needs to become closer aligned with the political process of change, so that our new teachers will be able to guide new societal leaders, through education they will get to know urgent social problematic situations of conflict, regional separatism and discrimination, and this requires teachers' participation*' (33:4). These comments align closely with the SJTE ideal of teachers as active and engaged intellectuals.

The above mentioned quotes accurately reflect on the present 'momentum for change' in the Normales. But, how do trainers see their own roles as agents of change? Benardo explains: '*as a trainer in pedagogy I try to train the new teachers with a capacity to read their reality, the socio-cultural reality, so that they can engage in a dialectical relation with it. Now it is time to reflect, to change, and to search for new politics and new pedagogies*' (108:3). According to an urban colleague of Benardo, '*we talk with our students about values, about the role of education in our society, and about their role as permanent actors in change processes. We are training future teachers, so that they can make a change in society. If not, they have no reason to be here in the Normal'* (48:25). In the rural institute, a senior trainer reflected how, in order to become an agent of change himself, he would start with *'critically analysing my own reality, to think about what kind of citizens this country will need, how we can make use of our human and natural resources. In order to do this, we as educators, we have to be committed to the new movement, the new political changes. I will think about how to train our new teachers in such a way they construct a reflexive educational praxis themselves, so that education can become the engine of change of this society'* (43:20). Clearly in support of the new government plans, this trainer also stated how *'for me, the biggest satisfaction of being a teacher trainer is when your students after some years are able to engage in the same reflexive processes, and have become active subjects, people who can innovate, who can make a change'* (43:14). During the course of my four years of fieldwork, the director of this same rural institute exchanged the countryside surroundings for the concrete blocks of the MoE in La Paz. Here, we met again: *'Do you remember when I was still director of the Normal, we had sent some texts elaborated by trainers and students to the Ministry?'*, he asked as I nodded in confirmation. *'We are now recollecting this information, these experiences of changing our mentalities, and this is essential. For a long time, teachers have been trained to fulfil the goals of the neoliberal project. What we need is a cultural-intellectual 'Pachakuti', a return to the older times, and we need a radical change of attitudes and commitment, a decolonial attitude'* (107:5).[145] These quotes follow the new governments' ideological discourse of a decolonised and communitarian education system, and while some of them portray trainers' *ideas* on *future* strategies, or recently started tactics, they still provide some evidence of the willingness of a small part of trainers to bring the ASEP reform about.

In contrast, an urban trainer sees less hope for Normales to become institutes that train future agents of change. He reflects on the current situation as follows: *'You see Mieke, in Bolivia we continue with a state of egoism. We have not opened our eyes to the rest of the world'*. Referring to the earlier criticised 'fixed profession' (chapter 6), he continued to state that *'here you can just become a teacher, a trainer, and that is that, no further obligations* (47:19). Then he talked about an inspirational speech given by an older Japanese professor during a conference on the reconstruction of Japan after the bombing of Hiroshima. *'He said, in Japan we cannot live without a crisis. When there is a crisis, they [the Japanese] see this as a new opportunity for change, as this allows them to remain in a constant state of alertness. I am impressed by this, as here in Bolivia, it seems the people are sleeping if there is no crisis, and we only wake up to react when there is a crisis'* (47: 39). Complementing this rather negative view of educators' apathy in the Normales, a former socialist politician, Normal director during the University administration and academic sees *'teachers as the most conservative force in Bolivia'*. Based on his long-term experience in the education sector, he is sceptical about the possibilities for future and current teachers to be(come) agents of change: *'for decades, teachers have struggled for their secure job positions, their welfare arrangements. They have a lot of priviliges to defend'* (23). Teachers therefore have, in his view, resisted political processes of change since their unions *'have made their institutes untouchable to changes. Change cannot enter the Normales, change cannot be implemented, because there is no evaluation system for teachers, there is no in-service training programme. This way, change is not possible'* (23). This links back to the analysis in chapter 6 of a sense of institutional inertia, the 'fixed profession' that automatically promotes teachers according to years of experience without an adequate evaluation and support system, as well as the relatively powerful position of the unions when it

---

[145] *Pachakuti* was introduced in chapter 1 as a traditional Andean ritual and phase of change.

comes to transforming the Normales and wider education system. From this data, we can conclude how the ideological state discourse and its proponents define teachers as active 'soldiers for liberation and decolonisation', while the reality in and beyond the Normales is less favourable to bring these changes about.

How do the student teachers themselves see their roles as agents of change? From the survey data, it became clear that around one-third of both urban and rural students, when talking about their motivations, mentioned the words 'change', 'progress', 'improvement' and 'development'. Bearing in mind the discussion in chapter 8 about how particularly these 'written-down' answers tend to be rather 'politically correct', they still reflect an interesting discourse adopted by these students, about both societal and educational changes and improvements, as illustrated in Textbox 7.

Textbox 7. Student teachers' motivations as agents of change

- *'I want to teach the children and youngsters, who form the future of Bolivia, I want to awaken them from their sleepiness, that was caused by colonialism and capitalism'*
  (24-year old male urban student)

- *'I want a different, equal and unified Bolivia, because I have the opportunity to incentivate changes. I want to develop critical and reflexive persons. It makes me feel happy to see a child with (realistic) dreams'*
  (26-year old female urban student)

- *'Education in Bolivia is subordinated, and society reflects this education system. I want to contribute to this educational change, to improve our society'*
  (21 year old male rural student)

- *'Unfortunately, the bad economic situation in our country has created a more economic interest in the teaching profession, rather than a vocational one. I need to be part of an improvement of education, for changing this nation'*
  (21-year old male urban student)

- *'I want to share knowledge that is helpful for our society, in an equal way, without discrimination, to help to unify my country on the basis of my ideology'*
  (25 year old female rural student)

- *'This country needs people who can make a difference, who can change this colonising education system that has been oriented at only a few'*
  (22 year old male urban student)

- *'I feel that the changes in our lives come with a revolution in my country, not with arms, but with a change in attitude of the new generations. This can only be reached through study. So, yes, as a teacher I can help in this process'*
  (26 year old male urban student)

Source: survey data Simon Bolivar and Paracaya, first and third year students, August-September 2008, responses to the open question: 'Why do you want to become a teacher?'

Interestingly, these quotes do not so much have a direct resonance with the current government's discourse, most probably because many of the teacher students, including for instance Elisa, had very little knowledge of the details of the ASEP reform. Still, in their idealistic and hopeful comments they do express a wish for bringing change, reflecting the unused vocational and socio-political motivations as defined in chapter 8. This idealism was also clearly expressed by a female teacher student at the urban institute, who was determined that she could make a difference as a teacher, '*We will be able to change things. It only takes one to make a change, is what I tell my students. Like Mahatma Gandhi, he made a big change, and John Lennon, with his music he had his way to change, and in Bolivia there are so many men who did a lot as well*' (18:13). Moore (2008), in this regard, wrote how pre-service teachers in her study in New York would sometimes have 'illusions of grandeur' to the effects they will have beyond their classrooms, as they have no clear idea (yet) of what types of opposition they might face and they are unsure how to go about achieving this. Moore therefore argues that teacher education programmes need to provide a better informed definition of social justice understandings in their subject teaching, as well as a better understanding of the ideological nature of schooling and science, and the role of teachers within them (Moore 2008:206). As illustrated in chapter 5, the new outline of the Bolivian ASEP teacher education curriculum includes subject matters such as political ideology, which could potentially include these types of discussions, but further research would have to highlight how, and in what ways, this results in practice.

Not all students have these 'illusions of grandeur', as they also reflected on the challenges of becoming an agent of change. Elisa, for instance, in a group interview with two other female students, talked about the difficulties young, female teachers face in order to really make significant changes in schools. '*Making a difference is difficult. Just because we are young, and female, they think we don't know. Because of the colonial times, the Aymara parents are very closed, they are not open to any type of innovation, they won't let us*' (16:71). Hence, when new teachers start their teaching career in schools, the 'illusions of grandeur' often quickly disappears. '*With a lot of enthusiasm, we see new teachers arriving in the schools in the provinces*', an ex-trainer now working in a donor organisation explains, '*it is very rewarding to work with this group of people. But the bad thing is that after a while they become tired, and their work quality diminishes. That is why a good school director is so crucial, when she/he provides good opportunities to develop, these young teachers normally continue to function very well, they have the highest possibility to make a change*' (77:11). A 28 year old female teacher, and a graduate from Simón Bolívar (specialising in literature teaching), verifies the idea that a good and cooperative relationship between beginning teachers and the principal is very important. She experienced a '*clash of ideas*' with the director of the rural school she first started to work in, and had a difficult time in those first years to implement her innovative ideas. Nevertheless, she felt that she had made a change in the lives of her students, as she tried to make them think critically about the 'obvious' choice to also wanting to become a teacher: '*When I started teaching there in 2007, about 70% of all last year students said they wanted to become a teacher. In the class of 2008, in the end around 60% wanted to become a teacher, and in 2009, [this was the case for] only 30% of the students. This was the case because I started to ask them why. They responded: 'because it is a secure job, because my parents are also teachers, and because we like the way you teach us'. I realised we are really a point of reference for these youngsters. So I was very satisfied with this last generation of the 2009 students, because they had a different view on the world. I studied the newspapers with them, and we always discussed the different types of professions we would find. Now, they also wanted to study medicine, become psychologists and airplane designers*' (100:19). In 2010, she returned to work in a secondary school in El Alto, after almost four years of teaching in the rural community. Here, she experienced another difficulty, as she was assigned a teaching post outside of her specialisation and was expected to work more hours than she would get paid for (100: 7).

This situation unfortunately reflects a reality for many teachers. Another graduate from Simón Bolívar had worked for two years in a rural school, '*where I really learned how to teach*' (111:1). On her return to work in a school in El Alto, she experienced the same situation as her colleague, in that she was appointed a position for a subject matter that she had not been trained for. When asked if she felt that the Normal had prepared her well for the job, she responded: '*They give you the content knowledge, in an isolated way. When we were leaving the Normal to go and work, me and my colleagues found out we were missing many things. Only in the first years in the province did we really start to develop*' (111:8). This teacher was not alone in feeling unprepared when leaving the Normal. In accordance with views of other in-service teachers, she reflected how this situation obviously does not contribute to improve the low quality of education in remote areas, let alone her confidence in acting as a 'soldier of change'.

Union leader and primary school teacher Dilma, while drawing an 'actor map' in my notebook (see also chapters 4 and 6), explained: '*If society were a house, then we would need to radically transform its foundation, which is the economic structure of the country. The upper part of the house is breaking down, and they [the government] try to fix it with a bit of paint, you see? But in reality, what needs to be changed is the foundation. The actors in this foundation are the motors of transformation; it's the people. But we have to work hard to 'ideologise' them, to 'conscientise' and to prepare them for our struggle*' (49).[146] One of the directors of the urban Normal, uses a similar argumentation to explain why changing the Normal is such a difficult undertaking: '*They say the young generation will bring about changes, but in reality many of them do not want to change anything. Therefore, the dedication to pedagogical innovation, the creativity, should not only be incorporated by the management levels, they also have to engage with the basis [las bases] of the institute. Because if there is no will at the basis to change, if the people do not want to change, we cannot change the Normal, they will resist*' (17:20). This comment stands in stark contrast to the group of students who were quoted above, as showing a commitment to change. Drawing from the discussion of the institutional obstacles for change discussed in chapter 6, the idea that the Normales are difficult to change because students (and trainers) are simply not willing to do so, is therefore a little nuanced and lacks a comprehensive analysis of both structural and agential factors.

Thus, several trainers see an important role for Bolivian teachers to be(come) actors of change, a discourse which is potentially strengthened by the current governments' talk of change. There is, nevertheless, also a shared concern for the obstacles to future teachers' change-agent role, both consisting of institutional obstacles, as well as agential unwillingness or apathy. Many students had a rather idealistic view of themselves as future 'actors for change' in an educational, as well as a social sense. Still, a number of students and young teachers also reflected critically on the often limited space that they (will) really have in their future job to 'change things' and it was mentioned how permanent teacher formation throughout teachers' careers could improve the opportunities for teachers to be actors for change. In line with the new government policies, both trainers and students referred to 'changing attitudes' as an important step towards a new

---

[146] An academic researcher in La Paz reflected how Dilma's 'hard work' to convince the teachers has to do with the fact that '*Evo increased their salaries, which is why they do not come to demonstrate*' (78:24).

(decolonised) society, showing the importance of the discursive level of social change. Hence, perceptions vary on what a Bolivian teacher as agent of change should look like and also what her/his space for manoeuvre is to bring about both educational innovations and societal changes.

9.3 Obstacles and niches for teachers' individual and collective strategies

Teachers' choices and agency should be understood within the limits or opportunities of the specific strategic selective context. To some extent, teachers have the freedom to either uncritically follow a prescribed routine that might contribute to various processes of conflict (chapter 3) to actively challenge injustices or to follow a 'middle way'. When making such decisions, both identities and motivations play a crucial role. Building from the SRA, an analytical distinction can be made between intuitive and explicit strategic action; in reality, most strategies combine both intuitive and explicit strategic actions (Hay, 2002a: 132-133).[147] Hay's (2002a) case that actors face an uneven distribution of opportunities and constraints – resulting in a strategic selective context – might help to understand the differences in opportunities for rural and urban teachers in Bolivia. Several rural students, for example, expressed their concern for limited career options, as training programmes are often exclusively provided in urban areas. Besides, constrained by unequal power relations, empowered individuals and groups can only disrupt oppressive policies, practices and perspectives as far as their position in the social order allows them (North, 2008: 1192). Considering the fairly low social status of Bolivian teachers, and the complex and changing socio-political reality, the data of this study shows how being an agent of change – or, perhaps, against change – in the teacher education field of Bolivian is a rather complex issue.

In the literature that deals with Bolivian education 'before Morales', there seems to be a shared opinion about the paradoxical and ambiguous roles of educators in reproducing the structures of a hidden curriculum; strengthening instead of withstanding the ongoing 'castellanisation' of education (see for instance Regalsky and Laurie, 2007: 232). In other words, *'those that have been forced to memorise the world are not likely to change it'*; rather, they are more likely to reproduce reality (Cochran-Smith 2004: 206). Gamboa Rocabado writes how even under the new Bolivian regime, *'for many public policy specialists and reformers, it is nowadays still unthinkable that indigenous groups and farmers can actually be historical actors of change'* (2009: 70). As argued in chapter 8, we need to rethink this homogenising, reproducing and passive idea of the Bolivian teacher. From a Gramscian perspective, we should consider that education is *not* a mere aparatus of the state and that educators are strategic subjects (Talavera Simoni, 2011). Hence, we should rethink Bolivian teachers' roles in relation to their agency – either for or against the current governmental policies. For the purpose of this study, when analysing possibilities and obstacles to the teachers' role as agents for or against change, Giroux's (2003b) idea of rethinking teachers' roles as transformative intellectuals, instead of mere 'messengers' of a system, is interesting. Often, policy-makers display little confidence in teachers' intellectual and moral abilities, and they tend to ignore teachers' roles in preparing active and critical citizens. Giroux therefore argues that teachers should join public debates, engage in self-critique and collectively organise to struggle

---

[147] 'Intuitive strategies' are related to a 'practical consciousness' of routines, habits, rituals or other forms of un-reflexive action, and 'explicitly strategic actions' imply more conscious attempts to bring about individual and collective intentions and objectives (Hay, 2002a: 132-133).

for their rights and status in society. In Bolivia, we can see a history of resistance among teachers – either through individual efforts or collective organised unions. Here, historically embedded attitudes of resistance, as well as critical and reflexive attitudes and socio-political aspirations, become important incentives for a teacher to act or to remain passive; to support, passively follow or resist Morales' new ASEP education policy lines, sometimes regardless of their more general political support to the MAS.

The Normales and future teachers' individual strategies

In what ways are student teachers' 'voice' or active agency stimulated in their training? In line with the outcomes of Delany-Barmann's research in 2005 (2010: 197), during my fieldwork I found that in many cases students' voice in the classrooms of Normales was limited to individual or group presentations, that often literally reproduced the content that was provided on photocopied texts. In the absence of textbook material in most of the classrooms, the photocopied material forms the textual basis for many of the classes in both Normales, this way supporting one or several independent and well-earning photocopy-shops on the institutes' premises. The texts included documents prepared by the trainers (such as an observation check-list for the PDI course) and photocopies made of (parts of) books on educational content, pedagogy, didactics etc. Besides these photocopies, the blackboard is used to transfer content into students' notebooks. These rather traditional and reproducing teaching techniques – also known as 'banking education' – obviously do little to engage critical thinking and expression of the voice of these student teachers.

In complete contrast to these traditional techniques, I also observed classes in which some forms of dialogue and interaction were stimulated. Particularly in social science classes, discussions on Bolivia's colonial history and its current global role were topics of debate, often based on the readings of Eduardo Galeano's classic work of 'Open Veins of Latin America' (1971). Due to the relatively large classes (usually between 20 and 40 students), the number of students that were actively engaged in these types of debates and discussions was naturally limited and often the same students spoke up, as most trainers showed little engagement in general to involve the rest. Possibly, my presence as an observer might have influenced these situations, perhaps leading some trainers to adopt interactive techniques they do not normally use, or possibly choosing a strategy of letting the 'good' students talk. In one instance during my last visit in May 2010, a first year urban male student was clearly used to speaking up in class. Clearly in favour of the current governments' 21st Century socialist orientation, he commented on the role of teachers in Bolivia's current 'Boom', that 'led to the current immersion in socialism, for which we as teachers are going to fight.' With a strong voice, he carried on: 'we are already doing so in our 'practicas' [internships]. [We work] for the construction of 'the new man', as Che Guevarra called it, to break down the deprivations caused by the capitalist man. With a high moral, we as teachers are bringing forward the socialisation and revaluation of all of our knowledges' (105:4). In contrast to most of the students I met in 2007 and 2008, this student was evidently aware (and supportive) of the ASEP discourse.

I found it especially interesting that during this last fieldwork visit (May 2010), in which I shared my preliminary findings in order to discuss them and receive feedback, I encountered several examples of open forms of 'voice' in two feedback discussions with first and second year students in the urban Normal. In their open and critical reactions to both my findings, as well as the intentions of my research, it was obvious that they had become used to posing these types of

222

critical questions. The same first year male student quoted above, whom I did not meet in my earlier visits as he was not yet enrolled, for instance commented how he was bothered by '*foreigners coming here to look at us*'. He continued to state that many of 'the foreigners' come to Bolivia only during very brief and isolated visits, to disappear without leaving any type of feedback behind (105:7). He thus wondered about the rationale behind my research. He continued by reflecting how '*we are all sons of the working class. Part of the problem now, apart from that our cultural and ideological roots have been taken away, is that we have been educated with a very low quality. What we know, is perhaps more because of our own efforts. Without wanting to offend you, we just learned from the book Open Veins of Latin America, how Holland was one of those colonisers. I sometimes get very angry with those outsiders coming to look at us as if we were animals in a zoo. And then they are astonished about our culture, about our Pachamama, without even understanding what is the Pachamama*' (105:6). While being a challenging and insightful experience for myself, I also realised that this openly critical attitude of a few of the students in particular showed their desire for active engagement and critical reflection. I had a similar experience with a rural trainer, who was well aware of how the results of a (foreign) study could be used at the central level of the MoE, with potential funding consequences. Delany-Barmann describes a similar experience of students' suspicion towards external researchers, as students were aware that such research observations '*might come back to them in the form of policy*' (2010: 197).

During my engagement with final year students during their PDI final project, I encountered some examples of how future educators attempted to improve existing structures that trigger forms of violence and conflict in educational settings. Drawing from the critical pedagogical literature on action research (see for instance Greenman and Dieckmann, 2004; Kane, 2002; Noffke, 1997; Price, 2001), it can be argued that the internship period and the related pedagogical innovation project (PIP) could help teacher-students to understand and reflect not only on their 'educational role' (Torres del Castillo, 2007), but also on their broader socio-cultural and political roles as future agents for change. A final year student at the urban teacher training institute, for instance, passionately defended his final 'innovation' project, aiming at improvement of 'human relationships' at the primary education level.[148] He explained how '*I have seen how children are afraid of their teachers. I have seen that traditional and hierarchical relations still exist. I want to explore how these relations between teachers and students can improve, in order for children to develop and learn in an environment of trust and peace. I want to use this final research project for my future work*' (66). A female colleague of his explained to me that she aims to develop methods to strengthen young childrens' abilities to protect themselves from sexual abuse. Based on her experience as a volunteer for a local education oriented NGO, one afternoon she invited me to come and see how she and her colleagues use story telling and a theatre approach to teach young students about the dangers of sexual harassment.

Unfortunately, these newly trained teachers, with a commitment to innovate and improve education after graduation, are confronted with a rather restrictive strategically selective context, as highligted in the former section. It seems like a majority group of 'older' teachers choose the 'routine' path, or an intuitive strategy of 'practical consciousness', instead of the more 'explicitly strategic actions' and a conflictive and difficult path of innovation and/or resistance. With an eye on the future of these newly trained teachers as potential actors of change in *and beyond* the

---

148 The student also joined the photo-workshop, see chapter 7.

classroom, in the next section I turn to discuss some of the possible strategies in-service teachers can adopt in countering the five dimensions of conflict defined in chapter 3.[149]

Discussing in-service teachers' individual strategies

Linked to the first and second dimensions of conflict, observations and conversations in different schools revealed structures of discrimination and exclusion of indigenous, darker coloured children with different mother tongues. Since discrimination in Bolivia is not only directed towards indigenous people, but extends to gender and class issues and regional prejudices, it is necessary for teachers to adopt a 'multiple consciousness of difference', meaning differences among indigenous peoples and differences within the (non-) indigenous individuals (D'Emilio, 1996: 22, 59). In the context of the ASEP project, one of the main challenges for Bolivian teachers is to promote a multiple perception of diversity, focused on commonalities, rather than following '*more inward-looking and potentially segregationist*' (Howard, 2009) or '*paralysing and exclusionary*' (Van Dam and Salman, 2009) forms of intraculturalism. Speiser argued that educators should work towards 'unity in diversity': '*within the framework of a segregationist society one can claim success if the educators have developed interest, readiness and a capacity to dialogue with those whom they consider to be different*' (2000: 235-236). Ten years later, 'unity in diversity' is a fundamental part of the new education law (Article 3.1, ASEP law 2010). The catchphrase of bringing 'unity in diversity', nonetheless, often sounds better than how it materialises in educational reality. Based on insights from critical race theories, with a 'unity over difference approach' there is a danger of promoting essentialism and static identities (North, 2006), or in the case of the current politics in Bolivia, a danger of an essentialised notion of 'indigenous-ness' or 'Andean-centrism' (Postero, 2007).[150]

From the literature on 'education and conflict' we can learn how teachers can actively resist against discrimination, stereotyping and the polarising discourses of identity politics – relating to the third dimension of conflict. Moreover, teachers should help students to adopt a 'hybrid identity' (Davies, 2006a), in order to deal respectfully with one's own and others 'differences' (in language, ethnicity, culture, sexuality, religion and so forth). Davies' work on 'interruptive democracies' and her pedagogical 'XvX model', demonstrate the importance of such an open and critical discussion on hybrid identities, emphasising the need for humour, creativity and play 'to interrupt dogma' (Davies, 2008; Davies, 2005a). Creativity in many of the Bolivian schools, for instance during music, dance and arts classes, is sometimes adopted in a somewhat folkloristic manner. Following the insights of critical pedagogy on SJTE, dialogue, critical thinking and reflexivity need to be included more seriously, especially with regards to the development of critical and reflexive citizens (Giroux, 2003b; Burns, 1996; Bush, 2000; Apple in Scott, 2008). In this line of argument, Davies writes about the importance of the stimulation of free speech, and critical media and satire analysis in schools, to open up critical discussions about extremist points of view without avoiding offence – yet evading humiliation (2008: 124, 149).

---

149 These dimensions included: 1) poverty and inequality of opportunities; 2) discrimination and exclusion; 3) separatist discourses and identity politics; 4) mistrust in the state & between societal groups; and 5) popular protests and violent clashes between the state & social movements.

150 While seeking 'sameness' or 'unity' in the name of equality, often harmful group stereotypes remain unchallenged and the complex, political and developing nature of individual's identities are overlooked (North, 2006: 517) in uncritical forms of education. Bartlett rightly warns for the danger of uncritically accepting 'indigenous knowledge' as something static, which could reinforce forms of cultural relativism by teachers (2005: 363).

In relation to the fourth dimension of conflict, another strategy for teachers to enhance educational (and hence societal) changes in the Bolivian tense context would be to increase levels of trust (at different scales). Mistrust often leads to difficult processes of dialogue and cooperation between educational actors at the school/community level, as shown in chapter 1. For instance, Bolivian (indigenous) parents complain about non-traditional and time consuming 'innovative' teaching methods that stimulate creativity or play, and towards the strengthening of indigenous languages next to Spanish. This is often explained by parents' *'cultural and pragmatic perceptions'* and preferences for traditional/modernising forms of education (Yapu 1999 in Howard, 2009). In her study of three EIB Normales in Bolivia in 2005, Delany-Barmann (2010: 196) further discusses the difficult and even contradictory role of teachers in trying to bring forward a bilingual and inter(intra-)cultural type of schooling, while parents and teachers themselves often have serious doubts about the rationale and usefulness of these innovations. Teachers often feel frustrated and ambivalent towards their new roles as placed on them through reforms, both because they might disagree with the policy's rationale, or because they feel unprepared or not proficient enough in indigenous languages to fullfil these tasks, a situation that continues to raise concerns for the implementation of ASEP. Hence, there also lies an important task for the MoE and Normales in supporting teachers in being prepared for this task. As shown in chapter 8, while future teachers are trained differently in urban and rural teacher training centres, all teachers are obliged to teach at least two years in 'province'. Considering that the first few years of teaching are the hardest, these two years in a rural school must be a huge challenge for students trained in an urban context, without adequate tools to communicate and adapt to a local context unknown to them. Thus, regardless of the efforts of intercultural and bilingual teacher training programmes in the EIB Normales, a large part of the future teachers are not prepared enough to teach in a non-Spanish and rural context, diminishing the chances for teachers to potentially convince parents of the benefits of inter-/intracultural and bilingual education.

With regards to the strategic selective environment of the schools in which (future) teachers work, there is often a lack of trust between teachers and parents, organised in the *'juntas escolares'* or parental commissions. Due to the relative power of these parents associations over teachers, instead of working together conflicts are prone to occur. On the positive side, these parents associations provide an instrument for a larger control on teachers' work, and on what happens inside the school walls. Although problematic, such an institutionalised control measure is a democratic necessity. For example, violence in the form of physical punishment has been – and in some cases still is – common in schools to punish low-performing or disobedient students. These castigations became illegal in the 1994 reforms, in line with the goal to increase the number of girls attending school. Teachers have been reported to be expelled by the parents associations because of – true or false – accusations of maltreatment of students. Teacher unions argue that they feel constrained by the increasing levels of power of the parental commissions. In contrast, a Bolivian political scientist believes teachers should be confronted with an even tighter control system: *'when a rural teacher – and this happens quite often – abuses a girl, the only thing that happens is he will be changed to another school, as he is protected by his union'* (23). Chapter 3 also described how mistrust between different groups of users of school buildings can lead to increasing tensions. When teachers show how to share or respect others' belongings, they could provide a better model for children on how to 'learn to live together' (Sinclair, 2004). Thus, dialogue between the different actors involved could help to ensure a culture of trust and understanding, instead of (pedagogical) misunderstandings and unbalanced power plays.

This section reveals how, on the individual level, it is a huge challenge for future teachers to become a critical and reflexive generation that will inspire students, parents and the older generation of in-service teachers to improve classroom practices and to resist, instead of reproduce, historical discriminatory educational practices. In response to the first four dimensions of conflict defined in chapter 3, teachers would ideally adopt and stimulate others to have hybrid identities and foster a critical and open dialogue about differences and respect for diversity in an atmosphere of trust. Their training is crucial for a solid preparation, to stimulate an innovative and reflexive attitude and to foster latent motivations into active forms of agency.

Teachers' collective strategies

'*Individually, we have no power. Together, we can do anything*', is an often used phrase in the city of El Alto, a birthplace of Bolivian popular resistance (Dangl 2007: 140). Similarly, research shows how teachers' individual strategies of resistance often cannot be sustained alone and need a strong community that reinforces alternative perspectives and the joint questioning of dominant messages (Achinstein and Ogawa, 2006). Coming back to Benardo's story, in a feedback discussion with eight other urban trainers in May 2010, it became clear how he was isolated in his critique of the urban unions' demand for another salary increase of 12% (instead of the 5% that was promised). His criticism of the union is rare, since these critiques are often not openly expressed out of fear to be 'voted out' of the system. In individual conversations, Benardo showed a strong commitment to changing the current teaching practices in the Normal along the decolonising and inter-intracultural lines of the ASEP law. He also thought of himself as someone who could, and had to, make changes. However, this was not easy and was mostly limited to working with the students in his classroom. Although Benardo does not stand alone on a national level, within the institute he is clearly an exception and his agency is therefore limited. This section consequently explores the more collective strategies adopted by Bolivian teachers.

Bolivian teachers are a very 'visible' social group. Not only because of their very important and responsible job, but also because they make themselves heard through demonstrations and strikes. Chapter 6, for example, showed how in 2005 unsatisfied students and staff from some of the teacher training institutes effectively used pressure mechanisms (strikes, demonstrations) to enforce an end to the administrative role of Universities in their institutes. Similar to many other countries worldwide, Bolivian teachers are often viewed quite negatively by society as being resistant and under-qualified professionals. This is especially the case when classes are suspended because of 'unionised' activities. Policy makers, not excluding those in Bolivia, rather avoid these types of teachers' resistance and consequently teachers' individual agency is advanced to the detriment of collective teacher action and voice, hence downplaying the power of teacher unions (Vongalis-Macrow, 2007: 428-433). We should, however, also consider how these collective forms of teacher resistance towards state initiatives can be a productive and necessary counter-voice in the political arena, since collective interest might be used to overcome powerlessness of certain social groups '*by pooling their resources and thereby constituting themselves as strategic actors*' (Hay, 2002b).

Relating to the education field, Giroux passionately argues how '*educators should work to form alliances with parents, community organizers, labor organizations, and civil rights groups at local, national, and international levels to understand better how to translate private troubles into public actions, arouse public interest in pressing social problems, and use collective means to democratize more fully the commanding institutional economic, cultural, and social structures that dominate our societies*' (Giroux, 2003a: 13). In this line of thought, Sleeter (1996) stresses how the role of social movements should be recognised in the definition of critical pedagogical approaches, while Yogev and Michaeli argue that teacher training needs to include both community involvement in training programmes, as well as students' engagement in civic projects in communities (2011: 318). These approaches to a collective form of agency are particularly relevant to the Bolivian case. On the one hand because social movements – from radical to moderate indigenous organisations and from women's organisations to radical right-wing movements – have an active role in Bolivian politics and social life; and on the other hand, because of the recent shift of focus towards respecting and including indigenous rights and knowledge into educational policies. Based on the authors refered to above, possibilties for strengthening teachers' collective agency would probably lie in overcoming the lack of dialogue between teachers – and particularly the urban union – and different actors involved in the Bolivian education field.

We should avoid simplistic black-and-white accounts of teachers' resistance being either positive or emancipatory, versus negative and un-principled. There exists a growing body of literature that calls for a more nuanced view on the tensions between teachers' 'good sense' and their 'principled resistance' (see chapter 2). Rather than putting aside teachers' resistance as a psychological deficit or basic reluctance, teachers' *can* also respond from their professional principles (Achinstein and Ogawa, 2006). The students of the rural Normal, for instance, in 2005 took serious measures to demand better teachers, as they organised demonstrations and a roadblock at the main highway to insist on an institutionalisation process (41:13) to get teachers that would respond to their learning expectations (32:7). However, according to a student who was involved in the protests, the current processes of institutionalisation (chapter 6) did not deliver good teachers: '*the changes they did made it worse, but we will demonstrate again if necessary. Here we created the blockade [pointing in the direction of the highway], we stayed until we got into a battle with the police, all this we have suffered for what? To end up in a similar situation*' (41:13). The fact that students and teachers alike have continued to adopt these 'popular pressure methods' (such as strikes, demonstrations, road blocks and hunger strikes), regardless of the outcomes of their struggle, reflects a strong historical culture of popular resistance.

In contrast to these examples of 'principled collective action', on the more negative side teachers can also resist promising policy initiatives, as happened in both Mexico and Japan, where teacher unions have successfully obstructed reforms that were intended to improve educational quality (Tatto, 2007: 269-270). In addition, union struggles can also directly affect the education system negatively, resulting for instance in high numbers of cancelled school days because of strikes and demonstrations in Bolivia: 37 days in 1995; 24 in 1996; 15 in 1997 and 22 in 1998 (Talavera Simoni, 1999). Talavera's recent work (2011) shows that Bolivian teacher resistance from the urban union resembles the situations in Mexico and Japan, as their strategies focus on improving working conditions and salary issues, rather than that they are rooted in professional principles for improving educational quality.[151] Jansen (2001a) explains how teachers' professional and political identities can be completely different and yet exist alongside each other. In the case of South Africa, '*conservative professional behaviour (e.g. teacher dominated classrooms, test-driven instruction, corporal punishment) co-existed neatly with radical political behaviour (e.g. mass activism of teachers on conditions of service, salaries and political change)*' (2001a: 243). This divide, between the professional and the political, was reinforced by the ways in which progressive teacher unions defined the terrain of activism for teachers: curriculum matters were not, until recently – both in South Africa and in Bolivia – regarded as grounds for political contestation by teachers as professionals (Jansen 2001a).

A decent salary is a common collective point of struggle for teachers all around the globe. As proclaimed particularly by the urban Bolivian teachers' union, teachers' salaries are too low in relation to the responsibility and heaviness of the job, forcing them into extra jobs. Considering the immensely responsible job for teachers as Bolivia's 'soldiers of change', even a government supporting rural trainer feels '*considering the importance of teachers vocation and social commitment, this vocation is still very badly paid, we sacrifice ourselves for this job, without hopes for compensation*'(43:10). However, it could also be argued that amidst other societal problems (unemployment and severe poverty) the new government is at least providing a better level of working conditions when compared to other sectors. Moreover, in the past years (under Morales), teachers' salaries have increased significantly by 37%: with 7% in 2006; 6% in 2007; 10% in 2008; and 14% in 2009. This data was published by the Bolivian MoE (2009), also stating that former governments in the past two decades only increased salaries by 3-3.5% after strikes and demonstrations. About a decade ago, Talavera (1999: xiii, 127-129) argued how the public debate about salary scales needed to open up to overcome the persistent struggle between the government and the teacher unions, and that the (urban) union leaders had to learn how to debate and negotiate, and not only think about 'the survival of the union'. The recent raise in salaries, together with some ex-union members appearing in a relatively high positions within the MoE, might indicate a potential opening towards dialogue between parties involved. Some first steps towards more open dialogue between the rural union and the MoE have been taken in the past years. The strategy of dialogue of Bolivia's rural union to some extent reflects what Weiner (2008) describes as unions' 'holistic social justice campaigns', working towards educational improvements benefitting the life opportunities of children and working against injustices in society as a whole, rather than focusing on material conditions only.

Looking at the collective level of teachers' strategies, this section shows how Bolivia's teachers unions form a crucial political counter-voice. Improving teachers' collective strength could be realised through forming alliances with other stakeholders (parents, community organisations, labour organisations and civil rights groups at local, national, and international levels) and creating a constructive dialogue with authorities. Based on insights from the SJTE literature, Bolivia's rural union's strategy of dialogue illustrates a shift from a sole focus on mostly 'practical concerns' (including salaries and retirement) to working towards educational improvements that work against injustices in society as a whole.

---

[151] As argued in chapter 5, a more nuanced view on the position of both the urban and the rural union is more valid nowadays. Especially the rural union has shown an interest in negotiating the new educational policy plans of the Morales government.

9.4 To conclude – Bolivian teachers' limited agency in a potentially enabling context: soldiers of liberation or guards of continuation?

'Recognizing teachers as engaged and public intellectuals means that educators should never be reduced to technicians just as education should never be reduced to training' (Giroux, 2003b: 48)

In this section I connected the outcomes of the different book parts to the analysis of teachers' agency presented in this chapter. Throughout the book, it becomes clear how Bolivian teachers see themselves confronted with processes of change and continuity. Their life and work is embedded in, and dialectically related to, the tense and discriminatory 'strategically selective context'. In addition, unclear policy lines, a persistently changing MoE staff and continuing mistrust in the state and its institutions (including the teacher training institutes) make it difficult to forecast whether teachers can really become actors for – or against – change. Based on the outcomes of Part III of the book, Bolivia's Normales are perceived as islands and are difficult to transform. The conservative attitude of teacher training institutes is a more general phenomena, as both within and beyond Bolivia they are considered 'untouched monopolies' (Tatto, 2007: 14). Continuing structures of corruption, discrimination and traditional teaching styles in the two Normales studied here add up to this situation.

Moreover, Part III showed how power plays at different levels and between a range of education actors contribute to the complexity of the strategic selective context that Bolivian (future) teachers are positioned in. While the MoE tries to maintain its central position in the education sector, it also struggles with internal and external forms of opposition to its radically new policy lines for decolonisation. Debates continue on how to interpret and deal with the (more and more divergent) positions of the two teachers' unions and even the right to the existence of the division between an urban and a rural confederation. What is clear, is the considerable level of influence in the governance of the Normales, particularly with regard to the relationship between the La Paz federation and the Normal Simón Bolívar. This structural context elaborated in Part III obviously affects the strategies of Bolivia's trainers, teacher students and teachers. Therefore, I argue that it is unfair to exclusively hold these educators responsible for the failures of political reform initiatives, let alone the successes of a social transformation project, as they face numerous structural constraints. Often, they face low social status while they work long hours in multiple jobs to support their families, while they miss(ed) out on a proper pre-service training and a permanent source of support to help them stay motivated and updated. Especially now – in the highly tense and conflictive Bolivian context – we need an understanding of the space available to Bolivian (future) teachers and factors underlying the choices teachers make, in order to develop their strategies that either intendedly or unintendedly support or resist current policies. This way, the study endeavours to respond to the need for research on the effects of changing and heterogenous policy environments with varying degrees of control on teachers' agency (Achinstein and Ogawa, 2006).

In contrast to these continuing structural constraints, this research shows how Bolivia's new socio-political situation also opens up new possibilities for processes of transformation; in the Normales, in schools and eventually in wider society. These emerging possibilities for change particularly become clear from the discussion of the (potential) agential factors for change, discussed in Part IV of the book. Chapter 6 has shown a changing profile of Bolivia's teacher students, influenced by two contextual developments: firstly a lack of job opportunities leads to an increased age and in many cases wider experiences of students who enter the Normal; and secondly, a growing societal and political recognition of indigenous culture and languages stimulates students to develop a growing awareness and acceptance of their own ethno-cultural and linguistic background. Nevertheless, the Normales seem to miss and misunderstand the opportunity behind these developments. On the one hand there lies a potential benefit with regards to training a group of older, higher skilled and more experienced students, which is largely ignored or rejected. On the other hand, students' development of a greater socio-cultural awareness, acceptance and self esteem in relation to their formerly often discriminated cultural-ethnic background, opens a niche for critical reflection and awareness, yet the Normales do not sufficiently reflect on and work with these changing profile and identities of students. In other words, teachers' changing profiles and identities are an unused opportunity for change.

Following Hay's (2002a) SRA, actors' motivations are crucial in their passive or active strategies and these motivations are influenced by the ideologies and discourses around them, and vice versa. This chapter illustrated how the new government's discourse on 'teachers as agents of change' was primarily reflected in the narratives of those trainers that are supportive of the ASEP reform, who are presumably also better informed about it. Interestingly, while students' sometimes idealistic accounts also reflected the need for them to become change agents, perhaps because of their lack of familarity of the ASEP law, there was less of a clear link with the decolonisation discourse of the government. This links to the fact that a substantial group of interviewed student teachers, besides economic motivations, also showed a pedagogical-vocational and socio-political commitment, constituting a potential yet unused aspiration among a group of students at the Normales (chapter 7). Teacher education programmes need to focus on developing these vocational and political commitments (see for instance Yogev and Michaeli, 2011: 315). Thus, instead of simply blaming this majority of (future) teachers for a lack of commitment and vocation to the teaching profession and socio-political transformation, I argue that the structural constraints of the (pre-service and in-service) teacher training system largely fails to address and stimulate teachers' motivations to provide good education and become actors of change.

In response to why some teachers are not 'acting as change agents', we should critically look at who is designing educational policies and curricula, and the rationales behind these policies. We cannot expect teachers to implement academically constructed programmes for change that do not relate to the daily struggles and reality in schools (North, 2008: 1200). Nor can we expect educators to become partners in the governments' politics of change and hence to live up to their educational *and* societal responsibility, when they do not receive high quality training, a higher social status and a reasonable compensation. Considering the amount of incertainty and resistance among a considerable part of Bolivia's teachers, the Bolivian government needs to take Fraser's third dimension of social justice (representation) more seriously, in its attempts to engage Bolivia's teaching force in the new reform process.

Inherent to the ongoing developments in the Bolivian context, we are left with some imperative questions. Is the new decolonising political approach indeed relevant to *all* of Bolivia's citizens, as the law proclaims, or should we consider it as a new imposition for a part of the population? Will the present 'discursive turn' in the Bolivian political arena indeed promote a more enabling context for teachers and students to openly announce and discuss their hybrid identities, or will exclusionary forms of 'identity politics' be reinforced? Is Morales' 'politics of change' indeed a positive environment for changes to happen, for teachers to take centre stage in processes, and a dialogue working against negative forms of conflict and towards social justice? There is some hope. We should not forget the potential among future teachers, about those that have a changing identity and (latent) motivation to become an actor of change; one student-teacher told me how his own negative educational experience – of non-motivating and uninspiring teachers – became his main reason to become a teacher himself, in order to *change*. This future teacher embodies a larger agential potential, of future teachers with good aspirations to become 'soldiers of liberation', rather than reproducing reality as guards of continuation.

10

Concluding and theoretical reflections:
Bolivian future teachers between decolonisation and demonstration

'Pachakuti, or hegemony, always takes hard work by creative actors in every era' (Postero, 2007: 22)[152]

10.1 Bolivian teacher education: continuity, change, discourses & practices

The present Bolivian attempts to attain a counter-hegemonic state ideal, and a continuing 'organic crisis' in which this new hegemony is not yet institutionalised, indeed needs the 'hard work' of 'creative actors' in order to become a sustainable alternative to the more exclusionary forms of state that Bolivia has experienced previously. It is however, as this thesis shows, questionable whether Morales' ambitious vision of Bolivia's teachers as the *'soldiers for liberation and decolonisation'* is a helpful utopia in this quest for an alternative and decolonised society. The answer to this question is two-fold: on one hand, the new and 'extended' policy image of teachers as change agents, their continuously increasing wage, a discursive policy commitment to social justice oriented goals and a prioritisation of (pre-service) teacher education are exceptional developments for Bolivia's teaching profession and education system, considering a global education policy move in the opposite direction. On the other hand, empirical findings question the degree to which Bolivian teachers can effectively design their strategies as 'liberating teachers' in a context of continuous structural impediments; and whether they are socio-politically motivated – or even informed and involved enough – in policy design and implementation to adopt such strategies for change as envisioned by the government. Ramiro, the 'Aymara almost-teacher' introduced at the start of this book, reflected on his views of the future in a recent email exchange (May 2011), which I have summarised in Box 8.

---

[152] *Pachakuti* was introduced in chapter 1 as a traditional Andean ritual and phase of change.

Ramiro's and other similar stories inspired the exploration presented in this research of Bolivia's future teachers (enabling and restricting) pre-service education. These stories encouraged me to explore future teachers' (continuous and changing) identity constructions and motivations, and subsequently their potential space for manouevre to develop (continuing or changed) strategies in a context of demanding and changing policy reform and socio-political tension and transformation. Consequently, this thesis took the case of Bolivian pre-service teacher education – including its *institutes* and its *actors* – in an urban and a rural context to explore:

How do Bolivian pre-service teacher education institutes and actors develop strategies for or against socio-educational transformation that is envisaged by the new Plurinational constitutional regime?

Building from the answers to the five guiding questions (see introduction) in the five respective book parts, in this chapter I aim to respond to this main research question. Drawing from the data and analysis of this research, and a range of theoretical insights presented in chapter 2 and the introductions to Book Parts III, IV and V, in this chapter I aim to respond, and perhaps contribute modestly, to the development of these theoretical understandings. In an attempt to give an overview of the two main lines of argumentation used throughout this thesis, Table 7 illustrates the nexus between continuity-change and discourse-practice. The following section relates the issues presented in Table 7 back to the earlier theoretical discussions.

CONTINUITY	&	CHANGE

DISCOURSES & PRACTICES

DISCOURSES

CONTINUITY	CHANGE
❖ Education for All ❖ Intercultural education ❖ Gender equity ❖ (Quasi-)decentralisation ➢ Professionalisation agenda for Teacher Education	❖ Plurinational Constitution ❖ ASEP law ❖ *Vivir bien* ❖ Decolonisation ❖ Intracultural education ❖ Productive & communitarian education ➢ Social Justice agenda for Teacher Education

| **Structural institutional 'obstacles'**
❖ insufficient institutional infrastructure
❖ Normales as islands
❖ closed/fixed teaching profession
❖ corruption and political favours
❖ discrimination
❖ traditional teaching styles
❖ inertia
❖ failure to enhance critical thinking and reflexivity through the PDI course | **Structural niches for change**
❖ national democratic representation of indigenous majority
❖ former social movement/union leaders now staff in MoE
❖ increasing teacher salaries
❖ prioritisation of teacher education
❖ institutionalisation process: attempt to bring transparency in staff appointment and training initiatives for teacher trainers — creating a potential link to cooperation with Universities
❖ PDI as a *potential* transformative & reflexive space (action-research) |

PRACTICES

| **Agential factors of continuity**
❖ majority teachers female and lower class
❖ majority mother tongue is Spanish
❖ economic motivations prevale
❖ low levels of trust
❖ negative and conservative societal image of teachers and Normales
❖ educators' rather professional idea of the ideal teacher | **Agential change factors**
❖ new policy image of a professional, socio-politically engaged and emotionally/ethically prepared ideal teacher
❖ increasing age and experience of student teachers
❖ amplified ethno-cultural awareness and identity construction
❖ future teachers' latent vocational and socio-political motivations |

| **Continuing strategies**
❖ teaching as a way out of poverty
❖ routine teaching manners
❖ urban union's resistance
❖ urban Normal's hesitant adaptability to reform | **Changing strategies**
❖ opening dialogue rural union/CEPOs/Government
❖ rural Normal's open attitude to ASEP
❖ heterogeneity of trainers' individual responses to reform plans, not necessarily in line with the inertia of the urban institute or resistance of teacher unions
❖ ASEP potentially opening up new space for transformative strategies |

Table 7, overview of main outcomes of the research

10.2 Relating empirical findings and theory

Bolivia's new regime under the presidency of Evo Morales is seeking to create a new social, political and economic composition of Bolivian society, with education being a core instrument for that transformation. As part of a wider regional Latin American shift to the political left, through a new Plurinational constitution, the government adopts a radical discourse-for-change, which is exemplified by the recent approval of the new decolonising education reform ASEP. As detailed in chapter 5, the ASEP reform is both unique and contested. It is unique in the sense that in contrast to wider global developments of market-driven education reforms, Bolivia seeks an endogenous path to educational and social development, based on a revolutionary ideological discourse of decolonisation and *'vivir bien'*. Rather than shortening teacher training, reducing teachers' salaries and downgrading teachers' societal roles, as we see in many countries around the globe, Bolivia is instead increasing teachers' training programme from three and a half to five years, the government is pushed by teachers' unions to increase wages and president Morales has declared teachers to be *'the soldiers of liberation and decolonisation'*. This new revolutionary reform is, however, not uncontested either, as challenges for its implementation linger and various oppositional groups openly question its legitimacy and relevance. Structural socio-economic and educational inequalities (urban-rural, lowland-highland) persist despite a rhetoric of change, perpetuating ongoing tensions in Bolivian society.

This thesis explores how the current government's 'politics of change' are played out in the 'socio-political battle field' of pre-service teacher education institutes, where several structural obstacles to transformation remain in existence. It argues how the new hegemonic project of decolonisation of the current government is not fully institutionalised; as with regards to the education sector, internal struggles still exist within the MoE and various groups of stakeholders (including for instance teachers, parents and the Catholic Church) remain actively opposed to parts of the new reform. However, this thesis also highlights the various potential spaces for transformation, as designers and proponents of the ASEP reforms finally see a turn around of deep historical injustices for the majority indigenous population. The research thus contrasts strong instances of continuity with niches for change, as illustrated in Table 7 above.

Continuity and change in Bolivian discourses around teacher education

While present day reality in the two Normales included in this research continue to be characterised by rather traditional practices – in terms of their organisation, teaching methods and materials (further elaborated below) – at a discursive level a radical shift has taken place. Through the decolonisation of the teacher education system as one of the key reform goals, a revolutionary transformation of the entire education sector is envisaged, along the lines of an inter-/intracultural, plurilingual, communitarian and productive education approach. The key role for teacher education was emphasised by a MoE official as follows: *'Social justice, inclusion and decolonisation are all pillars of the new teacher training programme, and the whole new education reform of Bolivia. Teacher education institutes need to incorporate the new curriculum for teacher education, so they can materialise these philosophical and theoretical underpinnings of the ASEP law'* (44:4). While many social justice oriented political approaches in the US context are focused around economic redistribution (North, 2008: 1198), the current education reform plans in Bolivia are exceptional because of a clear emphasis on recognition and representation issues related to the claims of the indigenous movement struggles. Based on interviews and documentation analysis, I argue that the notion of *'vivir bien'* is crucial to a Bolivian understanding of a social justice oriented (teacher) education system (Article 3.1 ASEP Law, Ministerio de Educacion de Bolivia, 2010b), that aims to work towards a society based on solidarity, equal rights and opportunities for all citizens.

The *rationale* of Bolivia's education reform can be considered 'revolutionary', as it seeks not only to produce genuine improvements in people's lives, but also to build popular political capacity (Rodriguez-Garavito et al, 2008: 24). Its discursive aims are also 'transformative', as it strives for a restructuring or deconstruction of the educational status quo (Fraser, 1995). During these processes of transformative remedies, disrespect – particularly for the indigenous population – is redressed by transforming the underlying 'cultural-valuational' structures. Through transformatory remedies to social injustice, existing group identities and differentiations can be destabilised and the self-esteem of currently disrespected groups is often raised, while *'everyone's* sense of belonging, affiliation and self* would change (original italics Fraser 1995: 82-83, 87). This is at least partly the case in Bolivia, where my research shows how tensions rise between indigenous and non-indigenous citizens from the different low-land, high-land or central regions of the country, while indigenous identities are more openly 'adopted' by Bolivia's future teachers, reclaiming their cultural and linguistic heritage, including surnames and ways of dressing in formal settings. The outcomes of this thesis, however, question the degree to which the rethoric of a 'revolutionary transformation', that is envisaged to start in Bolivia's Normales, will actually be implemented considering a range of structural and agential obstacles (see Table 7).

Drawing from Frasers' feminist theory of a three-dimensional conceptualisation of social justice (chapter 2), I argue how at the *discursive level* the new ASEP Reform, as embedded within a broader politics of change and Plurinational constitution, indeed strives for more justice in terms of economic redistribution, cultural recognition – and a revaluation of the heterogenous indigenous heritage – and political representation. Current policy discourses emphasise a broad interpretation of justice, including for instance environmental justice and gender justice, both in wider society as well as in education spaces. As a consequence of these changing political discourses, the policy approach to teacher education similarly shifted towards a social justice orientation. The discourse of the ASEP policy and (available versions of the) curriculum-in-design relate to the more critical interpretations in the literature on SJTE, both in its socio-political goals of redistribution, recognition and representation, and in its methodological and pedagogical approaches that emphasise critical reflection and action research.

When applying the typology of the 'three agenda's for teacher education' (elaborated in chapter 2, see for instance Cochran-Smith, 2004; Sleeter, 2009; Zeichner, 2009) to the situation in Bolivia, it can be argued that the 1994 Reform primarily fitted the professionalisation agenda, with an emphasis on teachers' professional pedagogical base. Bolivia's new policy still follows the professionalisation agenda, while at the same time it attempts to pursue a social justice and critical inter-/intracultural rationale, as illustrated in Table 7. The new law is clearly not following the deregulation agenda; for instance the government has increased the length of teacher training instead of reducing it. In this sense, Bolivia is a clear exception to the 'global rule' of neoliberal marketisation of teacher education, that leads to shorter training programmes that prepare teachers as *'technicians to raise students' test scores while moving away from teachers' professional knowledge and quality'* (Sleeter, 2009: 612). In a recent publication a MoE official makes Bolivia's alternative revolutionary orientation more explicit:

'The main priority of the new teacher will be to critically understand social reality and their new social contexts. From the point of view of liberation and construction of historical consciousness, a teacher should go beyond the usual simple thematic content, the repetition and memorisation of meaningless dates and events, the eternal blackboard, chalk and pads, but rather incorporate appropriate new technologies in the educational context. Teacher education should establish an epistemological break with the prevailing pedagogical tradition, reaffirming a strong ideological and political training, with a clear position on the role and functions of the teacher as a protagonist in transforming Bolivian communities and a keeper of personal ethics and professional integrity' (Del Granado, 2011).

In this new state vision for teacher education, Normales are seen as 'research institutes'. In order to reach this goal not only the curriculum is revised, but also the educational management is transformed, since *'the curriculum itself is not synonymous with transformation'* (Del Granado, 2011). Here, it is relevant to return to the main dilemma of teacher education (Tatto 2007) as discussed in chapter 2, namely whether teacher training is required to bring about critical reflection and extensive professional autonomy or whether teaching is seen as a more procedural, scripted activity that asks teachers to only deliver the standards of a prescribed curriculum. The current ideological discourse of the ASEP law and its proponents are visibly commanding a more extensive role for teachers than merely following a prescribed curriculum. In line with the SJTE criteria (chapter 2), the ASEP law (2010) underlines the importance of critical reflection of teachers and the importance of research within the teacher education programme. Two MoE officials responsible for the new teacher education programme under ASEP confirmed the view that research and critical reflexive thinking, particularly through the practical and research 'PDI-course', are core elements of the five-year training cycle (101:3 and 102:4).

In addition, according to new legislation, teachers are expected to engage in community life and actively undertake (action) research to *'solve productive and social problems, to promote scientific, cultural and linguistic diversity, and to participate side by side with the local population in all processes of social liberation, in order to create a society with more equity and social justice'* (Article 91 of the new constitution, 2008: 20). This discursive and policy shift to a 'research methodology', particularly in Bolivia's PDI course, aims therefore to apply the SJTE criteria of critical thinking and reflexivity through action research methodologies (Liston and Zeichner, 1990; Price, 2001; Zeichner, 2009). Though these types of action research ideally enable (future) teachers to produce and control knowledge in order to act upon educational and societal changes, it depends on the quality of the practical experience and the level of support the teacher students receive, during 'guided enquiry' in schools, as to whether these actually help to build a social justice awareness and understanding, or whether it will function as a reproduction of the status quo, merely reinforcing rather than challenging negative stereotypes (McDonald and Zeichner, 2009: 604; Sleeter, 2009: 619-620). The analysis of the implementation of the PDI course in chapter 6 illustrated a limited system of guidance and support for student teachers during their internships and research periods, resulting in an untapped potential for critical reflection and socio-political critical awareness, and consequent strategies to act upon them, even though this is part of the official ASEP policy discourse.

Continuity and change in Bolivian teacher education practices

Regardless of the apparent discursive shift towards a more social justice oriented teacher education system, there is still a large gap between ASEP's social justice oriented ideology and the reality in Bolivian Normales and schools. This was confirmed in one of the feedback discussions with teacher trainers and students in the rural institute, where it was argued that having a good new law is one thing, but changing it into a reality is another (121). Thus, the various structural and agential factors produce a somewhat complicated reality for these justice ideals to materialise and for SJTE to shift from an idelogical discourse into teacher education practice (as illustrated in Table 7).

Structural factors of continuity and change

As became clear from chapter 5, there is an impasse in the whole education sector because of the recent approval of the ASEP law and a lack of clear conceptualisations, guidelines and curricula to accompany the new plans. In line with the challenges of ASEPs implementation discussed in chapter 5, there is a genuine danger that the critiques on the former reform of 1994 – an overemphasis on the theoretical and ideational and too little on the practical implementation – will be repeated again now ASEP has started to be implemented in the teacher education sector. The big shift in comparison to the reform process of the 1990s, is that teacher education is now seen as the first step towards reforming the whole education system. Yet, while ASEP prioritises teacher education, it has difficulties in accomplishing full information sharing, participation and 'ownership' of the changes in all Normales.

Dictated by continuing economic insecurity and poverty, youngsters and unemployed professionals alike claim their right to enter the Normales, as they continue to perceive the teacher profession as a useful path to upward social and economic development. The MoE, however, predicts high unemployment rates of graduates as too many teachers have recently graduated from Normales and there are not enough jobs. Furthermore, though Bolivian teachers might not be challenged by the same problems and limitations inherent in the global and market-driven 'crisis in the teaching profession' discussed in the introduction of the thesis, we can nevertheless still speak of a crisis in the Bolivian teacher profession. While teachers' salaries have increased and welfare arrangements have been assured, their status remains low and teacher training institutes are still considered conservative islands in wider society. In addition, for many of Bolivia's pre-service and in-service teachers, the current situation of an 'impasse' or 'crisis' understandably frustrates them, as they remain in a state of limbo, unsure of what the future reform and curricula will bring. Still, this uncertain situation, together with an intensification of entrance procedures and a longer duration of the teacher education programme, does not deter many Bolivians from pursuing a (first or second) career in education, taking a range of measures to ensure their successful entrance to one of the Normales.

Supportive and oppositional actors of the new ASEP reform perform their power plays at different (institutional, local and national) levels of the teacher education system. Drawing from 'actor maps' that were visualised by various respondents, the Normales come out as complex socio-political battle fields – or strategic selective contexts (Hay 2002a; Robertson forthcoming) – where different power relations are played out. The MoE plays a central role in that it primarily finances, guides and (only to some extent) controls the Normales. Both interviews and actor maps revealed how the MoE and (primarily the urban) union are caught up in a trial of strength with regards to their influence in the Normales, positioning the Normales at the frontline of socio-political struggles. Tensions continue to augment, for instance over the monopoly of the teaching profession for *normalistas* – those trained in the Normal – thus exluding University graduates. As already highlighted in chapter 4, Tatto et al (2007b) similarly discuss how in the case of Mexico, the Normal Schools have not changed nor lost their position due to the support of the teachers' union (Tatto, 2007: 16). The power of the Bolivian MoE in the Normales is being limited, negotiated and mediated by the supportive, or resistant, influence of unions and social movements such as the CEPOs. At the same time, the relative power of the unions is also being 'attacked' through the processes of institutionalisation mentioned above. The Normales, as *'complex and emergent sites of struggle and contestation'* (Jessop, 2005: 28), mediate between these sometimes opposing power relations, as the institutes are positioned on the verge of ASEP's transformation from an ideological policy into an educational reality.

The historically embedded institutional cultures and political strategies of the different stakeholders involved are not necessarily creating an enabling environment for governments' policies, which aim for a radical restructuring of teacher education in terms of the governance mechanisms, as well as a socio-political redirection of its curriculum. Continuing structural institutional obstacles to change include: insufficient institutional infrastructure; traditional teaching techniques; discrimination; corruption; strong hierarchies; a lack of democratic institutional governance; and engagement with the wider community (chapter 6). The breach between ASEP's social justice oriented ideology and the reality in Bolivian Normales is further illustrated in the application of Sleeters SJTE framework to Bolivian teacher education 'actions' at the end of chapter 7. Firstly, while recruitment measures have been revised in order to recruit better and more motivated future teachers, regardless of their background, the entrance exam still tests memorisation skills and interviews are still limited in both time and scope. Secondly, while the new policy discourse encourages inter-/intracultural and multilingual (teacher) educational approaches as well as socio-political awareness raising, in reality these ideas have (yet) barely reached the classrooms of the Normales. Thirdly, the impact of the promising PDI course, and the continuing attention to these types of research methodologies in Bolivian teacher education, is limited due to a lack of guidance and critical reflection.

Building on the insights of former studies (Concha et al, 2002; Lozada Pereire, 2004) as well as several interviews with Bolivian academics, I argue that new directions should be sought for different forms of collaboration between Universities and Normales in order to build Normales as 'research oriented institutes', as is envisioned by the current government. Currently, there is little trust or willingness for such a collaboration from the side of the Normales, as the enforced external administration by Universities is still fresh in their memories. If the various actors involved could take seriously the idea of critical and reflexive teachers-as-researchers that is supported in the SJTE literature, new forms of cooperation between Normales and Universities, or other research institutes, would be indispensable. In this area there is a need for future research. In developing such new forms of collaboration, the *normalista* arguments against too heavily theoretical University influence should be acknowledged, while at the same time Universities' comparative strength deserves recognition. Finally, the ongoing institutionalisation process provides another potential space for improvement as it aims to enhance the transparency of teacher placements and at the same time to ensure a better qualified teacher trainer force. Yet, according to the critical views of both students, trainers and MoE officials, this process so far has not been fully succesful in terms of its actual transparency, while it has also resulted in a loss of effective instruction time in both Normales. There is, in my view, a need for a selection process based on trainers' demonstrable qualifications, rather than political affiliations or the 'automatic' gained qualification points according to trainers' years in the profession.

Agential factors of continuity and change

Part IV of the book analysed the continuities of a number of 'agential factors' (see Table 7). First, the majority of teachers are still female, speak Spanish as their mother tongue and come from lower classes. Consequently they see the teaching profession as an important way out of poverty. In contrast to the general negative view in Bolivia, of students *only* entering the Normales because of financial reasons, the interviews and survey results revealed a more nuanced picture of how both urban and rural students expressed various kinds of pedagogical-vocational and socio-political related reasons for entering the teaching profession. Moreover, while Yogev and Michaeli (2011: 315) claim that teacher education programmes need to focus on developing these vocational and political commitments, this is not so much the case in the two Normales examined so far, thus forming an under-utilised potential. Besides, there are generally low levels of trust between the various educational actors at different scales and both teacher students and their trainers have rather negative and narrow views of each others' motivations to be(come) educators. In contrast, at the national level, the policy discourse embeds a new policy image of a professional, socio-politically engaged and emotionally/ethically prepared ideal teacher, as was discussed above.

While in the literature the need for reflexive processes of identity construction is emphasised as a key element of transformative teacher education programmes (e.g. Clarke, 2009; Price, 2001; Beauchamp and Thomas, 2009; McDonald and Zeichner, 2009), this receives a lack of attention and understanding in Bolivian teacher education practices and policy. While Bolivia's teachers' at all levels of experience are faced with a rapidly changing context of a Latin American 'indigenous awakening', a continuous unequal society and economy and an upcoming new education reform, they demand 'flexible' identities in order to deal with these changing landscapes (Clandinin et al, 2009: 142; Welmond, 2002: 24-26), yet in reality they receive little support in terms of pre-service and in-service training. This study found that there is a changing teacher student profile marked by two of these contextual developments: firstly a lack of job opportunities leads to an increased age and, in many cases, wider experiences of students who enter the Normal and, secondly, a growing societal and political recognition of indigenous culture and languages stimulates students to develop a growing awareness and acceptance of their own ethno-cultural and linguistic background. Teacher education institutions – as well as national level policy-makers – seem to miss and misunderstand the opportunity behind these developments. I argue that on the one hand, there lies a potential benefit with regards to training a group of older, highly skilled and more experienced students. On the other hand, due to processes of 're-ethnisation' and 're-identification' students develop a greater awareness, acceptance and self esteem in relation to their formerly often discriminated cultural-ethnic background. While, in the literature, pre-service training is described as an ideal starting point to create awareness of the need to develop and reflect on the ongoing shifts in identities of future teachers' complex identities (Beauchamp and Thomas, 2009: 176, 186), this is rarely taken up by Bolivian teacher education practices.

Continuing and changing strategies

With the aim to take into consideration both the structural (Part III) and agential factors (Part IV), Part V aims to shows what space for manoeuvre – or agency – is left for (future) teachers in order to adopt strategies that work for or against educational *and* societal change. Chapter 9 analyses the possibilities and challenges Bolivian teachers face in their work within Bolivia's challenging context of continuing tensions, discrimination and instability. Being a teacher in Bolivia, thus, means being caught up in a context of social and political conflicts, since the choice between 'marches' or 'maths' is often not really a free, but rather a strongly politicised choice, as was illustrated in the case of teacher students' and trainers' 'forced' participation in demonstrations (chapter 9).

Actors' motivations are crucial in their passive or active strategies and these motivations are influenced by the ideologies and discourses around them and vice versa (Hay, 2002a). As argued in chapter 8, we need to rethink the homogenising, reproducing and passive idea of the Bolivian teacher. Many actors in the education field, including policy makers, teacher trainers, student teachers and teachers themselves, *perceive* educators to be potential or actual agents of change (chapter 9). These discourses are possibly strengthened by the current government's talk of change, particularly for those trainers who are supportive of the ASEP reform and who are presumably also better informed about it's content. Even though quotes from teacher students do not directly appear to align with the current government's ASEP discourse, and many still have very little knowledge of the ins and outs of the ASEP reform, in their idealistic and hopeful 'illusions of grandeur' (Moore 2008) they do express a wish for bringing change, reflecting the under-utilised vocational and socio-political motivations mentioned above. As illustrated in chapter 5, the new outline of the ASEP teacher education curriculum includes subject matters such as political ideology, which could potentially become a space for critical reflection to help future students to make sense of their potential roles as change agents, but further research would have to highlight if and how this results in practice. Some respondents spoke of how permanent teacher formation for in-service teachers could improve the chances for teachers to be actors for change, as it was recognised by various actors that changing existing practices in schools remains a huge challenge. Notwithstanding Morales' 'politics of change', many Bolivian schools tend to be more conservative rather than open to new ideas and change; as a large group of in-service teachers choose a 'routine' path, rather than a more conflictive and difficult path of innovation and/or resistance. Considering that many of these in-service teachers at some point also function as 'guiding-teachers' in the internship and research trajectories of future teachers (the PDI programme), it is thus questionable whether these internship experiences of guided teaching and fieldwork will actually help to build a social justice awareness and understanding, or if it will function as a reproduction of the status quo, merely reinforcing, rather than challenging, negative stereotypes (McDonald and Zeichner, 2009: 604; Sleeter, 2009: 619-620).

In terms of (future) teachers individual strategies, I found that in many cases students' voice in the classrooms of Normales was limited to individual or group presentations, often literally reproducing the content that was provided on photocopied texts or the blackboard. While in many classrooms these 'banking education' teaching techniques continue to exist and evidently do little to engage critical thinking and expression of students' voice, I also observed classes in which some forms of dialogue and interaction were stimulated, often still naturally limited due to the relatively large class sizes. Nevertheless, during two feedback discussions with first and second year students in the urban Normal during the last fieldwork visit, I did see more open forms of 'voice', as the critical reactions to both my findings and the intentions of my research made it clear that these students had already become used to posing these types of critical questions. Though these examples are limited and perhaps do not represent a wider trend (yet), they do indicate how the discourse of critical and engaged teachers is starting to be reflected in some spaces within Bolivia's Normales.

Drawing from an interdisciplinary body of literature, as well as interviews and observations of this study, chapter 9 discussed possible strategies for Bolivia's (future) teachers as 'agents of change', to counter the different dimensions of the Bolivian socio-political conflict (defined in chapter 3). By taking on a critical and reflexive stance towards 'difference' and by helping themselves, and their students, to adopt hybrid identities (Davies, 2006a; Davies, 2008), teachers can ideally provide a counteracting force to forms of exclusionary 'identity politics'. Another strategy for teachers to enhance educational (and hence societal) changes in the Bolivian tense context is to increase levels of trust and dialogue in the strategic selective environments of the schools and other education institutes (including Normales), where there is often a lack of confidence between the various actors involved, including teachers, parental commissions, unions, (indigenous) educational organisations and lower or national level government institutions. However, in order to do so teachers themselves need to believe in their own capacities and skills, as regardless of the efforts of intercultural and bilingual teacher training programmes in the EIB Normales a large number of future teachers are, for instance, not prepared enough to teach in a non-Spanish and rural context, diminishing the chances for teachers to potentially convince parents and the community of the benefits of inter-/intracultural and bilingual education, or a decolonised, communitarian and productive curriculum. Their training, both pre-service and in-service, is crucial for a solid preparation, to stimulate an innovative and reflexive attitude and to foster latent motivations into active forms of agency for transformation.

Policy makers, not excluding those in Bolivia, rather avoid teachers' collective forms of action and resistance (Vongalis-Macrow, 2007: 428-433). Collective forms of teacher resistance towards state initiatives can, however, also be a productive and necessary counter-voice in the political arena. As we should avoid simplistic black-and-white accounts of teachers' resistance as being either negative and un-principled versus positive or emancipatory, this study acknowledges both the conservative as well as the more transformative outcomes of Bolivian teachers' collective actions. Research also shows how teachers' individual strategies of resistance can often not be sustained alone and the need for a strong community that reinforces alternative perspectives and the joint questioning of dominant messages (Achinstein and Ogawa, 2006). This was exemplified by the story of Benardo, a senior urban teacher trainer who showed a strong commitment to changing the current teaching practices in the Normal along the decolonising and inter-intracultural lines of the ASEP law. He felt, however, limited to an individual strategy 'within the four walls of the classroom' only. Although Benardo does not stand alone on a national level, within the institute he is clearly an exception and his individual agency is therefore limited. Similarly, the idea that '*Individually, we have no power and together, we can do anything*' has convincingly proved its strength in the city of El Alto, sometimes also referred to as the birthplace of Bolivian popular resistance (Dangl 2007: 140).

Collective action is therefore not uncommon for Bolivian teachers. A decent salary is a common collective point of struggle for teachers all around the globe and – as proclaimed particularly by the urban Bolivian teachers' union   Bolivian teachers' salaries are too low in relation to the responsibility and demands of the job, forcing them to take on extra jobs. This study contrasts these views with the observation that teachers' salaries have continuously been increased since Morales entered into government. Together with ex-union and indigenous movement members taking up relatively high positions in the MoE, and a changing strategy of dialogue of the rural teachers' unions, these developments might indicate a potential opening of more dialogue between the parties involved over the systematic issues of conflict in the education sector (e.g. salary issues, pension arrangements, reform implementation and so forth).

It is thus for Bolivian teachers not an easy, nor a straightforward choice to develop their strategies in the various arrays of tensions and pressures between decolonisation and demonstration. As long as in the majority of practices, observed in the two Normales included in this research, continue in a routine manner of banking education, teacher students will continue to experience that instead of actually *learning* their new profession; they instead *attend* classes (Bonal, 2007) in order to get their certificate and thus a life long assurance of a salary. Also, as long as teachers' pre-service education does not radically transform in itself, and an in-service system of training and support continues to fail to stimulates teachers to engage in innovative and transformative ways of teaching, we can hardly blame Bolivia's educators for sticking to their strategies of survival and routine, in the absence of clear, supported and awarded alternatives.

In summary, amidst long historical processes of continuity, the current socio-political transformations in Bolivia have meant an opening up of potential niches for change both inside and around the socio-political 'battle-field' of the Normales. The continuing and routine strategies exist alongside the limited, but existing, individual (in the case of the urban Normal) and rural collective support initiatives for the ASEP reform of trainers and management staff. Illustrated in Table 7, these 'niches for change' for instance consist of: the rural unions' new strategy of dialogue with the MoE and the CEPOs; increased (national level) democratic representation of the indigenous majority; an increased ethno-cultural awareness and identity building among those that identity with being indigenous; former social movement staff now working in the MoE; and last, but not least, the PDI-course as a potential transformative and reflexive space for future teachers. Hence, we already see the first shifts in policy prioritisation of teacher education, and new and emerging individual and collective strategies that in some cases resist, and in some cases enhance the project of transformation of the government under Evo Morales.

10.3 Contributions to the field & suggestions for future research

In this final section, I intend to abstract six important issues that this thesis hopes to contribute to transdisciplinary debates on the politics of education in situations of social transformation and conflict, and in particular the dialectical relationship between teachers and socio-educational transformation. Building from these insights, I also recommend several areas for future investigation.

Firstly, this study recognises the value of Latin American coloniality debates in their aim to understand and at the same time deconstruct historical structures of injustices. Yet it urges for closer engagement with various, not to be ignored, counter-voices from the Latin American ground. As argued throughout the book, the Bolivian government pursues these ideals through a politics of change and decolonisation of the education system, to create a socially just society in which all citizens can 'live well' (*vivir bien*). The empirical outcomes of this study, however, illustrate how the 'decolonial ideal' is not embraced by various groups of social actors in Bolivia, among which: groups of parents who would rather see their children being taught in Spanish; urban teachers who perceive the communitarian and productive aspects of the ASEP law to be irrelevant to their contexts; and Catholic education organisations who fear being excluded from a non-religious oriented education system. Bearing in mind these forms of resistance and counter-strategies, it is debatable whether the government's attempts to reform education through decolonisation is a legitimate strategy, or perhaps a new form of imposition as some respondents expressed. Future exploration is needed to investigate whether and how the actual implementation of ASEP's discourse for SJTE – in terms of critical and reflective thinking and a meaningful intercultural dialogue – are indeed realised in teacher education practices, or whether the government's political ideology of decolonisation turns out to become another form of dogmatism in the classrooms of Bolivia's Normales. In the process of further developing these valuable and necessary debates on '*alternatives of knowledge and alternatives of action*' (Sousa Santos 1998: 130), a sincere engagement with these actual counter-voices 'against decolonisation' becomes a crucial field for future inquiry and theory building.

Secondly, based on the findings of Parts III and IV, and in line with a critical realist point of view, I argue that discourse and policy, such as the new ASEP law, do more than just '*leaving a trace in practice*', as Jansen suggests in his work on 'political symbolism' and its effect of non-reform (2001b: 212-213). The data of this study partly speaks against Jansen's analysis. While for the case of South Africa Jansen found a lack of integration of national policy statements, and a lack of coherence between a wide range of policy documents (2001b: 203), this study shows more coherence between Bolivia's constitution, the National Development Plan and the ASEP education reform. In addition, while Jansen's observation of heavy international influence in policy design was still true for Bolivia's 1994 Reform, its current ASEP policy is said to be of pure Bolivian-owned design. In resemblance to the case of post-Apartheid South Africa, the first period of the Morales government's attempts to reform and decolonise Bolivian education can indeed largely be characterised as 'political symbolism', however it does not mean this discourse only created 'non-reform'. I argue that we can take this analysis a step further, by applying Dale's multiscalar 'politics of education' approach, and that, by analysing that, what happens in the (teacher) education sector is inherently embedded in broader socio-political and economic processes of transformation. This way, we can see how the broader socio-political discourse and actual changing societal arrangements impact future teachers' new ways of self-identification and a cultural-linguistic re-recognition of their indigenous roots (chapter 7) and how an enduring economic situation of insecurity fuels an even larger influx to the entrance exams for Normales (chapter 6). Besides, a changing political arena with ever more flexible and fading boundaries between the current government and social movements such as the CEPOs, and even the rural branch of Bolivia's teacher union, impact the different approaches and readiness for adaptability to the new envisaged decolonial education system in the rural and the more resistant urban Normales included in this research. The fact that Bolivia's rural and urban institutes respond differently to the 'political symbolism' of the government, and express different levels of engagement and ownership of the ASEP project, leads me to conclude that Jansen's 'political symbolism' explanation of non-reform could be nuanced or advanced by including a more holistic and multilevel analysis of the complexities of power plays, interests and actors involved in (teacher) education in similar situations in transformation.

Thirdly, the case of Bolivian Normales illustrates how teacher education institutes should be considered as sites of embedded social and political struggle and as spaces where various actors both inside and outside of the institute play out their socio-political and educational conflicts. Or, as Robertson argues, we could view teacher education institutes *as a complex terrain and outcome of discursive, material and institutionalised struggles over the role of education in the social contract* (Robertson forthcoming). Teacher education institutes are characterised in the literature as somewhat paradoxical spaces, where instances of conservatism and transformation meet (see for instance Tatto, 1999 & 2007b on Mexico, Jansen, 2001a on South Africa and Yogev and Michaeli, 2011 on Israel). This contradictory position is also reflected in Bolivia's Normales. To a certain degree, this study thus confirms the existing conservative societal image of Bolivia's Normales. This is in line with Yogev and Michaeli's claim that in turbulent social and political contexts teacher education institutes frequently stick to relatively conservative models – providing *'an illusion of security'* – hampering innovative and transformative forms of teacher preparation (2011: 315). However, the picture is more complex. Drawing from a critical realist approach (Jessop, 2005: 41), the study has attempted to uncover the visible *empirical domain of reality,* the *actual* (in)visible events and processes as well as the invisible, yet *real* structures, mechanisms and powers inside and around Bolivia's Normales. Based on a multiscalar analysis of the present Bolivian socio-political and educational context, and drawing from the Cultural Political Economy perspective on education (CPE/E, Robertson forthcoming), this research brings forward a more nuanced picture of teacher training institutes as heterogeneous spaces (Tatto 2007) of struggle and contestation, in which potential new spaces for transformation do appear. The study confirms the importance of semiosis in processes of social transformation, as the niches for change occur at the verge of the new ASEP policy discourse and the slowly opening and changing strategies of individual trainers, the rural union and the indigenous education councils (CEPOs).

Fourthly, while in its policy design and social justice oriented discourse the new Bolivian government seems to respond to a transformative approach to teacher education (Yogev and Michaeli 2011: 317-318), Bolivia's current teacher education practices largely fail to implement a transformative model that stimulates teachers to become 'transformative intellectuals' (Giroux 2003b). Following Gramscian thinking on the potential transformative role of 'organic intellectuals' in the education field, Michaeli and Yogev argue for such a transformative teacher education model, that *'is intended to train teachers as "involved intellectuals" whose professional identity is based on strong intellectual self-image, awareness of social activism, and commitment to public activity'* (2011: 313). The theoretical chapter 2 highlighted several key 'indicators' of a SJTE programme, including an enhancement of teachers' agency through an action research programme for critical thinking, reflexivity and fostering meaningful intercultural dialogue. These 'indicators' correspond with Bolivia's new vision of a longer, more intensive and academically qualified teacher education system that trains future teachers to become *'critical, reflective, innovative and 'research-oriented professionals'* (Article 33.1, ASEP law). Through its action research methodology, the PDI course provides a potential space to enhance critical thinking, reflexivity and consequently teachers' active agency for change, but for the most part its current implementation fails to do so. Part IV illustrated how regardless of the potentials of a changing, more experienced and culturally more aware future teacher generation, with latent vocational and socio-political motivations, there is little evidence of actual practices that stimulate an engaged and committed ideal Bolivian teacher. Yogev and Michaeli continue to argue that in order to do so, teacher training institutes need to reconceptualise their roles and responsibilities beyond the field of education, challenging the reproducing hegemonic conservative educational ideologies and practices (2011: 322). Part III of this study shows how – in contrast to the new policy guidelines – Bolivian Normales are still very closed institutes, or 'islands', with limited connection to, or engagement with, its surrounding environment. In addition, interviews with young in-service teachers revealed how, in many schools, teachers are faced with a similar conservative environment. Thus, the new 'revolutionary' ASEP curriculum and other reform documents as products of the governments' 'political symbolism' (Jansen 2001b) do not necessarily translate directly into changed practices. The developing nature and early stage of the recently designed and approved ASEP Reform did not allow this research to make statements about the *effects of strategic actions* of actors in the field of teacher education and therefore these boxes and arrows were included in the conceptual scheme with dotted lines (see chapter 2).

Fifthly, without ignoring the continuity of traditional and non-transformative practices in Bolivia's Normales, we should stay away from the simplistic conclusion that Bolivia's educators are therefore a conservative crowd. Building from insights on the importance and interrelatedness of structures, agents and agency, I aim to open up debates that place the blame for a low quality education and a low-committed teaching force on teachers, by arguing that we need to understand the causes of these developments in the wider structural context of (pre- and in-service) teacher training and support, as well as the broader socio-political and economic environment. This claim not only holds for Bolivian teacher education, but has relevance to other education levels and other countries as well. It is unfair to solely hold these educators responsible for not being prepared and equipped to provide quality teaching and/or training. In the case of Bolivia, yet also in many contexts elsewhere, teachers lack a permanent source of support to ensure that they remain motivated and updated, while they face low social status, miss out on a proper pre-service training and often combine multiple jobs to support their families.

Sixthly, following from the conclusions presented in this thesis, it is fair to state that the ideals and foundations embedded in the critical, and often US-based, literature on SJTE are certainly closely linked to Bolivia's discursive policy turn as I have argued above. Yet, its actual implications for the transformation of Bolivian teacher education practices is limited due to a range of continuing structural and agential challenges (Table 7). The application as an analytical instrument for discourse analysis has proven useful in this thesis, even though the Bolivian context is very distinct from the US context, for instance, where most of the literature is developed, or other contexts where a market driven approach aims to (de)professionalise the teaching profession instead of Bolivia's (discursive) attempts to extend teachers' socio-political roles. The actual level of implementation of the ASEP reform is still in its premature phase, and future and further critical ethnographic study is needed in order to further develop a SJTE framework that is particularly applicable to highly unequal, diverse and socio-politically tense contexts in the global South, such as Bolivia.

A follow up on the implementation phase of the ASEP curriculum in the Normales would be an interesting area for future research, as the field of teacher education in Bolivia remains under-studied and deserves broader attention. Due to the limitations of this study in terms of the inclusion of only two out of the 27 Normales (let alone the new 'Academic Units') for pre-service teacher education, it would be interesting to conduct similar qualitative and critical ethnographic research in other Normales. In addition, more research is needed in order to better understand the precise funding mechanisms of the Normales, as precise financial data was hard to locate and this might bring more insight into issues of power and negotiation between institutes and other (non-)governmental actors.

In addition to the need for more research in the field of Bolivian teacher education, I think an exploration of the further developments of the implementation phase of the ASEP project in the education sector as a whole – including its institutional governance and implications, continuing power-plays, and educators' perceptions, motivations and strategies – naturally forms a new area for future research. Investigation is also required in order to analyse and understand how the various socio-political tensions and dimensions of conflicts are played out at different education levels, including the early phases of (pre)primary education up to the higher levels of vocational and university education. As a follow up of this study, it would be particularly interesting to explore teachers' early transition from pre-service to in-service teaching and the clashes between new teachers coming from the Normales and those already working in school settings. Considering the warning signs of growing unemployment among trained teachers, future research could also explore the effects of this situation, as well as to explore the continuing struggles between the MoE and youngsters, and their parents, over 'the right to enter the Normal'. In light of Morales' 'politics of change', and various sources of literature (including this study) suggesting that in-service teachers prefer to follow a routine manner of 'traditional teaching', prospective studies could potentially shed more light on in-service teachers' points of view and strategies with regard to the new Reform, and the broader socio-political goals of their government towards 'decolonisation and liberation'. Similarly, there is a need to better understand the changing and developing identities, motivations and strategies of Bolivia's in-service teachers located across the countries' nine departments and across the different scales of the education arena.

Finally, I end by sharing the following quote from Benardo, one of the most engaged and experienced urban teacher trainers I had the honour to get to know. After a series of interviews and conversations with this trainer over the course of the fieldwork visits, in May 2010 we sat down at the kitchen table, reflecting on the preliminary findings I had just told him about:

> *'Bolivia's context today has totally changed. It means that at present, what we called the 'Normalista' teacher, with their own theoretical frame, their own paradigm, with the passage of time this [type of teacher] does not respond anymore to the necessities of this country... we now see this [educational] structure did not solve the major problems of this country, the fundamental social, economic, cultural and educational problems. That is why we need studies, we need a diagnostic to understand where we find ourselves now, what state teacher education – which lies at the core – is in. And from those understandings, we need to formulate new policies that will help to remedy these major problems, towards a quality education. Such [studies] help me to reflect, to solve [issues], not only with the mind but also with the heart. Therefore, I think your research, let's say, could be a perfectly fitting glove'* (108:1).

I can, of course, only wish that I have, perhaps partly, lived up to these reflections.

REFERENCE LIST

Achinstein, B. and R. T. Ogawa (2006). "(In)Fidelity: What the Resistance of New Teachers Reveals about Professional Principles and Prescriptive Educational Policies." Harvard Education Review, 76(1), pp. 30-63.

AECID (2007). Programa de formación e innovación institutional y academica dirigido a los Institutos Normales Superiores (INS) públicos de Bolivia, Agencia Espanola de Cooperación Internacional, unpublished document.

Aikman, S. (2011). Educational and indigenous justice in Africa. International Journal of Educational Development, 31: pp.15-22.

Al Jazeera (2008a). Talk to Jazeera – Evo Morales. Bolivia, YouTube: http://www.youtube.com/watch?v=zOdPP1ruHdk .

ALBA (2008). Cochabamba Declaracion. Ministerio del Poder Popular para la Educacion Superior, Gobierno Bolivariano de Venezuela.

ALBA (2009a). Managua Declaración. Ministerio del Poder Popular para la Educacion Superior, Gobierno Bolivariano de Venezuela.

ALBA (2009b). Cronología del Proyecto Gran-nacional ALBA-Educación. Ministerio del Poder Popular para la Educacion Superior, Gobierno Bolivariano de Venezuela.

Albó, X. (2005). "Bolivia revolutionises bilingual education." ID21 insights, Retrieved 13-09-07, from http://www.id21.org/insights/insights-ed05/art04.html .

Albó, X. and A. Anaya (2003). Ninos alegres, libres, expresivos. La audacia de la educación intercultural bilingüe en Bolivia. La Paz, CIPCA and UNICEF.

Almudevar, L. (2007). Pressure for Bolivian 'people's president'. BBC newspaper article, 06-08-2007, Sucre, Bolivia.

Altinyelken, H. K. (2010). "Pedagogical renewal in sub-Saharan Africa: the case of Uganda " Comparative Education 46(2): pp. 151-171.

Anaya, A. (2009). Magisterio y Reforma Educativa en Bolivia. Sindicatos Docentes y Reformas Educativas en America Latina: Bolivia, Rio de Janeiro, SOPLA, Conrad Adenauer Stiftung.

Appadurai, A. (2006). "The right to research." Globalisation, Societies and Education, 4(2): pp. 167-177.

Apple, M. W. (1982). Reproduction and Contradiction in Education: an Introduction. Cultural and Economic Reproduction in Education, M. W. Apple, Routledge & Kegan Paul Books: pp. 1-31.

Apple, M. W. (2009). Foreword. Teacher Education and the Struggle for Social Justice. New York and London, Routledge, Taylor & Francis: pp. ix-xii.

Asamblea Constituyente de Bolivia (2008). Nueva Constitucion Politica del Estado, available at http://www.presidencia.gob.bo/download/constitucion.pdf .

Assies, W. and T. Salman (2003). "Bolivian Democracy: Consolidating or Disintegrating?" Focaal European Journal of Anthropology, 42: pp. 141-160.

Auala, R. K. (2005). A profile of the new teaching profession. The ideal teachers' profile. Capacity building of teacher training institutions in Sub-Saharan Africa. UNESCO: pp. 179-185.

Avalos, B. (2002). "Teacher Education: Reflections, Debates, Challenges and Innovations." Prospects : quarterly review of education, 32(3): pp. 1-8.

Banks, J. A. (2004). "Essays – Teaching for Social Justice, Diversity, and Citizenship in a Global World." The Educational forum, 68(4): pp. 289-298.

Bartlett, L. (2005). "Dialogue, Knowledge and Teacher-Student Relations: Freirian Pedagogy in Theory and Practice." Comparative Education Review, 49(3): pp. 344-364.

Bates, T. R. (1975). "Gramsci and the Theory of Hegemony." Journal of the History of Ideas, 36(2): pp. 351-366.

Baud, M. (2007a). "Indigenous Politics and the State, The Andean Highlands in the nineteenth and twentieth centuries." Social analysis, 51(2): pp.19-42.

Baud, M. and R. Rutten, Eds. (2004). Popular Intellectuals and Social Movements. Framing protests in Asia, Africa and Latin America. International Review of Social History, supplement 12. Cambridge, Cambridge University Press.

BBC (2006), 'Evo Morales sworn in as spiritual leader', video reporting, http://news.bbc.co.uk/2/hi/americas/8473899.stm (last accessed 01-04-2011).

Beauchamp, C. and L. Thomas (2009). "Understanding teacher identity: an overview of issues in the literature and implications for teacher education." Cambridge Journal of Education, 39(2): pp. 175-189.

Bieler, A. and A. D. Morton (2004). "A critical theory route to hegemony, world order and historical change: neo-Gramscian perspectives in International Relations." Capital & Class, 28: pp. 85-113.

Bonal, X. (2007). "On global absences: Reflections on the failings in the education and poverty relationship in Latin America." International Journal of Educational Development, 27: pp. 86-100.

Boyles, D., T. Carusi, et al. (2009). Historical and Critical Interpretations of Social Justice. Handbook of Social Justice in Education. W. Ayers, T. Quinn and D. Stovall. New York and London, Routledge: pp. 30-42.

Brienen, M. (2002). "The Clamor for Schools – Rural education and the Development of State-community Contact in Highland Bolivia 1930-1952." Revista de Indias, LXII(226): pp. 615-650.

Brienen, M. (2007). "Interminable Revolution Populism and Frustration in 20th Century Bolivia." SAIS review, 27(1): pp. 21-33.

Brienen, M. (2011). The Clamor for Schools – Indigenous Communities, the State, and the Development of Indigenous Education in Bolivia, 1900-1952. University of Leiden, PhD thesis manuscript, July 2011.

Burawoy, M. (1998). "The Extended Case Method." Sociology Theory, 16(1): pp. 4-33.

Burawoy, M. (2004). "Public sociologies: contradictions, dilemmas, and possibilities." Social Forces, 82(4): pp, 1603-1618, http://www.soc.umn.edu/~hartmann/courses/burawoy_20070118135613.pdf .

Calzadilla Sarmiento, R. (2009). Presentation of the Bolivian ambassador in The Hague on the Bolivia's poltics and future. University of Amsterdam, Graduate School of Social Sciences, 22 October 2010.

Canessa, A. (2004). "Reproducing racism: Schooling and race in highland Bolivia." Race Ethnicity and Education, 7(2): pp. 185-204.

Canessa, A. (2006). "Todos somos indígenas: Towards a new language of national political identity." Bulletin of Latin American Research, 25(2): pp. 241-263.

Carspecken, P. F. (2001). Critical Ethnographies from Houston: Distinctive Features and Directions. Critical ethnography and education, P. F. Carspecken and G. Walford. Oxford, Elsevier Science Ltd: pp. 1-26.

Castles, S. (2001). "Studying Social Transformation." International Political Scince Review, 22(1): pp. 13-32.

CEPAL (2005). Los pueblos indígenas de Bolivia: diagnóstico sociodemográfico a partir del censo del 2001. Santiago de Chile, CEPAL: Comision Economica para America Latina y el Caribe.

Chaves, M. and M. Zambrano (2006). "From blanqueamiento to reindigenizacion: Paradoxes of mestizaje and multiculturalism in contemporary Colombia." Revista Europea de Estudios Latinoamericanos y del Caribe, 80(abril de 2006): pp. 5-23.

Clandinin, D. J., C. A. Downey, et al. (2009). "Attending to changing landscapes: Shapong the interwoven identities of teachers and teacher educators." Asia-Pacific Journal of Teacher Education, 37(2): pp. 141-154.

Clarke, M. (2009). "The Ethico-politics of Teacher Identity." Educational Philosophy and Theory, 41(2): pp. 185-200.

Cochran-Smith, M. (2004). "Defining the outcomes of teacher education: what's social justice got to do with it?" Asia-Pacific Journal of Teacher Education, 32(3): pp. 193-212.

Cochran-Smith, M., J. Barnatt, et al. (2009). Teacher Education for Social Justice: Critiquing the critiques. Handbook of Social Justice in Education. W. Ayers, T. Quinn and D. Stovall. New York, London, Routledge: pp. 625-639.

Concha, C., M. L. Talavera Simoni, et al. (2002). Informe Final: Evaluacion Academica e Institucional/Administrativa de los Institutos Normales Superiores. La Paz, December, unpublished evaluation document.

Congreso Nacional de Educación (2006). Especial: Congreso National de Educación en Sucre, Julio 2006. Ministerio de Edución de Bolivia, 3(15).

Contreras, M. E. and M. L. Talavera Simoni (2003). The Bolivian Education Reform 1992-2002: case studies in large-scale education reform. Washington, The World Bank.

Contreras, M. E. and M. L. Talavera Simoni. (2004a, 13-02-08). "La reforma educativa Boliviana 1992-2002: del escepticismo a la esperanza". Obtained from http://www.unesco.cl/medios/biblioteca/documentos/conflictividad_bolivia_reforma_e ducativa_boliviana_1992_2002_escepticismo_esperanza.pdf .

Contreras, M. E. and M. L. Talavera Simoni (2004b). Examen Parcial. la reforma educativa Boliviana 1992-2002. La Paz, PIEB.

Cox, R. (1996). Approaches to World Order. Cambridge, Cambridge University Press.

Crehan, K. (2002). Gramsci, Culture and Anthropology. Berkeley, Los Angeles, University of California Press.

CTEUB (1957-2007). Reglamento de Escalafón Nacional del Servicio de Educación y Reglamento de Faltas y Sanciones. CTEUB.

CTEUB (2006). La Escuela Para Rescatar la Patria, Documento aprobado en el congreso nacional de educación urbana. Sucre, CTEUB.

CTEUB and Ministerio de Coordinación con Movimientos Sociales y la Sociedad Civil (2007). Debate sobre la educación Boliviana: análisis de concordancias entre el proyecto de 'nueva ley de educación Boliviana 'Elizardo Perez Avelino Sinani' y la propuesta 'la escuela para rescatar la patria' del magisterio urbano de Bolivia, unpublished document.

Cummings, W. K. (1999). "The InstitutionS of Education: Compare, Compare, Compare!" Comparative Education Review, 43(4): pp. 413-437.

D'Emilio, L. (1996). Voices and processes towards pluralism: Indigenous education in Bolivia. New Educaction Division Documents, no. 9. Stockholm, SIDA & UNICEF.

Dale, R. (1994). Applied Education Policy or Political Sociology of Education? in: D. Halpi and B. Troyna, Researching education policy: ethical and methodological issues. London/Bristol (USA), Falmer Press: pp. 31-41.

Dale, R. (2000). "Globalization and education: demonstrating a common world education culture or locating a 'globally structured educational agenda". Educational Theory, 50 (4): pp 427-448.

Dale, R. (2005). "Globalisation, knowledge economy and comparative education." Comparative Education, 41(2): pp. 117-149.

Dale, R. (2006). "From comparison to translation: extending the research imagination?" Globalisation, Societies and Education, 4(2): pp. 179-192.

Dale, R. (2010). Retroducting and Reconstructing 'Education and Conflict', Lecture at farewell function for Dr Mario Novelli, University of Amsterdam, 31 August 2010.

Dale, R. and S. Robertson (2004). "Interview with Boaventura de Sousa Santos." Globalisation, Societies & Education, 2(2): 147-160.

Dangl, B. (2007). The Price of Fire: Resource Wars and Social Movements in Bolivia. Oakland, Edinburgh, Baltimore, AK Press.

Dangl, B. (2010). Dancing with Dynamite: Social Movements and States in Latin America. Oakland, Edinburgh, Baltimore, AK Press.

Davies, L. (2005a). Making education more inclusive: democracy building and citizenship for all. Expert meeting on quality of education, University of Amsterdam, unpublished paper.

Davies, L. (2005b). "Schools and war: urgent agendas for comparative and international education." Compare: A Journal of Comparative Education, 35(4): pp. 357-371.

Davies, L. (2006a). "Global citizenship: abstraction or framework for action?" Educational Review, 58(1): pp. 5-25.

Davies, L. (2006c). Education for Positive Conflict and Interruptive Democracy. In: H. Lauder, P. Brown, J.-A. Dillabough and A. H. Halsey, Education, globalization, and social change. Oxford [etc.], Oxford University Press.

Davies, L. (2008). Educating against extremism. Stoke on Trent, UK and Sterling, USA, Trentham Books.

De Koning, N. (2005). The Decline of the West A case study of Intervultural and Citizenship Education in Bolivia. International Development Studies, unpusblished Master thesis, Amsterdam, University of Amsterdam.

Del Granado Cosio, T. (2006). Politica Educativa, Normales Y Formadores de profesores. El caso del instituto Normal Superior "Simón Bolívar". Magíster en Investigación Educativa, Universidad Academia de Humanismo Cristiano, unpublished thesis.

Del Granado Cosio, T. (2007). Without title. Documento de trabajo sobre formación docente. La Paz, unpublished, referencing approved by author.

Del Granado Cosio, T. (2011). "La formación docente, factor clave para la mejora educativa." Boletin de Cultura de Paz, 3 (1), El reto de incorporar Cultura de Paz en el diseño curricular escolar, http://cedoin-gtz.padep.org.bo/upload/diseno-curricular.pdf: p.11.

Delany-Barmann, G. (2010). "Teacher Education Reform and Subaltern Voices: From Politica to Practica in Bolivia." Journal of Language, Identity and Education, 9(3): pp. 180-202.

Democracy Now (2010). Bolivian President Evo Morales on Climate Debt, Capitalism, Why He Wants a Tribunal for Climate Justice and Much More. Online Video: http://www.democracynow.org/2009/12/17/bolivian_president_evo_morales_on_clim ate .

Domingo, P. (2005). "Democracy and New Social Forces in Bolivia." Social forces, 83(4): pp. 1727-1743.

Drange, L. D. (2007). "Power in Intercultural Education:"Education in Bolivia – from Oppression to Liberation"?" Journal of Intercultural Communication,(15): pp. 1-11 as printed from website.

Duffield, M. (2001). Global governance and the new wars – the merging of development and security. London [etc.], Zed Books.

Edwards Jr., D. B. (2010). "Critical Pedagogy and Democratic Education: Possibilities for Cross-Pollination." The Urban Review, 42(3): pp. 221-242.

Education International (2007). Education International Barometer of Human & Trade Union Rights in Education, available from http://www.ei-ie.org/barometer/en/profiles_detail.php?country=bolivia.

Escobar, A. (2007). "Worlds and knowledges otherwise." Cultural studies 21(2): pp. 179-210.

Estado Plurinacional de Bolivia (2009). DECRETO SUPREMO N°29894, Estructura organizativa del Poder Ejecutivo del Estado Plurinacional Evo Morales, available at: http://www.minedu.gob.bo.

Fairclough, N. (2005). "Discourse Analysis in Organization Studies: The Case for Critical Realism." Organizational Studies, 26(6): pp. 915-939.

Feldfeber, M. (2007). "La regulacion de la formacion y el trabajo docente: un alaysis critico de la "agenda educativa" en America Latina." Revista Educacao & Sociedade, 28(99): pp. 444-465.

Femia, J. (1975). "Hegemony and Consiousness in the Thought of Antonio Gramsci." Political Studies, XXIII(1): pp. 29-48.

Fraser, N. (1995). "From Redistribution to Recognition? Dilemmas of Justice in a 'Post-Socialist' Age." New Left Review, I(212, July/August 1995): pp. 68-93.

Fraser, N. (2005a). "Reframing justice in a globalizing world." New Left Review, (36): pp.69-88.

Fraser, N. (2005b). "Mapping the Feminist Imagination: From Redistribution to Recognition to Representation." Constellations : an international journal of critical and democratic theory, 12(3): pp. 295-307.

Freire, P. (1970). Pedagogy of the oppressed. London [etc.], Penguin Books.

Freire, P. (1977). Pedagogie in ontwikkeling, Brieven aan Guinee-Bissau. Baarn, Anthos, Uitgeverij de Toren, original title: Cartas a Guine Bissau: Registros de uma experiencia em processo.

Gamboa Rocabado, F. (2009). De las criticas contra el sistema al ejercicio del poder: Los movimientos sociales indigenas y las politicas de Reforma Educativa en Bolivia. Global Monitoring Report on Education UNESCO.

Gandin, L. A. and M. W. Apple (2002). "Challenging neo-liberalism, building democracy: creating the Citizen School in Porto Alegre, Brazil." Journal of Education Policy, 17(2): pp. 259-279.

Giroux, H. (2003a). "Public Pedagogy and the Politics of Resistance: Notes on a critical theory of educational struggle." Educational Philosophy and Theory, 35(1): pp. 5-16.

Giroux, H. (2003b). Teachers as Transformative Intellectuals. In: A. S. Canestrari and B. A. Marlowe, Educational foundations: An anthology of critical readings., Sage: Chapter 21, pp. 205-212.

Gramsci, A. (1971). Selections from the Prison Notebooks. London, Lawrence and Wishart.

Grant, C. A. (2009). Bottom-Up Struggle for Social Justice: Where Are The Teachers? In: W. Ayers, T. Quinn and D. Stovall, Handbook of Social Justice in Education. New York, London: pp. 654-656.

Gray Molina, G. (2009). The Challenge of Progressive Change in Bolivia: Run-up to the 2009 Elections, CEDLA lecture 6-11-2009, University of Amsterdam. Amsterdam.

Greenman, N. P. and J. A. Dieckmann (2004). "Considering criticality and culture as pivotal in transformative teacher education " Journal of Teacher Education, 55(3): pp. 240-255.

Griffiths, T. G. (forthcoming). Higher Education and socialism in Venezuela: Massification, development and transformation. In: T. G. Griffiths and Z. Millei, Socialism and education: Historical, current and future perspectives. Dordrecht, Netherlands, Springer.

Grosfoguel, R. (2007a). La descolonizacion de la economia politica y los estudios postcoloniales: transmodernidad, pensamiento fronterizo y colonialidad global. Educación superior, interculturalidad y descolonización. S. (ed). La Paz, CEUB and Fundacion PIEB: pp. 87-124.

Grosfoguel, R. (2007b). "The epistemic decolonial turn." Cultural studies, 21(2): 211.

Hale, C. (2002). "Does Multiculturalism Menace? Governance, Cultural Rights and the Politics of Identity in Guatemala". Journal of Latin American Studies, 34, pp. 485-524.

Hall, I. (2009). "What Causes What: The Ontologies of Critical Realism." International Studies Review, 11: pp. 629-630.

Hamilton, M. L. and J. Clandinin (2011). "Becoming researchers in the field of teaching and teacher education: editorial." Teachers and Teacher Education, 27: pp. 681-682.

Harris, J. (2007). "Bolivia and Venezuela: the democratic dialectic in new revolutionary movements." Race & Class, 49(1): pp. 1-24.

Harvie, D. (2006). "Value production and struggle in the classroom: Teachers within, against and beyond capital." Capital & class : bulletin of the Conference of Socialist Economists, (88): pp. 1-32.

Hatton, N. and D. Smith (1995). "Reflection in teacher education: towards definition and implementation." Teaching and Teacher Education, 11(1). pp. 33-49.

Hay, C. (2002a). Political analysis. Basingstoke [etc.], Palgrave.

Hay, C. (2002b). "Globalisation as a Problem of Political Analysis: Restoring Agents to a 'Process without a Subject' and Politics to a logic of Economic Compulsion." Cambridge Review of International Affairs, 15(3): pp. 379-392.

hooks, b. (1994). Teaching to transgress education as the practice of freedom. New York [etc.], Routledge.

Howard, R. (2009). "Education reform, indigenous politics, and decolonisation in the Bolivia of Evo Morales." International Journal of Educational Development, 29: pp. 583-593.

Howard, R. (2010). "Language, Signs and the Performance of Power, The Discursive Struggle over Decolonization in the Bolivia of Evo Morales." Latin American Perspectives, 37(5): pp. 176-194.

Instituto Normal Superior Simón Bolívar (2008). Orientaciones generales para la entrevista, photocopied interview manual.

Jansen, J. D. (2001a). "Image-ining teachers: policy images and teacher identity in South African classrooms." South African Journal of Education, 21(4): pp. 242-246.

Jansen, J. D. (2001b). "Political symbolism as policy craft: explaining non-reform in South African education after apartheid" Journal of Education Policy, 17(2): pp. 199-215.

Japan Internacional Cooperacion Agency (JICA) and Ministerio de Educación de Bolivia (2007). Working documents of the II Encuentro internacional de maestros y maestras. Intercambio de practicas pedagogicas. II Encuentro internacional de maestros y maestras, La Paz, PROMECA – Proyecto de mejoramiento de la calidad de la enseñanza escolar.

Jessop, B. (2004a). Institutional Re(turns) and the Strategic Relational Approach. Governing local and regional economies. Institutions, Polictics and Economic Development. A. Wood and D. Valler. Aldershot, UK, Ashgate Publishing Limited, also available online: http://www.lancs.ac.uk/fass/sociology/papers/jessop-institutional-(re)turns.pdf: pp. 23-56.

Jessop, B. (2004b). "Critical Semiotic Analysis and Cultural Political Economy." Critical Discourse Studies, 1(2): pp. 159-174.

Jessop, B. (2005). "Critical Realism and the Strategic-Relational Approach." New Formations, 56: pp. 40-53.

Jessop, B. (2007a). State power: a strategic-relational approach. Cambridge [etc.], Polity.

Journeyman Pictures (12 May 2008). The Struggle For A New Constitution - Bolivia, http://www.youtube.com/watch?v=qIYo4ZD9JTw&feature=related.

Kaldor, M. (1999). New and Old Wars: Organized Violence in a Global Era Stanford, California, Stanford University Press.

Kane, R. G. (2002). "How We Teach the Teachers. New Ways to Theorize Practice and Practise Theory." Prospects, 32(3): pp. 347-364.

Kennemore, A. and Weeks, G. (2011). "Twenty-First Century Socialism? The Elusive Search for a Post-Neoliberal Development Model in Bolivia and Ecuador." Bulletin of Latin American Research, 30 (3): pp. 267-281.

Klein, N. (2007). The shock doctrine – the rise of disaster capitalism. London [etc.], Allen Lane.

Krinsky, J. (2007). "Review: The politics of protest. Social movements in America, by David Meyer." Contemporary Sociology-A Journal of Reviews, 36(5): pp. 487-488.

Kohl, B. (2006). "Challenges to Neoliberal Hegemony in Bolivia." Antipode, pp. 304-326.

Kohl, B. and R. Bresnahan (2010). "Bolivia under Morales: consolidating Power, initiating Decolonization." Latin American Perspectives, 37(5): pp. 5-17.

Kohl, B. H. and L. C. Farthing (2006). Impasse in Bolivia: neoliberal hegemony and popular resistance. London [etc.], Zed Books.

Korthagen, F. A. J. (2001). Linking practice and theory, the pedagogy of realistic teacher education. Mahwah, Lawrence Erlbaum Associates.

Kosar Altinyelken, H. (2010). Changing Pedagogy: A comparative analysis of reforms efforts in Uganda and Turkey. PhD thesis, Faculty of Social and Behavioural Sciences. Amsterdam, University of Amsterdam.

La Prensa (16-03-2010). No más cupos para las normales. La Prensa. La Paz.

La Prensa (18-03-2010a). Educación eleva a 9000 los cupos para normales. La Prensa, La Paz.

La Prensa (18-03-2010b). Expertos capacitan a profesores. La Prensa. La Paz.

La Prensa (22-12 2010). Maestros aprenderán medicina tradicional e ideología política, available at http://www.laprensa.com.bo/noticias/22-12-2010/noticias/22-12-2010_1220.php.

La Razon (07-08-2006). Álvaro García pide a la Asamblea un país con igualdad y unidad. La Razon. La Paz.

La Razon. (10-09-2008). Gobierno acusa a Costas y Marinkovic de gestar golpe. La Razon. La Paz.

La Razon (13-09-2000). Suman once los muertos en Pando, 9 por impacto de bala. La Razon. La Paz.

La Razon (17-09-2009). El rector de la Normal obliga a marchar. La Razon. La Paz.

La Razon (31-03-2011). Aguilar: lío de las normales está zanjado. La Razón. La Paz.

Latinobarómetro (2007). Informe Latinobarómetro 2007, Banco de datos en línea, Retrieved 07-04-08, from www.latinobarometro.org.

Laurie, N., R. Andolina, et al. (2003). "Indigenous professionalization: transnational social reproduction in the Andes." Antipode, 35(3): pp. 463-491.

Lazar, S. and J.A. McNeish (2006). "The Millions Return? Democracy in Bolivia at the start of the twenty-first century. Introduction." Bulletin of Latin American Research, 25(2): pp. 157-162.

Lewis, M. (2009). Linguistic map of Bolivia, www.ethnologue.com, © SIL International.

Limachi, V. (2008). Evaluacion Quinta Version Maestria en EIB. Cochabamba, PROEIB ANDES.

Liston, D. P. and K. M. Zeichner (1990a). "Teacher-education and the social context of schooling – issues for curriculum development " American Educational Research Journal, 27(4): pp. 610-636.

Liston, D. P. and K. M. Zeichner (1990b). "Reflective teaching and action research in preservice teacher-education " Journal of Education For Teaching, 16(3): pp. 235-254.

Lopes Cardozo, M. T. A. (2008). "Sri Lanka: in peace of in pieces? A Critical Approach to Peace Education in Sri Lanka." Research in Comparative and International Education, 3(1): pp. 19-35.

Lopes Cardozo, M. T. A. and Soeterik, I.M. (2008), Memorandum Del Ecuentro Internacional sobre Descolonialización y Desafíos Educativos: Reflexiones desde Bolivia y Brasil, 24 de Octubre de 2008, UMSA - La Paz, http://educationanddevelopment.files.wordpress.com/2009/02/memorandum-del-encuentro-internacional-sobre-descolonizacion-y-educacion.pdf.

Lopes Cardozo, M. T. A. (2009). "Teachers in a Bolivian context of conflict: potential actors for or against change?" Globalisation, Societies and Education, special issue on 'New perspectives: Globalisation, Education and Violent Conflict', 7(4): pp. 409-432.

Lopes Cardozo, M. T. A. and J. Strauss (forthcoming 2012). From the local to the regional and back: Bolivia's politics of decolonizing education in the context of ALBA, in: T. Muhr (ed). *Resistance to Global Capitalism: ALBA and the Bolivarian Revolution in Latin America and the Caribbean,* Rethinking Globalizations Series, Routledge.

Lozada Pereira, B. (2004). La Formación Docente en Bolivia, informe de Consultaría. La Paz, UNESCO-IESALC (Instituto Internacional de la UNESCO para la educación Superior en América Latina y el Caribe) en cooperacion con Ministerio de Educacion de Bolivia.

Luke, A. (1996). "Text and Discourse in Education: An Introduction to Critical Discourse Analysis." Review of Research in Education, 21: pp. 3-48.

Lynn, M. and R. Smith-Maddox (2007). "Preservice teacher inquiry: Creating a space to dialogue about becoming a social justice educator." Teaching & Teacher Education, 23(1): pp. 94-105.

MacLure, M. (1993). "Arguing for Your Self: Identity as an Organising Principle in Teachers' Jobs and Lives." British Educational Research Journal, 19(4): PP. 311-322.

Madison, D. S. (2005). Critical ethnography: method, ethics, and performance, Thousand Oaks, London, New Delhi, Sage.

Malaver, L. and M. F. Oostra (2003). Bolivia: mensen, politiek, economie, cultuur, milieu. Amsterdam, Koninklijk Instituut voor de Tropen.

Martin, J. (1997). "Hegemony and the crisis of legitimacy in Gramsci." History of the Human Sciences, 10(1): pp. 37-56.

Mathers, A. and M. Novelli (2007). "Researching Resistance to Neoliberal Globalization: Engaged Ethnography as Solidarity and Praxis." Globalizations, 4(2): pp. 229-249.

McDonald, M. and K. M. Zeichner (2009). Social Justice Teacher Education. In: W. Ayers, T. Quinn and D. Stovall, Handbook of Social Justice in Education. New York and London, Routledge: pp. 595-610.

McLaren, P. (1989). Life in schools, an introduction to critical pedagogy in the foundations of education. New York [etc.], Longman.

McLaren, P. and R. Farahmandpur (2005). Teaching against global capitalism and the new imperialisma critical pedagogy. Lanham, Md [etc.], Rowman & Littlefield.

McNeish, J.A. (2006). "Stones on the Road: The Politics of Participation and the Generation of Crisis in Bolivia." Bulletin of Latin American Research, 25(2): pp. 220-240.

McNeish, J.A. (2007). "REVIEW Now We Are Citizens: Indigenous Politics in Postmulticutural Bolivia, by Nancy Grey Postero." Journal of Latin American Studies, 39(4): pp. 889-891.

Medinaceli, B. (2007). Subsistema de Formacion Permanente En la perspectiva de una educacion descolonizadora, comunitaria y productiva. La Paz, PowerPoint presentation presented at the 'Encuentro Internacional de maestros y maestras', Direccion de Gestion Docente, Ministerio de Educacion.

Mesa, C. (2008). Un espiritu quebrado. El País, newspaper article, 19-09-2008, Madrid.

Mignolo, W. D. (2000). "The Many Faces of Cosmo-polis: Border Thinking and Critical Cosmopolitanism." Public Culture, 12(3): 721.

Mignolo, W. D. (2007a). Cambiando las eticas y las politicas del conocimiento: logica de la colonialidad y postcolonialidad imperial. In: Saavedra (ed), Educación superior, interculturalidad y descolonización. La Paz, CEUB and Fundacion PIEB: pp. 55-85.

Mignolo, W. D. (2007b). "Introduction: Coloniality of power and de-colonial thinking." Cultural Studies 21(2): pp. 155-167.

Ministerio de Educación de Bolivia (1999). Evaluacion del proceso de transformacion de siete Escuelas Normales en Institutos Normales Superiores, resumen de resultados INS Simón Bolívar La Paz. Economia y educacion SRL, Ministerio de Educacion, donacion del Reino de Suecia No TF-24826 BO.

Ministerio de Educación de Bolivia (2007). Lineamiento reglatorios sobre PDI. Taller de socializacion de normas, unpublished document.

Ministerio de Educación de Bolivia (2009). *Bolivia tiene 137.817 maestros, el 60% son mujeres y el 40% varones*. Published on http://www.minedu.gov.bo/minedu/showNews.do?newsId=1542, La Paz, Bolivia.

Ministerio de Educación de Bolivia (2010a). Ministerio de Educación firma convenio con normalistas y soluciona conflicto, available online: http://www.minedu.gov.bo/minedu/showNews.do?newsId=1851, last visited 08-02-2010.

Ministerio de Educación de Bolivia (2010b). Ley no. 70 de Educacion ASEP – Revolucion en la Education, availble at: http://www.minedu.gob.bo/Portals/0/leyeducacion.pdf.

Ministerio de Educacion de Bolivia (2010c). Website of the Ministry of Education of Bolivia, http://www.minedu.gob.bo, information downloaded on 22-12-2010.

Ministerio de Educación de Bolivia (2010d). Presidente "El maestro es el soldado de la liberación y descolonización de Bolivia", downloaded 20-12-2010, http://www.minedu.gob.bo/Inicio/tabid/40/EntryId/56/Presidente-El-maestro-es-el-soldado-de-la-liberacion-y-descolonizacion-de-Bolivia.aspx#.

Ministerio de Educación de Bolivia (2011). Presidente: "Sin educación, es imposible pensar que Bolivia salga adelante", downloaded 02-02-2011, http://www.minedu.gob.bo/Inicio/tabid/40/EntryId/70/Presidente-Sin-educacion-es-imposible-pensar-que-Bolivia-salga-adelante.aspx#.

Ministerio de Planificacion del Desarollo (2006-2010). Lineamientos estrategicos Plan Nacional de Desarollo. La Paz.

Molina, F. (2008). "Bolivia: la geografia de un conflicto." Nueva Sociedad, 218 (noviembre-diciembre de 2008): pp. 4-13.

Moore, F. M. (2008). "Agency, Identity and Social Justice Education: preservice Teachers' Thoughts on Becoming Agents of Change in Urban Elementary Science Classrooms." Research in Science Education, 38: pp. 589-610.

Morales, W. Q. (2004). A brief history of Bolivia. New York, NY, Checkmark Books.

Morrow, W. (1998). Multicultural education in South Africa. In: W. Morrow and K. King, Vision and reality., University of Capetown press.

Morton, A. D. (1999). "On Gramsci." Politics, 19(1): pp. 1-8.

Muhr, T. (2008b). Venezuela: Global counter-hegemony, geographies of regional development and higher education for all, Faculty of Social Sciences. Bristol, University of Bristol. PhD thesis.

Muhr, T. (2009). Guest lecture on 'Challenging the commoditisation of education and 'decentralisation' as we know it. Nicaragua and the ALBA', BA course Education and International Development. 07-10-2009, University of Amsterdam.

Muhr, T. and A. Verger (2006). "Venezuela: Higher Education for All." Journal for Critical Education Policy Studies, 4(1), http://www.jceps.com/index.php?pageID=article&articleID=63.

North, C. (2006). "More Than Words? Delving Into the Substantive Meaning(s) of "Social Justice" in Education." Review of Educational Research, 76(4): pp. 507-535.

North, C. (2008). "What Is All This Talk About "Social Justice"? Mapping the Terrain of Education's Latest Catchphrase." Teachers College Record, 110(6): pp. 1182-1206.

Novelli, M. (2004). Trade Unions, Strategic Pedagogy and Globalisation: Learning from the anti-privatisation struggles of Sintraemcali. Faculty of Social Sciences, Graduate School of Education. Bristol, University of Bristol. PhD thesis.

Novelli, M. (2006). "Imagining research as solidarity and grassroots globalisation: a response to Appadurai (2001)." Globalisation, Societies and Education, 4(2): pp. 275-286.

Novelli, M. (2009). Colombia's Classroom Wars - Political violence against education sector trade unions. Brussels, Education International.

Novelli, M. and M. T. A. Lopes Cardozo (2008). "Conflict, education and the global south: New critical directions." International Journal of Educational Development, 28: pp. 473-488.

Nucinkis, N. (2004). Situación de la Educación Intercultural Bilingüe en Bolivia. Documento preparado para el seminario-taller "Balance y Perspectivas", World Bank & PROEIB ANDES: 66.

Palmer, P. J. (1997). "The Heart of a Teacher, Identity and Integrity in Teaching." Change magazine, 29(6): pp. 14-21.

Pawson, R. (2002). "Evidence-based Policy: The Promise of 'Realist Synthesis'." Evaluation, 8(3): pp. 340-358.

Petras, J. (2006). "A Bizarre Beginning in Bolivia: Inside Evo Morales's Cabinet." Retrieved 08-04-16, from http://www.worldproutassembly.org/archives/2006/02/a_bizarre_begin.html.

Pigozzi, M. (1999). Education in emergencies and for reconstruction: A developmental approach. New York, UNICEF, http://reliefweb.int/sites/reliefweb.int/files/resources/00C2D7D60B301365C1256C7C003F9B25-unicef-education-1999.pdf.

Pilar Unda, M. (2002). "The experience of the teaching expedition and teacher networks: new modes of training?" Prospects, XXXII(3): pp. 333-345.

Postero, N. (2007). "Andean Utopia's in Evo Morales' Bolivia." Latin American and Caribbean Ethnic Studies, 2(1): pp. 1-28.

Price, J. N. (2001). "Action research, pedagogy and change: the transformative potential of action research in pre-service teacher education." Journal of Curriculum Studies, 33(1): pp. 43-74.

Proyecto de Ley ASEP (2007). Proyecto de la nueva ley de educación Avelino Sinani Elizardo Perez, revised version for the commission of Human Development. Ministerio de Educacion Culturas y Desportes de Bolivia.

Proyecto de Ley ASEP (2006). Nueva Ley de Educacion Boliviana, Avelino Siñani Elizardo Pérez. Ministerio de Educacion Culturas y Desportes de Bolivia. La Paz, at the time available at http://www.minedu.gov.bo/minedu/nley/nuevaley14sept.pdf, later on replaced with newer documentation.

Quijano, A. (2007). "Coloniality and modernity-rationality." Cultural studies, 21(2): 168.

Rama, C. (2004). Prologo; La formacion de docentes en America Latina, de las Normales a las Universisdades ?Solucion o Problema? In: B. Lozada Pereira. la Formacion Docente en Bolivia, informe de Consularia. La Paz, UNESCO-IESALC (Instituto Internacional de la UNESCO para la educación Superior en América Latina y el Caribe) en cooperacion con Ministerio de Educacion de Bolivia.

Reagan, T. (2005). Non-Western educational traditions: indigenous approaches to educational thought and practice. New Jersey, Lawrence Erlbaum Associates.

Regalsky, P. and N. Laurie (2007). "... whose place is this? The deep structures of the hidden curriculum in indigenous education in Bolivia." Comparative Education, 43(2), pp. 231-251.

Ritchie, J. and J. Lewis (2003). Qualitative research practice – a guide for social science students and researchers. London, Sage.

Robertson, S. L. (2000). A Class Act: Changing Teachers' Work, the State, and Globalisation. New York, Falmer Press.

Robertson, S. L. (2011). Locating Teachers in the World Bank's Global Positioning System. Paper prepared for CIES Conference Montreal, 1-5 May 2011, Panel 'The Local/Global Reform of Teaching and Teacher Education, Part 1'.

Robertson, S. L. (forthcoming). Untangling Theories and Hegemonic Projects in Researching Education and the knowledge economy. In: Reid et al. (eds), Companion to Research in Education, Springer.

Robinson, M. (2005). Teacher preparation for diversity in classrooms and schools: towards a research agenda. Expert meeting on quality of education, University of Amsterdam, unpublished version.

Robinson, M. and W. McMillan (2006). "Who teaches the teachers? Identity, discourse and policy in teacher education." Teaching and Teacher Education, 22: pp. 327-336.

Rodriguez-Garavito, C., P. Barrett, et al. (2008). Utopia reborn? Introduction to the study of the new Latin American left. In: P. Barrett, D. Chavez and C. Rodriguez-Garavito, The New Latin American Left – Utopia Reborn. London, Pluto Press: pp. 1-41.

Saavedra, J. L., Ed. (2007). Educación superior, interculturalidad y descolonización. La Paz, CEUB and Fundacion PIEB.

Salman, T. (2006). "The Jammed Democracy: Bolivia's Troubled Political Learning Process." Bulletin of Latin American Research, 25(2): pp. 163-182.

Salman, T. (2008). "Reinventing Democracy in Bolivia and Latin America: Review Essay." European Review of Latin American and Carribean Studies, 84(April 2008): pp. 87-99.

Scott, D. (2008). Michael Apple on structure. In: D. Scott, Critical Essays on Major Curriculum Theorists. Oxon (UK) and New York, Routledge: pp. 65-71.

Seitz, K. (2004). Education and conflict: the role of education in the creation, prevention and resolution of societal crises – consequences for development cooperation, German Technical Cooperation/Deutsche Gessellschaft fur Technische Zusammenarbeit (GTZ, now GIZ).

Seligson, M. A., A. B. Cordova, et al. (2006). Democracy Audit: Bolivia 2006 Report, LAPOP – Latin American Pulblic Opinion Project, USAID, Vanderbilt University.

Semali, L. (2001). "Review of REAGAN, T. & MAHWAH, N. (2000) Non-Western Educational Traditions: alternative approaches to educational thought and practice (New Jersey, Lawrence Erlbaum Associates)." Comparative Education Review, 45(4): pp. 643-646.

Sivak, M. (2008). Jefazo, retrato intimo de Evo Morales. Santa Cruz de la Sierra, Editorial Sudamericana S.A. & Editorial Imprenta El Pais.

Sleeter, C. E. (1996). "Multicultural Education as a Social Movement." Theory into Practice, 35(4, special issue on 'Multicultural Education: Cases and Commentaries (autumn 1996)): pp. 239-247.

Sleeter, C. E. (2009). Teacher Education, Neoliberalism, and Social Justice. In: W. Ayers, T. Quinn and D. Stovall, Handbook of Social Justice in Education. New York, London, Routledge: pp. 611-624.

Society for International Development (2011), Development: Education for Transformation. December 2010, Palgrave Macmillan Journals. 53 (4): pp. 449-572.

Sousa Santos, B. d. (1998). "Oppositional Postmodernism and Globalizations." Law and Social Inquiry, 23(1): pp. 121-139.

Sousa Santos, B. d. (2008). Depolarised pluralities. A left with a future. In: P. Barrett, D. Chavez and C. Rodriguez-Garavito, The New Latin American Left – Utopia Reborn. London, Pluto Press: pp. 255-272.

Speiser, S. (2000). "Becoming an intercultural primary school teacher: experiences from Bolivia." Intercultural Education, 11(3): pp. 225-237.

Strauss, J. (2010). Engaging Plurinationalism: A critical look at Bolivia's new education reform, International Development Studies, University of Amsterdam, unpublished Masters thesis.

Tabulawa, R. (2003). "International Aid Agencies, Learner-centred Pedagogy and Political Democratisation: a critique." Comparative Education, 39(1): pp. 7-26.

Talavera Simoni, M. L. (1999). Otras voces, otros maestros: aproximación a los procesos de innovación y resistencia en tres escuelas del Programa de reforma educativa, ciudad de La Paz, 1997-1998. La Paz, PIEB, Programa de investigación estratégica en Bolivia.

Talavera Simoni, M. L. (2002). "Innovation and Resistance to Change in Bolivian Schools." Prospects, 32(3): 0.

Talavera Simoni, M. L. (2009). Los hijos de Rouma. In: E. Aillon Soria, R. Calderon Jemio and M. L. Talavera Simoni, A cien anos de la fundacion de la Escuela Nacional de Maestros de Sucre (1909), Miradas retrospectivas a la eduacion publica en Bolivia. La Paz, Bolivia, Universidad Mayor de San Andres, Carrera de Historia: pp. 57-84.

Talavera Simoni, M. L. (2011). Educacion Publica y Formacion de las Culturas Magistrales en Bolivia 1955-2005. CIDES, La Paz, Universidad Mayor de San Andres. Doctorado Multidisciplinario en Sciencias del Desarollo.

Tapia, L. (2008). Bolivia. The left and social movements. In: P. Barrett, D. Chavez and C. Rodriguez-Garavito, The New Latin American Left – Utopia Reborn. London, Pluto Press: pp. 215-231.

Tatto, M. T. (1997). "Reconstructing teacher education for disadvantaged communities." International journal of educational development, 17(4): pp. 405-415.

Tatto, M. T. (1999). "Improving Teacher Education in Rural Mexico: The Challenges and Tensions of Constructivist Reform." Teaching and teacher education: an international journal of research and studies, 15(1): pp. 15-35.

Tatto, M. T. (2007). Reforming teaching globally. Didcot, Symposium Books.

Tatto, M. T., S. Schmelkes, et al. (2007b). Mexico's Educational Reform and the Reshaping of Accountability on Teachers' Development and Work. In: M. T. Tatto, Reforming Teaching Globally. Oxford, Symposium Books: pp. 139-168.

Taylor, S. G. (2004). "Intercultural and bilingual education in Bolivia: the challenge of ethnic diversity and national identity." Documneto de trabajo no.01/04. Retrieved February 2004, from http://www.iisec.ucb.edu.bo/papers/2001-2005/iisec-dt-2004-01.pdf.

Torres del Castillo, R. M. (2007). "Nuevo papel docente - Que modelo de formacion y para que modelo educativo? ." Online publication, downloaded from http://saberes.wordpress.com/2007/08/04/nuevo-papel-docente-%c2%bfque-modelo-de-formacion-y-para-que-modelo-eductivo/.

Tuhiwai Smith , L. (1999). Decolonizing methodologies: research and indigenous peoples. London, Zed Books.

UNESCO (2011). EFA Global Monitoring Report 2011 – The hidden crisis: armed conflict and education. UNESCO. Paris.

United Nations (2004). Map of Bolivia, UN Department of Peacekeeping operations, http://www.un.org/Depts/Cartographic/map/profile/bolivia.pdf.

UNNIOs (2004). Por una educación indigena originaria. Hacia la autodeterminación ideológica, política, territorial y sociocultural. UNNIOs - Unidad Nacional de las Naciones Indigenas Originarias. La Paz, Santa Cruz, G.I.G.

Urquiola, M., W. Jiménez, et al. (2000). Los maestros en Bolivia: impacto, incentivos y desempeño. La Paz, Sierpe Publicaciones.

Vaillant, D. (2010). "Capacidades docente para la educacion de manana." Pensamiento Iberoamericano, 7: pp. 113-128.

Van Dam, A. (2006). Lerend doen en doende leren: Bolivia's interculturele onderwijshervorming in proces.In: W. Hoogbergen and D. Kruijt, Functionele alfabetisering: lessons learned. Maastricht, Shaker Publishing: pp. 119-135.

Van Dam, A. and T. Salman (2003). Andean transversality: identity between fixation and flow. In: T. Salman and A. Zoomers, Imagining the Andes: shifting margins of a marginal world. Amsterdam, Aksant: pp. 14-39.

Van Dam, A. and T. Salman (2009). Interculturalidad, policulturalidad y creolización – una reflexión y un caso. Dinámicas Interculturales en contextos (trans)andinos. d. K. Munter, M. Lara and M. Quisbert. Oruro, CEPA/ VLIR-UOS: pp. 77-96.

Van Dam, A. and M. Poppema (2005). Researching quality of education for all in the South: main issues and current gaps. Expert meeting on quality of education, University of Amsterdam, unpublished version.

Verger, A. and M. Novelli (2010). Transnational Advocacy Coalitions' Strategy and Political Outcomes in the Global South: A Comparative Analysis of the GCE. Paper presented at the ISA Göteborg, Sweden, July 16, 2010.

Von Gleich, U. (2008). La nueva formacion de docentes en Educacion Intercultural Bilingüe en Bolivia. In: G. Dietz et al. Multiculturalismo, educación intercultural y derechos indígenas en las Américas Quito, Abya-Yala: pp. 85-115.

Vongalis-Macrow, A. (2007). "I, Teacher: re-territorialization of teachers' multi-faceted agency in globalized education." British Journal of Sociology of Education, 28(4): pp. 425-439.

Walkington, J. (2005). "Becoming a teacher: encouraging development of teacher identity through reflective practice." Asia-Pacific Journal of Teacher Education, 33(1): pp. 53-64.

Wallerstein, E. (2000). Cultures in Conflict? Who are we? Who are the others?, http://fbc.binghamton.edu/iw-hk-pao.htm, accessed 01-04-2011.

Walsh, C. (2007a). "Shifting the geopolitics of critical knowledge." Cultural studies, 21(2): pp. 224-239.

Walsh, C. (2007b). Interculturalidad y colonialidad del poder: un pensamiento y posicionamiento otro desde la diferencia colonial. In: Saavedra (ed). Educación superior, interculturalidad y descolonización. La Paz, CEUB and Fundacion PIEB: pp. 175-213.

Weiler, H. N. (2003). "Diversity and the Politics of Knowledge. Remarks prepared for an international Policy Forum on "Planning for Diversity: Education in Multi-Ethnic and Multicultural Societies" at IIEP, Paris, June 19-20, 2003." Retrieved 19-20 June 2003.

Weiner, L. (2008). Building the International Movement We Need: Why a Consistent Defense of Democracy and Equality is Essential. In: M. Compton and L. Weiner, The global assualt on teaching, teachers and their unions. New York, USA and Houndmills, UK, Palgrave Macmillan: 237-250.

Welmond, M. (2002). "Globalization Viewed from the Periphery: The Dynamics of Teacher Identity in the Republic of Benin." Comparative Education Review, 46(1): 37-65.

World Bank (2009). Country data Bolivia, http://data.worldbank.org/country/bolivia, last accessed 09-11-10.

World Bank (2009). Status of Projects in Execution – FY09 SOPE Bolivia. Operations Policy and Country Services.

Yapu, M. (2009). La calidad de la educacion en Bolivia. Tendencias y puntos de vista. La Paz, Plan Internacional Inc. Bolivia, coordinated by Terres des Hommes.

Yashar, D. J. (1998). "Contesting Citizenship: Indigenous Movements and Democracy in Latin America." Comparative politics, 31(1): pp. 23-42

Yogev, E. And Michaeli, N. (2011). "Teachers as Society-Involved "Organic Intellectuals": Training Teachers in a Political Context." Journal of Teacher Education, 62(3), pp. 312-324.

Zibechi, R. (2010). Dispersing power, Social movements as anti-state forces. Oakland, Edinburgh, Baltimore, AK Press.

Zeichner (2009). Teacher Education and the Struggle for Social Justice. New York and London, Routledge, Francis & Taylor.

Zeichner, K. M. (2003). "The adequacies and inadequacies of three current strategies to recruit, prepare, and retain the best teachers for all students." Teachers College Record, 105(3): pp. 490-519.

Zoomers, A. (2006). "Pro-Indigenous Reforms in Bolivia: Is there an Andean Way to Escape Poverty?" Development and change, 37(5): pp. 1023-1046.

Zuazo, M. (2008). Como nacio el MAS? La ruralizacion de la politica en Bolivia. La Paz, Bolivia, Fundacion Ebert.

APPENDIX 1. ROLE AS A RESEARCHER

Research cannot be totally value free, and people being studied will naturally be affected by the research done. In my role as a researcher, I have aimed for 'emphatic neutrality' by being reflexive on these processes, and by making assumptions and theoretical frameworks transparent (Ritchie and Lewis, 2003). The work of a social scientist, then, is also not value free. There are some biases I carry with me, being a *young western white woman*, and being born and raised in the Netherlands, and having, for instance, a certain idea of what it means to 'be on time' (my patience has been tested many times). On the other hand, my sympathy for and belief in the potential of progressive social (and political) movements and agents, particularly in the global South, has obviously been influential in some of my decisions, not least to focus my PhD research on the current socio-educational developments in Bolivia in the first place. This sympathy has, as will become clear from the analysis and outcomes of this study, not stopped me from critically looking into the potentials *and* pitfalls of Bolivia's ideologically progressive route, as well as the opportunities and obstacles of teacher training institutes and the main actors within them to either support or resist the (not always) progressive processes of change.

The fact that my own age is relative close to the majority of the teacher students has had positive effects of understanding and trust especially with the students, as well as some difficulties in gaining access to, and being taken seriously by, some of the 'higher positioned' staff from the Normales and Universities. In addition, being a young *woman* in a sometimes *'machisto'* environment has been challenging.[153] My 'foreignness' equally provided me with access to sources which Bolivian researchers might not have had easy access to (as was pointed out to me by my local Bolivian supervisor), yet it has also resulted in remaining in the role of an 'outsider'.[154] Relating to the participant observations, I found it interesting and sometimes challenging to function in the different roles of a 'participant'. In those cases where I could join a conference (which included other non-Bolivians) it was easier to feel and be perceived as any other participant. However, in all other cases my role as a researcher has remained one of an outsider that intervenes in a situation, yet with increasing levels of trust, engagement and openness from both sides. Finally, in discussions with various people I realised even more clearly the privilege of being able to produce a funded PhD in a context where obtaining a scholarship for a PhD is quite rare.

---

[153] In my field notes and diary I wrote down various experiences and frustrations on the way – young and older – male respondents openly commented on the fact that I was doing fieldwork 'alone' (without my partner physically being there) and more comments of a similar kind.

[154] Although in the first instance (especially with phone calls or emails) my 'Latino-*sounding*' surname was sometimes helpful, my appearance make the fact that I am a non-Bolivian quite clear.

APPENDIX 2. LIST OF INTERVIEWS, DISCUSSIONS AND WORKSHOPS

The numbers of interviews below do *not* correspond to the references I make in the text to the Atlas Ti codification (number of interview: quotation) after each quote, so as to ensure better anonymity of respondents.

LPZ = La Paz, CCBA = Cochabamba, UE = *Unidad Educativa* (primary school), MoE = Ministry of Education, SB = Normal Simón Bolívar, P = Normal de Paracaya, W = Normal de Warisata

Number	Respondents' affiliation/organisation	Date, location
Fieldwork 1		
1	Staff member, Dutch Embassy in LPZ	03-10-'07, Scheveningen (NL), expert meeting
2	Member of the Commisión Constitucional	11-10-'07, LPZ, Cafe Wagamama
3	Staff member MoE, Gestión Docente	12-10-'07, LPZ, in office
4	Staff member Plan Bolivia, Education section	15-10-'07, LPZ, in office
5	Researcher & Lecturer UMSA	16-10-'07, LPZ, my living room
6	Teacher & unionist Confederacion LPZ	16-10-'07, LPZ, Casa social de los maestros
7	Teacher/Director primary school (UE) in LPZ	17-10-'07 and 9-10-'08, teachers' living room and trip to school
8	Researcher Convenio Andres Bello	18-10-'07, Reunión Internacional de los Maestros, Hotel Europa, LPZ
9	Demonstration urban teachers' union: video and notes	19-10-'07, casa social de los maestros/centro LPZ
10	Two staff members of Spanish cooperation - AECID	22-10-'07, LPZ, in office/Embassy
11	Union leader CTEUB, national head quarters	23-10-'07, LPZ, in office
12	Group interview union members CONMERB, national head quarters	23-10-'07, LPZ, group interview in office
13	Two staff members/researchers of CEBIAE	23-10-'07, LPZ, in office
14	Director UE Rosmarie Barientos	24-10-'07, LPZ, in office
15	Trainer SB, Pedagogia	24-10-'07, LPZ, classroom SB
16	Trainer SB, Literatura, Directora Primaria	25-10-'07, LPZ, in office
17	Staff member MoE, Gestión Docente, Formación Permanente	29-10-'07, LPZ, in office
18	Ex-Trainer Normal Paracaya	CCBA, 05-11-'07, Hotel

19	Researcher and lecturer, PROEIB ANDES	06-11-'07, CCBA, in office
20	Director General & Academic Director Normal La Catolica	06-11-'07, CCBA, in office
21	Trainer Normal La Catolica	06-11-'07, CCBA, in office
22	Trainer Normal La Catolica	06-11-'07, CCBA, in office
23	Seven students Normal La Catolica, third year	06-11-'07, CCBA, in their communal room, interview and dancing
24	Ex-staff member of Dutch Embassy in LPZ	12-11-'07, LPZ, in office
25	Two staff members of CENAQ/CEPOS in Sucre	15-11-'07, Sucre, Hotel
26	Leader and coordinator of CEPOS	15-11-'07, Sucre, Hotel
27	Trainer Normal Universidad Pedagogica	16-11-'07, Sucre, in office
28	Directora Primaria, Normal Universidad Pedagogica	16-11-'07, Sucre, in classroom
29	Trainer/researcher, Normal Universidad Pedagogica	16-11-'07, Sucre, in office
Fieldwork 2		
30	Staff member MoE, Educational planning	05-06-'08, LPZ, in office
31	MoE, Director Gestión Docente, former TT	05-06-'08, LPZ, in office
32	UNICEF staff member, education section	05-06-'08, LPZ, in office
33	Trainer SB, lenguajes y literatura, secundaria	09-06-'08, LPZ, office SB
34	Two trainers SB, PDI	10-06-'08, LPZ, PDI office
35	Staff member MoE, Gestión Docente	11-06-'08, LPZ, in office
36	Trainer SB, ciencias sociales primaria	16-06-'08, LPZ, Cantina SB
37	Researcher, Ex-trainer, Curriculum developer	17-06-'08, LPZ, Gardín botánico, LPZ
38	Trainer SB, aprendizaje, curriculum	18-06-'08, LPZ, classroom SB
39	Trainer SB, psicologia	18-06-'08, LPZ, Comedor SB/classroom
40	Staff member AECID, responsible for teacher education	24-06-'08, LPZ, in office
41	Researcher and ex-Minister	24-06-'08, LPZ, in office
42	Trainer SB Ingles & Directora UE 'Piloto'	25/28-06-'08, LPZ, classroom/Director's house over lunch

43	Staff member MoE, politicas interculturales, former CEPOs leader	26-06-'08, LPZ, cafe Fridolin
44	Trainer SB, Ingles	26-06-'08, LPZ, sala de docentes
45	Three students SB, Ingles 2°	27-06-'08, LPZ, classroom
46	Academic Director Normal SB	30-06-'08, LPZ, in office
47	Student, SB Ingles 2°	30-06-'08, LPZ, SB premises outside
48	Four students, SB Ingles 2°	30-06-'08, LPZ, comedor 'city centre' over lunch
49	Student, SB Ingles 2°	01-07-'08, LPZ, comedor SB
50	Student, SB Ingles 2°	02-07-'08, LPZ, SB premises outside
51	Four students, SB Ingles 2°	02-07-'08, LPZ, Living room, Alto Obrajes
52	Researcher and lecturer, UMSA, Political sciences	02-07-'08, LPZ, in office, 'casa Montes', UMSA
53	Researcher, ex-trainer, CEPOS member	03-07-'08, LPZ, cafe Fridolin
54	Researcher and lecturer in History, UMSA	07-08-'08, LPZ, in office, casa Montes UMSA
55	Member of CENAQ/CEPOS	19-08-'08, Paracaya, Outside workshop room
56	Workshop on ASEP of CEPOS for TT Paracaya	19-08-'08, Paracaya
57	Two students P, postulantes	20-08-'08, Paracaya, premises outside
58	Three students P, postulantes	20-08-'08, Paracaya, premises outside
59	Three students P, postulantes	20-08-'08, Paracaya, premises outside
60	Trainer P, Liderazco, Etica/responsabilidad	21-08-'08, Paracaya, outside comedor
61	Trainer P, Lenguages originarias	26-08-'08, Paracaya, premises outside
62	Trainer P, coordinador PDI	26-08-'08, Paracaya, in office
63	Students P, 6° PDI	26-08-'08, Paracaya, in front of classroom
64	Researcher and lecturer PROEIB ANDES	27-08-'08, CCBA, in office
65	Academic Director Normal	28-08-'08, Paracaya, in office
66	Two students P, 6° Polivalentes	28-08-'08, Paracaya, premises outside
67	Student P, 6° Polivalentes, PDI	28-08-'08, Paracaya, classroom
68	Trainer P, Expresion y creatividad	28-08-'08, Paracaya, outside of comedor

69	General Director P	28-08-'08, Paracaya, in office
70	Students P, 3° Polivalentes	01-09-'08, Paracaya, Library
71	Trainer P, PDI	01-09-'08, Paracaya, in office
72	Trainer SB, Ingles & Pedagogia	12-09-'08, LPZ, sala de docentes SB
73	Staff member MoE, Director Gestión Docente	15-09-'09, LPZ, in office
74	Demonstration in response to violence in Pando: photos, transcriptions and notes	16-09-'08, LPZ, Centro LPZ
75	Ministra de Educación, MoE	16-09-'08, LPZ, in office
76	Trainer SB, Coordinador PDI	17-09-'08, LPZ, in office
77	Trainer and Director Primaria SB	18-09-'08, LPZ, in office
78	Two unionists, Conferederacion LPZ, CTEUB	19-09-'08, LPZ, in office, casa social de los maestros
79	Trainer SB, curriculum design, member of 'commision episcopal'	22-09-'08, LPZ, in classroom
80	Academic director Normal Enrique Finot	30-09-'08, LPZ/SCZ, phone interview
81	Director UE Ignacio Calderon, Fe y Alegria	01-10-'08, LPZ, in office
82	Docente Guia 2B, UE Colegio Italia Armando Cortez	06-10-'08, LPZ, in classroom
83	Docente Guia 5B, UE Colegio Italia Armando Cortez	06-10-'08, LPZ, in classroom
84	Director UE Colegio Italia Armando Cortez	13-10-'08, LPZ, in office
85	Two students UMSA, sciencias de Educacion + studying at SB	14-09-'08, LPZ, UMSA classroom
86	Padres de Famila (PPFF), UE Colegio Italia	15-09-'08, LPZ, classroom
87	Docente Guia 4A, UE Colegio Italia Armando Cortez	15-09-'08, LPZ, classroom
88	Docente Guia 3A, UE Colegio Italia Armando Cortez	15-09-'08, LPZ, classroom
89	Directora UE Colegio Agustin Aispiazu	17-09-'08, LPZ, in office
90	Researcher and lecturer, Education sciences, UMSA	20-10-'08, LPZ, Allianca Francesa
91	General Director SB	27-10-'08, LPZ, in office
92	Researcher Convenio Andres Bello (Cubano)	30-10-'08, LPZ, in office
93	General Director Normal Warisata	05-11-'08, Warisata, in office

94	Three students W, 3° Matematica	05-11-'08, Warisata, premises outside
95	Three students W, 2° & 3°	05-11-'08, Warisata, library
96	Researcher, indigenist/feminist social movement leader	08-11-'08, LPZ, in her living room
97	Staff member MoE, Gestión Docente	10-11-'08, LPZ, in office
98	Staff member Seduca LPZ, ex trainer PINS-EIB	10-11-'08, LPZ, Cafe Fridolin
99	Staff member and researcher German Cooperation – GTZ	11-11-'08, LPZ/correo electronico (meeting + answers via email)
Fieldwork 3		
100	Ex-student SB, teacher colegio secundaria El Alto	28-04-'10, LPZ, Café Plaza San Pedro
101	Director General Gestión Docente, MoE	28-04-'10, LPZ, in office
102	Staff member MoE, Gestión Docente	28-04-'10, LPZ, in office
103	Student SB, Ingles/Aymara	01-05-'10, LPZ, living room
104	Trainer SB, Ingles	03-05-'10, LPZ, SB comedor
105	Feedback discussion students SB, first semester	03-05-'10, LPZ, in class
106	Staff member MoE, Gestión Docente, Formacion permanente	04-05-'10, LPZ, in office
107	Staff member MoE, Curriculum Gestión Docente, ex-director Paracaya	04-05-'10, LPZ, in office
108	Feedback discussion, students SB, Aymara third semester	05-05-'10, LPZ, in class
109	TT SB, Pedagogia	05-05-'10, LPZ, living room
110	Ex-student SB, teacher primaria en provincia (carretera a Copacabana)	05-05-'10, LPZ, SB fotocopiadora
111	Staff member MoE, unidad de financiamiento	06-05-'10, LPZ, in office
112	Staff member MoE, unidad de infraestructura	06-05-'10, LPZ, in office
113	Researcher and lecturer, education sciences UMSA	07-05-'10, LPZ, café cuidad
114	Staff member MoE, politicas interculturales, ex-CEPOs	07-05-'10, LPZ, in office
115	Trainer SB, Curriculum	10-05-'10, LPZ, SB sala de coordinacion primaria
116	Feedback discussion trainers SB	10-05-'10, LPZ, SB sala de coordinacion primaria
117	Feedback discussion students SB, Ingles third	10-05-'10, LPZ, in class

	semester	
118	Researcher, Convenio Andres Bello	11-05-'10, LPZ, Hotel Radisson, during the 'encuentro sobre decentralizacion'
119	Ex-student SB, Teacher primaria in El Alto	13-05-'10, LPZ, living room
120	Feedback discussion students P fifth semester	17-05-'10, Paracaya, premises outside
121	Large feedback discussion/presentation with students, trainers and directors in P	17-05-'10, Paracaya, sala de reuniones
122	General Director Normal Enrique Finot	19-05-'10, Santa Cruz, in office
123	Feedback discussion with students, sixth semester	19-05-'10, Santa Cruz, School garden Enrique Finot

AMID*St*
Amsterdam Institute for Metropolitan
and International Development Studies

Proyecto de Investigación Doctorado - PhD

Un investigación de la formación de los
maestros/as del nivel primario en un contexto
Boliviano de diversidad y desigualdad

Mieke Lopes Cardozo

UNIVERSIDAD DE AMSTERDAM

Roeterseiland - Building G
Nieuwe Prinsengracht 130
1018 VZ Amsterdam
Los Países Bajos

Tel : +31 (0)2 05 25 4089/4063
Correo: mlopescardozo@fmg.uva.nl

Estimado/a señor/a,

Mi nombre es Mieke Lopes Cardozo y soy ciudadana de Holanda. Trabajo como investigadora doctoral en la Universidad de Amsterdam. Nuestro grupo universitario se dedica al tema 'calidad de la educación en contextos de diversidad'. Mi investigación trata de la formación docente de los maestros/as del nivel primaria.

Durante mi proyecto de 4 años, visitaré Bolivia algunas veces. La investigación se desarrollaré en múltiples niveles: al nivel político, al nivel académico, al nivel de los institutos de formación docente y al nivel escolar. En el año 2009 organizaré un encuentro con las personas involucradas e interesadas para que puedan conocer los resultados de mi trabajo y hacerme llegar su opinión.

Si usted tiene cualquier pregunta sobre mi proyecto de investigación, por favor, contáctame: mlopescardozo@fmg.uva.nl. Aunque la mayoría de mis publicaciones serán en Ingles, escribiré un resumen de mi trabajo en español. Las publicaciones y otros productos relacionados estarán disponibles en mi sitio de Web:
http://educationanddevelopment.wordpress.com/members/mieke-lopes-cardozo/

Es importante que sepa que si usted participa en mi investigación, su anonimidad será garantizada si así lo desea.

Muchas gracias por su colaboración, su tiempo y su interés en mi investigación.

Mieke Lopes Cardozo

UNIVERSITEIT VAN AMSTERDAM

APPENDIX 4. EXAMPLES OF INTERVIEW GUIDES

The interview questions were designed based on semi-structured interviews in the first fieldwork period, and discussed with the local supervisors. The questions were posed in various orders, and depending on the interview only a selection of these questions were covered. Direct questions on the issues of 'compromiso social', critical reflection and social justice were only posed during the last two months of fieldwork visit 2, so as to first analyse whether the topics would be raised by respondents themselves (which was the case).

Guía para las entrevistas: non-estudiantes

1. Nueva ley
1a. ¿Qué piensa usted de la nueva ley?
1b. ¿Cómo va a influir la nueva ley la formación docente en las Normales?
1c. ¿Piensa usted que este nueva ley mejorara la situación del pais?

2. Actores principales
2a. ¿Cuál son los actores mas importantes que influyen FD en Normales?
   Posibilidad de crear una mapa institucional por los respondientes
2b. ¿Cuál son los actores mas importantes que resisten la nueva ley, en relación con formación docente?
2.c ¿Cuáles actores promueven/resisten formas transformadoras en la formación docente?

3. Metas
3. ¿Cuál son las metas mas importantes de la formación docente del nivel primario?

4. Motivaciones de estudiantes de las Normales
4a. ¿Porqué los estudiantes quieren ser maestros/maestras?
(Opcional) 4b. ¿Tienen un compromiso social?

5. Maestro/a ideal
¿Cuál son las tres características mas importantes de un maestro/a ideal?

6. Cambios (institucionales & sociales)
6a. ¿Qué cambiaría si usted fuera el director/la directora del Normal? (o la ministra)
6b. ¿Cuál cambios serian los mas importantes?
6c. ¿Cómo organizaría estos cambios?
6d. ¿Cree usted que los profesores del instituto estan comprometidos a los cambios sociales/institucionales?
6e. ¿Piensa que los futuros maestros pueden ser actores de cambio?
6f. ¿Qué tipo de cambios necesita este pais?
(Opcional) 6g. ¿Piensa(s) que los estudiantes aprenden un pensamiento critico social?

7. PDI
7a. ¿Cuál es su opinión sobre PDI? Es importante? Porque?
7b. ¿Cómo esta implementado PDI?
7c. ¿Que debería cambiar en PDI?

(Opcional!) 8. Justicia social y formacion docente
8a. ¿Qué significa justicia social para usted?
8b. ¿Piensa que el tema de justicia social tiene un vinculo con la formacion de futuros maestros?
8c. ¿Piensa que el tema de justicia social es parte de la formacion de los futuros maestros dentro de las Normales?
8d. ¿Y es justicia social incorporado en la educacion Boliviana en general (no solo en el nivel politico, pero tambien al nivel practico?)

1. Motivaciones

1a. ¿Porqué quieres ser maestro/maestra?
1b. ¿Porqué los otros estudiantes quieren ser maestros/maestras?
(Opcional) 1c. ¿Tienen/s un compromiso social?

2. Nueva ley

2a. ¿Qué piensa(s) (usted) de la nueva ley?
2b. ¿Piensa(s) (usted) que este nueva ley mejorara la situación del pais?

3. Maestro/a ideal

¿Cuál son las tres características mas importantes de un maestro/a ideal?
¿Piensas que profes en el instituto tienen estas caracteristicas?

4. Metas

¿Cuál son las metas mas importantes de la formación docente del nivel primario?

5. Cambios (institucionales & sociales)

5a. ¿Qué cambiaría si tu fueras el director/la directora del Normal? (o la ministra)
5b. ¿Cuál cambios serian los mas importantes dentro del instituto?
5c. ¿Cómo organizaría estos cambios?
5d. ¿Cree usted que los profesores del instituto estan comprometidos a estos cambios?
5e. ¿Piensas que los futuros maestros pueden ser actores de cambio?
5f. ¿Qué tipo de cambios necesita este país?
5g. ¿Piensa(s) que los estudiantes se forman con un pensamiento critico?

6. Actores principales

6.a ¿Cuáles actores promueven/resisten formas transformadoras en la formación docente? (opcional: dibujo de los actores)

7. PDI

7a. ¿Cuál es su opinión sobre PDI? Es importante? Porque?
7b. ¿Cómo esta implementado PDI? *Pregunta para los estudiantes desde el tercer ano*
7c. ¿Cuál son tus/sus experiencias de PDI?
7d. ¿Recibes bastante apoyo/supervision durante su practica y proyecto de investigacion?
7e. ¿Que debería cambiar en PDI?

(Opcional!) 8. Justicia social y formacion docente

8a. ¿Qué significa justicia social para ti?
8b. ¿Piensas que el tema de justicia social tiene un vinculo con la formacion de futuros maestros?
8c. ¿Piensa que el tema de justicia social es parte de la formacion de los futuros maestros dentro de las Normales?
8d. ¿Y es justicia social incorporado en la educacion Boliviana en general (no solo en el nivel politico, pero tambien al nivel practico?)

APPENDIX 5. EXAMPLES OF SURVEY QUESTIONS

This survey was conducted in both Normales during August and September 2008. In total, 164 first and third year students participated in Simón Bolívar, and 159 first and third year students in Paracaya. The trainers' survey was only conducted in the urban Normal, where 19 trainers participated. The outcomes were inserted in excel and analysed accordingly, and the contact details of some of the student and trainers were used to get in touch with them again in the third fieldwork period.

Cuestionario para los estudiantes del INS Simon Bolívar

Por favor rellena individualmente. Muchas gracias por su collaboración!

---

1. Nombre:

---

2. Edad: _____ años

---

3. Hombre/Mujer (Tachar lo que es incorrecto)

---

4. Detalles
   4a. Teléfono de casa: _____
   4b. Celular: _____
   4c. Correo(s) electrónicos: _____
   _____
   4d. Dirección: _____
   _____

---

5. Año de estudio en el Instituto Normal:
   ○ Semestre inicial
   ○ Primer año
   ○ Segundo año
   ○ Tercer año

---

6. Educación anterior:
   ○ Hasta el nivel secundario
   ○ Otros estudios:
      ○ Estudio técnico ¿Cuál estudio? _____
      ○ Estudio universitario ¿Cuál estudio?_____

---

7. ¿Creció en un lugar urbano/rural? (Tachar lo que es incorrecto)

---

8. ¿Ahora vive en la ciudad/provincia? (Tachar lo que es incorrecto)

9a. ¿Qué lengua materna habla? _____

9b. ¿Qué más idiomas habla?_____

---

10. ¿Con qué cultura nacional se identifica?_____

11a. ¿En el futuro dónde prefería trabajar: un lugar urbano/rural?(Tachar lo que es incorrecto)
11b. ¿Por favor escriba las tres razones más importantes por las cuales quiere trabajar en un lugar urbano/rural?

1. _____

2. _____

3. _____

12. ¿Porqué quiere ser maestra/o?

_____

_____

_____

_____

13. Por favor escriba las tres características más importantes de un buen(a) maestra/o:

1. _____

2. _____

3. _____

14. Experiencias con la Práctica Docente e Investigación? Indique abajo si, no o neutro.

	Si	No	Neutro
a. ¿Participa en los cursos de Práctica Docente e Investigación?	0	0	0
b. ¿Se siente preparado(a) para la realización de su práctica?	0	0	0
c. ¿Considera que la práctica fortalece su preparación?	0	0	0
d. ¿Considera que la investigación mejora su aprendizaje?	0	0	0
e. ¿Está bien organizada la Practica Docente e Investigación?	0	0	0
f. ¿Recibe buena atención de los profesores en el INS?	0	0	0
g. ¿Recibe buena atención de los docentes guías en la(s) escuela(s)?	0	0	0
h. ¿Hay una evaluación de su practica?	0	0	0
i. ¿Considera que la Práctica Docente e Investigación es necesaria?	0	0	0

Por favor rellena individualmente. Muchas gracias por su colaboración!

1. Nombre:_____

2. Edad: _____ años

3. Hombre/Mujer (Tachar lo que es incorrecto)

4. Detalles
    4a. Teléfono de casa: _____
    4b. Celular: _____
    4c. Correo(s) electrónicos: _____
    _____
    4d. Dirección: _____
    _____

5. Especialidad/area de trabajo: _____

6a. Estudios anteriores (es posible indicar mas opciones)?:
    ○ Normal
    ○ Ciencias de la Educacion
    ○ Otros estudios:
        ○ Estudio técnico ¿Cuál estudio? _____
        ○ Estudio universitario ¿Cuál estudio?_____

6b. Estudios actuales? _____

7a. Años de servicio dentro del magisterio? _____
7b. Año de egreso de la Normal? _____
7c. Formación en cual Normal? _____
7d. Otro ocupación además de la docencia en la Normal? _____
_____

8. ¿Creció en un lugar urbano/rural? (Tachar lo que es incorrecto)

9a. ¿Qué lengua materna habla? _____

9b. ¿Qué otro idioma habla?_____

10. ¿Con qué cultura nacional se identifica?_____

APPENDIX 6. EXAMPLES OF ACTOR MAPS

Actor map 1: Teacher trainer

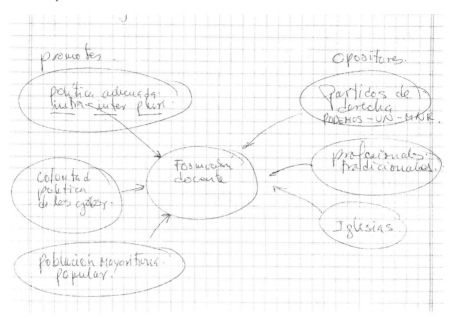

Actor map 2: Teacher trainer

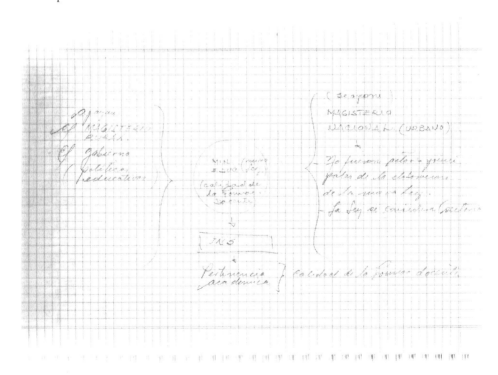

Actor map 3: Ex-trainer (EIB) and academic researcher

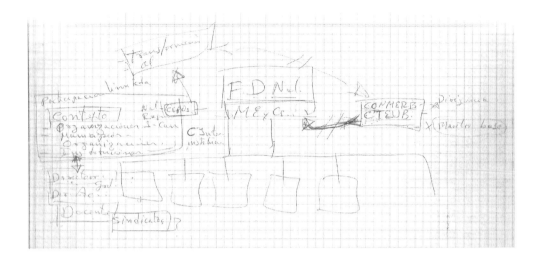

Actor Map 4: Ministry official at the Teacher Education Department

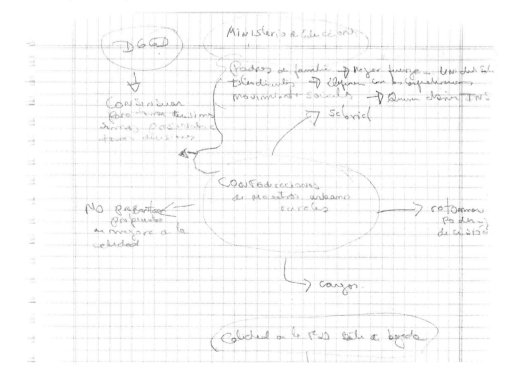

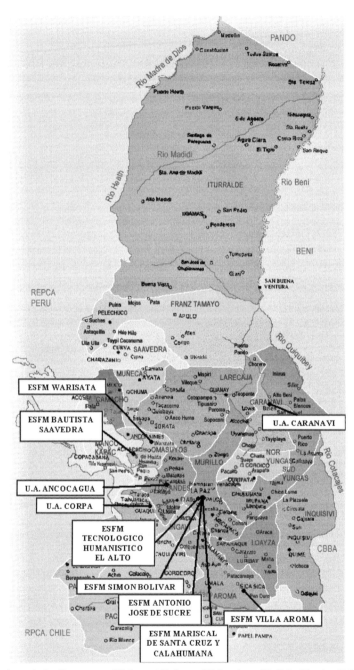

Map 4, Institutes in La Paz, source: Webpage Ministry of Education of Bolivia, Teacher Education Department; http://www.dgfm-bo.com/pages/mapas/la_paz.php.

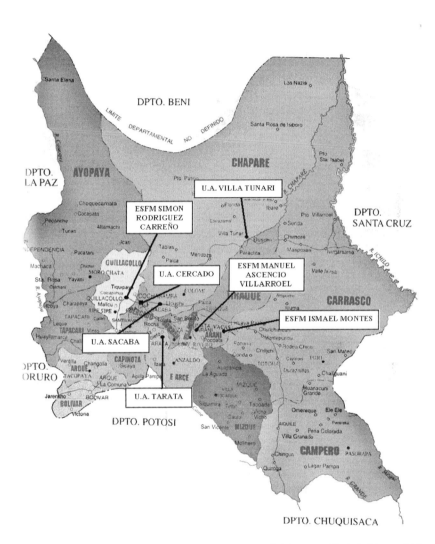

Map 5, Institutes in Cochabamba, source: Webpage Ministry of Education of Bolivia, Teacher Education Department; http://www.dgfm-bo.com/pages/mapas/cochabamba.php.

ABOUT THE AUTHOR

 Mieke T.A. Lopes Cardozo studied International Relations at the University of Utrecht, with a minor in Conflict Studies and Latin American Studies. She continued her studies in the Msc programme International Development Studies at the University of Amsterdam, with a specialisation in the area of 'Education and Development', for which she conducted research in Sri Lanka on the state of peace education and graduated cum laude. During and after her studies, Mieke worked at UNICEF in the Netherlands in the communication and education department. Having lost her heart to both academia and the Latin American continent, she started her PhD research on Bolivia in May 2007, in the context of the 'IS-Academie' co-funded project of the University of Amsterdam and the Dutch Ministry of Foreign Affairs. As of May 2011, Mieke is employed as a researcher and lecturer for the IS-Academie programme at the Amsterdam Institute for Social Science Research of the University of Amsterdam. She teaches in the BA course on Education and International Development, as well as the BA Introductory course on International Development Studies and MA course on Education and Development in Diverse Societies. Her reseach is focused on the themes of education for social justice, teacher education, teacher agency, progressive education reforms, critical approaches to multicultural and intercultural education, peace education and international education and conflict policies.

Bolivia related publications:

Lopes Cardozo, M.T.A. (2008), 'De onechte wereld van het schoolboek,' in: <u>Heilige Huisjes: Anders kijken naar Internationale Samenwerking</u>, 2nd June 2008, Dutch Ministry of Foreign Affairs.

Lopes Cardozo, M.T.A. (2009), Teachers in a Bolivian context of conflict: potential actors for or against change?, special issue on 'New perspectives: Globalisation, Education and Violent Conflict', <u>Globalisation, Societies & Education</u>, 7 (4), pp. 409-432.

Lopes Cardozo, M.T.A. (2009), 'De onderwijzer, een onmisbare schakel', winning essay of the writing competition Heilige Huisjes 2009. Published in <u>Onze Wereld</u>, # 7/8, July/August 2009, pp. 36-37. Also published in: <u>Heilige Huisjes, Essaybundel 2009</u>, 'Onderwijzen is meer dan lesgeven aleen', 24th June 2009, Dutch Ministry of Foreign Affairs and Onze Wereld.

Lopes Cardozo, M.T.A. (forthcoming 2011), '<u>Transforming pre-service teacher education in Bolivia: from indigenous denial to decolonisation?</u>', paper for UKFIET Conference, September 2011, panel: 'Indigenous knowledges in a globalising world'.

Lopes Cardozo, M.T.A. (forthcoming 2011/2012), 'Decolonising the education system in Bolivia – ideology versus reality' in: Griffiths, Tom G. And Zsuzsa Millei (eds), <u>Education and socialism: Historical, current and future perspectives</u>, Springer.

Lopes Cardozo, M.T.A. and Strauss, J. (forthcoming 2012), 'From the local to the regional and back: Bolivia's politics of decolonizing education in the context of ALBA' in: Muhr, T. (ed), <u>Resistance to Global Capitalism: ALBA and the Bolivarian Revolution in Latin America and the Caribbean</u>, Rethinking Globalizations Series, Routledge.

Lopes Cardozo, M.T.A. (forthcoming 2012), 'Bolivian teacher education as a socio-political battle field', special Issue edited by Lene Buchert, Constructing Knowledge and Understanding Education and Conflict, <i>Prospects</i>, UNESCO/Springer.

Other publications:

Lopes Cardozo, M.T.A. (2008), 'Sri Lanka: in peace or in pieces? A Critical Approach to Peace Education in Sri Lanka', <u>Research in Comparative and International Education</u>, 3 (1), pp. 19-35.

Novelli, M. and M.T.A. Lopes Cardozo (2008), 'Conflict, education and the global south: New critical directions', <u>International Journal of Educational Development</u>, 28 (4), pp. 473-488.

Lopes Cardozo, M.T.A. and A. May (2009), 'Teaching for peace – overcoming division? The potential contribution of peace education in reconciliation processes in the cases of Sri Lanka and Uganda', in: <u>Opportunities for Change</u>, edited by Susan Nicolai, UNESCO-IIEP.

Lopes Cardozo, M.T.A. and M. Novelli (2011),<u>GMR background paper: Dutch Aid to Education and Conflict</u>, UNESCO, http://unesdoc.unesco.org/images/0019/001907/190708e.pdf.

Novelli, M. and M.T.A. Lopes Cardozo (forthcoming, 2011/2012), 'Globalizing Educational Interventions in Zones of Conflict: The Role of Dutch Aid to Education and Conflict', in: H. Kosar-Altinyelken, M. Novelli and A. Verger (eds), <u>Global Education Policy and International Development: New Agendas, Issues and Policies</u>, Continuum.

9 789059 725737